AF828980

Monetary Policy and Central Banking in the Middle East and North Africa

This book contains new information and fresh analysis of monetary policy, central banking and exchange rate regimes in the Middle East and North Africa. Part I covers central banking and monetary policy, while Part II covers monetary policy and exchange rate regimes. Some chapters cover the whole region – for example, Gisolo reports an assessment of central bank independence for nearly all the MENA countries, Schnabl and Schobert investigate the operations of debtor central banks in the region, Achkar and Shahin examine the effect of exchange rates on inflation for each country in the region, and Adam and Cobham estimate the effect on countries' trade of alternative exchange rate regimes. Other chapters focus on individual countries – for example, Dibeh examines the nature and origin of central bank independence in the Lebanese case (against the background of the region as a whole), Zouache and Ilmane consider the changing status of the Algerian central bank, while Boughrara, Boughzala and Moussa analyse the vulnerability of the Tunisian banking system to shocks under inflation targeting, and Hatipoglu and Alper estimate an augmented Taylor rule for Turkey under inflation targeting. Rossi proposes an alternative route to monetary integration for MENA countries, while Bangaké, Desquilbet and Jedlane compare the different types of exchange rate arrangement open to the Maghreb countries.

David Cobham is Professor of Economics at Heriot-Watt University in Edinburgh, UK. His main research area is monetary policy, particularly the UK, but he also has an interest in Middle East economies. He has published papers in *Economic Journal, Oxford Bulletin of Economics and Statistics, World Development, International Finance* and other journals.

Ghassan Dibeh is currently Associate Professor of Economics at the Lebanese American University in Byblos. He is the editor of *Review of Middle East Economics and Finance*. His research interests include macroeconomics, political economy, financial economics and econophysics. His papers have appeared in *Physica A, Review of Political Economy, Energy Economics, Journal of International Development* and *Middle Eastern Studies*.

The Routledge Political Economy of the Middle East and North Africa Series

Series editor: Hassan Hakimian

Senior Lecturer in Economics at Cass Business School, City University, London.

Editorial Board: Jacques Charmes, Professor of Economics and Director of the Social and Health Sciences Department at L'Institut de Recherche pour le Développement (IRD), Paris. **David Cobham**, Professor of Economics at Heriot Watt University, UK. **Nu'man Kanafani**, Associate Professor of Economics at the Department of Economics and Natural Resources, The Royal Veterinary and Agricultural University, Denmark. **Massoud Karshenas**, Professor of Economics at the School of Oriental and African Studies (SOAS), University of London, UK. **Jeffrey B. Nugent**, Professor of Economics at the University of Southern California, Los Angeles, USA. **Jennifer Olmsted**, Associate Professor of Economics at Drew University, New Jersey, USA. **Karen Pfeifer,** Professor of Economics at Smith College, Northampton, Massachusetts, USA. **Wassim Shahin**, Professor of Economics and Dean of the Business School at the Lebanese American University (LAU), Byblos, Lebanon. **Subidey Togan**, Professor of Economics and Director of the Centre for International Economics at Bilkent University, Ankara, Turkey.

1 **Trade Policy and Economic Integration in the Middle East and North Africa**
Economic boundaries in flux
Edited by Hassan Hakimian and Jeffrey B. Nugent

2 **State Formation in Palestine**
Viability and governance during a social transformation
Edited by Mushtaq Husain Khan

3 **Palestinian Labour Migration to Israel**
Land, labour and migration
Leila H. Farsakh

4 **Islam and the Everyday World**
Public policy dilemmas
Edited by Sohrab Behdad and Farhad Nomani

5 **Monetary Policy and Central Banking in the Middle East and North Africa**
Edited by David Cobham and Ghassan Dibeh

Monetary Policy and Central Banking in the Middle East and North Africa

Edited by David Cobham and
Ghassan Dibeh

Routledge
Taylor & Francis Group
LONDON AND NEW YORK

First published 2009
by Routledge
2 Park Square, Milton Park, Abingdon, Oxon OX14 4RN

Simultaneously published in the USA and Canada
by Routledge
270 Madison Ave, New York, NY 10016

Routledge is an imprint of the Taylor & Francis Group, an informa business

© 2009 Editorial selection and matter; David Cobham and Ghassan Dibeh; individual chapters, the contributors

Typeset in Times New Roman by Pindar NZ, Auckland, New Zealand
Printed and bound in Great Britain by MPG Books Ltd, Bodmin, Cornwall

All rights reserved. No part of this book may be reprinted or reproduced or utilised in any form or by any electronic, mechanical, or other means, now known or hereafter invented, including photocopying and recording, or in any information storage or retrieval system, without permission in writing from the publishers.

British Library Cataloguing in Publication Data
A catalogue record for this book is available from the British Library

Library of Congress Cataloging-in-Publication Data
Monetary policy and central banking in the Middle East and North Africa / edited by David Cobham & Ghassan Dibeh.
p. cm. — (The Routledge political economy of the Middle East and North Africa series ; 5)
Includes bibliographical references and index.
ISBN 978-0-415-47643-0 (hbk : alk. paper) — ISBN 978-0-203-88455-3 (ebook) 1. Monetary policy—Middle East. 2. Monetary policy—Africa, North. 3. Banks and banking, Central—Middle East. 4. Banks and banking, Central—Africa, North. I. Cobham, David P. II. Dibeh, Ghassan, 1963-
HG1206.M66 2008
339.5'30956—dc22 2008027767

ISBN 10: 0-415-47643-0(hbk)
ISBN 10: 0-203-88455-3 (ebk)

ISBN 13: 978-0-415-47643-0 (hbk)
ISBN 13: 978-0-203-88455-3 (ebk)

Contents

Illustrations

Tables

Figures

Notes on contributors

Christopher Adam is Reader in Development Economics at the University of Oxford. His research concentrates on issues of short-run macroeconomic management and external adjustment and transformation in low-income economies. He has been a regular visiting scholar at the Research Department of the IMF and from 2003–2005 served as External Macroeconomic Adviser to the Policy Division of the UK Department for International Development (DFID).

Elias El-Achkar is Director of Research and Statistics at the Association of Banks in Lebanon. He has authored and co-authored policy articles related to the banking sector and the financial markets in Lebanon and MENA countries and academic articles on monetary policy and exchange rates. Dr El-Achkar has also offered courses in Banking and Finance at major universities in Lebanon and presented academic and policy research in international conferences and seminars.

C. Emre Alper is Professor of Economics at Bogazici University, Istanbul, Turkey. His areas of interest include international finance, applied macroeconometrics and monetary economics. Currently he is working on several research projects including the effects of the composition of government spending and the composition of its financing; money, search and specialization; the use of extended Kalman filters for Taylor Rule estimation in emerging markets; and the effects of oil and natural gas prices on real economic activity in Turkey.

Chrysost Bangaké is Research Associate at the Laboratory of Economics of Orléans (France). His main research area is monetary integration in Africa and monetary regimes. He has also worked on the economies of the Maghreb. He was previously assistant professor at the University of Orléans.

Adel Boughrara is Associate Professor at the University of Sousse and a member of the BESTMOD Laboratory, University of Tunis. He has also been an associate visiting professor at the UAE University. His research interests span monetary policy and applied econometrics.

Mongi Boughzala is Professor at the University of Tunis El Manar (Tunisia). He has a PhD from the University of Minnesota. His main interest is in public economics and economic policy, including monetary policy, labour and trade issues. He has been closely concerned with the economic policies of Tunisia and other Middle Eastern and North African countries.

David Cobham is Professor of Economics at Heriot-Watt University. His main research area is UK monetary policy, but he has also worked on European monetary integration, central bank independence, financial systems and the economies of the Middle East. He was a Senior Houblon-Norman Fellow at the Bank of England in 2001.

Jean-Baptiste Desquilbet is Professor of Economics at the University of Artois (France). His main field of interest is the theory of monetary policy and monetary regimes (central bank independence, the currency board regime, transmission channels). He has also studied Lebanese monetary policy.

Ghassan Dibeh holds a BA in Physics and a PhD in Economics from the University of Texas at Austin, Texas. He is currently Associate Professor of Economics in the Department of Economics at the Lebanese American University in Byblos. He is the editor of the journal *Review of Middle East Economics and Finance*. His research interests include macroeconomics, political economy, financial economics and econophysics. His research has appeared in the journals: *Physica A*, *Review of Political Economy*, *Energy Economics*, and the *Journal of International Development* and *Middle Eastern Studies*.

Enrico Gisolo is a Senior Economist at the Bank of Italy, where he deals with the supervision of national banking and financial intermediaries. He previously held positions at the European Central Bank and at the European Commission where he was in charge of international economic and financial relations with some MENA countries. His research interests range from financial and monetary policy topics to developing economy issues, particularly in the MENA region.

Ozan Hatipoglu is Assistant Professor of economics at Bogazici University. His areas of research include macroeconomics, growth theory, monetary economics and applied econometrics. He has written on the role of exchange rates in Taylor rules, the estimation of unobserved variables in economics via recursive Bayesian methods such as dual extended Kalman filters, the relationship between innovation-driven growth and income inequality and the political economy of the informal sector.

Hassouna Moussa is Professor at Acadia University, Canada. He has a PhD from the University of Minnesota. His main research interest is monetary policy and financial institutions. He has also carried out research on the Tunisian economy, and on the economies of a range of other countries.

Mohamed-Cherif Ilmane is Professor of Economics at the Institut Algérien des Hautes Etudes Financières, Algiers, Algeria. He was formerly vice-governor of the central bank of Algeria from 1990 to 2001. His fields of interest are banking, macroeconomics and finance.

Nabil Jedlane is Assistant Professor of Economics at Cadi Ayyad University (UCAM), Morocco. His main research area is exchange rate regimes, but he has also worked on monetary integration and the economies of the Maghreb. He is a Research Associate at the Laboratory of Economics of Orléans, France.

Sergio Rossi is Professor of Economics at the University of Fribourg, Switzerland. He has a DPhil degree from the University of Fribourg and a PhD degree from University College London. His research interests are in the area of monetary macroeconomics. He has authored and edited a number of books, contributed several chapters to books, and published widely in academic journals.

Gunther Schnabl is professor of international economics and economic policy at the University of Leipzig, Germany. His main research area is exchange rate and monetary policy in emerging markets. He has worked for the European Central Bank and has been a visiting researcher at Stanford University, Deutsche Bundesbank and Bank of Japan.

Franziska Schobert is financial markets adviser at the Centre for Technical Central Bank Cooperation of the Deutsche Bundesbank in Frankfurt, Germany. Her main research area is central banking in emerging markets.

Wassim Shahin is Dean of the School of Business and Professor of Business Economics at the Lebanese American University, Byblos, Lebanon. He has authored, co-authored and edited three books, several monographs, and over twenty academic articles dealing with monetary policy, banking, exchange rates, budgetary politics and the application of economic methodology to hostage-taking activities. He is the founding editor of the *Review of Middle East Economics and Finance* and serves on the editorial board of several academic journals.

Abdallah Zouache is Lecturer in Economics (maître de conférences) at the University Jean Monnet, Saint-Etienne, France. He is a member of the economic research centre of the University of Saint-Etienne (Creuset-Cnrs). His fields of interest are macroeconomics, monetary policy, history of economic ideas, growth and development.

Preface

This book presents selected papers from the workshop on 'Monetary Policy and Central Banking in the Middle East and North Africa: Policies, Politics and Prospects', held at the 8th Mediterranean Research Meeting organised by the European University Institute's Robert Schuman Centre for Advanced Studies, on 21–25 March 2007 in Montecatini Terme, Italy. The workshop was designed to encourage papers on a number of areas of monetary policy and central banking in the MENA region: the recent and ongoing development of monetary policy frameworks in MENA countries; the political economy of central banking and monetary policy in the MENA region and the impact of monetary policies on the real economy; and the exchange rate regime choices facing MENA countries, particularly in the light of the possible impact of the Euro–Med Agreements and the eurozone on monetary policy design in the region.

We would like to thank the Robert Schuman Centre, its director Professor Stefano Bartolini, and Imco Brouwer, the scientific coordinator of the Mediterranean Research Meeting, for the opportunity to organise this workshop at the Meeting and for their hospitality. We are grateful to the workshop participants whose papers appear in this volume and who made the workshop both interesting and amicable. And we would also like to thank the two 'listening participants', Angela DiMaria from the Banca d'Italia and Michael Sturm from the European Central Bank, who enriched the discussions with their insightful comments.

Finally, we are grateful to Hassan Hakimian, the series editor, for his advice and comments at different stages of the process, and to Peter Sowden, our editor at Routledge.

David Cobham and Ghassan Dibeh
20 October 2008

1 Introduction

David Cobham and Ghassan Dibeh

Monetary policy, including monetary policy frameworks, central bank independence and exchange rate regimes, is an area in which both academics and policymakers have made enormous strides in the last two decades. The main thrust of work in both academic institutions and central banks has been towards a better understanding of what monetary policy can and cannot do and how it can best be designed. Most of this work has focused on the industrial countries and on a small number of developing countries, mostly in Latin America, while the economies of the MENA region remain under-researched in this respect. As regards monetary policy frameworks, economists at the Central Bank of Turkey have produced a number of research papers (eg Emir *et al.*, 2000; Ozatay, 2005) and other economists have made important contributions (eg Celasun and Rodrik, 1989; Canova and Favero, 2005). Pesaran (2000) has studied money demand in Iran and found a structural break between the pre- and post-revolutionary periods which has implications for monetary policy. Bonato (2008) has studied the monetary causes of inflation in Iran during the period 1988–2006. Some work has been done on monetary policy in Lebanon (e.g. Dibeh, 2002; Makdisi, 2004) and in Egypt (e.g. Abdel-Khalek, 2001; Ikram, 2006). However, the quantity of research on these countries is limited and that on other Arab countries is even more so. For example, the Bank of England survey (Mahadeva and Sterne, 2000), which gives basic information on monetary policy targets and central bank independence for some 90 countries, includes only Bahrain, Egypt, Jordan, Kuwait, Lebanon and Turkey from the MENA region, which means it excludes the Maghreb countries, Libya, Syria, Iraq, Iran, Saudi Arabia, Qatar, Oman and the UAE.

Research on the political economy of central banking and monetary policy has highlighted the importance of politics and institutions in the determination of monetary policy in both developed and developing countries. According to various perspectives in this line of investigation, the role of social and political groups, central bank independence (CBI), and private sector preferences are all important in the determination of central bank policy stances such as inflation-fighting or output stabilisation (Epstein, 1992; Cukierman, 1992; Henning, 1994; Franzese, 2002).

Maxfield (1998) has also shown that in developing countries the international dimension to the politics of central bank independence and currency values is significant. Moreover, the resultant monetary policy adopted by central banks, such as inflation-targeting or commitment to output stabilisation, has important social and economic effects.

Elson and Cagatay (2000) have shown that in the 1990s a 'deflationary bias' in macroeconomic policy in many developing countries caused high interest rates, tight monetary policies and fiscal restraint with a negative impact on unemployment. In this respect, debates on the appropriate institutional and legal set-up of central banks can shed light on the interaction between central banking and economic development. In a recent paper, Epstein (2005) has argued that central banks have historically played an active role as agents of economic development. Moreover the relationship between central bank independence, democracy, transparency and accountability (Blinder, 1998) has obvious relevance for MENA countries, where CBI is typically low (and transparency and accountability lower).

In the MENA region the political economy of monetary policy has not received much attention. Sadek, Jarehi and Latifah (1996) assessed the independence of a small number of Arab country central banks. Abdel-Rahman (2000) used Partisan Theory to study the effect of the different policy stances of political regimes on output growth, inflation and political cycles, focusing on finance and monetary policy in the MENA region.

Dibeh (2002) studied the inflationary period of the 1980s and early 1990s in Lebanon and the role of different social and economic groups in engendering inflation and currency collapse during this period. Mitchell (1999) linked the monetary restraints practised in the 1990s in Egypt to the triumph of neo-liberalism in framing the economic discourse in Egyptian society. A recent study has linked political violence and currency markets in Egypt, a relation that may have significant monetary policy implications (Fielding and Shortland, 2005). However, a comprehensive evaluation of CBI in the MENA region has not been available until now, and for many countries there were no serious case studies available either.

Substantial progress has been made in recent years in analysing the advantages and disadvantages of different exchange rate regimes, for both industrial and developing countries. Calvo and Reinhart (2002) identified the 'fear of floating' which means that many governments which claimed that their currencies were floating were in fact intervening heavily in one way or another in the foreign currency markets. Levy-Yeyati and Sturzenegger (2005), Bailliu *et al.* (2003) and Reinhart and Rogoff (2004) produced classifications of *de facto* as opposed to *de jure* exchange rate regimes, and various authors studied the macroeconomic impact and durability of different regimes (e.g. Bailliu *et al.* 2003; Husain, Mody and Rogoff, 2005).

The importance of investigating alternative exchange rate regimes for the MENA region cannot be overstated given the recent developments in international currency markets, especially the weakening of the dollar which has fuelled inflation in some MENA countries. Most MENA countries have pegged their currencies more or less continuously to the US dollar, although more of their trade is typically with European Union countries than with the US. In this respect, Frankel and Rose (2002), noting that Egypt and Turkey had more trade with the eurozone than with the dollar zone, predicted on that basis that they would gain more from joining the European Economic and Monetary Union (EMU) than from dollarisation.

The Euro–Med Agreements which have been signed in recent years between the European Union (EU) and Algeria, Egypt, Jordan, Lebanon, Morocco, the Palestinian Authority, Syria and Tunisia are likely over the next decade to have a significant positive influence on the flows of trade and investment between the EU and these MENA countries. In addition, the emergence of the euro and the eurozone mean that there is now, for the first time, a substantial and viable alternative anchor currency for these countries and, indeed, for the other MENA countries. This peg-switching alternative is not, of course, the only alternative in the choice of exchange rate regime for MENA countries. Some observers have highlighted the need for greater flexibility in MENA exchange rates as a means of establishing more flexible open economies in the region (Jbili and Kramarenko, 2003), while currency substitution and (partial) dollarisation have been investigated by Shahin and Freiha (2005), for Lebanon and Egypt, and Civcir (2005) for Turkey.

The papers in this book address in different ways the above areas of monetary policy, central banking and exchange rate choice in the MENA region. Part 1 covers central banking and monetary policy, Part 2 monetary policy and exchange rate regimes. In chapter 2, Ghassan Dibeh examines the political economy of central banking in the MENA countries, with particular reference to Lebanon. He presents empirical relationships between central bank independence and inflation in MENA, and then focuses on the political economy of the Lebanese central bank mainly during the formative years of the *Banque du Liban* between 1964 and 1971. The analysis shows that CBI may be necessary for low inflation but it is certainly not sufficient, and a wider range of factors affect macroeconomic outcomes in the MENA countries.

In chapter 3 Enrico Gisolo presents an analysis of CBI in a large sample of countries which includes most of the MENA region (plus Malta and Cyprus), using a methodology constructed at the International Monetary Fund (IMF) by Lybek (1999) and Gutiérrez (2003). His findings show that CBI is indeed relatively low in these countries and confirm the previous evidence (on a much smaller sample) that the relationship between CBI and inflation is weak.

In chapter 4 Gunther Schnabl and Franziska Schobert examine the monetary policy operations of central banks in MENA countries. Following work by McKinnon and Schnabl (2004a, 2004b) on East Asia, they distinguish between 'creditor' central banks such as those of the US and the eurozone, which typically supply liquidity to the markets, and 'debtor' central banks such as those in most transition and developing economies which typically mop up the excess liquidity arising from foreign exchange market intervention in the presence of payments inflows. Schnabl and Schobert show that most MENA region central banks are firmly in the latter category, and identify the differing ways in which they intervene.

In chapter 5 Abdallah Zouache and Mohamed-Cherif Ilmane investigate the evolving independence of the Algerian central bank which, from having in the 1970s and 1980s been something close to the Soviet Gosbank, has experienced over the last two decades first high and then decreasing *de jure* independence, associated with fluctuating *de facto* independence. Their analysis shows that the *de jure/de facto* distinction is crucial in Algeria, and that institutional constraints of different kinds are often more important than the legal statutes for the practical independence of a central bank.

Adel Boughrara, Mongi Boughzala and Hassouna Moussa examine the feasibility of introducing a formal monetary framework of inflation targeting in Tunisia. They first consider the issue of institutional adequacy, with respect to the Tunisian central bank (which is insufficiently independent, accountable or transparent), the Tunisian banking system (which has a high ratio of non-performing loans) and the pressures in Tunisia towards fiscal dominance. They then analyse the impact on the banking system of a move to inflation targeting, in the context of shocks to inflation and to supply; they find that such shocks lead to rises in the ratio of non-performing loans which imply increases in the fragility of the financial system. Their analysis therefore places a question mark against the inflation targeting proposal.

In the first chapter of Part 2, Christopher Adam and David Cobham present gravity model estimates of the trade effects of alternative exchange rate regimes for MENA countries, drawing on other work where they have developed the ability to handle a wide range of bilateral exchange rate regimes in a way that takes proper account of the 'multilateral trade resistance' effects. Their simulations for the MENA countries suggest that for most MENA countries their trade would be higher if they anchored on the euro rather than, as at present, on the dollar.

In chapter 8 Elias El-Achkar and Wassim Shahin examine the relationship between exchange rate policies and inflation for 18 MENA countries over a 30 year period. Their results indicate that exchange rate regimes (where they distinguish between pegged and non-pegged regimes) have no significant relationship with inflation, but exchange rate variability is negatively related to inflation. These findings provide interesting contrasts with those of other researchers for developing and industrial countries.

In chapter 9 Chrysost Bangaké, Jean-Baptiste Desquilbet and Nabil Jedlane consider the choices facing the Maghreb countries, using a three-country model in which they can analyse the effects on welfare (evaluated in terms of unemployment, inflation and transactions costs) of a range of scenarios: all three countries allow their currencies to float; the two small countries peg to the larger country; the two small countries form a monetary union which floats against the larger; and so on. Their analysis identifies the various advantages and disadvantages of the different choices and the factors on which these magnitudes depend.

In chapter 10 Ozan Hatipoglu and C. Emre Alper model the behaviour of an inflation-targeting emerging market central bank under floating exchange rates, namely the Central Bank of Turkey (CBT) since 2001. They estimate an augmented Taylor rule with time-varying parameters by means of a dual extended Kalman filter. Their findings indicate that in this case the real exchange rate gap should not be included directly in the rule itself, though exchange rates obviously influence expected and observed inflation and output; and that the CBT has reacted more aggressively to inflation as time goes on (it may have been concerned earlier about fiscal dominance).

Finally, in chapter 11 Sergio Rossi proposes a means by which the MENA countries could embark on monetary integration by introducing a common currency (the 'MENA dinar') to be used in transactions between MENA central banks and a MENA settlement institution, rather than adopting a single currency on the pattern of the Economic and Monetary Union in Europe. His proposal requires countries to offset surpluses or deficits on trade with purchases or sales of securities. It would, he argues, promote exchange-rate stability between MENA countries and encourage capital inflows, notably in the form of foreign direct investment.

In sum, these papers offer a mix of region-wide and country-specific studies which should bring about a step improvement in our understanding of the institutions and operations of monetary policy and the strategic choices it faces in the Middle East and North Africa.

References

Abdel-Khalek, G. (2001) *Stabilisation and Adjustment in Egypt: Reform or De-Industrialisation*. Cheltenham: Edward Elgar.

Abdel-Rahman, M. (2000) 'Political Regime Structures, Macroeconomic Policy Outcomes, and Instrument Use in the MENA Region', Economic Research Forum, Research Paper #0405.

Bailliu J., Lafrance, R., and Perrault, J-F. (2003) 'Does Exchange Rate Policy Matter for Growth?' *International Finance*, 6: 381–414.

Blinder, A. (1998) *Central Banking in Theory and Practice*. Cambridge, Massachusetts: MIT Press.

Bonato, L. (2008) 'Money and Inflation in the Islamic Republic of Iran', *Review of Middle East Economics and Finance*: 4, The Berkeley Electronic Press: http://www.bepress.com/rmeef/vol4/iss1/art3.

Calvo, G., and Reinhart, C. (2002) 'Fear Of Floating,' *Quarterly Journal of Economics*, 117: 379–08.

Canova, F., and Favero, C. (2005) Monetary Policy in the Euro Area: Lessons From Five Years of ECB and Implications for Turkey, *Centre for Economic Policy Research, Discussion Paper* no. 5101.

Celasun, M., and Rodrik, D. (1989) Debt, Adjustment and Growth: Turkey, in J.D. Sachs, and S. M. Collins (eds). *Developing Country Debt and Economic Performance, Volume 3: Country Studies—Indonesia, Korea, Philippines, Turkey*. Chicago: University of Chicago Press.

Civcir, I. (2005) 'Dollarisation and its Long-run Determinants in Turkey', in Neaime and Colton (2005).

Cukierman, A. (1992) *Central Bank Strategy, Credibility, and Independence: Theory and Evidence*. Cambridge, Massachusetts: MIT Press.

Dibeh, G. (2002) 'The Political Economy of Inflation and Currency Depreciation in Lebanon: 1984–1992,' *Middle Eastern Studies*, 38: 33–52.

Elson, D., and Cagatay, N. (2000) 'The Social Content of Macroeconomic Polices,' *World Development*, 28: 1347–64.

Emir, O.Y., Karasoy, A., and Kunter, K. (2000) 'Monetary Policy Reaction Function in Turkey', *Working Paper, Research Department*, Central Bank of the Republic of Turkey.

Epstein, G. (1992) 'Political Economy and Competitive Central Banking,' *Review of Radical Political Economics,* 24: 1–30.

Epstein, G. (2005) 'Central Banks as Agents of Economic Development,' paper presented at UNU-WIDER Conference on Institutions and Economic Development: Theory, History and Contemporary Experiences, Helsinki, April 18–19, 2005.

Fielding, D., and Shortland, A. (2005) 'How Does Political Violence Affect Confidence in a Local Currency? Evidence from Egypt,' *Journal of International Development*, 17: 841–66.

Frankel, J., and Rose, A. (2002) 'An Estimate of the Effect of Common Currencies on Trade and Income', *Quarterly Journal of Economics*, 117: 437–66.

Franzese, R. (2002) *Macroeconomic Policies of Developed Democracies*. Cambridge, Massachusetts: Cambridge University Press.

Gutierrez, E. (2003) 'Inflation, Performance and Constitutional Central Bank Independence: Evidence from Latin American and the Caribbean'. *International Monetary Fund Working Paper* 03/53.

Henning, C.R. (1994) *Currencies and Politics in the United States, Germany and Japan*. Washington: Institute of International Economics.

Husain, A.M., Mody, A., and Rogoff, K.S. (2005) 'Exchange rate regime durability and performance in developing versus advanced economies', *Journal of Monetary Economics*, 52: 35–64.

Ikram, K. (2006) *The Egyptian Economy, 1952–2000: Performance, Policies and Issues*. London: Routledge.

Jbili, A., and Kramarenko, V. (2003) 'Choosing Exchange Rate Regimes in the Middle East and North Africa' International Monetary Fund http://www.imf.org/external/pubs/ft/med/2003/eng/jbili/jbili.htm.

Levy-Yeyati, E., and Sturzenegger, F. (2005) 'Classifying Exchange rate Regimes: Deeds vs. Words', *European Economic Review*, 49: 1603–35.

Lybek, T. (1999) 'Central Bank Autonomy, and Inflation and Output Performance in the Baltic States, Russia, and Other Countries of the Former Soviet Union, 1995–97'. *International Monetary Fund Working Paper* 99/4.

McKinnon, R., and Schnabl, G. (2004a) 'The East Asian Dollar Standard, Fear of Floating, and Original Sin', *Review of Development Economics*, 8: 331–60.

McKinnon, R., and Schnabl, G. (2004b) 'The Return to Soft Dollar Pegging in East Asia? Mitigating Conflicted Virtue', *International Finance*, 7: 169–201.

Mahadeva, L. and Sterne, G. (2000) *Monetary Policy Frameworks in a Global Context*. London: Routledge.

Makdisi, S. (2004) *The Lessons of Lebanon: The Economics of War and Development*. London: I.B. Tauris.

Maxfield, S. (1998) *Gatekeepers of Growth: The International Political Economy of Central Banking in Developing Countries*. Princeton: Princeton University Press.

Mitchell, T. (1999) 'No Factories, No Problems: The Logic of Neo-Liberalism in Egypt,' *Review of African Political Economy*. 26: 455–68.

Neaime, S., and Colton, N. (eds) (2005) *Money and Finance in the Middle East: Missed Opportunities or Future Prospects*, vol. 6 of *Research in Middle East Economics*.

Ozatay, F. (2005) 'Monetary Policy Challenges for Turkey in European Union Accession Process', *Research Department*, Central Bank of the Republic of Turkey.

Pesaran, H.M. (2000) Economic Trends and Macroeconomic Policies in Post-Revolutionary Iran. In P. Alizadeh (ed), *The Economy of Iran: Dilemmas of an Islamic State*. London: I.B. Tauris.

Reinhart, C., and Rogoff, K. (2004) 'The Modern History Of Exchange Rate Arrangements: A Reinterpretation', *Quarterly Journal of Economics*, 119: 1–48.

Sadek, A., Jarehi, M. and Latifah, N. (1996) *Monetary Policy in the Arab Countries*. Abu Dhabi: Arab Monetary Fund Publications (in Arabic).

Shahin, W., and Freiha, F. (2005) Hysteresis in currency substitution: the Middle East and North Africa, in Neaime and Colton (2005).

Part I

Central banking and monetary policy

2 The political economy of central banking in the MENA region with special reference to Lebanon

Ghassan Dibeh

Introduction

Most Middle Eastern and North African (MENA) countries have either adopted or are in the process of adopting economic and financial market reforms that include the conduct of monetary policy and the role of central banks in the process of monetary policy making.[1] In this respect, the independence of central banks in relation to political authorities is considered an important aspect of any institutional monetary reform, as evidenced by central bank reforms conducted in Europe, Latin America and the transition economies in Europe (Walsh, 1995). The modern theory of optimal monetary policy was developed by Kydland and Prescott (1977) and Barro and Gordon (1983) where central banks maximise social welfare given an expectations-augmented Phillips curve.

This social planner approach shows that a central bank with an employment motive aiming at deviation of real output from potential output will generate an inflation bias. This inflation bias on the part of central banks can be mitigated according to Rogoff (1985) by delegating monetary policy not only to an independent central bank but also to a 'conservative' central banker. The conservative central banker has higher inflation-aversion than all other economic agents and groups in society and is protected from the political influences of various social groups by its legal and instrumental independence. The basic theoretical model of a conservative independent central bank predicts less inflation bias than a normal central bank.

This approach to central banking paved the way for new political economy models which consider the central bank's objective function as a political compromise between distributionally motivated advocates of employment and advocates of lower inflation (Cukierman, 1992). In these models, also, central bank independence is sufficient to generate a lower inflation bias. Early empirical work (Cukierman, 1992) which found a positive relationship between central bank independence and low inflation has been corroborated by many researchers for different economic regions and periods (Cukierman *et al.*, 2002; Dolmas *et al.*, 2000; Jacome and Vasquez, 2005; Loungani and Sheets, 1997; Sturm and de Haan, 2001).

In contrast, Posen (1995) has shown that central bank independence is neither exogenous nor sufficient for the generation of low inflation. Independent central bank preferences are determined endogenously by the financial sector's opposition to inflation. In this respect, the distributional effects of monetary policy become the prime determinant of the central bank's policy stance as winners and losers form the political basis for competing claims on policy preferences, where historically the financial sector has been the dominant group among the different groups that lobby for price stability both in the developed and developing countries.[2] The Posen proposition agrees with political economy models of monetary policy and central banking which show that competing claims on inflation, employment and output by different groups in the economy can influence the institutional status and policy objectives and outcomes of central banks. In many countries, for example, political setups were conducive to inflation (Davis, 1963; Beckerman, 1995; Blumenschein, 1995). Epstein (1992) develops a political economy model of central banking that takes into account various competing claims in the economy and their effect on the objective function of the central bank. Such a political economy methodology, which has been applied by Epstein (1982; 2003) and Epstein and Schor (1989, 1990) to the US and Italy allows for a more general analysis of the political determinants of monetary policy and central bank institutional design. For Epstein (1992), the wage-profit nexus and finance-industry relations, in addition to the international position and political independence of the central bank, form the basic building blocks of monetary policy-bias.

In other studies of the politics of monetary policy, Henning (1994), for example, shows that private sector preferences play an important role in external monetary policy making and exchange rate management. These preferences are also the outcome of the structural relationship between banking and industry. The public sector plays a role in exchange rate policy given the degree of independence of the central bank from the political authorities and the relative roles of the central bank and the ministries of finance in external monetary policy making.

Moreover, Maxfield (1997) argues that in developing countries the international dimension to the politics of central bank independence is significant. The international framework analyses the impact of the need for international creditworthiness and balance of payments equilibrium on the domestic politics of the different sectoral groups and the government in relation to the degree of independence of the central bank. Discussing several cases of central bank independence in developing countries, Maxfield (1997) reaches the conclusion that the greater a country's need for capital inflows and foreign investment, the higher is the push by the financial sector and the government for an independent central bank.

This chapter studies the political economy of central banking in the Middle East and North Africa, specifically the relationship between central bank independence and inflationary outcomes in a set of MENA countries. The chapter also studies the rise of central banking in Lebanon, the MENA country with a tradition of free market policies implemented by most governments in Lebanon in the post-independence period. Examples of studies of specific country experiences are given in Goodman (1992) for Western European countries, Livingston (1986) for the United States of America (USA), Cukierman (2007) for Israel and Makinen (2001) for a specific period in the case of Poland.

This special reference to the Lebanon experience investigates further what we can call the Posen Hypothesis (Posen, 1993; 1995) on the importance of political arrangements and especially the influence of the financial sector on the choice of a particular central banking regime. The lessons of the experience of Lebanon show that an independent central bank follows anti-inflationary policies more effectively in political-economic setups that are conducive to inflation-fighting. This corroborates the Posen hypothesis that political setups override central bank independence in generating inflationary or disinflationary biases in the economy. In such a model, central bank independence is endogenous to the political-economic matrix of relations.

The chapter is divided as follows. Section 1 investigates empirically the relationship between central bank independence as proxied by the Cukierman index and the central bank (CB) governors' turnover rate (TOR) and inflationary outcomes in the MENA region. Section 2 discusses Lebanese monetary policy in the period before the establishment of the Banque du Liban (BdL) and the political environment surrounding its establishment in 1964, especially the banking sector's opposition to it and the subsequent post-BdL monetary policy. Section 3 presents the political-economic matrix that contributed to the BdL's eventual status and stance and its transformation in the pre-civil war era between 1971 and 1975, especially with respect to capital-labour and finance-industry relations. Section 4 concludes.

1 Central Bank independence and inflation in MENA

The drive towards monetary reforms in the MENA region has been in place for some time now. The main reforms are aimed at eventually creating more independent central banks with more autonomy in their choice of monetary policy objectives such as inflation targeting. Such reforms are in line with the increase in CB independence in the world in the 1990s as a result of the increase in the importance of price stability, given the dismal performance of high inflation countries and

Table 2.1 Ranking of MENA central banks by the Cukierman index of independence in the 1990s and corresponding TORs

Economy	*CBI*	*TOR*
Lebanon	0.603	0.0
Egypt	0.5	0.0
Algeria	0.497	0.0
Libya	0.452	0.25
Tunisia	0.43	0.0
Jordan	0.426	0.25
Morocco	0.375	0.0
Syria	0.364	0.25

Sources: CBI from Sadek *et al.* (1996); TORs from Sturm and de Haan (2001).
Notes: TOR = Turnover rate.

globalisation (Cukierman, 2006). Table 2.1 shows the ranking of MENA countries by the Cukierman index of CB independence (CBI) in the 1990s.

The basic model which argues that cross-country differences in central bank independence cause a definite cross-country correlation in inflation is presented in Cukierman (1992). The Cukierman proposition states that the mean rate of inflation in a country is higher the lower the independence of the country's central bank. This proposition has been empirically tested for developed and developing countries with mixed results. Cukierman *et al.* (1992) have shown that there is a robust relationship between CBI measures and inflation in developed economies which breaks down for developing economies, where the TOR is significantly related to inflation. Bouwman *et al.* (2005), on the other hand, show that central bank independence as proxied by TOR is significantly related to inflation only in high inflation developing countries. Jacome and Vazquez (2005) have shown, however, that in Latin America increased central bank independence played a role in successful disinflations in the 1990s. Finally, Loungani and Sheets (1997) show that there is a robust negative relationship between CBI and inflation in twelve transition economies. The standard econometric model estimated for the MENA countries is the following:

$$q = \alpha + \beta\,(TOR) + u \tag{1}$$

where

$$q = \frac{\pi}{1+\pi}$$

is inflation transformed in order to reduce heteroescedasticity, a standard procedure in independence-inflation econometric tests (Cukierman, 1992; Jacome and Vazquez, 2005) where $0 \leq q \leq 1$.

First, the model is tested for 13 MENA countries that have data on turnover rates (TOR) for the periods 1980–1989 and 1990–1998.[3] The TOR index is a proxy for CBI and is widely used when there is a divergence between legal and actual central bank independence, especially in developing countries.

Table 2.2 shows that TOR is significant in the 1990s. Higher turnover rates are associated with higher inflation. However, the relationship between inflation and TOR is insignificant for the 1980s. To further investigate the relationship between central bank independence and inflation, the following econometric model was estimated

$$q = \alpha + \beta(CBI) + u \tag{2}$$

for the period in the 1990s given that the data on CBI is not widely available compared with the TOR. The results show that there is a positive significant relationship between Cukierman's CBI measure and inflation in MENA countries in the 1990s. Higher independence is hence associated with higher inflation. This result is based

Table 2.2 Estimation results for transformed inflation vs. TOR in MENA sample

Dependent variable: q	*1990–1998*	*1980–1989*
TOR	0.074	0.334
	(0.034)	(0.29)
Intercept	0.439	0.058
	(0.188)	(0.072)
R^2	0.331	0.107
No. of Observations	13	13

Sources: For inflation in MENA other than Lebanon, IFS database. For Lebanon, 1980–1994, IFS database; for 1995–1997, data tables in Eken and Helbling (1999); for 1998, Bank Audi (2005). For Tunisia in 1980–1982, the WPI is used instead of CPI. Numbers in parentheses are standard errors.

Notes:
TOR = Turnover rate.

Table 2.3 Estimation of the effect of CBI on inflation in MENA sample

Dependent variable: q *Regressors:*	*1990–1998*
CBI	0.667
	(0.176)
Intercept	–0.206
	(0.081)
R^2	0.704
No. of Obs.	8

Note: Numbers in parentheses are standard errors.

on a limited sample. However, the basic finding is broadly confirmed by Gisolo (2009) who finds an inconclusive relation between his new CBI index for the region and inflation.

The empirical findings in the MENA region for the effect of central bank independence on inflation are mixed. The results offer little support for the Cukierman proposition. This may be due to political-economic factors in MENA that render central bank independence or the turnover rate devoid of significant effects on monetary policy. One possible explanation is that produced by Cukierman (1992), which is a legalistic argument that legal independence in developing countries is not respected by totalitarian regimes or that 'adherence to the law is more rooted in developed democracies' (p. 454). In this respect, Dolmas *et al.* (2000) showed that in non-democracies the measure of legal central bank independence is of little significance while the TOR is significant at the 10 per cent level. On the other hand, the lack of robustness of inflation to CB independence in MENA countries may be a result of the lack of political-economic support for lower inflation despite the existence of independent central banks and market reforms.

2 The rise of the Banque du Liban

In Lebanon, the central bank is a relatively new institution. The Banque du Liban (BdL) was established in 1964 during the modernist Chehab regime more than twenty years after Lebanon gained independence in 1943. It came on the heels of the civil war of 1958 which interrupted a period of relative stability and high growth at an average of 6.5 per cent annually in the period 1950–1956 (Issawi, 1964). The Chehab regime was the first administration in Lebanon's post-independence period that gave priority to development planning, public administration building and modernisation of the state apparatus.

By 1963, and due to increased government intervention in the economy, the budget was in deficit and the state policy had moved away from the traditional free market policies implemented by most governments in Lebanon in the post-independence period.[4] The establishment of the BdL was one of the modernisation projects of the regime. The BdL is still today one of the most independent central banks in the MENA region. Table 2.4 shows the degree of independence of the BdL given various measures of central bank independence for the 1980s and 1990s.

Prior to its establishment, central banking activities were conducted by a private bank, Banque de Syrie et du Liban (BSL), which issued the common Lebanese and Syrian currency. The BSL, by and large a French institution, was established in 1919 to take over the note issue in Lebanon after the collapse of the Ottoman Empire. This institutional setup had been a convenient one for the main financial players: the commercial banks and the BSL itself. The BSL acted more as an issuer of the currency than a modern central bank with macroeconomic policy objectives or regulatory powers. The BSL's objective was the stability of the currency.

Table 2.4 Various measures of CB independence in Lebanon, MENA and World

	BdL	*MENA*	*Developing Countries*	*Developed Countries*
Cukierman Index[a] (1980s)	0.4	0.277[b]	0.34[c]	0.37[d]
TOR (1980s)	0.2	0.2 [e]	0.265[f]	NA
TOR (1990s)	0	0.07[e]	0.190[f]	NA
Cukierman Index[g] (1990s)	0.603	0.435[h]	NA	NA

Sources: Averages are calculations by author from cited sources: [a]Index from Cukierman *et al.* (1992). [b]MENA={Egypt, Qatar, Morocco} sample from Cukierman *et al.* (1992). [c]Developing countries sample from Cukierman *et al.*(1992)—including Israel, Turkey and NICs. [d]Developed countries from Cukierman *et al.* (1992). [e]MENA={Algeria, Bahrain, Egypt, Jordan, Iran, Kuwait, Libya, Morocco, Qatar, Syria, Tunisia} sample from Sturm and de Haan (2001). [f]Developing Countries sample of 80 countries from Sturm and de Haan (2001). [g]Index calculated by Sadek *et al.* (1996), [h]MENA={Algeria, Egypt, Jordan, Libya, Morocco, Syria, Tunisia} sample from Sadek *et al.* (1996).

Notes:

a TOR=Turnover Rate of Central Bank governors.

b Cukierman Index=an index of legal independence of central banks with 0 for least independent and 1 for most independent.

According to one of its presidents the role of the BSL was to guarantee 'the safety of money, so that no abuse of credit leads to inflation' (Badrudin, 1984, p. 31).

The BSL followed a conservative note issuing policy with 100 per cent gold coverage of the note issue. At the time, the gold coverage and monetary stability were considered of the utmost importance to the confidence of economic actors in the Lebanese financial system (Persen, 1958). The gold coverage objective of the BSL was accompanied by the reliance of the economy on capital inflows to finance a chronic deficit in its foreign trade accounts. The banking system and the economy became outward-oriented, forming a financial centre for the whole Middle East (Badrudin, 1984).

The gold coverage with free capital mobility formed a quasi-gold standard. Foreign capital flows determined the main macroeconomic variables: the exchange rate, inflation and output fluctuations.[5] The quasi-gold standard cohabited well with the assignment of money issuing rights to a private institution. The BSL adhered to its narrow note-issuing role. Output stabilisation was not a policy option for the BSL during its tenure, even during the deflationary cycle between 1950 and 1954. The discount rate, under BSL control, was left to be determined by the market in order to guarantee the stability of the Lebanese pound through the mechanisms of the quasi-gold standard.[6]

The commercial banking system grew at a tremendous rate during the 1950s as a result of the banking secrecy law enacted in 1956 and the influx of capital from neighbouring countries. This ultimately led to the decline of the relative share of the BSL in the banking sector by the time the BdL was introduced in 1964. In the early 1950s the BSL held around 50 per cent of deposits and 70 per cent of advances and discounts. However, by March 1964 it held only 15 per cent of total deposits (Asseily, 1967). Moreover, the BSL's profit rate fell from an average of 12 per cent in 1954 to around 4 per cent by 1964 (Badrudin, 1984).

The introduction of the BdL was, however, met by opposition from the financial sector led by the Association of Lebanese Bankers (ABL) (Badrudin, 1984), and it was only after many amendments were introduced into the newly established money and credit code (MCC) that the ABL accepted the establishment of the BdL.[7] The ABL feared an increase in regulation and control of the banking sector by the new public monetary authority. Owen (1976) observed that Chehab 'created a central bank and instituted some control over Lebanon's free for all banking system' (p. 29).[8]

Up to this period, the commercial banks were subject to the Commercial Code which governed other commercial establishments. This state of affairs was seen by Guenther (1964) as 'curious and incongruous.' The planned MCC, which would govern the banking system and its relationship to the BdL, was the locus of a contest between the state and the commercial banks. The commercial banks fought a fierce battle with the government in defence of banking secrecy and in an attempt to maintain the financial sector's dominance of the Lebanese economy.

In an ABL letter to the prime minister during the discussion over the MCC, the ABL said 'The Lebanese Banks' Association considers that any attempt to touch the Banking Secrecy law is an attempt to change the foundations of our economic system'(Asseily, 1967:21).

The BdL was established despite such opposition but its legal and instrument independence was enhanced as a result of the ABL's opposition. The ABL opposed many proposals by the government regarding the institutional structure of the BdL. A proposal by the government's planning board that the director of the ministry of finance be a representative of the government on the central council of the BdL with powers to hold for ten days any decision taken by the council was met with opposition from the ABL. The actual law came out against such a proposal and the two members of the central council from the government ministries would not, by law, represent the views of their government. In addition the ABL was able to introduce into the BdL structure the requirement that the governor and his deputies be specialists in money and banking and the institution of a loose relationship between the government and the BdL.

Moreover, the BdL was not given the authority to require commercial banks to hold statutory reserves, which deprived it of one of the main tools of monetary policy.[9] Furthermore, article 100 of the MCC forbad the BdL from discounting commercial, industrial, and agricultural bills with terms exceeding 90 days (Asseily, 1967), which further constrained the BdL. Hence, as a result of such opposition, the BdL was established as a Rogoff-type central bank, an independent,

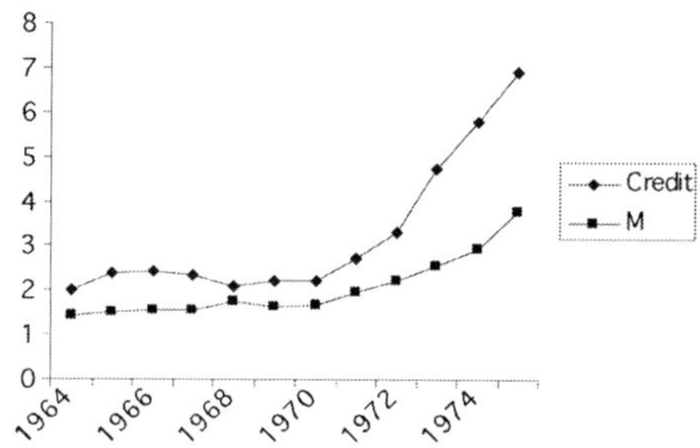

Figure 2.1 The growth of credit and money supply in the post-BdL period.

Source: IFS database.

Figure 2.2 The discount rate in Lebanon 1950–1979.

Sources: For the years 1950–1963, calculations by author from monthly data on the BSL discount rate given in Asseily (1967). For 1964–1979, IFS database.

anti-inflationary institution with the highest weight given to the stability of the value of the currency.[10]

In addition, the basic principles of the MCC were tailored to ensure that the central bank did not interfere with the fundamental principles of a free financial system. A former deputy governor of the BdL said, 'Lebanon should pay the price of freedom in order to remain an international centre, with regard to capital movements.' (Badrudin, 1984, p. 43). During the sixties, the BdL largely followed a noninterventionist policy except during the Intra crisis which threatened the banking system with wholesale bankruptcy. This incident enhanced the regulatory functions of the BdL through increased control of the banking industry. However, on the macroeconomic level, the BdL did not wield any of the traditional tools of monetary policy especially for output stabilisation.[11]

The conduct of monetary policy in 1964–1971 reflected the independent status of the newly formed central bank which had a clear anti-inflation bias.[12] In the 1960s, the growth rate of the economy weakened (Mallat, 1980). However, monetary aggregates grew at lower rates than before 1964. During the pre-1964 period, the M1 growth rate averaged 12.6 per cent while during the period 1964–1971, M1 grew at an average rate of 2.5 per cent (Saidi, 1981). Figure 2.1 gives the evolution of money supply and private credit in Lebanon during the period 1964–1975. It clearly shows a credit and money crunch during the 1964–1970 period. The BdL's passive policy in 1964–1971 was reflected in the constant discount rate policy followed by the BdL despite the credit crunch and the slowdown in economic activity during this period. Figure 2.2 shows the evolution over time of the discount rate for the BSL and BdL periods. The BSL quasi-gold system where inflation was determined by the exchange rate and economic activity was a function of capital flows was not broken by the BdL.[13]

3 The political economy of the BdL

In section 2 the financial sector was shown to have been instrumental in influencing the legal status of the BdL as an independent central bank. This overwhelming influence of the financial sector confirms the Posen hypothesis. This section undertakes further investigation of the other components of the political-economic matrix in Lebanon during the formative years of the BdL. The political-economic matrix of relations that might influence the central bank's status and policy objectives are the relationship between industry and finance, the wage-profit nexus and the position of Lebanon in the international economy (Epstein, 1992).[14]

Finance-industry relations

The relationship between finance and industry during the period up to the establishment of the BdL was governed by the liberal policies espoused by Lebanese governments in the post-independence period which favoured the development of a finance-biased liberal economy. The 1949 monetary law combined with an official gold-buying policy during the second world war and the liberalisation of the foreign exchange market in 1948 paved the way for the Lebanese economy to become the regional financial centre. The industrialists were dealt a major blow when the Syrian-Lebanese Customs Union was dissolved in 1950, an event that Owen (1976) considered the major decisive element in the economic orientation of Lebanon in the post-independence period. The trade and finance orientation caused commercial activity to increase by 56.4 per cent between 1950 and 1957 (Owen, 1976) and the share of finance in the Net National Product (NNP) doubled from 3.8 per cent to 7.0 per cent between 1948 and 1957 (Gates, 1989).

The dominance of trade and finance in the Lebanese economy did not hamper greatly the development of an industrial sector which, after a negative shock resulting from the abolition of the customs union, was able to develop into a sizable export-oriented sector (Gates, 1989). However, industry remained relatively weak in the political-economic nexus of Lebanon. In 1971, for example, an attempt by the government to raise import duties on some goods was met with a ten day general strike by Beirut traders and shopkeepers and the eventual reversal of the government's policy. However, the finance-industry relationship was very weak during the 1960s. The banking sector was not a major source of industrial finance. Industrial establishments relied on internal revenues and familial relationships in raising capital for investment (Smith, 1974).

Moreover, the banks were prohibited by the MCC from transforming short-term deposits into the long-term contracts that industrial development needs (Karam, 1979). However, a relatively small amount of the credit that was extended to the industrial sector took the form of long-term credit through the act of refinancing short-term (90 days) papers. In general, the share of credit granted to the industrial sector was low compared to commercial loans; it hovered during this period around 13 per cent of all credits advanced to the economy by commercial banks (this in a period when the economy was suffering from a credit crunch). Hence the financial system's interests were highly independent from industry. This independence and the general finance-bias in the Lebanese economy pushed the financial sector to take a very conservative stance on stable prices and the currency.

The position of Lebanon in the international economy

Closely connected with the rise of the financial sector and the subsequent finance-industry relations is the position of Lebanon in the international economy. In the discussion of the finance-bias of the Lebanese economy, it was seen that Lebanon became a financial centre for the Middle East. The rise of the banking system combined with political stability in Lebanon (Persen, 1958) formed the prerequisites for a growing and vibrant economy. Maxfield (1987) has already shown through several case studies of developing countries that the more open the economy is and the greater is the need for capital inflows and foreign investment, the higher will be the independence of the central bank.

This hypothesis exactly fitted Lebanon during the 1950s and 1960s. Lebanon during this period maintained a flexible exchange rate system which was unique during this period, as most countries followed the IMF fixed exchange rate system.

Such a place in the international economy obliged Lebanon's monetary authorities, whether the BSL or the BdL, to follow monetary policies that did not threaten the economy with capital outflows which would destabilise the whole system.

The financial crisis of Lebanon in the mid 1960s is a case in point. The crisis was mainly a liquidity crisis that ended with the collapse of the largest bank in Lebanon, *Intra Bank*. The crisis showed the vulnerability of the Lebanese financial system to international economic events. The crisis was caused by the massive outflow of capital from Lebanon in the period 1965–66 as a result of the interest rate differential created by the policies of the US and UK monetary authorities, which led to unprecedented interest rate hikes on the US dollar and the British pound (Ghattas, 1970).

Capital-labour relations

According to Epstein and Schor (1989) in 'countries that experience high levels of labour militancy, shifts in the distribution of income towards wages, or social unrest, the independence of the central bank is crucial to the policy response' (p. 147). In 1962, the establishment of a new association of workers, the General Confederation of Workers of Lebanon, led to higher demands by workers who were becoming more organised (Warburg, 1964). Although by 1967 only 25 per cent of Lebanon's labour force was unionised and the dominance of family, village and sectarian associations weakened class-based politics, as argued at the time by Khuri (1969), the 1960s witnessed the germination of an effective workers' movement that was strengthening its position in both the political and economic spheres.

Capital-labour relations during this period were tense for several reasons: first, labour militancy was increasing and there was a significant rise in the number and frequency of strikes and disputes compared to the 1950s. The number of labour disputes rose from 208 annually in 1955 to 1068 in 1963 and the number of strikes rose from 4 in 1955 to 36 in 1963, with a peak of 58 in 1959 (Khalaf, 1965). Labour unions were pushing for and obtaining higher wages during the period from 1961 to 1966. In addition, collective bargaining was instituted in 1964 by a legislative decree that gave workers more bargaining power vis-à-vis management.

Second, employers were not in total control of the labour process, which affected negatively corporate profitability.[15] Although during the 1960s rural workers had departed in increasing numbers to the cities and hence constituted a large pool of reserve labour to be tapped by the industrialists (Smith, 1974), workers were not receptive to the process of industrialisation. Management complained of absenteeism, slackness, damage to equipment, and lack of commitment to work on the part of the workers (Khalaf, 1967). Thus, the lack of a culture of industrialisation led to a slowing of the processes of labour-saving mechanisation and the deskilling of craft workers. The low level of productivity-augmenting investment rendered wages, although absolutely low, costly due to the low productivity of unskilled labour (Guenther, 1964).[16]

Mallat (1980) reports that between 1955 and 1965 there were increasing pressures for higher salaries and wages which were showing 'anti-economic upward trends', prompting the government to rationalise what Mallat called 'the social excesses of labour' (p. 212). In addition to the specific increase in labour militancy in the 1960s, there was a general trend in the 1960s for the usage of strikes, riots and violence as means for achieving political and economic goals amongst various sections of the population (Suleiman, 1972).

Hence, there is sufficient evidence to doubt that the process of industrialisation could have continued at a faster rate without endangering the profitability of the industrial sector. The rate of industrialisation was, however, impressive in the 1960s compared to the 1950s when employment in industry increased very sluggishly from 35013 workers in 1955 to 39000 workers in 1960 (Raphaeli, 1967). This trend accelerated in the 1960s. In 1964, the number of establishments was at 6300 (Smith, 1974), which increased to 11000 by 1971 (Dubar and Nasr, 1976). Problems of finance, the resistance of the working class to the discipline of industrialisation, and the increasing intensity of industrial conflict may have prevented the industrialists from pursuing a higher growth strategy.

Given the productivity problems and the lack of linkages between production and demand in the local market, we can assume that the wage-relation was Marxian (any growth oriented strategy would have decreased the profit share). The growth of real wages decreased in 1964–1966 and stabilised after 1966. At the same time, during the period 1964–1971, the trend in relative shares in industry showed a secular rise in the profit share. Measured by the ratio of profits to wages, the share of capital increased from 177 per cent in 1964 to 204 per cent in 1971 (Akel, 1985). Without yearly time series data, the effect of the deflationary policy on the cyclical component of the relative shares cannot be accurately discerned. However, since the minimum real wage increased from 1965 to 1966, followed by real wage stagnation in 1967–69, we can assume that the effect of the passive monetary policy on wages was an important element in the secular rise of the profit share during the period 1964–71. Hence, with regard to monetary policy, it is safe to assume that within the parameters of the prevailing political-economic and social structure, the industrialists were generally neutral towards the *de facto* disinflationary policy of the BdL.

Transformation in the political-economic matrix

The political-economic developments in the period following the establishment of the BdL also shed some light on its political economy. During the period 1971–75 before the start of the civil war, there was a qualitative change in the matrix of relations between different social groups and in the fundamental relations between economic variables, signalling the rise of a new political-economic regime.

The most important development was the convergence of interests between the industrialists and the financial sector as more credit was forthcoming to the industrial sector (Hani, 1984).

The influx of unprecedentedly large amounts of capital inflows (Badrudin, 1984) during the early 1970s and an increase in the demand by the Arab Gulf states for Lebanese goods (Chaib, 1981) led to this fusion of interests between industry and finance. The banking system in this period lost its fear of inflation and growth as the profitability of the industrial sector started to reflect positively on the profitability of banks. Credit to the industrial sector increased in that period at a 27 per cent annual rate (Makdisi, 1979) which propelled the industrial sector to become a major component of the Lebanese economy.

From 1971 to 1973, industrial investment totalled 350 million LL. (Lebanese pounds), which represented 30 per cent of the total capital stock (Dubar and Nasr, 1976). Given that finance and industry were becoming more integrated during this period, both parties would have had a genuine interest in a non-interventionist monetary policy. The economy was being transformed from the 'gold standard' to what Lipietz (1986) called a credit economy. The monetary authorities responded with only limited measures against inflation. The BdL's policy during this period was overwhelmed by massive capital inflows. During the period 1971–74, high liquidity rendered the discount rate policy of the BdL ineffective despite repeated increases in the discount rate.

These developments (higher credit, capital inflows, BdL policy failure) led to higher rates of inflation. These inflationary tendencies were validated by the practices of the banks, the industrial sector, and the import conglomerates.[17] First, the import oligopolies were practicing an over-pricing strategy; they marked up the price of imports above the increases in world-price levels (Makdisi, 1979). Second, the growth in short-term industrial credit, with the added cost of 2 per cent fees for revolving credit (Smith, 1974), added tremendously to the costs of production. Third, given the increased monopolisation and concentration of the industrial sector (Dubar and Nasr, 1976), these increased costs were transferred to prices through higher mark-ups. These practices led to inflationary pressures in the economy exceeding 8 per cent annually.

Inflation transformed what was a Marxian wage relation formed by capital-labour relations in 1960s into a Keynesian one resulting in a redistribution of income. Although the real wage showed an increase during the period 1971–1973 (followed by a sharp drop in 1974), the rate of surplus value increased by 4.3 per cent in the years 1972 and 1973 and by 0.8 per cent in 1974 (Akel, 1985). Hence, the increase in real wages during that period did not lead to a lowering in the profit share but, on the contrary, economic growth, investment, and export expansion led to an increase in the profit share of employers.

4 Conclusions

The relationship between central bank independence and inflationary outcomes in the MENA region has been similar to that in other developing countries or non-democracies. Central bank independence, although necessary for low-inflationary outcomes, is not sufficient. Political setups accommodating central bank inflation objectives may play a decisive role in the ultimate policy outcome of central banks, as Posen (1993) argued. This paper has shown that central banking in Lebanon has enjoyed from its inception in 1964 a high level of independence from the political authorities and this independence was supported by a political-economic setup conducive to price stability. In the formative years of the BdL, capital-labour relations, finance-industry relations and the position of the economy in the international economy provided the political support for the BdL's disinflationary bias.

Notes

1 The monetary authorities in Morocco and Tunisia, for example, have shifted their monetary policy from targeting the nominal exchange rate to targeting the real exchange rate in an effort to maintain the competitiveness of their economies (Dropsy and Grand, 2004). For reforms in Egypt, see Galal and Lawrence (2005).

2 In his comments on Posen's paper, Alesina (1995) argued that the impact of the financial sector's opposition to inflation can be incorporated into Rogoff's model by its impact on the value of the inflation-aversion weight in the central bank's loss function.

3 Data from Sturm and de Haan (2001). The countries are: Algeria, Bahrain, Egypt, Iran, Jordan, Kuwait, Lebanon, Libya, Morocco, Qatar, Sudan, Syria and Tunisia.

4 The intimate relationship between the *laissez-faire* thinking and the economic regime implemented during the post World War II period has been analysed by many students of post-independence political and economic thought in Lebanon (Issawi, 1964; Shehadi, 1987; and Traboulsi, 2002). The state's economic policy and the predominant schools of economic thought in Lebanon were vehemently Classical in the period from 1943 until the advent of the Chehab regime. One of the major achievements of the regime was the strengthening of the Ministry of Planning which instituted the first five-year development plan for the period 1962–1967 (Raphaeli, 1967). In retrospect, Saidi (1981) faults the creation of the Central Bank as an 'externality' that contributed to the bank failures that occurred in the period 1964–1967.

5 For a discussion of the gold standard in the industrialised countries and its effect on inflation and output dynamics, see Lipietz (1986) and Boyer (1990a, 1990b).

6 To investigate the role of the discount rate during this period, the following equation was estimated for 1950–1962:

$$D_t = \alpha + \beta(\frac{\Delta y}{y})_t + \gamma(E)_t$$

where D = discount rate, y = GDP and E = exchange rate (LP/$). The coefficient of Gross Domestic Product growth was insignificant while the coefficient of the exchange rate was significant, lending support to the idea that the discount rate was passive during this period.

7 ABL is the French acronym for the Association of Lebanese Banks.

8 There is a similar incident in central banking history in Germany. The shopkeepers and farmers favoured the nationalisation of the ReichBank while the bankers preferred private ownership because of fear of inflationary policies (Goodman, 1992).

9 According to Banaian *et al.* (1983) statements and laws concerning the independence of the central banks are important indicators of CB independence. Moreover, Uusitalo (1984) stressed the importance of evaluating the relative autonomy of CB with respect to government and the parliament. For example, who appoints the members of the central organs of the central bank and to whom they are responsible are important questions that would determine eventually the institutional-legal relationship between the state and the central bank.

10 For historical analyses of the rise of central banks in the United States, France, Germany, and Italy from a political economy perspective, see Livingston (1986) and Goodman (1992).

11 Makdisi (1979) argued that the main declared and undeclared policy objectives of the Lebanese government during the 1960s were price stability, maintenance and expansion of existing foreign exchange reserves, and balance of payments equilibrium.

12 As a sign of the Banque du Liban's policy orientation the items discussed in the BdL council meeting in June 1964 represented clearly the bias of the central bank. The items were: stimulation of bank credit to the real estate sector to solve the problems of frozen investment, encouraging foreign savings and attracting foreign capital by removing taxes on bank deposits, and reducing corporate profit taxes (Badrudin, 1984).

13 The practices of the banking system were also governed by a conservative and outward-looking stance. Commercial banks were, for example, taking advantage of the high interest rates on the Euro-dollar and Euro-sterling markets during 1965–66. Between September 1965 and September 1966, the foreign assets of Lebanese banks rose by 30 per cent (Ghattas, 1970). These practices were in part responsible for the financial crisis of 1966 which resulted in a further outflow of capital and tightening of the local money market.

14 Empirically Epstein (1992) has shown that the political economy matrix of increased central bank independence, speculative finance and Marxian wage relations led to higher output gaps in eight OECD (Organisation for Economic Co-operation and Development) countries in the 1980s.

15 For a discussion on the relationship between control of the labour process and the profitability of the capitalist enterprise, see Edwards (1979).

16 In the 1950s, the banks were the monopoly source of credit to the agricultural sector, which led to the channeling of resources to large commercial agriculture at the expense of the small farmer (Gates, 1989). Small producers were thrown out of work, which also explains the mass exodus from the rural areas to the cities that created a large army of labour.

17 Moreover, a militant labour movement combined with increased left-wing activity also contributed to the creation of a political-economic environment conducive to inflation.

References

Akel, M. (1985) 'The Laissez Faire Economy and its Effect on Absolute and Relative Impoverishment in Lebanon'. *At-Tarik*, 4 September, pp. 81–98 (in Arabic).

Alesina, A. (1995) Comment, in B. Bernanke and J. Rotemberg (eds), *National Bureau of Economic Research Macroeconomics Annual 1995*, pp. 287–95. Cambridge, Massachusetts: MIT Press.

Alesina, A. and Gatti, R. (1995) 'Independent Central Banks: Low Inflation at no Cost'. *American Economic Review,* 85: 196–200.

Asseily, A. (1967) *Central Banking in Lebanon.* Beirut: Khayat Press.

Badrudin, A. (1984) *The Bank of Lebanon*. London: Frances Pinter.

Banaian, K., Laney, L.O., and Willet, T.D. (1983) 'Central Bank Independence: An International Comparison'. *Federal Reserve Bank of Dallas Economic Review*, March, pp. 1–13.

Bank Audi (2005) Country and Market Update: http://www.audi.com.lb/geteconomy/economic/cm2005.pdf.

Barro, R.J. and Gordon, D.B. (1983) 'A Positive Theory of Monetary Policy in a Natural Rate Model'. *Journal of Political Economy*, 91: 589–610.

Beckerman, P. (1995) 'Central Bank 'Distress' and Hyperinflation in Argentina, 1989–1990'. *Journal of Latin American Studies*, 27: 663–82.

Blumenschein, F. (1995) 'The Positive Economic of Inflation in Brazil'. *Development and Change*, 26: 651–86.

Bouwman, K., Jong-A-Pin, R., and de Haan, J. (2005) 'On the Relationship Between Central Bank Independence and Inflation: Some More Bad News'. *Applied Financial Economics Letters*, 1: 381–5.

Boyer, R. (1990a) 'Formalising Growth Regimes' in G. Dosi (ed.), *Technical Change and Economic Theory.* New York: Pinter.

Boyer, R. (1990b) 'Technical Change and the Theory of Regulation' in G. Dosi (ed.), *Technical Change and Economic Theory*. New York: Pinter.
Chaib, A. (1981) 'Economic and Other Determinants of Exports and Export Structure: A Cross-Section Analysis of Lebanese Data'. *Banque du Liban, Bulletin Trimestriel,* No. 11: 14–19.
Cukierman, A. (1992) *Central Bank Strategy, Credibility, and Independence: Theory and Evidence*. Cambridge, Massachusetts: MIT Press.
Cukierman, A. (2006) Central Bank Independence and Monetary Policymaking Institutions: Past, Present and Future. *Proceedings of the Annual Meeting of the Chilean Economic Society*, September 2005, Vina del Mar, Chile.
Cukierman A. (2007) De Jure, De Facto, and Desired Independence: The Bank of Israel as a Case Study, in N. Liviatan and H. Barkai (eds.), *The Bank of Israel, Vol. 2, Selected Topics in Israel's Monetary Policy*, Oxford: Oxford University Press.
Cukierman, A., Miller, G.P., and Neyapti, B. (2002) 'Central Bank Reform, Liberalisation and Inflation in Transition Economies–An International Perspective'. *Journal of Monetary Economics*, 49: 237–64.
Cukierman, A., Webb, S., and Neyapti, B. (1992) 'Measuring the Independence of Central Banks and Its Effect on Policy Outcomes'. *World Bank Economic Review*, 6: 353–98.
Davis, T.E. (1963) 'Eight Decades of Inflation in Chile, 1879–1959: A Political Interpretation'. *Journal of Political Economy*, 71: 389–97.
Dibeh, G. (2002) 'The Political Economy of Inflation and Currency Depreciation in Lebanon: 1984–1992'. *Middle Eastern Studies*, 38: 33–52.
Dolmas, J., Huffman, G., and Wynne, M.A. (2000) 'Inequality, Inflation and Central Bank Independence'. *Canadian Journal of Economics*, 33: 271–87.
Dropsy, V. and Grand, N. (2004) 'Exchange Rate and Inflation Targeting in Morocco and Tunisia'. Paper presented at the Economic Research Forum meetings, December 11–3, Beirut.
Dubar, C., and Nasr, S. (1976) '*Les Classes Sociales au Liban'*. Paris: Presses de La Fondation Nationale de Sciences Politiques.
Edwards, R. (1979) *Contested Terrain: The Transformation of the Workplace in the Twentieth Century*. New York: Basic Books.
Eken, S., and Helbling, T. (eds) (1999) 'Back to the Future: Postwar Reconstruction and Stabilisation in Lebanon'. International Monetary Fund Occasional Paper, No.176.
Epstein, G. (1982) Federal Reserve Politics and Monetary Instability, in E. Stone and E. Harpham, (eds.), *The Political Economy of Public Policy*. Beverly Hills: Sage Publications.
Epstein, G. (1992) 'Political Economy and Competitive Central Banking'. *Review of Radical Political Economics,* 24: 1–30.
Epstein, G. (2003) 'Alternatives to Inflation Targeting Monetary Policy for Stable and Egalitarian Growth: A Brief Research Summary'. *Working Paper* No. 62, Political Economy Research Institute.
Epstein, G. (2005) Central Banks as Agents of Economic Development. Paper presented at UNU-WIDER Conference on Institutions and Economic Development: Theory, History and Contemporary Experiences, Helsinki, April 18–19, 2005.
Epstein, G., and Schor, J. (1989) The Divorce of the Banca d'Italia and the Italian Treasury: A Case Study of Central Bank Independence, in P. Lange, and M. Regini, (eds.), *State, Market, and Social Regulation: New Perspectives on the Italian Case,*. New York: Cambridge University Press.
Epstein, G., and Schor, J. (1990) Corporate Profitability as a Determinant of Restrictive Monetary Policy: Estimates for the Postwar United States, in T. Mayer. (ed.), *The Political Economy of American Monetary Policy*. New York: Cambridge University Press.
Fry, M. (1998) 'Assessing Central Bank Independence: Do Actions Speak Louder than Words'. *Oxford Economic Papers*, 48: 39–51.
Galal, A. and Lawrence, R.Z. (2005) 'Anchoring Reform with a US–Egypt Free Trade

Agreement'. *Policy Analyses in International Economics*, 74. Washington, DC. IIE publications.

Gates, C. (1989) 'The Historical Role of Political Economy in the Development of Modern Lebanon'. *Papers on Lebanon* 10, Centre For Lebanese Studies, Oxford:UK.

Ghattas, E. (1970) 'Lebanon's Financial Crisis in 1966: A Systemic Approach'. *Middle East Economic Journal*, 25: 31–44.

Gisolo, E. (2009) The Degree of Legal Independence of the Mediterranean Central Banks: International Comparison and Macroeconomic Implication, in D. Cobham and G. Dibeh (eds.), *Monetary Policy and Central Banking in the Middle East and North Africa*. Routledge: London.

Goodman, J.B. (1992) *Monetary Sovereignty: The Politics of Central Banking in Western Europe*. Ithaca: Cornell University Press.

Guenther, H.P. (1964) 'Banking in Lebanon'. *The Banker,* 114, July, pp. 442–448.

Hani, K. (1984) 'Some Characteristics of Industrial Growth in Lebanon, 1974–1984'. *At-Tarik*, 43(6), 70–85 (in Arabic).

Henning, C.R. (1994). *Currencies and Policies in the United States, Germany, and Japan*, Washington; Peterson Institute for International Economics.

Issawi, C. (1964) 'Economic Development and Liberalism in Lebanon'. *The Middle East Journal*, 18: 279–92.

Jacome, L.I., and Vazquez, F. (2005) 'Any Link between Legal Independence and Inflation? Evidence from Latin America and the Caribbean'. International Monetary Fund Working Paper 05/75.

Karam, F.S. (1979) '*Commercial Banking in Lebanon'*. Unpublished Masters Report, University of Texas at Austin.

Khalaf, S. (1965) 'Industrial Conflict in Lebanon'. *Human Organisation*, 24: 25–31.

Khalaf, S. (1967) 'Industrialisation and Industrial Conflict in Lebanon'. *International Journal of Comparative Sociology*, 8: 89–98.

Khuri, F.I. (1969) 'The Changing Class Structure in Lebanon'. *Middle East Journal*, 23: 29–44.

Kydland, F.E., and Prescott, E.C. (1977) 'Rules Rather Than Discretion: The Inconsistency of Optimal Plans'. *Journal of Political Economy*, 85: 473–92.

Lipietz, A. (1986) *The Enchanted World*. New York: Verso.

Livingston, J. (1986) *Origins of the Federal Reserve System: Money, Class, and Corporate Capitalism: 1890–1913*. Ithaca: Cornell University Press.

Loungani, P., and Sheets, N. (1997) 'Central Bank Independence, Inflation and Growth in Transition Economies'. *Journal of Money, Credit and Banking*, 29: 381–99.

Makdisi, S. (1979) *Financial Policy and Economic Growth: The Lebanese Experience.* New York: Columbia University Press.

Makinen, G.E. (2001) 'An Independent Central Bank and an Independent Monetary Policy: The Role of Government Budget–The Case of Poland 1924–26'. *Public Budgeting and Finance*, 21: 22–34.

Mallat, R.A. (1980) *Fiscal Policy for Social Justice and Economic Development in Lebanon.* Beirut: Aleph.

Maxfield, S. (1997) *Gatekeepers of Growth: The International Political Economy of Central Banking in Developing Countries*. New Jersey: Princeton University Press.

Owen, R. (1976) The Political Economy of Grand Liban, 1920–70, in R. Owen. (ed.), *Essays on the Crisis in Lebanon*. London: Ithaca Press.

Persen, W. (1958) 'Economic Development Since 1950'. *Middle East Journal*, 12: 277–94.

Posen, A. (1993) Why Central Bank Independence Does Not Cause Low Inflation: There is No Institutional Fix for Politics, in R. O'Brien (ed.), *Finance and the International Economy*. Oxford: Oxford University Press.

Posen, A. (1995) 'Declarations Are Not Enough: Financial Sector Sources of Central Bank Independence' in B. Bernanke and J. Rotemberg, (eds.), *National Bureau of Economic*

Research Macroeconomics Annual 1995, pp. 253–274, Cambridge, Massachusetts: MIT Press.

Posen, A. (1998) 'Central Bank Independence and Disinflationary Credibility: a Missing Link'. *Oxford Economic Papers*, 50: 335–59.

Raphaeli, N. (1967) 'Development Planning: Lebanon,' *Western Political Quarterly*, 20: 714–28.

Rogoff, K. (1985) 'The Optimal Commitment to an Intermediate Monetary Target'. *Quarterly Journal of Economics*, 100: 1169–90.

Sadek, A., Jarehi, M., and Latifah, N. (1996) *Monetary Policy in the Arab Countries*. Abu Dhabi: Arab Monetary Fund Publications (in Arabic).

Saidi, N. (1981) 'Flexible Exchange Rates and Competitive Banking: an Interpretation of Lebanon's Monetary Experience, 1950–1977'. *Banque du Liban, Bulletin Trimestriel*, 9: 28–39.

Schor, J. (1985) Wage Flexibility, Social Wage Expenditures, and Monetary Restrictiveness, in M. Jarsulic (ed.), *Money and Macro Policy*. Boston: Kluwer.

Shehadi, N. (1987) 'The Idea of Lebanon: Economy and State in the Cénacle Libanais' in Papers on Lebanon, no. 5. Centre For Lebanese Studies: Oxford, UK.

Smith, H. (1974) *Area Handbook For Lebanon*. Foreign Area Studies, American University: Washington DC.

Sturm, J-E. and de Haan, J. (2001) 'Inflation in Developing Countries: Does Central Bank Independence Matter?' *Cesifo Working Paper* no. 511. Munich.

Suleiman, M.W. (1972) 'Crisis and Revolution in Lebanon'. *Middle East Journal*, 26: 11–24.

Traboulsi, F. (2002) *Silat Bila-Wasel: Michel Chiha and the Lebanese Ideology*. Beirut: Riyad Rayess Publishers (in Arabic).

Uusitalo, P. (1984) 'Monetarism, Keynesianism, and the Institutional Status of Central Banks'. *Acta Sociologica*, 27: 31–50.

Walsh, C. (1995) Recent Central Bank Reforms and the Role of Price Stability as the Sole Objective of Monetary Policy, in B. Bernanke and J. Rotemberg (eds.), *National Bureau of Economic Research Macroeconomics Annual 1995*, pp. 237–252, Cambridge, Massachusetts: MIT Press.

Warburg, G. (1964) 'Lebanon's Trade Union Federations'. *New Outlook*, 7: 59–70.

3 The degree of legal central bank independence in MENA countries

International comparisons and macroeconomic implications

Enrico Gisolo

Introduction

Central bank independence (CBI) has been a widely explored field of research for industrialised countries since the seminal work of Alesina (1988). During the first half of the 1990s other prominent papers (see section 1 below) helped to characterise more clearly the concept of independence in order to provide an adequate taxonomy of the phenomenon and to explore the alleged relation between central bank independence and macroeconomic performance, which is particularly complex in the current context of increasing globalisation.[1]

However, there has been relatively little analysis of central bank independence in developing and emerging economies. Two recent contributions from the IMF propose a simplified methodology to calculate the *de jure* independence in some developing regions. But until now there has been no assessment of the degree of legal independence for the central banks of the countries of the south shore of the Mediterranean Sea.

Limiting the analysis to *de jure* independence involves both advantages and shortcomings. The first, rather obvious, advantage is that the evaluation has to be based only on legal documents, without considering any political or institutional arrangements (usually informal and complex) or any actual procedures or practices not clearly established in law. In other words, the assessment can be factual and the information set limited to a small number of easily available sources. Another advantage is that one can consider only well established and legally enforced rules, which are likely to prevail against informal procedures in the case of serious conflicts between different institutional bodies.

Moreover, what the law states is likely to became actual, even if it is not yet fully implemented, once appropriate enforcement mechanisms are set up. Thus the examination of central bank laws, insofar as the government authorities are committed to their fulfilment, can help to determine the future degree of central bank independence.

On the other hand, there may also be cases, for instance that of Israel in the Mediterranean region, where established practices can give guidance for the legislative authorities in preparing future laws. However, this is probably an exception which is not likely to prevail in transition economies.

There is also an obvious disadvantage in considering only central bank charters: this does not allow us to apprehend the current degree of independence and this may result in a misperception of the actual framework in which monetary policy is currently conducted. It is also true that any consolidated informal institutional agreement is likely, sooner or later, to become law when it is politically and institutionally validated (with a possible temporal delay that depends on the institutional framework). Overall, however, the legal approach should be considered a suitable one.

The aim of the present paper is to assess the degree of *de jure* central bank independence enjoyed by the central banks of the south shore of the Mediterranean Sea (which belong to the Euro–Mediterranean Partnership[2]) and of some other Middle East countries, and to shed some light on the macroeconomic outcomes associated with different degrees of independence. The chapter is organised as follows: section 1 briefly reviews the literature on central bank independence, section 2 describes the approach followed by this study, section 3 presents the results, section 4 sheds some light on the macroeconomic impact of central bank independence in the countries considered, and section 5 concludes.

1 A brief survey of the literature on central bank independence

A comprehensive review of the large body of literature on central bank independence goes beyond the aim of the present work. But it is worth noting here that several empirical studies of industrialised economies provide evidence that higher central bank autonomy is associated with lower average inflation (see, for example, Grilli *et al.*, 1991, or Cukierman, 1992). Since 1970, during the post Bretton Woods period, the industrialised countries which accorded greater legal autonomy to their central banks also experienced lower average inflation, while this seems not to have negatively affected average real growth. However, the correlation between legal autonomy and lower inflation did not appear, at least until the end of the 1990s, to be empirically significant in developing countries. Nonetheless, some more recent studies have introduced new variables in the empirical studies and the results have not always been so clear-cut (see, for example, Campillo and Miron, 1997, or de Haan and Kooi, 2000).

For a brief but complete survey of studies regarding industrialised countries, which is also interesting for its consistent comparison of different indicators and for the innovative multivariate methodology presented by the authors, see de Haan *et al.* (2003). For a more comprehensive review of the literature, with some insight also on developing countries, see Gutiérrez (2003).

The remainder of this section will deal with some recent works focused on emerging markets economies.

Lybek (1999) initially set the stage for an indicator of central bank *de jure* independence suitable for emerging economies. His study deals with countries of the former Soviet Union in the period 1995–1997. As regards the index used, it embodies most of the elements found in other similar indexes, but, in addition, it is specifically tailored to suit the guidelines followed by the Monetary and Exchange

Affairs Department and the Legal Department of the International Monetary Fund when they provide technical assistance.

Gutiérrez (2003) argues that the alleged lack of correlation between legal central bank independence and inflation in emerging economies may depend on the lower level of enforcement of the law in these countries relative to industrialised ones and, thus, considers only the provisions embodied in the legal documents of the highest rank (constitutions), where he finds evidence that those countries in Latin America and the Caribbean that entrench the independence of central banks in their constitutional charters, exhibit a better inflation performance. The index of legal independence employed is basically the same as in Lybek (1999), with a slight modification in the scale of the evaluation scores.

Dvorsky (2000) measures the degree of legal and actual central bank independence in five Central and Eastern European transition economies (namely, the Czech Republic, Hungary, Poland, Slovakia and Slovenia) using the Cukierman (1992) and the Grilli, Masciandaro and Tabellini (1991) indices for legal independence and the turnover rate of central bank governors to proxy the degree of actual central bank independence. The main conclusion of the paper is that, together with central bank independence, other requirements were needed (such as structural reforms and a proper coordination of fiscal and monetary policies) to fight inflation effectively in those countries, join the European Union and, at a later date, adopt the euro as the currency.

Sturm and de Haan (2001) analyse whether central bank independence affects inflation in an extensive set of developing countries, based on the turnover rate of central bank governors, covering the 1990s. They find that, in general, central bank independence does not appear significant in explaining inflation when they control for various inflation-related variables, except in the case of very high-inflation countries.

Beblavý (2003) uses a different approach to central bank independence, presenting the results of a questionnaire proposed personally by the author to the deputy central bank governors of the Czech Republic, Hungary, Poland and Slovakia, in order to assess which they thought were, out of the various criteria proposed in the literature, the most important indicators of central bank independence. As a control sample the author uses the analogous information provided for industrialised countries by Masciandaro and Spinelli (1994). The main results are that central bankers from both groups agree strongly on the importance of two aspects of central bank independence: goal independence and freedom to implement these goals (together with the freedom to determine the terms and limit the amount of the credit granted to the government).

In a recent work Arnone *et al.* (2006) analyse certain aspects of central bank independence based on an upgrade of the Grilli, Masciandaro and Tabellini index as of the end of 2003 for a rather extended set of OECD, developing and emerging economies. For a sub-set of countries the work assesses the change in central bank autonomy between 1992 and 2003, based on a methodology inspired by that of Cukierman (1992). The evidence shows a significant improvement in central bank autonomy, particularly for developing countries. Moreover, the increase in central banking independence seems to follow a common pattern, consisting of three stages: first the establishment of the political pre-conditions, secondly the development of a certain degree of operational autonomy and thirdly the confirmation of independence and/or its formalization through the appointment of high profile senior managers and by the enactment of appropriate laws. These results confirm the validity of the approach of the present work which considers the legislative step as a milestone, both prospectively or as a result of a recognised process, on the road to achieving a suitable degree of central bank independence.

2 Methodology and brief regional overview

Methodology

The methodology followed in the present work is derived from Gutiérrez (2003), who drew heavily on the simplified approach to assessing central bank independence in emerging market economies originally proposed by Lybek (1999). According to this method, only the legal situation is taken into account, without any consideration of the general monetary policy framework as determined by (informal) agreements and common practices.

The methodology evaluates central bank independence along five dimensions: *Central bank objectives*, *Policy formulation*, *Political autonomy*, *Economic autonomy* and *Accountability*. Each dimension presents a different number of sub-dimensions (two in the case of Central bank objectives and Accountability, four in the case of Policy formulation and Economic autonomy, seven in the case of Political autonomy). Each sub-dimension presents an evaluation scale of three to five degrees to each of which a score ranging from minus one (-1) (higher degree of dependence) to one (1) (higher degree of independence) is associated. Aggregation of scores by dimension is made by summing the sub-dimension scores.

As already indicated, there are two possible versions of the IMF methodology, one as in Lybek (1999), the other as in Gutiérrez (2003). Basically the two methodologies coincide, apart from the scale of the scores. The second one appears to be more suitable since it allows for negative evaluations on single aspects of independence, and thus seems to present a higher discriminatory power.

Some slight modifications of the Gutiérrez analysis benchmarks have been necessary to apply the methodology to the Mediterranean countries. These modifications have been kept to a minimum, in order to preserve the comparability of the results of the present analysis with other studies. A comprehensive description of the revised methodology is reported in Appendix 1. It is worth noting that the present study does not consider, as Gutierrez (2003) does, the constitutions, since the practice of embodying central bank provisions in constitutions is not present in the Mediterranean region. Instead, ordinary laws have been considered. Obviously, the fact that the independence of the central banks of the region considered in the present study is enshrined in a law or even a decree and not in the constitution does not safeguard these provisions to the same extent from frequent legislative reforms. In order to reduce the analyst-sensitivity of the results, the evaluation of legal independence according to the criteria for each country has sometimes been re-scaled by subtracting from it the relevant average value. In these cases (all except the total results in figures 1 and 2, which are absolute values) the results should be interpreted on a comparative basis rather than on an absolute one.

Like any other index for measuring independence, that used in the present study can be considered subjective. Indeed, Mangano (1998) claimed there was an important 'subjectivity' bias, deriving from an interpretation bias, when the results of the most commonly used indicators (those of Grilli, Masciandaro & Tabellini (1991), and Cukierman (1992)) were compared. In fact, the claim that the construction of indexes is likely to involve subjectivity is hard to reject.

The legal documents that have been used, which reflect the major legal developments in the South Mediterranean region, are summarised in Table 1.

Table 3.1 Legal central bank provisions in the South Mediterranean countries

Algeria	Ordonnance relative à la monnaie at au credit, no. 03-11, 26 August 2003
Cyprus	Central Bank of Cyprus Law of 2002, no. 138(1) 2002
Egypt	Presidential Decree no. 64 of 2004, promulgating the Statute of the Central Bank of Egypt, based on Law of the Central Bank, the Banking Sector and Money, promulgated by Law no. 88 of 2003
Israel	Bank of Israel Law, 5714–1954, effective from December 1954
Jordan	Law no. 23 of 1971, Law of the Central Bank of Jordan, as amended by Laws no. 37 of 1989, 14 of 1991, 10 of 1992, and 16 of 1992
Lebanon	Code of Money and Credit, promulgated by Legislative Decree no. 13513 of 1 August 1963
Libya	Law no. 8 of 1425(M)*/1996 and Law no. 1 of 1993 Concerning Banking, Currency and Credit
Malta	Central Bank of Malta Act, Chapter 204, Act XXX1 of 1967, as amended by Acts X and XXIX of 1968, XVII and XX of 1971, XXIV of 1972, XIX and LVIII of 1974; Legal Notice 148 of 1975; and Acts XX of 1981, XIII of 1983, XXXVIII of 1986, XI of 1988, XIV and XXVI of 1984, XXIV of 1995, IX and XVI of 1997, XVII of 2002 and III of 2004
Morocco	Statutes of Bank Al-Maghrib, Dahir no. 1.59.233 hijra 1378 (30 June 1959). Also Dahir bearing law no. 1-93-147 of 6 July 1993 Relating to the Activity and Control of Credit Institutions
Palestinian Authority	Law of 16 December 1997
Tunisia	Law no. 58-90 of 19 September 1958, establishing the Central Bank of Tunisia
Turkey	Law on the Central Bank of the Republic of Turkey, no. 1211, date of acceptance 14 January 1970, as amended by Law no. 4651 of 25 April 2001

A brief regional overview of the Mediterranean region

Some Mediterranean countries have experienced in recent years, or are still going through, legal developments in central bank laws. Generally these developments have led to an improvement of *de jure* independence. In some cases (Malta, Cyprus and Turkey) the reforms were related to the EU accession process. In some others, they can be seen in the wider framework of a move towards structural reform and financial system liberalisation and modernisation. Morocco's parliament has been discussing since late 2005 a widely announced but not yet definitively approved new law on central banking activity, whose general outlook is expected to increase substantially the independence of the Bank Al-Maghrib. Egypt has very recently modified the statute of its central bank. One exception in this move towards greater independence is Algeria, where the legal framework was changed (in 2001 and 2003) in ways that enhance to some extent the influence of the government on the activities of the central bank.

Finally, it is worth noting that there are several features of the Mediterranean region, some common to the region as a whole, and others specific to a particular country, that may help in understanding the results of the study. The diversity within the region is important, since this set of countries brings together the Maghreb-Mashreq ones with Israel, Malta, Cyprus and Turkey, which feature different characteristics:

1 The recent economic history of the Maghreb-Mashreq countries, for example, has undoubtedly influenced the degree of independence of its central banks; most of the countries in the region had adopted centrally-directed economic models, in which the official sector had a very important role in the economy. Therefore, a transition towards a market-oriented and private sector-led economy has been initiated in recent years – and is still continuing – with structural reforms including deregulation, liberalisation, promotion of competition etc. With respect to the financial sector, these reforms have aimed at increasing central bank independence, privatisation, liberalisation of interest rates, etc. Thus, the move towards central bank independence has to be framed in this context, in which the public sector is starting to withdraw itself from heavy interference in the private sector, but the process is still ongoing.

2 The accession of Malta and Cyprus to the EU in May 2004 undoubtedly contributed to the modification of their Central Bank laws in the direction of more independence. Indeed, during the convergence process both the European Central Bank (ECB) and the European Commission guided these countries towards the modification of their statutes in order to achieve full compliance with those of the ECB. The same applies, though under a different process since the accession procedure is not so advanced, to the case of Turkey.

3 Israel is probably the only country that cannot be classified into any of the above mentioned blocks. As a developed country, its Central Bank might be expected to be very independent, but this is not the case in legal terms.

4 At the same time, exchange rate regimes also matter: if central banks are really independent but the country has an open capital account and a fixed exchange rate regime, in practice it is very difficult for the central bank to actively pursue its main objectives independently (i.e. the so-called "impossible trinity"). Furthermore, with a currency board, for example, there is not much room for an independent national monetary policy. However, there are no such cases in this region. Some countries have evolved towards a more flexible exchange rate, in line with developments in a wide range of other countries. The exchange rate regimes of the countries considered (excluding Palestine[3] and Malta and Cyprus due to their accession status) are as follows:

- Soft pegs: Morocco;
- Hard pegs: Jordan, Lebanon;
- Exchange rate bands: Israel (free floating *de facto*: exchange rate band around 50 per cent);
- Managed floating exchange rates: Algeria, Tunisia, Egypt (though officially classified as floating);
- Independently floating exchange rate: Turkey.

As regards Libya, it pursues (like other oil producing countries such as Iran, Nigeria and Venezuela) an exchange rate regime which has some sort of tie to the value of the dollar, although it does not fit exactly under any of the above mentioned categories.

The following paragraph examines the results in the light of the above mentioned peculiarities.

3 Results

The Mediterranean region

The preliminary application of the methodology to the 12 Mediterranean countries considered (excluding Syria[4] and including Libya), led to the results set out in Appendix 1 and graphically displayed in Figure 3.1. The ranking of countries is determined by their degree of independence.

While some of the results are intuitively understandable, others are probably different from what might have been expected, possibly because *de facto* independence is sometimes very different from what merely legal considerations would imply. A notable example of this is the case of Israel in which the *de facto* independence is much greater than the *de jure* independence (see Box 1), which is the opposite of the case of the Palestine Monetary Authority, whose *de jure* independence is much greater than its *de facto* independence – except for the political autonomy criterion – mainly due to the delicate socio-political situation and to the fact that Palestine does not issue its own currency.

Box 3.1 Central bank independence in Israel

The degree of actual independence that the central bank of Israel enjoys is higher than what the law would suggest. A suitable measure of central bank independence is the weighted index used in Cukierman, Webb and Neyapti (CWN, 1992). The index features a normalised average of 16 characteristics ranging from 0 (lower independence) to 1 (highest independence). More recently, Cukierman (2007) analysed the degree of actual independence enjoyed by the Bank of Israel year by year, as well as the legal score in the original charter of 1954, after the relevant amendment of 1985 and after the implementation of the modifications proposed in 1988 by the Levin Committee (Chart 3). This Committee was composed of independent experts appointed by the Israeli Prime Minister in 1987 to issue recommendations aimed to align the central bank statute to the best international practice. The Committee recommended, among other things, that price stability be set as the overriding goal for monetary policy.

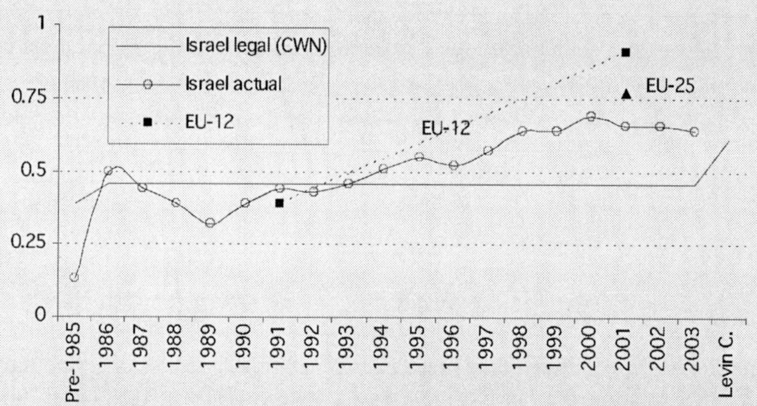

Box figure 3.1 Israel – legal vs. actual independence.

Source: Author's calculations based on data from Cukierman.

The issue of the independence of the central bank of Israel also came to the attention of the European Central Bank (ECB), which was requested to evaluate an amendment proposed by the Ministry of Finance (*Draft Bank of Israel Law, amendment No. 20, 5762–2002*), in the context of the Association Agreement between the EU and Israel. The ECB assessment stated that the Bank of Israel Law and the amendment proposed would have been basically inconsistent with the EU Treaty and the ESCB Statute. Also the IMF, in its 2004 Article IV Consultation, highlighted the need to amend the law to 'reflect international best practice regarding monetary policy objectives and procedures, along the lines of the recommendations of the Levin Committee'.

In 2005, after years of unsuccessful attempts, a proposed new Bank of Israel law was finally drafted by the government. Parliamentary approval is still pending. Key principles of the proposed new law include the creation of a monetary committee responsible for interest rate decisions; the formation of a management board responsible for oversight of administrative matters and the establishment of price stability as a primary policy objective. The proposed law should finally reconcile *de facto* and *de jure* central bank independence and fulfill the recommendations of the Levin Committee.

According to the figure, the new EU member States, Cyprus and Malta, rank among the first places. Tunisia also seems to have a very independent law, while the case of Algeria is an anomaly that derives from the use of the methodology, as explained in the following paragraph. Morocco ranks in the last position, which explains why it is in the process of modifying its central bank law to make the Bank Al-Maghrib more independent. As for the second worst result, Jordan, this is due mainly to the strong governmental involvement in the appointment and dismissal of the governor and members of the Board.

Apart from considerations on the measured level of independence, the graph also displays an important characteristic of any law: its internal coherence. In fact, a given level of independence might be less effective when some highly positive components face some other significantly negative ones compared to the case in which all the components are coherently positive. With this respect the case of Algeria shows, perhaps surprisingly, a good example of a coherently balanced law, despite the recent modification designed to reduce the independence of the central bank and the methodological caveats that will be put forward below, in the discussion of political autonomy.

As the Gutierrez methodology does not coincide with that used by the Eurosystem to assess compliance with the Treaty, we also show a weighted version of the index, in which the weights for the criteria have been assigned according to the importance given to them in the compliance assessment[4] pursued by the European Central Bank (ECB) with respect to accession countries. The results are shown in Figure 3.2.

A paradoxical consideration is that, once we consider the ECB-criteria weighted indicator, the ranking of Cyprus and, to a larger extent Turkey, decrease,

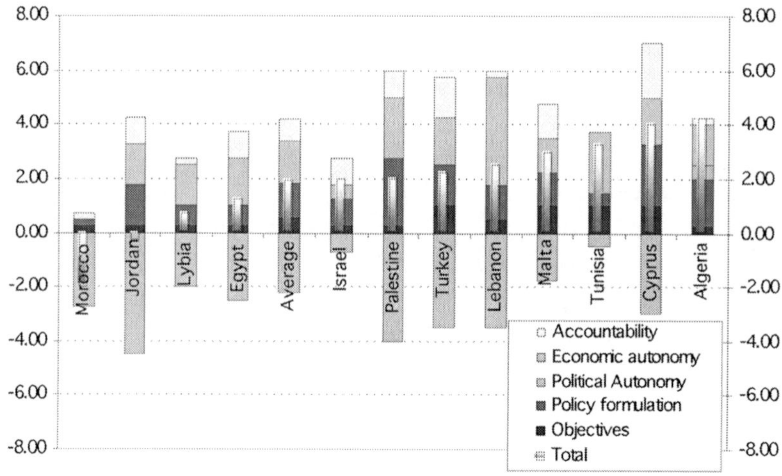

Figure 3.1 Assessment of central bank independence (absolute values).

Source: Author's calculations.

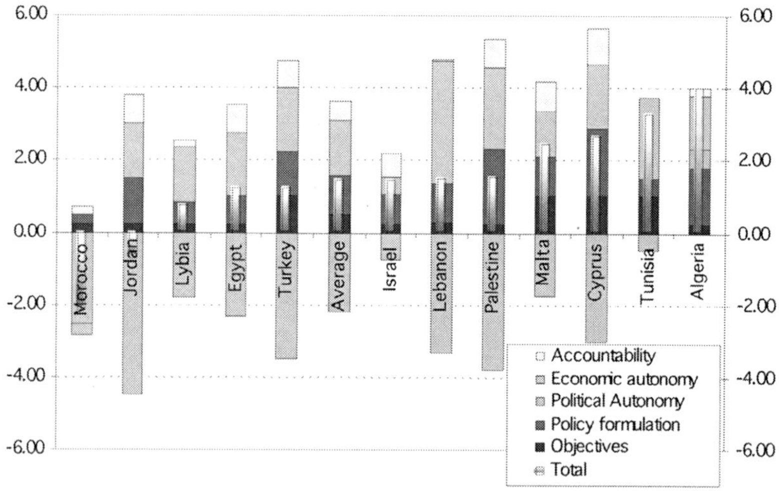

Figure 3.2 Assessment of CB independence (weighted) (absolute values).

Source: Author's calculations.

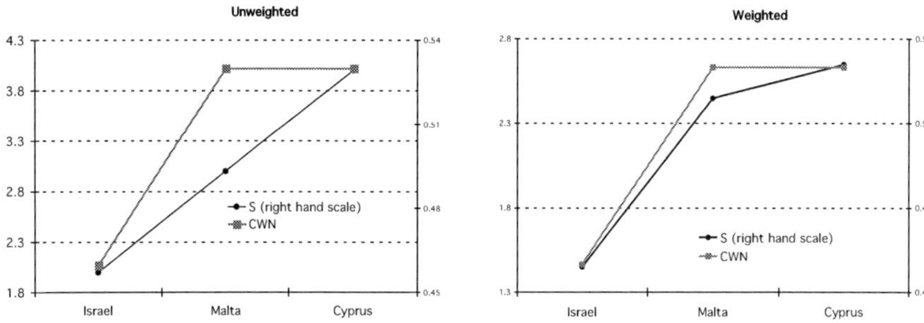

Figure 3.3 Comparison between CWN and S (Cyprus, Malta and Israel) (absolute values).

Source: Author's calculations.

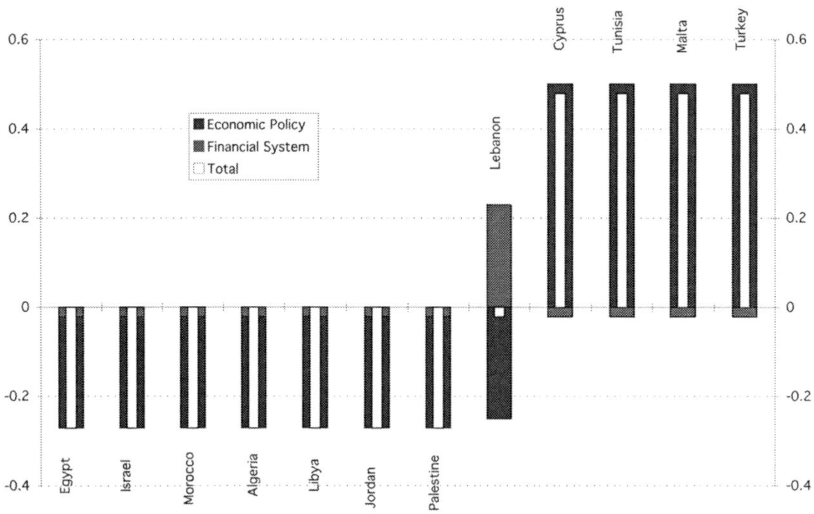

Figure 3.4 Legal central bank independence: objectives (difference from average).

Source: Author's calculations.

notwithstanding the efforts undertaken by these countries to implement the *acquis communautaire*. This is surprising, as these two countries have been considered as complying with the EU criteria. The source of the difference is methodological in nature and concerns the political criterion, or 'personal independence' in the ECB's terminology, in several aspects:

- Concerning the term of office of the Governor and the Board, the ECB criteria establish a minimum term of office of five years as acceptable, whereas for Gutierrez (2003) the benchmark is established through the comparison of the term with that of the appointing body (it should be longer).

- Concerning the competent authority to appoint the Governor and Board members, the ECB criteria do not establish which is the competent authority, while according to Gutiérrez (2003) it should not be the Executive alone or the Executive must not have a predominant role.

As a result, Turkey and Cyprus can be in full compliance with these ECB criteria and at the same time do not reach fully satisfactory results according to the Gutiérrez methodology.

On the other hand, if we consider the three countries for which we have both the Cukierman, Webb and Neyapti (1992) indicator (CWN), updated to 2001, and the score developed in the present study (S), namely Cyprus, Malta and Israel, the weighted version of the latter seems, apart from a scale factor, to present more similarity with the former (see Figure 3.3).

In the remainder of this section, the results of the assessment for each dimension of evaluation are presented and briefly discussed (for details of the methodology applied, see Appendix 2).

For the rest of the paper the scores are presented in terms of differences from the respective average, in order to emphasise the comparative dimension of the analysis.

Central bank objectives

This dimension of the evaluation analyses the situation concerning economic policy and the financial system. As for economic policy, it is very near to the ECB's definition of independence (which depends on the extent to which price stability is the overriding goal for monetary policy). The component relative to the financial system is based on the rationale that when the law attributes to an independent authority the supervision of the financial intermediaries, the autonomy of the central bank as regards the conduct of monetary policy is higher, because the monetary authority is not committed to different, potentially conflicting, goals. Accordingly, the countries that recently joined the European Union (Malta, and Cyprus) as well as the candidate country, Turkey, have higher degrees of autonomy, together with one of the Maghreb countries, Tunisia, while all the other countries show an unsatisfactory level of independence as regards the determination of the objectives of monetary policy (Figure 3.4). This is also the ranking in total terms, since the second objective does not really discriminate among countries, with the notable exception of Lebanon.

The second aspect, the financial system, considers whether supervision is explicitly delegated to an autonomous agency, granting a better mark if this is the case. Nonetheless, it is not universally accepted that the separation of supervision from the Central Bank is necessary for independence or better on effectiveness grounds.[5] Indeed, the ECB criteria on independence refer to this issue in the financial independence provisions, which state that the decisions made by the supervisory authorities within the CB but through an independent decision-making body of the central bank should not endanger the finances of the central bank as a whole.

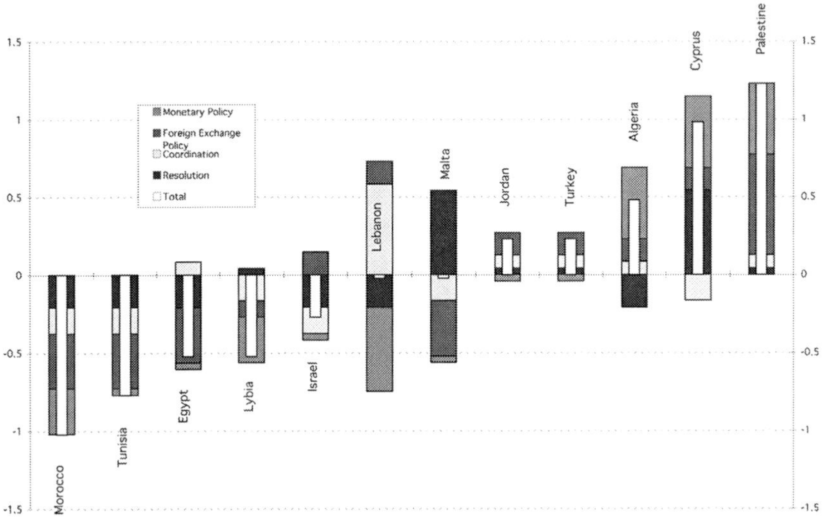

Figure 3.5 Legal central bank independence: policy formulation (values compared to the average).

Source: Author's calculations.

In fact in the present study this criterion does not tell us much, since all central banks are ranked equally, because most of them are in charge of supervision themselves, or do not make a reference to the issue. The exception is Lebanon, which has established an independent Banking Control Commission. I considered that this Commission could not be regarded as an "autonomous government agency" since its budget must be ratified by the Higher Banking Council, whose chairman is the Central Bank governor, and thus this contingent financing could interfere with the conduct of its functions. This is the reason why in total terms Lebanon is around the average, but on the "weighted criteria" according to the ECB this exception diminishes in importance.

Policy formulation

Apart from the fact that long run price stability should be regarded as the pre-eminent objective for monetary policy, an important component of central bank independence is the capacity to formulate concrete policies independently from the government. From this perspective, this criterion analyses the situation regarding monetary policy, foreign exchange policy, coordination of policies and resolution of conflicts.

In global terms, Cyprus and Turkey show a satisfactory independence level, while Malta is slightly below the average, even if joining the European Union is likely to further insulate the implementation of monetary policy from excessive governmental pressures. Algeria and Jordan also show a comparatively high degree of independence in policy formulation, while the legislation of the other countries seems to be more binding on this issue (see Figure 3.5). Palestine gets a surprisingly high mark here, but this is explained by having a good law which gives the Palestine Monetary Authority (PMA) a responsibility in the conduct of monetary and exchange rate policy which is obviously not matched by reality: the PMA does not issue its own currency, so obviously we are referring here to a merely legal and not *de facto* autonomy.

Concerning the specific objective of Monetary Policy, there are subtle differences in the wording used by each Central Bank Law which hide differences in the degree of power of the Central Bank: the ranking goes from "outline" the monetary policy (Lebanon), to "shape" it (Israel), to "give its opinion" (Morocco).

Political autonomy

Political autonomy is the dimension that in this study presents the widest range of scores, due to the fact that it is the sum of two components related to the position of the governor and the position of the other members of the board (Figures 3.6 and 3.7).

As shown in Figures 3.1 and 3.2, political autonomy is the only dimension that is globally negative for all countries, with the notable exception of Algeria. In the case of Algeria, however, it should be noted that the fact that there is no reference in the law to the term of office of the governor and vice-governors, and no reference to the grounds for dismissal, tends to raise Algerian CBI because of the scores applied; I have evaluated these aspects with a zero ("0"), which means that there is no reference in the law, while most other countries have negative scores on these issues. Nonetheless, since the articles mentioning the fixed term of office for the

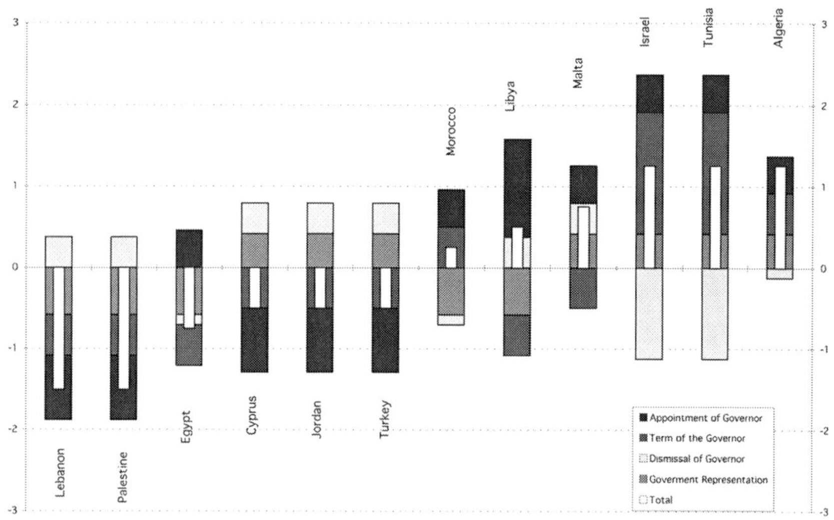

Figure 3.6 Legal central bank independence: political autonomy (governor) (difference from average).

Source: Author's calculations.

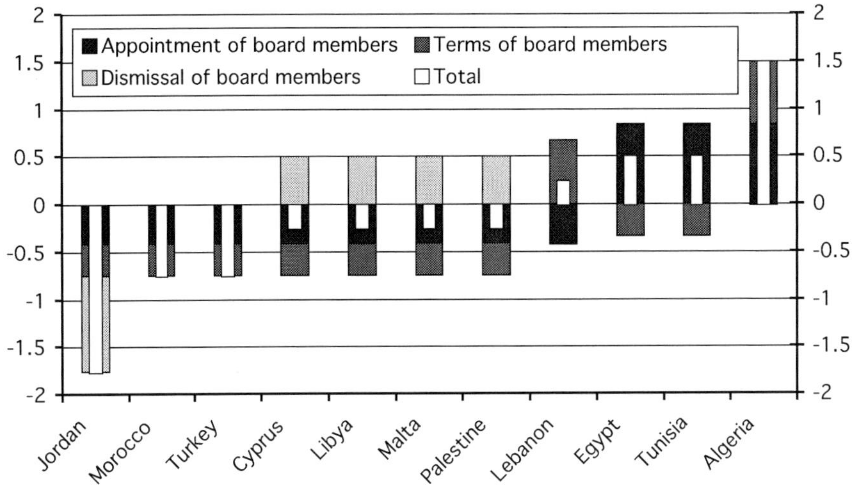

Figure 3.7 Legal central bank independence: political autonomy (board) (difference from average).

Source: Author's calculations.

Governor and vice-governors were expressly deleted from the law in a reform that took place in 2001, we might consider here that the deletion in fact grants powers to the Executive to freely dismiss the governor and Board members at any time, and that their term is shorter or equal to that of the Executive, in which case the assessment would be negative.

At the same time, the EU members and the EU candidate country do not rank very high on this aspect, which reflects the methodological difference between the ECB criteria and the Gutiérrez ones concerning the term of office of the governor and Board of Governors and their appointments.

Israel has not been included in Figure 3.7 since it is the only central bank in the region which does not have a Board of Governors, nor a Monetary Policy Committee.

As stressed before, legal indices of central bank independence are often incomplete and noisy indicators as laws are not able to specify explicitly the distribution of powers between central bank and political authorities under all contingencies (and, even when the laws are quite explicit, actual practices may deviate from them). Cukierman (1992), for example, argues that legal independence measures may be a better proxy for effective independence in industrial countries than in emerging market economies. Thus, as an alternative, Cukierman (1992) and Cukierman *et al.* (1992) used as a proxy of (actual) central bank political independence in the 1980s the actual average term of office of the governor, assuming that, at least up to some threshold, the longer this term is, the higher is the independence of the central bank from politicians. Following this line of thinking, Sturm and de Haan (2001) built an extensive data set of the *turnover rate* (TOR) of governors for 90 emerging market economies during the 1980s and the 1990s.[8]

Figure 3.8 plots a TOR-based indicator (TOR_{av} - TOR_i), namely the difference between the average TOR in the Mediterranean region and the TOR in each of the 12 Mediterranean countries considered in this study, as well as in the 90 emerging economies as a whole. By construction, positive values of this index correspond to higher political independence and vice versa. Besides the values for the entire period considered by Sturm and de Haan (2001), values for the two sub-periods 1980–1989 and 1990–1998 are also reported. Countries are ranked, in ascending order, following the value of the respective TOR-based indicator for the period 1980–1998. It is clear from Figure 3.8 that the overall numbers for the Mediterranean region are better, in terms of central bank independence, compared to the whole sample of emerging economies (only Libya and Turkey show average figures worse than the average of the 90 emerging countries). While most of the countries have experienced an improvement in the degree of independence of the central bank from politics (which has been significant in countries such as Algeria, Egypt, Israel and Tunisia), for Jordan, Malta and Syria the opposite holds.

Furthermore, the TOR can be helpful in evaluating whether there is a correlation between the indicator of legal political independence shown in Figures 6 and 7 and a measure of the actual degree of political independence, which can be proxied by the TOR-based indicator. Figure 3.9 plots the dismissal of the governor component of the political independence indicator, as well as the TOR-based 1980–98 indicator.

It is worth noting that the countries considered can be clearly split into two subsamples: Algeria, Morocco, Cyprus, Lebanon and Malta present a positive correlation between the turnover of the governor and the relative legal provisions, while the other countries show a negative correlation. In particular Libya, Jordan, Tunisia and Israel show a turnover rate higher than the one that would have been implied by the legal framework, while the opposite holds for Turkey and Egypt.

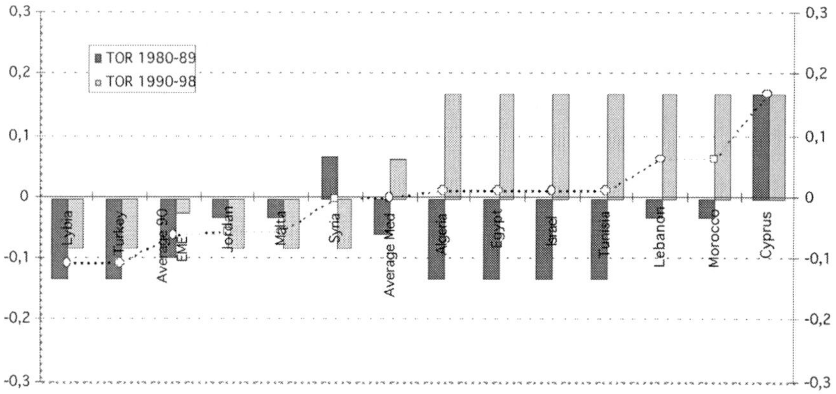

Figure 3.8 Turnover rate of governors (1980–1998) (difference from average).

Source: Author's calculations based on data reported in Sturm and de Haan (2001).
Note: Countries are ordered by TOR 1980–98 (dotted line, right scale).

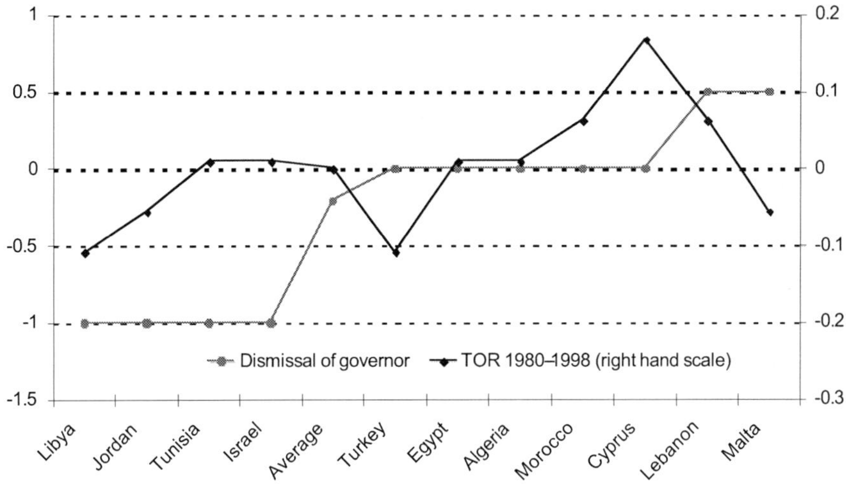

Figure 3.9 Legal vs. actual (TOR) political autonomy (dismissal of governor) (average values).

Source: Author's calculations.

Economic autonomy

As regards the economic autonomy attributed by law (which basically coincides with whether central banks have dedicated capital, their independence of judgment in financing the government and their ability to operate freely on the capital markets) the Mediterranean sample is almost equally divided into two. Lebanon, Palestine, Tunisia, Turkey, Egypt and Cyprus seem to enjoy the highest level of economic independence, while Jordan, Libya, Malta, and, to a larger extent, Morocco and Israel present a level of legal economic independence below the average (Figure 3.10). Nonetheless, the situation in Morocco in this regard is about to change according to the new law which is being elaborated.

Lebanon ranks first here because it is the only country that states that the Central Bank cannot operate with non-financial institutions (i.e. undertake quasi-fiscal activities) and also establishes clear limits on credit to the government, which is only allowed in extraordinary circumstances and subject to safeguards.

Accountability

According to the index used in the present work, the majority of central banks present a satisfactory (above average) level of accountability, in terms of the publication of statements and audit procedures. The EU member countries, together with Turkey, rank first on this criterion. On the other hand, Tunisia, Lebanon, Morocco, Algeria and Libya appear to have almost no accountability.

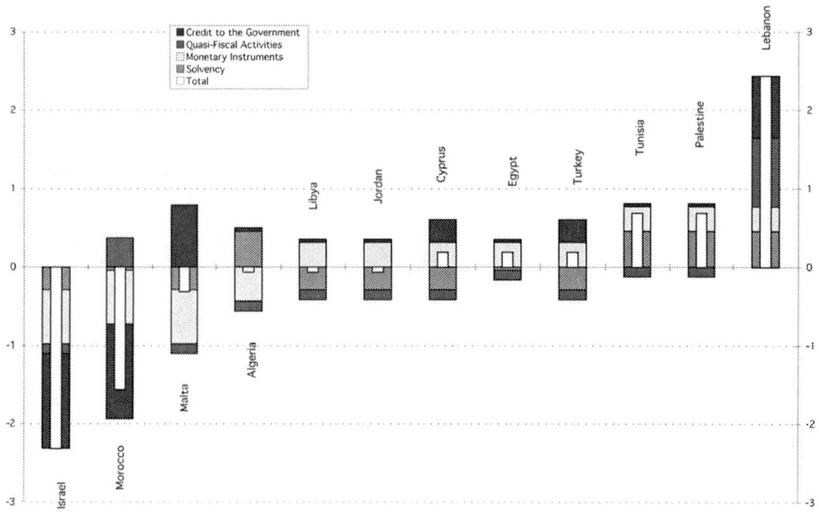

Figure 3.10 Legal central bank independence: economic autonomy (difference from average).

Source: Author's calculations.

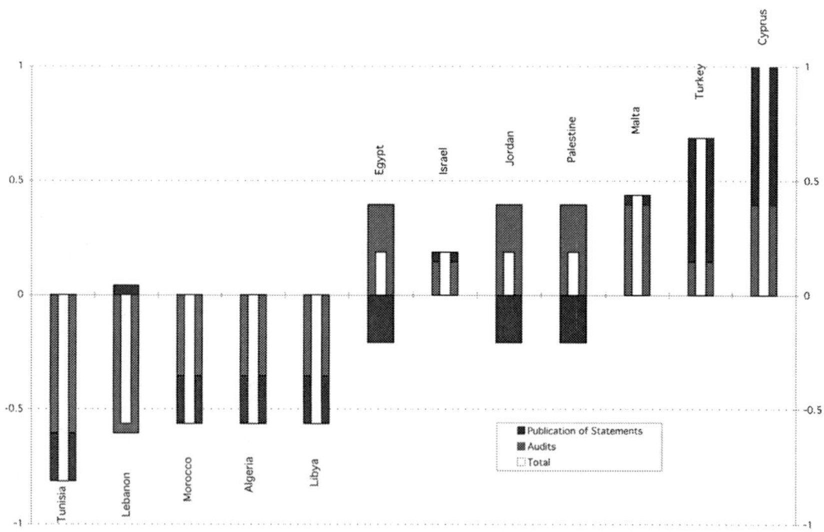

Figure 3.11 Legal central bank independence: accountability (difference from average).

Source: Author's calculations.

Syria, Iran and the United Arab Emirates

Syria, although it participates in the Barcelona process, can be considered more similar to (and compared with) other Middle Eastern countries, namely Iran and the United Arab Emirates (UAE). The inclusion of Saudi Arabia has not been possible due to the unavailability of an official English translation of its monetary law.

The legal documents considered in the present analyses are as follows:

1 Syria: Law No.23 of 2002, concerning the 'Central Bank and the Basic Monetary Order';
2 UAE: Union Law No. 10 of 1980, concerning the 'Central Bank, the Monetary System and the Organisation of Banking';
3 Iran: the Law on the Central Bank of Iran, approved on Tir 18, 1351 (July 9, 1972).

The results of the analyses are reported in Figure 3.12 and Appendix 1. Not surprisingly, Syria is the least independent of the countries considered: before 2002 the Central Bank of Syria was in fact not much more than a special branch of the Ministry of Economics and Finance, while the current formulation of the central bank law still maintains aspects of substantial dependence on the executive.

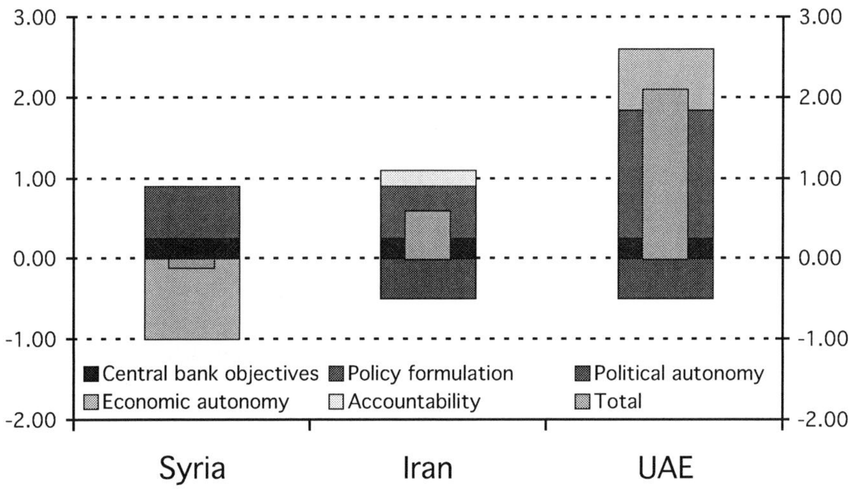

Figure 3.12 Syria, Iran, UAE: weighted independence index and its components.

Source: Author's calculations.

4 The macroeconomic impact of central bank independence

The Mediterranean region

The previous section of this chapter reported the results of an extensive analysis of the charters of the central banks of the southern shore of the Mediterranean Sea and thus gave a picture of the degree of central bank legal independence in the area. Nevertheless, as stated above, legal independence does not necessarily imply actual independence, at least in the short run. To make a preliminary assessment of the extent to which legal independence may correspond to actual, an analysis of the relationship between the calculated independence indicator and the average inflation over the past ten years may prove to be useful. The results of such an analysis are reported in Figure 3.13 which plots the independence indicator and the average inflation rate.[6]

As mentioned, the central bank of Israel enjoys a degree of actual independence higher than the one suggested by the legal indicators. Bearing in mind this consideration, Figure 3.13 clearly shows how (amongst the central banks of the countries of the Barcelona Process *for which data are both reliable and comparable*), we can identify a group of five which shows the expected correlation between the legal independence indicator and inflation (Egypt, Israel, Cyprus, Malta and Tunisia) and two central banks whose actual anti-inflation behaviour seems stronger than that implied by the legal indicator (Jordan and, even more, Morocco). On the other hand, Algeria shows a higher-than-expected medium-term inflation rate when compared to the legal independence enjoyed by its central bank.

By comparing the legal independence indicators with a measure of the medium term excess money growth (EMG), defined as the average difference between the growth rate of quasi-money and that of GDP over the last ten years (as in Figure 3.14) the following conclusion can be drawn: EMG is highly correlated with inflation, as might be expected, except for Morocco and Jordan. This may imply a different interpretation of the behaviour of the national central banks: they may have actually pursued an expansionary monetary policy that has been only partially translated into prices due to some deflationary pressures. In other words, they may have not been as conservative as the analysis of medium term inflation would suggest.

Notwithstanding the fact that economic theory does not present any conclusive argument in favour of the view that inflation, at least within common recorded values, may lower growth, there is a quite widespread consensus that when inflation is under control, the market's uncertainties are reduced, the price formation mechanism is thus more effective and, as a consequence (provided that the market mechanisms are working) the resulting better allocation of resources (through price adjustments) should foster long term growth. The evidence from the last ten years in the countries considered does not contradict this common understanding. In fact, if we exclude Algeria, where prolonged episodes of civil war during the last decade have reduced medium-term growth rates, a trade-off seems to exist between the ten year average inflation rate and the same period growth rate. A relevant exception seems to be represented by Egypt, at least if we do not consider the high

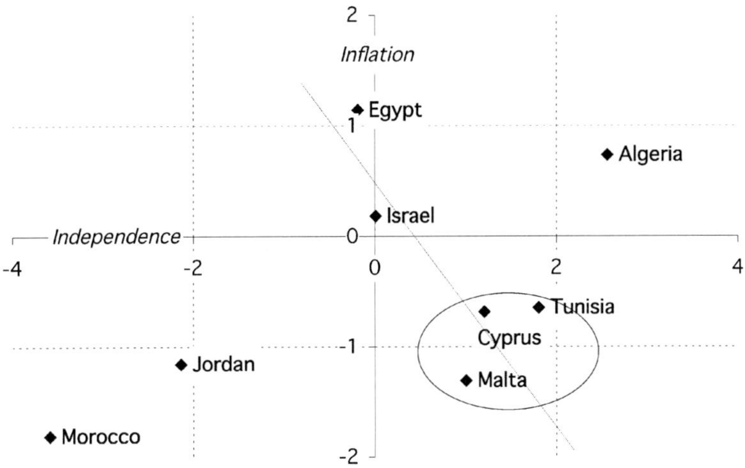

Figure 3.13 Weighted legal independence index vs. average inflation (1996–2005).

Source: Author's calculations and IFS data (IMF). Note: values are standardised around the average.

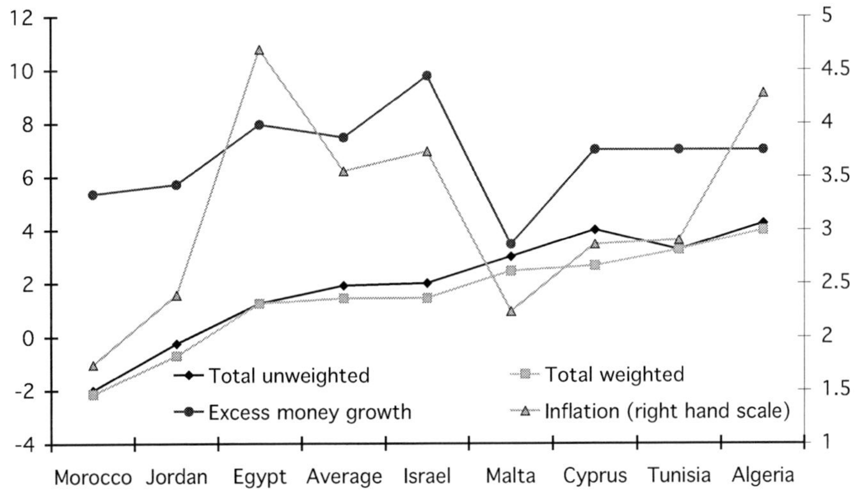

Figure 3.14 Mediterranean: independence indicator, EMG and inflation (1996–2005) (index and ten year average).

Source: Author's calculations and data from IFS.

devaluation of the currency in 2003, which contributed to the vigorous recent rise of inflation (Figure 3.15).

The available data suggest that a strong commitment to reducing inflation seems to be conducive to a better long term macroeconomic performance (except for Malta, where relative low inflation seems not to have implied faster growth), that is, the expected relation between long run inflation and growth seems to be verified in the majority of the countries considered.

Syria, Iran and the United Arab Emirates

The preliminary results on the impact of central bank independence on macroeconomic performance in Syria confirm the general picture obtained for the South Mediterranean countries.

In fact, there seems to exist a clear positive correlation between central bank independence and growth, as shown in Figure 3.16.

On the other hand, an alleged direct relationship between central bank independence and inflation seems more difficult to identify. Figure 3.17 plots the weighted CBI index against the 25–year average inflation rate.[7] While a trade-off between CBI and inflation cannot be clearly identified, it is possible to argue that the less independent central banks (Syria, Iran) have experienced, on average, a substantially higher level of inflation compared to the UAE.

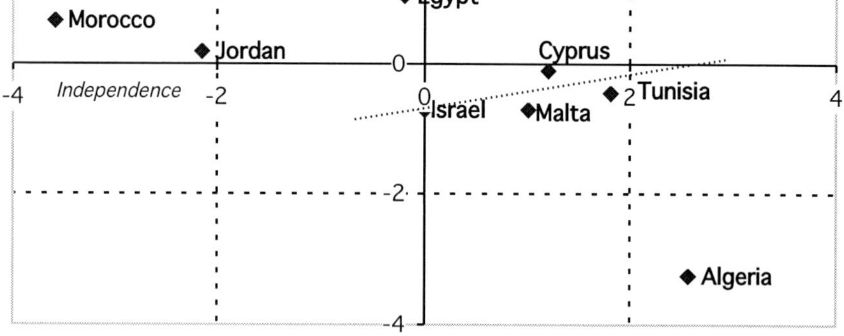

Figure 3.15 Weighted legal independence index vs. average growth (1996–2005).

Source: Author's calculations and IFS data. Note: values are standardised around the average.

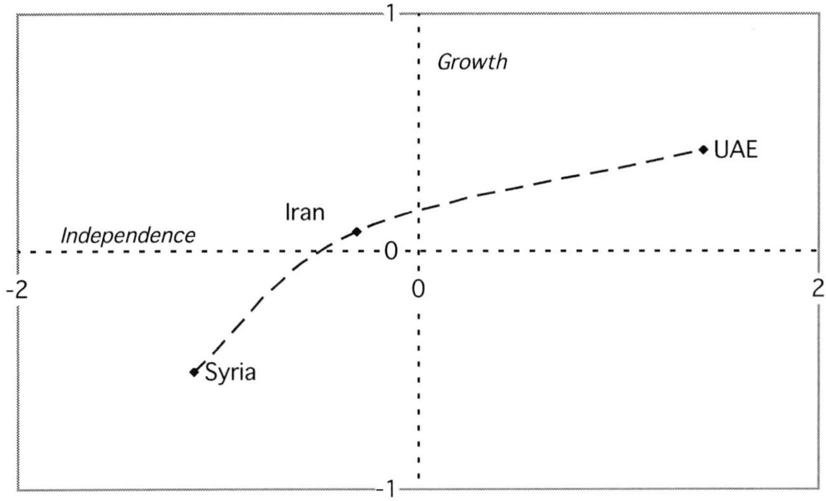

Figure 3.16 Syria, Iran, UAE: weighted independence index vs. growth (1996–2005).

Source: Author's calculations and IFS data. Note: values are standardised around the average.

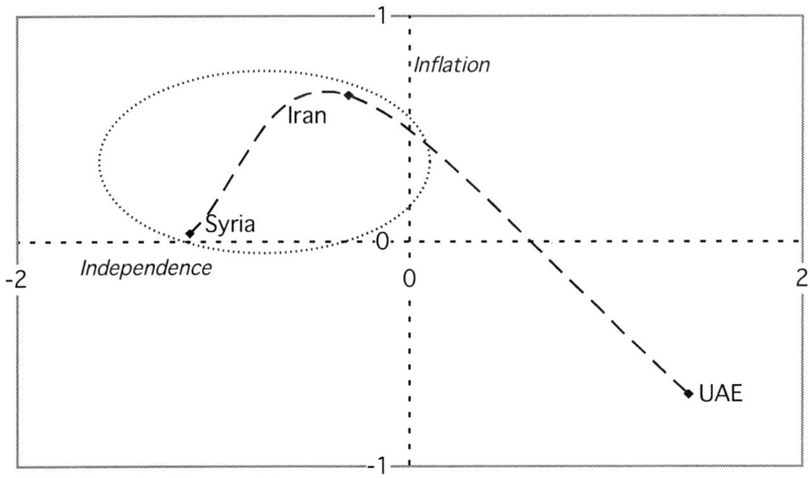

Figure 3.17 Syria, Iran, UAE: weighted independence index vs. inflation (1981–2005).

Source: Author's calculations and IFS data. Note: values are standardised around the average.

5 Concluding remarks

Central bank independence, as resulting from legal provisions, has been analysed, together with its relation with overall macroeconomic performance, in a number of studies. Notwithstanding the arguments against, there is a broad consensus on the fact that central bank independence should (at least in industrialised countries) make for lower inflation, and thus foster growth. The nexus between *de jure* central bank independence and its possible macroeconomic implications has been explored rather less for emerging economies, though some recent attempts have shed some light on this in some developing areas, including Latin America, the Baltic states and the Commonwealth of Independent States (CIS) republics, Eastern and South-Eastern Europe. Nevertheless, an assessment of central bank independence for the MENA countries had not been conducted so far. The present work represents a first investigation of the situation in this area. From a country-specific point of view, the present study shows that very few laws succeed in reaching a balanced equilibrium between all the aspects of independence. Indeed, even the countries that have a positive assessment overall and that rank among the first on most criteria, such as Cyprus and Malta, show noticeable exceptions; for example, Cyprus ranks number nine in the case of Political Autonomy-Governor, and Malta ranks number ten in Economic Autonomy. The same could be said as regards Tunisia, which always ranks number two or three except for two important exceptions in which it is nearly the last country in the list: Policy Formulation (number 11) and Accountability (last one, number 12). Lebanon could be considered an average country, with two exceptions: it is the last one in the assessment of Political Autonomy-Governor, and the first one in Economic Autonomy. The same could be said about the Palestine Monetary Authority, with exceptions; it ranks first concerning Policy Formulation. At the lower rank in the sample, we find Egypt, Jordan, Libya and Morocco.

Further research is needed to understand better the extent to which the actual situation is coherent with the legal picture, even if this effort presents non-trivial challenges, mainly due to the lack of detailed information on internal procedures and unofficial agreements and relationships. An immediate field for further research on central bank behaviour in the MENA region could be a better assessment of other features of the central banks of the area (e.g. the degree of 'conservativeness' or, in other words, of the inflation-fighting commitment) and, consequently, a more in-depth exploration of the relationship between the features of the individual central banks and the respective country-specific macroeconomic developments.

Notes

1 For a general overview of central banking in the framework of economic globalisation, see Fry *et al.* (2000).

2 Libya has only observer status. The basic analysis excludes Syria, because the relative central bank law was not available (but see the later parts of sections 3 and 4).

3 Palestine is a rather peculiar case as it currently lacks a national currency: in the *status quo* three different currencies are used: the new Israeli *shekel*, the Jordanian *dinar* (used

more in the West Bank than in Gaza) and the US dollar, with the former being used for most retail transactions, and the latter two used mostly for saving deposits and for some durable good transactions. Against this background, the most likely development seems to be the creation of a new Palestinian currency anchored, either under a currency board or under a fixed but adjustable parity, to the shekel, the dinar and the dollar and/or the euro.

4 The weights, individually ranging from 0.2 to 1, are the following: Economic policy: 1; Financial system: 0.2; Monetary policy: 1; Foreign exchange policy 0.6; Coordination: 1; Resolution: 0.8; Appointment of Governor: 1; Term of the Governor: 1; Dismissal of Governor: 1; Government representation: 0.8; Appointment of Board Members: 1; Terms of Board Members: 1; Dismissal of Board Members: 1; Credit to the Government: 1; Quasi-fiscal activities: 0.4; Monetary instruments: 1; Solvency: 1; Publication of statements: 0.2; Audit: 0.8.

5 See, for example, Goodhart and Schoenmaker (1995).

6 Data are taken from the International Financial Statistics (IFS) of the International Monetary Fund. Due to the non-availability or poor quality of the data reported for inflation and GDP growth in the latest available version of the IFS, Palestine, Lebanon and Libya have been excluded from the present analysis. Turkey has been excluded as well because available data, although reliable, show a hyperinflation pattern, not common to the area, that seems to have come to an end only very recently.

7 Due to the extremely erratic profile of the variations of the consumer price index in Syria, which amounted on average to 18.8 per cent per annum in the period 1980–1995 and to 1.9 per cent in 1996–2005, a longer reference period has been chosen for this comparison.

References

Alesina A. (1988) Macroeconomics and Politics, in *National Bureau of Economic Research Macroeconomic Annual 1988*. Cambridge UK: Cambridge University Press.

Arnone, M., Segalotto, J-F. and Laurens, B. (2006) 'Measures of Central Bank Autonomy: Empirical Evidence for OECD, Developing, and Emerging Market Economies'. International Monetary Fund Working Paper 06/228.

Beblavý, M. (2003) 'Central Bankers and Central Bank Independence'. *Scottish Journal of Political Economy*, 50: 61–8.

Campillo, M., and Miron, J.A (1997) Why does Inflation Differ Across Countries? in C. Romer and D. Romer (eds.), *Reducing Inflation: Motivation and Strategy*. Chicago: Chicago University Press.

Cukierman, A. (1992) *Central Bank Strategy, Credibility and Independence*. Cambridge, Massachusetts: MIT Press.

Cukierman, A. (2007) De Jure, De Facto and Desired Independence: The Bank of Israel as a Case Study, in N. Liviatan and H. Barkai (eds.), *The Bank of Israel: Volume 2, Selected Topics in Israel's Monetary Policy*. Oxford: Oxford University Press.

Cukierman, A., Webb, S.B. and Neyapti, B. (1992) 'Measuring the Independence of Central Banks and its Effect on Policy Outcomes'. *World Bank Economic Review*, 6: 353–8.

Dvorsky, S. (2000) 'Measuring Central Bank Independence in Selected Transition Countries and the Disinflation Process'. Bank of Finland Institute for Economies in Transition. BOFIT Discussion Paper, No. 13.

Eijffinger, S.C., and Schaling, E. (1992) 'Central Bank Independence: Criteria and Indices' Research Memorandum no. 548. Department of Economics, Tilburg University.

Fry, M., Julius, D., Mahadeva, L., Roger, S., and Sterne, G., (eds.) (2000) *Monetary Policy Frameworks in a Global Context*. London: Routledge.

Goodhart, C., and Schoenmaker, D. (1995) 'Should the Functions of Monetary Policy and Banking Supervision be Separated?' *Oxford Economic Papers*, 47: 539–60.

Grilli, V., Masciandaro, D., and Tabellini, G. (1991) 'Political and Monetary Institutions and Public Financial Policies in the Industrial Countries'. *Economic Policy*, 13: 341–92.

Gutierrez, E. (2003) 'Inflation, Performance and Constitutional Central Bank Independence: Evidence from Latin American and the Caribbean'. International Monetary Fund Working Paper 03/53.

de Haan, J., and Kooi, W.J. (2000) 'Does Central Bank Independence Really Matter? New Evidence for Developing Countries Using a New Indicator'. *Journal of Banking and Finance*, 24: 643–64.

de Haan, J., Leertouwer E., Meijer E., and T.J. Wansbeek, (2003) 'Measuring Central Bank Independence: a Latent Variable Approach'. *Scottish Journal of Political Economy*, 50: 326–40.

Lybek, T. (1999) 'Central Bank Autonomy, and Inflation and Output Performance in the Baltic States, Russia, and Other Countries of the Former Soviet Union, 1995–97'. International Monetary Fund Working Paper 99/4.

Mangano, G. (1998) 'Measuring Bank Independence: A Tale of Subjectivity and of its Consequences', *Oxford Economic Papers*, 50: 468–492.

Masciandaro, D., Spinelli, F. (1994) 'Central Banks' Independence: institutional Determinants, Rankings andCentral Bankers' Views', *Scottish Journal of Political Economy*, 41: 434–43.

Sturm, J., and de Haan, J. (2001) 'Inflation in Developing Countries: Does Central Bank Independence Matter? New Evidence Based on a New Data Set'. Unpublished manuscript, Department of Economics, University of Groningen, The Netherlands.

Appendix 3.1 Scores

Unweighted	*Cyprus*	*Egypt*	*Israel*	*Lebanon*	*Morocco*	*Tunisia*	*Algeria*	*Libya*	*Malta*	*Jordan*	*Palestine*	*Turkey*	*Average*
Central Bank Objectives													
Economic Policy	1	0.25	0.25	0.25	0.25	1	0.25	0.25	1	0.25	0.25	1	0.50
Financial System	0	0	0	0.25	0	0	0	0	0	0	0	0	0.02
Total	1	0.25	0.25	0.5	0.25	1	0.25	0.25	1	0.25	0.25	1	0.52
Policy Formulation													
Monetary Policy	1	0.5	0.5	0	0.25	0.5	1	0.25	0.5	0.5	1	0.5	0.54
Foreign Exchange Policy	0.5	0	0.5	0.5	0	0	0.5	0.25	0	0.5	1	0.5	0.35
Coordination	0	0.25	0	0.75	0	0	0.25	0	0	0.25	0.25	0.25	0.17
Resolution	0.75	0	0	0	0	0	0	0.25	0.75	0.25	0.25	0.25	0.21
Total	2.25	0.75	1	1.25	0.25	0.5	1.75	0.75	1.25	1.5	2.5	1.5	1.27
Political Autonomy													
Appointment of Governor	–1	0.25	0.25	–1	0.25	0.25	0.25	1	0.25	–1	–1	–1	–0.21
Term of the Governor	–1	–1	1	–1	0	1	0	–1	–1	–1	–1	–1	–0.50
Dismissal of Governor	0.5	0	–1	0.5	0	–1	0	0.5	0.5	0.5	0.5	0.5	0.13
Government Representation (in the Board)	0	–1	0	–1	–1	0	0	–1	0	0	–1	0	–0.42
Total	–1.5	–1.75	0.25	–2.5	–0.75	0.25	0.25	–0.5	–0.25	–1.5	–2.5	–1.5	–1.00

(continued)

Unweighted	*Cyprus*	*Egypt*	*Israel*	*Lebanon*	*Morocco*	*Tunisia*	*Algeria*	*Libya*	*Malta*	*Jordan*	*Palestine*	*Turkey*	*Average*
Political Autonomy													
Appointment of Board Members	–1	0.25	0.25	–1	–1	0.25	0.25	–1	–1	–1	–1	–1	–0.58
Terms of Board Members	–1	–1	1	0	–1	–1	0	–1	–1	–1	–1	–1	–0.67
Dismissal of Board Members	0.5	0	–1	0	0	0	0	0.5	0.5	–1	0.5	0	0.00
Total	–1.5	–0.75	0.25	–1	–2	–0.75	0.25	–1.5	–1.5	–3	–1.5	–2	–1.25
Economic Autonomy													
Credit to the Government	0.5	0.25	–1	1	–1	0.25	0.25	0.25	1	0.25	0.25	0.5	0.21
Quasi–Fiscal Activities	0	0	0	1	0.5	0	0	0	0	0	0	0	0.13
Monetary Instruments	1	1	0	1	0	1	0.25	1	0	1	1	1	0.69
Solvency	0.25	0.5	0.25	1	0.5	1	1	0.25	0.25	0.25	1	0.25	0.54
Total	1.75	1.75	–0.75	4	0	2.25	1.5	1.5	1.25	1.5	2.25	1.75	1.56
Accountability													
Publication of Statements	1	0	0.25	0.25	0	0	0	0	0.25	0	0	0.75	0.21
Audits	1	1	0.75	0	0.25	0	0.25	0.25	1	1	1	0.75	0.60
Total	2	1	1	0.25	0.25	0	0.25	0.25	1.25	1	1	1.5	0.81
TOTAL SCORE	4	1.25	2	2.5	–2	3.25	4.25	0.75	3	–0.25	2	2.25	1.92

Weighted	*Cyprus*	*Egypt*	*Israel*	*Lebanon*	*Morocco*	*Tunisia*	*Algeria*	*Libya*	*Malta*	*Jordan*	*Palestine*	*Turkey*	*Average*
Central Bank Objectives													
Economic Policy	1	0.25	0.25	0.25	0.25	1	0.25	0.25	1	0.25	0.25	1	0.50
Financial System	0	0	0	0.05	0	0	0	0	0	0	0	0	0.00
Total	1	0.25	0.25	0.3	0.25	1	0.25	0.25	1	0.25	0.25	1	0.50
Policy Formulation													
Monetary Policy	1	0.5	0.5	0	0.25	0.5	1	0.25	0.5	0.5	1	0.5	0.54
Foreign Exchange Policy	0.3	0	0.3	0.3	0	0	0.3	0.15	0	0.3	0.6	0.3	0.21
Coordination	0	0.25	0	0.75	0	0	0.25	0	0	0.25	0.25	0.25	0.17
Resolution	0.6	0	0	0	0	0	0	0.2	0.6	0.2	0.2	0.2	0.17
Total	1.9	0.75	0.8	1.05	0.25	0.5	1.55	0.6	1.1	1.25	2.05	1.25	1.09
Political Autonomy													
Appointment of Governor	–1	0.25	0.25	–1	0.25	0.25	0.25	1	0.25	–1	–1	–1	–0.21
Term of the Governor	–1	–1	1	–1	0	1	0	–1	–1	–1	–1	–1	–0.50
Dismissal of Governor	0.5	0	–1	0.5	0	–1	0	0.5	0.5	0.5	0.5	0.5	0.13
Government Representation (in the Board)	0	–0.8	0	–0.8	–0.8	0	0	–0.8	0	0	–0.8	0	–0.33
Total	–1.5	–1.55	0.25	–2.3	–0.55	0.25	0.25	–0.3	–0.25	–1.5	–2.3	–1.5	–0.92

(continued)

Weighted	*Cyprus*	*Egypt*	*Israel*	*Lebanon*	*Morocco*	*Tunisia*	*Algeria*	*Libya*	*Malta*	*Jordan*	*Palestine*	*Turkey*	*Average*
Political Autonomy													
Appointment of Board Members	–1	0.25	0.25	–1	–1	0.25	0.25	–1	–1	–1	–1	–1	–0.58
Terms of Board Members	–1	–1	1	0	–1	–1	0	–1	–1	–1	–1	–1	–0.67
Dismissal of Board Members	0.5	0	–1	0	0	0	0	0.5	0.5	–1	0.5	0	0.00
Total	–1.5	–0.75	0.25	–1	–2	–0.75	0.25	–1.5	–1.5	–3	–1.5	–2	–1.25
Economic Autonomy													
Credit to the Government	0.5	0.25	–1	1	–1	0.25	0.25	0.25	1	0.25	0.25	0.5	0.21
Quasi-Fiscal Activities	0	0	0	0.4	0.2	0	0	0	0	0	0	0	0.05
Monetary Instruments	1	1	0	1	0	1	0.25	1	0	1	1	1	0.69
Solvency	0.25	0.5	0.25	1	0.5	1	1	0.25	0.25	0.25	1	0.25	0.54
Total	1.75	1.75	–0.75	3.4	–0.3	2.25	1.5	1.5	1.25	1.5	2.25	1.75	1.49
Accountability													
Publication of Statements	0.2	0	0.05	0.05	0	0	0	0	0.05	0	0	0.15	0.04
Audits	0.8	0.8	0.6	0	0.2	0	0.2	0.2	0.8	0.8	0.8	0.6	0.48
Total	1	0.8	0.65	0.05	0.2	0	0.2	0.2	0.85	0.8	0.8	0.75	0.53
TOTAL SCORE	2.65	1.25	1.45	1.5	–2.15	3.25	4	0.75	2.45	–0.7	1.55	1.25	1.44

Unweighted	*Syria*	*Iran*	*UAE*	*Weighted*	*Syria*	*Iran*	*UAE*
Central Bank Objectives				*Central Bank Objectives*			
Economic Policy	0.25	0.25	0.25	Economic Policy	0.25	0.25	0.25
Financial System	0.00	0.00	0.00	Financial System	0.00	0.00	0.00
Total	0.25	0.25	0.25	Total	0.25	0.25	0.25
Policy Formulation				*Policy Formulation*			
Monetary Policy	0.25	0.25	1.00	Monetary Policy	0.25	0.25	1.00
Foreign Exchange Policy	0.25	0.25	1.00	Foreign Exchange Policy	0.15	0.15	0.60
Coordination	0.25	0.25	0.00	Coordination	0.25	0.25	0.00
Resolution	0.00	0.00	0.00	Resolution	0.00	0.00	0.00
Total	0.75	0.75	2.00	Total	0.65	0.65	1.60
Political Autonomy (Governor)				*Political Autonomy (Governor)*			
Appointment of Governor	0.00	0.25	0.25	Appointment of Governor	0.00	0.25	0.25
Term of the Governor	0.00	–1.00	–1.00	Term of the Governor	0.00	–1.00	–1.00
Dismissal of Governor	0.00	0.50	0.50	Dismissal of Governor	0.00	0.50	0.50
Government Representation (Board)	0.00	0.00	0.00	Government Representation	0.00	0.00	0.00
Total	0.00	–0.25	–0.25	Total	0.00	–0.25	–0.25

(continued)

Unweighted	*Syria*	*Iran*	*UAE*	*Weighted*	*Syria*	*Iran*	*UAE*
Political Autonomy (Board)				*Political Autonomy (Board)*			
Appointment of Board Members	0.00	0.25	0.25	Appointment of Board Members	0.00	0.25	0.25
Terms of Board Members	0.00	–1.00	–1.00	Terms of Board Members	0.00	–1.00	–1.00
Dismissal of Board Members	0.00	0.50	0.50	Dismissal of Board Members	0.00	0.50	0.50
Total	0.00	–0.25	–0.25	Total	0.00	–0.25	–0.25
Economic Autonomy				*Economic Autonomy*			
Credit to the Government	–1.00	0.00	0.25	Credit to the Government	–1.00	0.00	0.25
Quasi-Fiscal Activities	0.00	0.00	0.00	Quasi-Fiscal Activities	0.00	0.00	0.00
Monetary Instruments	0.00	0.00	0.00	Monetary Instruments	0.00	0.00	0.00
Solvency	0.00	0.00	0.50	Solvency	0.00	0.00	0.50
Total	–1.00	0.00	0.75	Total	–1.00	0.00	0.75
Accountability				*Accountability*			
Publication of Statements	0.00	0.00	0.00	Publication of Statements	0.00	0.00	0.00
Audits	0.00	0.25	0.00	Audits	0.00	0.00	0.00
Total	0.00	0.25	0.00	Total	0.00	0.20	0.00
TOTAL SCORE	0.00	0.75	2.50		–0.10	0.60	2.10

Appendix 3.2 Methodology

Central bank objectives	*1*	*0.75*	*0.25*	*0*	*–1*
Economic policy	Price stability or stability of the internal and external value of the currency is the sole objective or primary objective	Monetary stability is given explicit priority	Price stability, monetary stability, or stability of the currency is explicitly mentioned as one of several objectives	There is no reference in the law	Only objectives other than price or monetary stability are mentioned
Financial system	Banking supervision is explicitly delegated to an autonomous government agency	The law mentions the existence of a banking supervision agency whose members are elected and/or appointed by the legislature	Banking supervision is delegated to an institution, although its functional autonomy is not established or if the existence of a banking supervision institution is mentioned	There is no reference in the law or banking supervision is performed by the central bank or one of its instrumental bodies	—
Policy formulation	*1*	*0.75*	*0.5*	*0.25*	*0*
Monetary policy	The central bank can explicitly formulate and determine monetary policy	—	The central bank executes monetary policy and participates in its formulation	The central bank executes monetary policy, or contributes to its execution	There is no reference in the law

(*continued*)

Foreign exchange policy	The central bank can formulate and determine the exchange rate consistent with its monetary policy	—	The central bank implements exchange rate policy and participates in its formulation	The central bank implements exchange rate policy	There is no reference in the law
Coordination	The central bank and the government shall inform each other or there are government representatives in its board that do not constitute a majority, but it is stated that the central bank is responsible for formulating monetary policy	The central bank coordinates with the government in the formulation and/or implementation of central bank policies	—	Policies are jointly set or the central bank participates in policy formulation	There is no reference in the law
Resolution	In case of conflict, when the government instructs the central bank to pursue a specific policy, both parties shall make statements, presented to the legislature or published	The central bank is not subordinated to government directives and central bank independence is strongly stated	The central bank does not accept orders, in particular areas its independence is strongly stated	It is stated that the central bank is autonomous or that the bank does not accept orders from the government in particular areas	There is no reference in the law or the Executive has the power to ask for a review/ modification of the central bank policy

Political autonomy (Governor)	*1*	*0.75*	*0.5*	*0.25*	*0*	*–1*
Appointment of Governor	[Nominated (appointed) by the Government and] appointed (confirmed) by Parliament	—	Appointed by the Board of Directors	Appointed by the Head of the State [on the recommendation of the Executive]	There is no reference in the law	The Executive alone is responsible for the appointment
Term of the Governor	Longer than the term of the body responsible for, or prominently involved in, the appointment	—	The term is defined in the law with a view to promote autonomy	—	There is no reference in the law	Equal or shorter than the term of the body responsible for, or prominently involved in, the appointment
Dismissal of Governor	Dismissal can take place only in case of breach of qualifications, misconduct, or poor performance, and if the latter can be clearly defined, ruled upon by the court or by an independent tribunal, and with the approval of the legislature	Dismissal can take place only in case of breach of qualifications, misconduct, or poor performance, and with the approval of the legislature	Dismissal can take place only in case of breach of qualifications, misconduct, or poor performance	Dismissal is approved by the legislative but the grounds are not clearly specified	There is no reference in the law or the Governor is supposed to stay in charge	The Executive alone can dismiss without further specifications

(*continued*)

Government representation	—	—	—	—	There is no reference in the law	The Government has direct representatives with voting rights
Political autonomy (Board Members)	*1*	*0.75*	*0.5*	*0.25*	*0*	*–1*
Appointment of Board Members	All members are [Nominated (appointed) by the Government and] appointed (confirmed) by Parliament	The majority of members are [Nominated (appointed) by the Government and] appointed (confirmed) by Parliament	—	The Head of State appoints (on the recommendation of the Executive)	There is no reference in the law	The Executive alone is responsible for the appointment of the majority of members
Terms of Board Members	Longer than the term of the body responsible for, or prominently involved in, the appointment	—	The term is defined in the law with a view to promote autonomy	—	There is no reference in the law	Equal or shorter than the term of the body responsible for, or prominently involved in, the appointment

Dismissal of Board Members	Dismissal can only take place in case of breach of qualifications, misconduct, or poor performance, andif the latter can be clearly defined, ruled upon by the court or by an independent tribunal, and with the approval of the legislature	Dismissal can only take place in case of breach of qualifications, misconduct, or poor performance, and with the approval of the legislature	Dismissal can only take place in case of breach of qualifications, misconduct, or poor performance	Dismissal is approved by the legislative but the grounds are not clearly specified	There is no reference in the law, or the executive alone can dismiss some of the board members
Economic autonomy	*1*	*0.5*	*0.25*	*0*	*–1*
Credit to the Government	Direct or indirect credit to the Government is prohibited, with the exception of extraordinary circumstances or in the context of Open Market Operations	Direct credit to the government is forbidden	Only temporary and/or limited overdrafts are allowed	There is no reference in the law	The central bank can grant credit to the government and limits are not clearly specified

(*continued*)

Quasi-fiscal activities	The central bank cannot operate with non-financial institutions, or cannot give credit or guarantees to non-financial institutions	The central bank can not give credit to non-financial institutions		There is no reference in the law	The bank can operate with non-financial institutions	—
Monetary instruments	The central bank can set its key interest rates on its own transactions without interference from the government and can freely conduct Open Market Operations	—	The central bank can freely conduct Open Market Operations	There is no reference in the law or the central bank can not conduct completely freely Open Market Operations	—	
Solvency	The central bank has financial autonomy or its own patrimony: its budget is not subject to executive or legislative approval, and the bank cannot be dissolved without parliamentary approval	The central bank has financial autonomy and its budget is not subject to executive or legislative approval	The central bank has financial autonomy or its budget is not subject to executive or legislative approval	There is no reference in the law or the central bank cannot conduct completely freely OMOs	The law establishes interest rate controls	

Accountability	*1*	*0.75*	*0.25*	*0*
Publication of statements	The central bank regularly reports to congress on the execution of policies. [The governor appears before the legislature to answer questions, at the legislature's request]	The central bank regularly reports to the Parliament on the execution of its policies	The Governor appears before the legislature to answer questions, at the legislature's request	There is no reference in the law or the central bank reports to the Executive
Audits	Independent external auditors audit the annual financial statement	The auditor general, or an non-independent third party, audits the annual statement and the audit report is released to the Legislature	The auditor general, or a non-independent third party, audits the annual statement and the audit report is released to the Executive	There is no reference in the law

4 Monetary policy operations of debtor central banks in MENA countries[1]

Gunther Schnabl and Franziska Schobert

Introduction

During the first few years of the new millennium the world experienced historically low levels of interest rates. Starting from 1999 the Bank of Japan kept the Japanese interest rate at zero to reactivate the ailing Japanese economy. After the burst of the IT-bubble in the year 2000, the Federal Reserve cut the federal funds rate to historically low levels and only started to increase interest rates during the year 2004. Albeit to a lesser extent, the European Central Bank also reduced interest rates considerably and only started to increase interest rates during the year 2006.

The liquidity conditions in the large industrial countries in North America, East Asia and Europe had a strong impact on the emerging market economies. As economic activity in the industrialised countries was (comparatively) weak and interest rates were low, investors discovered investment opportunities in the emerging markets where interest rates tended to be high(er). Driven by this 'hunt for yield', some emerging markets experienced an unprecedented degree of capital inflows. In other emerging markets and developing countries, foreign exchange inflows were driven by the global increase of commodity prices and thereby high export revenues.

The impacts of strong foreign exchange inflows into emerging market economies are diverse. While foreign exchange inflows contribute to lower interest rates and thereby higher investment, consumption and growth, monetary authorities may also face the threat of overinvestment, inflation and overheating. Then central banks may be inclined to absorb surplus liquidity from the domestic financial system to prevent risks to price and financial stability.

As will be shown in this chapter the central banks of emerging market economies can use a broad variety of instruments to withdraw liquidity from the markets. Whichever instrument is used, there will be an asymmetric pattern of monetary policy as between large industrialised countries and small emerging market economies. While the first ones are liquidity-providing (creditor central banks), the latter ones are liquidity-absorbing (debtor central banks).

In section 1 we will characterise the asymmetric world monetary system and its impact on exchange rate and monetary policies. We explain in general the reasoning for becoming debtor and creditor central banks. The case studies in section 2 will show how central banks in countries of the Middle East and North Africa (MENA) conduct monetary policy operations in this environment. Section 3 concludes.

1 Monetary and exchange rate policies by creditor and debtor central banks

The asymmetric nature of the world currency system

McKinnon and Schnabl (2004a, 2004b) stress the asymmetric nature of the world currency system. While the United States as the issuer of the most important international currency pursues an independent monetary policy, most countries outside Europe tend to stabilise exchange rates against the dollar. A similar situation applies to the euro area and its periphery. The European Central Bank is fully independent in monetary policy making, while at the periphery of the European Monetary Union the euro is widely used as an intervention, reserve, and pegging currency (European Central Bank, 2007).

The central banks of large countries issuing international currencies such as the European Central Bank and the Federal Reserve seldom participate in foreign exchange markets. Interest rate decisions are focused on domestic inflation, growth and interest rate smoothing. The exchange rate is (widely) left to market forces. Foreign exchange intervention takes place occasionally to calm 'disorderly market conditions'.[2] The large countries issuing international currencies can float their currencies freely for two main reasons. First, in large closed economies long-term fluctuations in the exchange rate level affect a comparatively small part of the economy. Second, highly developed capital markets provide a broad variety of instruments to hedge the foreign exchange risk of short-term payments flows.

In contrast, McKinnon and Schnabl (2004a, 2004b) provide the rationale for exchange rate stabilisation in small open economies with underdeveloped capital markets. They argue that emerging markets and developing countries cannot choose their monetary framework exogenously based on specific targets of economic policy making. Rather, the regime choice is endogenous, determined by several inherent and interdependent factors such as macroeconomic stabilisation, international trade, and the currency denomination of international capital flows.

In emerging market countries and developing countries exchange rate pegs help to anchor both inflation and inflation expectations and are an important tool for domestic price stabilisation. Even if low inflation in principle can be achieved within inflation targeting frameworks, exchange rate volatility feeds into domestic macroeconomic instability in small and open economies (McKinnon, 1963): as world market prices can be assumed to be given and imported goods take a large share in domestic prices, stabilising exchange rates is equivalent to stabilising the domestic price level.

Exchange rate stabilisation in emerging markets and developing countries is also motivated from international goods markets as transaction costs for international trade decline. From this perspective fixed exchange rates are particularly important for small open economies with a high share of international trade as percent of GDP as well as for highly integrated economic regions with strong intra-regional trade linkages such as Europe and East Asia (McKinnon and Schnabl, 2004a). In this context, invoicing habits also matter.

While the trade of the large industrialised countries tends to be invoiced in domestic currencies, the trade of emerging markets is overwhelmingly invoiced in international currency. Given this phenomenon of 'external currency pricing' (Cook and Devereux, 2006) (real) exchange rate devaluations fail to have an expansionary impact on the economy through rising exports, because exports are not immediately more competitive. While exports remain constant over the short term, imports collapse due to a rapid pass-through of the exchange rate change into import prices. As import volumes remain constant over the short term, nominal imports increase and the external balance deteriorates. Furthermore, over the longer term the depreciation will reduce the import demand of a country for imports. Therefore, there is an additional incentive to keep exchange rates stable.

Finally, underdeveloped capital markets as they are prevalent in emerging markets and developing economies (Eichengreen and Hausmann, 1999) provide an incentive for exchange rate stabilisation. Due to a long tradition of inflation and depreciation, which have partially resulted in a high degree of dollarisation or euroisation of the various economies, banks and enterprises cannot use the domestic currency to borrow or to lend internationally. International investors and debtors are unwilling to accept liabilities and assets denominated in local currencies. The foreign exchange risk of net international debt and assets remains widely unhedged.

The monetary authorities can provide a substitute for fragmented capital markets by exchange rate stabilisation (McKinnon and Schnabl, 2004a, 2004b). From a short-term perspective, reducing day-to-day exchange rate volatilities softens the risk for short-term payments flows. From a more long-term perspective, fixed exchanges rates contribute to macroeconomic and financial stability as fluctuations in the exchange rate level constitute a risk for the balance sheets of banks and enterprises. In particular, in the case of liability dollarisation, sharp depreciations lead to an increase in liabilities in terms of domestic currency. In highly euroised countries with a high stock of foreign debt, such as for instance Croatia, the incentive to avoid sharp exchange rate fluctuations is even stronger (Chmelarova and Schnabl, 2006).[3]

The asymmetric incentive for exchange rate stabilisation in anchor currency countries and in emerging market countries is reflected in both the balance sheets of central banks and the working mechanisms of monetary policies. While the European Central Bank and the Federal Reserve (henceforth creditor central banks) provide liquidity in their open market operations (OMOs), central banks of emerging market economies (henceforth debtor central banks) mainly supply liquidity by intervening in the foreign exchange market (i.e. by purchasing foreign assets). If the liquidity supply resulting from foreign exchange intervention is regarded as 'excessive', debtor central banks will absorb part of the liquidity by sterilisation operations.

A creditor central bank faces a liquidity deficit in the domestic banking system, whereas a debtor central bank faces a liquidity surplus. The definition of a liquidity deficit or surplus and therefore the definition of a creditor or debtor central bank depends crucially on the definition of autonomous factors. Autonomous factors affect liquidity and therefore they affect commercial banks' deposits held at the central bank, however, they do not belong to the monetary policy operations of the central bank.[4] They can be determined by the behaviour of the public, as in the case of banknotes in circulation, or by the exchange rate objectives of the central bank, as net foreign assets change due to foreign exchange interventions. If the sum of the autonomous factors is larger on the liability side than on the asset side of the central bank balance sheet this implies that the central bank faces a liquidity deficit in the domestic banking system and vice versa in the case of a liquidity surplus.

When, for example, net foreign assets are the only liquidity-providing autonomous factor and banknotes in circulation are the only liquidity-absorbing autonomous factor, the central bank will be in a creditor position if banknotes in circulation exceed net foreign assets. In contrast, net foreign assets will exceed banknotes in circulation in the case of a debtor central bank. A creditor central bank, therefore, will supply liquidity in its regular monetary policy operations by providing new balances on banks' accounts at the central bank, with which banks can refinance their business operations. In contrast, if foreign exchange interventions have already provided excess liquidity, a debtor central bank will need to absorb liquidity by its monetary policy operations, i.e. sterilisation operations. This implies an asymmetric causality in monetary policy making. While the monetary policy operations of the euro area and the US primarily steer domestic money market conditions, the monetary policy operations of emerging market central banks tend to respond to changes in liquidity conditions usually generated by concerns over exchange rate stability.

Creditor central banks

The working mechanism of monetary policy by creditor central banks and the respective impact on the central bank's balance sheets can be explained by referring to the stylised central bank balance sheet as shown in Table 4.1. The European Central Bank and the Federal Reserve issue base money by independent decisions on open market operations which supply liquidity to the financial system. As the economy grows and currency in circulation expands on the liability side, the central bank increases its volume of open market operations on the asset side of its balance sheet. Liquidity is mainly provided by increases in low-risk domestic assets based on outright purchases of domestic government bonds, repurchase agreements (repos) or collateralised lending to banks. Foreign assets remain widely unchanged.

Figure 4.1 shows the development of the most important balance sheet items for the Eurosystem since 1999. The balance sheet consolidates the balance sheets of national central banks participating in the European monetary union. The large stock of foreign reserves – in comparison to the US – is mostly due to the past history of exchange rate stabilisation under the Bretton Woods System and the

Table 4.1 Stylised Central Bank balance sheet

Assets	*Liabilities & Capital*
1. Net Foreign Assets (incl. gold)	3. Base Money 3.1 Currency in circulation 3.2 Deposits of commercial banks 3.2.1 Required reserves 3.2.1.1 Domestic currency 3.2.1.2 Foreign currency 3.2.2 Other deposits of commercial banks
2. Domestic Assets	4. OMO: Debt securities sold
2.1 Claims on central government	5. Liabilities to banks
2.1.1 Securities	5.1 OMO: reverse repos, deposit taking auctions
2.1.1.1 OMO: outright purchases	
2.1.1.2 Purchased by other procedures	5.2 Others
2.1.2 Others: loans, advances	6. Government deposits
2.2 Claims on the banks	7. Other liabilities
2.2.1 OMO: repos, collateralised lending	8. Capital and reserves
2.2.2 Others: credit, bail-out operations	
2.3 Claims on private sector	
2.4 Other assets	

Note: OMO = open market operations.

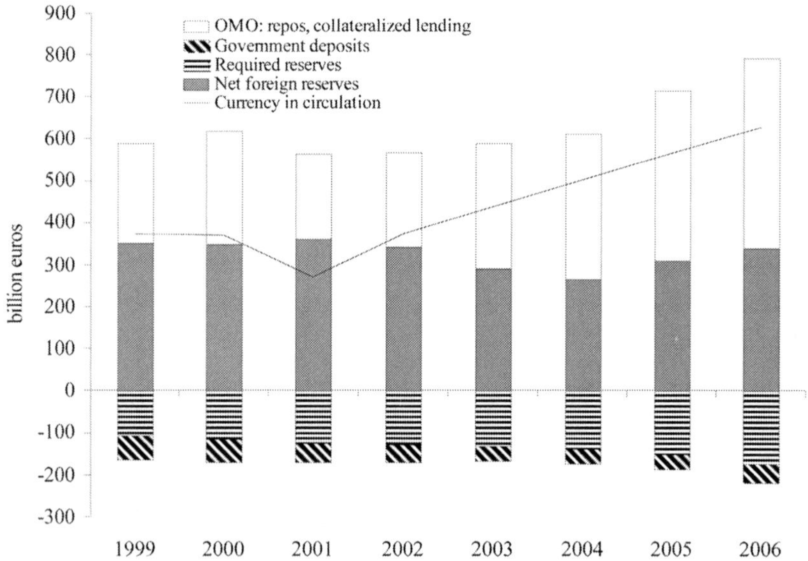

Figure 4.1 Consolidated balance sheet of the Eurosystem (1999–2006).

Source: ECB.

European Monetary System. Net foreign assets are the main autonomous factor on the asset side. Changes in net foreign assets, however, are low and mainly driven by valuation changes because the Eurosystem as a large and independently floating area hardly intervenes in the foreign exchange market.[5]

Currency in circulation and government deposits are the main autonomous factors on the liability side and the sum of the two exceeds net foreign assets. In fact, even without government deposits as an autonomous factor, currency in circulation exceeds net foreign assets and therefore puts the Eurosystem in a creditor position. Thus, the Eurosystem faces a liquidity deficit, and open market operations on the asset side such as repos and collateralised lending are the main liquidity-providing instruments, whereas currency in circulation is the main liquidity-absorbing item and expands together with open market operations on the asset side.[6]

Apart from currency in circulation, other items on the liability side are shown as negative figures in Figure 4.1. Reserve requirements develop steadily, reflecting the fact that the reserve ratio has remained constant since the creation of the Eurosystem. Minimum reserves in the Eurosystem contribute to the institutional framework of monetary policy implementation by stabilising interest rates in the money market and enlarging the structural liquidity shortage. In contrast to open market operations they are not used for actively implementing changes in the monetary policy stance. The size of government deposits is small, as many national central banks within the Eurosystem only provide essential fiscal agent functions to their governments, whereas most other banking services to the government are provided by commercial banks.

The Eurosystem provides an example of a typical creditor central bank, because the central bank faces a liquidity deficit in the domestic banking system which is mainly created and enlarged by the demand for currency. In this monetary policy setting, domestic interest rates are the operational targets of monetary policy which is conducted primarily with respect to domestic targets such as domestic price stability. International capital flows and exchange rates are allowed to adjust freely to these 'exogenous' interest rate changes. As a result, exchange rate volatility both in terms of levels and day-to-day returns is high. As the interest rate decisions of creditor central banks are focused primarily on domestic targets, foreign exchange intervention is rare. When it takes place it is sterilised because unsterilised intervention would impair the independence of domestic monetary policy making.[7]

Debtor central banks

Foreign versus domestic assets

The causality in monetary policy operations by debtor central banks tends to be in the reverse direction compared to the monetary policy operations of creditor central banks. Creditor central banks independently decide on monetary policy and therefore conduct their liquidity management usually by aiming at a domestic short-term interest rate as an operational target. Monetary policy operations by debtor central banks tend to react to exchange rate concerns which play a dominant role. Foreign exchange interventions against pressure for the appreciation of the domestic currency lead to autonomous increases of liquidity due to increases in net foreign assets. Monetary policy operations then react and sterilise the excess liquidity created by foreign exchange interventions.

Foreign exchange inflows can be driven by several factors such as foreign direct investment, short-term capital inflows attracted by high interest rates, remittances (as in Jordan or Lebanon) or current account surpluses (as in the oil exporting countries). As foreign exchange inflows lead to appreciation pressure, the central banks of emerging markets tend to intervene in the foreign exchange market thereby creating liquidity. The central banks may react to 'exchange rate driven' liquidity creation by sterilisation operations because they attempt to reach two goals at the same time: first, exchange rate stability as well as (second) price and/or financial stability.

This general pattern can be observed in many emerging market economies and is also reflected in the balance sheets of the MENA central banks. Typical debtor central banks such as the central bank of Jordan in our sample face a liquidity surplus in the domestic banking system which is created by foreign exchange market interventions. Net foreign assets are the main liquidity-providing autonomous factor and exceed currency in circulation as the main liquidity-absorbing autonomous factor. In the face of foreign exchange inflows, net foreign assets on the asset side of the central bank balance sheet increase. If the reserve accumulation remains fully unsterilised, changes in the stock of foreign reserves correspond to changes in base money. Then the liquidity supply to the domestic economy can become 'excessive' and the central bank may decide to withdraw liquidity from the market by sterilisation operations.

Additionally, the size of the liquidity surplus will depend not only on the size of the autonomous factors on the asset side, but also on the size of the autonomous factors on the liability side that absorb liquidity. The autonomous liquidity demand will be comparatively high in countries with a (history of a) sound macroeconomic environment and therefore a low degree of currency substitution. In this case, currency in circulation will be relatively high and increasing. In contrast, in countries with a long history of macroeconomic instability and inflation, domestic transactions may be widely based on international currencies. Then, as for instance in Lebanon or Israel, currency in circulation will be relatively low and hardly change with economic activity. Comparatively small liquidity expansions as created by foreign exchange interventions or fiscal financing will then create a comparatively large amount of surplus liquidity.

Therefore, a debtor central bank can also emerge in countries that face balance of payments deficits over some years, as long as the accumulated level of autonomous factors on the asset side, e.g. net foreign assets, exceeds autonomous factors on the liability side, e.g. currency in circulation. The level of foreign reserves may not emerge endogenously from foreign exchange inflows and exchange rate concerns, but it may be guided by a notion of what is an adequate level of foreign reserves. Given a sufficiently low demand for domestic currency, net foreign reserves can then quickly outweigh currency in circulation and even interventions that have accumulated only a minimum adequate level of foreign reserves will have already created a liquidity surplus in the domestic banking system.

Finally, and in addition to the liquidity creation due to reserve accumulation, central banks in emerging market economies may create (excessive) liquidity by purchasing government bonds. In this case domestic assets become a major liquidity-providing autonomous factor. For instance, in Egypt, a substantial part of central bank assets consists of government bonds, which – in contrast to the position at creditor central banks – usually reflects not monetary policy operations but a form of fiscal financing.[8] Liquidity creation takes place by non-monetary policy operations on the asset side, i.e. fiscal and quasi-fiscal operations. If this operation puts price stability at risk, the central bank absorbs liquidity partly by monetary policy operations on the liability side.

Liquidity-absorbing transactions

There are different forms of liquidity-absorbing monetary policy operations which are reflected on the liability side of the stylised central bank balance sheet in Table 4.1.[9] Item 3.2 includes 'required reserves' (item 3.2.1) and 'other deposits of commercial banks' (item 3.2.2). These other deposits of commercial banks may simply reflect excess reserves and thereby signal an unabsorbed liquidity surplus. But item 3.2.2 may also include more market-oriented monetary policy instruments other than required reserves, such as deposit facilities. Banks can use deposit facilities on their own initiative to place excess liquidity at a given interest rate at the central bank. Deposit facilities are therefore more market-oriented than required reserves, which often are not remunerated. Open market operations are considered as the most market-oriented monetary policy instruments and are reflected in items 4 and 5.1 (i.e. debt securities issued, reverse repos, or deposit taking auctions). They usually bear an interest rate that is close to a market rate.[10]

Because the rate of return of market oriented central bank sterilisation instruments competes with the other investment opportunities of commercial banks, the interest rate paid on market based sterilisation instruments needs to be close to the domestic market interest rate level. The downsides of market-oriented sterilisation instruments can be substantial sterilisation costs, in particular if the interest rate differential between emerging market economies and reserve currency countries is positive and high. Sterilisation costs can have an impact on the financial soundness of the central bank. Eventually the central bank's independence can be affected if sterilisation costs erode the central bank's capital base (Schobert 2006a).

Less costly ways to sterilise are reserve requirements. Central banks can use an active reserve requirement policy in order to absorb liquidity. It is less costly, because central banks can determine the respective remuneration rate at their own discretion or often decide not to remunerate it at all. The downside is that increasing and changing reserve requirements will lead to higher and more volatile interest rates and even financial disintermediation. As commercial banks may tend to circumvent reserve requirements with low remuneration the central bank may be forced to successively broaden the reserve base.

Alternatively, government deposits held at the central bank can restrict liquidity growth in the domestic banking system. Government deposits are usually regarded as an autonomous factor on the central banks' balance sheet in large industrial countries. In some countries, government deposits can nevertheless function like quasi-monetary policy operations, as changes in government deposits actively assist the liquidity management of the central bank. This instrument is common in countries in which the government receives a major share of the inflows in foreign currency. For example the revenues can originate from oil exports such as in Algeria and Iran, and are placed in so-called stabilisation funds held at the central bank.

Large privatisation receipts of the government can also be deposited at the central bank to avoid undue liquidity expansion, as for example in Tunisia in 2006. In both cases close cooperation between the central bank and the fiscal authorities is necessary as the degree of sterilisation will hinge strongly on government decisions to preserve the central bank's desired liquidity conditions. This can also be regarded as a downside, because an independent central bank would rather conduct its liquidity management without cooperating with the government.[11] The costs of this alternative way of restricting liquidity growth will correspond to the remuneration of the government deposits, if the deposits are interest-bearing.

2 Monetary policy operations at debtor central banks in MENA countries

Overview and data

The country study on debtor central banks in the MENA region includes Algeria, Egypt, Iran, Israel, Jordan, Kuwait, Lebanon, Morocco, Saudi Arabia, Syria, Tunisia and Turkey. Energy exports play a major role in Algeria, Iran, Kuwait and Saudi Arabia, which belong to the Organisation of Petroleum Exporting Countries (OPEC), as well as in Syria and Egypt, which are major non-OPEC oil exporting countries.[12] Exchange rates in these six countries as well as in Jordan and Lebanon are pegged or tightly managed to the US dollar. Tunisia and Morocco peg or tightly manage their currencies to a basket including the euro. Turkey and Israel officially claim floating exchange rates within an inflation targeting framework.

The central bank balance sheet data are collected from the financial statements of central banks or other statistical publications of the respective central bank with the exception of net foreign assets. Net foreign assets are calculated by using data for monetary authorities from the International Financial Statistics of the International Monetary Fund. To compare the structural differences across countries and over time we present annual data of the most important balance sheet items from 1997 until 2006 (depending on data availability). They include currency in circulation, net foreign assets, monetary policy operations, banks' and government deposits and – if applicable – other liquidity creating operations such as fiscal or quasi-fiscal operations.

Generally, required reserves are used as liquidity-absorbing monetary policy instruments by all central banks in the sample. All the central banks apart from Syria and Saudi Arabia report market-based sterilisation operations, though the size and activity differs widely both in cross section and over time (see Figures 4.2 to 4.4). Government deposits play an important role in the central banks' balance sheets in Algeria, Iran, Saudi Arabia, and Syria. Fiscal operations on the asset side are reflected in the balance sheet item 'claims on the government'. They usually include direct advances to the government, i.e. lending for budgetary purposes, or outright purchases of government securities for monetary policy purposes. The item 'claims on banks' can emerge, even if the banking system in aggregate has a liquidity surplus. It reflects either a malfunctioning of the interbank market, in the case of open market operations, or often bail-out operations or preferential loans to individual banks in the case of other credit operations.

Country analysis

Algeria, Iran, Kuwait and Saudi Arabia

The balance sheets of the central banks of Algeria, Iran, Kuwait, and Saudi Arabia as shown in Figure 4.2 reflect the fact that these OPEC countries depend heavily on oil export revenues. On the asset side of the central bank balance sheets net foreign assets dominate.[13] All four central banks are debtor central banks. Excess liquidity is absorbed mainly by reserve requirements and also by open market operations in the case of Kuwait.

In Algeria, Iran and Saudi Arabia, net foreign assets increase significantly together with government deposits. Liquidity creation due to the inflow of oil-related foreign exchange revenues is restricted by the 'parking' of these revenues in government deposits. In the cases of Algeria and Iran, government deposits reflect the working of the stabilisation funds that have existed in both countries since 2000 (Amuzegar, 2005). Saudi-Arabia has not yet officially announced a stabilisation fund. Liquidity creation from oil-related foreign exchange revenues is nevertheless restricted as government deposits increase with net foreign assets. Kuwait also uses a stabilisation fund, however, it is not held at the central bank. Therefore, the increase of net foreign assets at the central bank under-represents the increase of foreign reserve holdings due to oil-related foreign exchange revenues.

Kuwait is the only OPEC country in the sample that has actively used open market operations, i.e. the sale of Central Bank of Kuwait bonds, over recent years in order to sterilise excess liquidity.[14] In Iran the increase in net foreign assets is augmented by the increase of claims on the government. Despite high oil revenues, Iran continues to face budgetary pressures, which have presumably forced the central bank into financing the government.

Tunisia

As shown in the upper left panel of Figure 4.3 the asset side of the balance sheet of the Central Bank of Tunisia is dominated by foreign assets which have increased

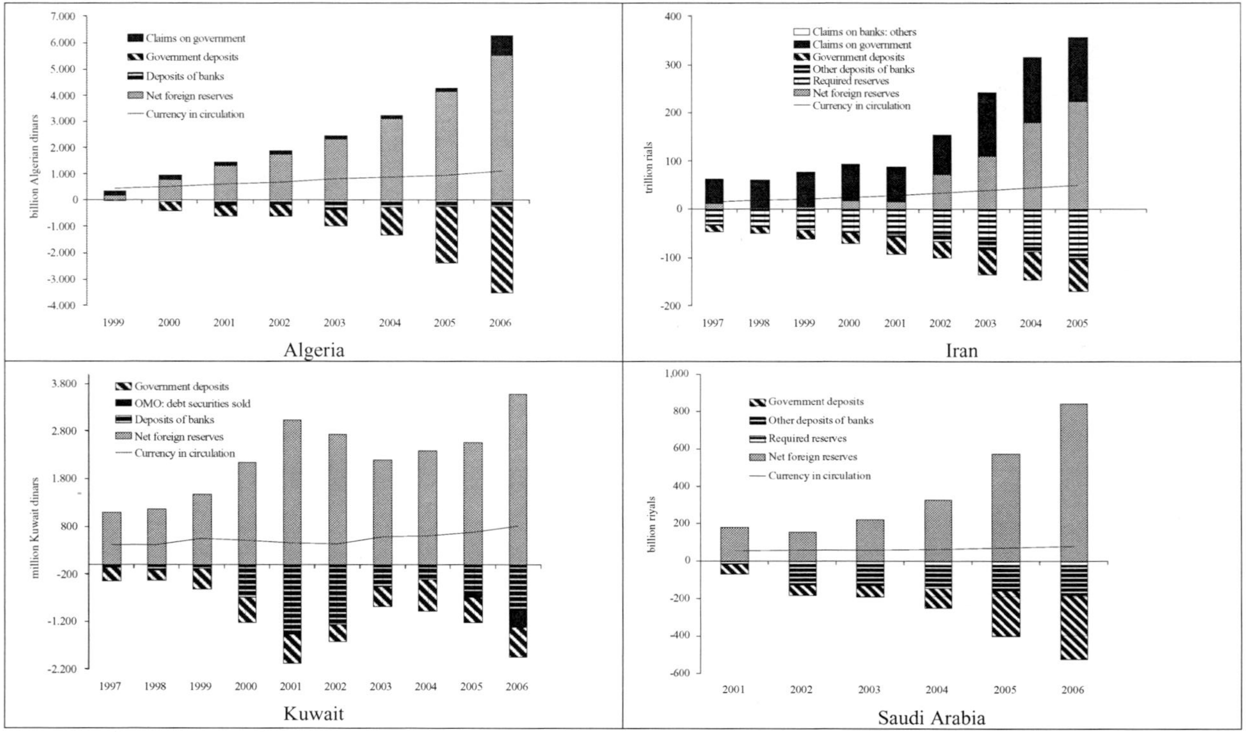

Figure 4.2 Central Bank balance sheets: Algeria, Iran, Kuwait, Saudi Arabia.

Source: National Central Banks, IMF.

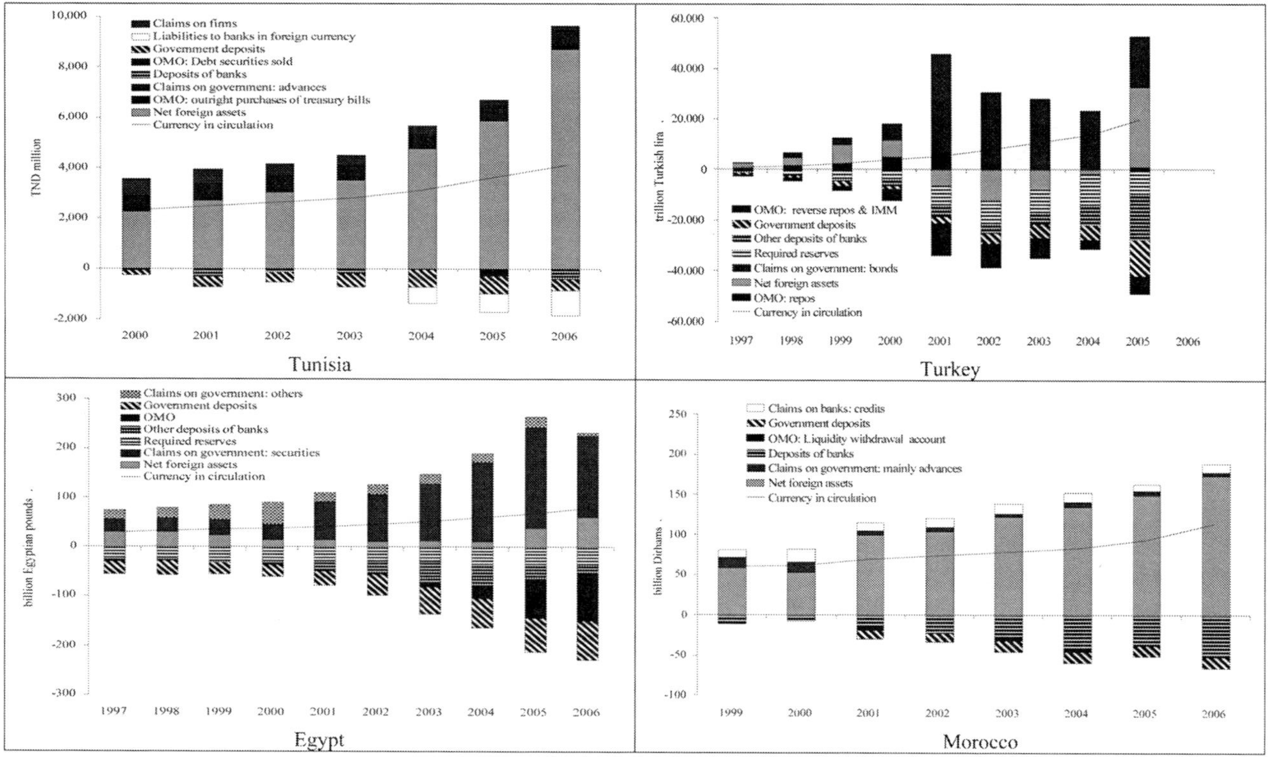

Figure 4.3 Central Bank balance sheets: Tunisia, Turkey, Egypt, Morocco.

Source: National Central Banks, IMF.

substantially since 2001 and exceed currency in circulation. The Central Bank of Tunisia has only marginally embarked on sterilisation operations. Open market operations have emerged only over the last few years; they are small in volume and are liquidity-providing, i.e. outright purchases of treasury bills, or liquidity-absorbing operations, i.e. the sale of central bank debt securities. Thus, open market operations are not systematically used to absorb a structural liquidity surplus in the domestic banking sector.

In particular, in 2006, liquidity creation from increases in net foreign assets due to the sale of state shares in *Tunisie Telecom* was restricted by an increase in a special government account. The foreign currency revenues were deposited on a pending account of the government that is reported as an adjustment item on the liability side of the central bank balance sheet not shown in Figure 4.3. Furthermore, the item 'liabilities to banks' that has emerged since 2004 includes foreign currency-denominated borrowing by the Central Bank of Tunisia in the money market and the sight deposits of Tunisian authorised financial intermediaries. It restricts liquidity growth due to the increase in net foreign assets.

Fiscal and quasi-fiscal operations are reflected in the items 'claims on the government' and 'claims on firms'. Claims on the government mainly include direct advances to the state.[15] Claims on government-related firms, namely claims on the National Oil Board and Cereal Board, were purchased from the National Agricultural Bank in 1996 and have continuously lost value.

Turkey

The central bank balance sheet of Turkey as shown in the upper right panel of Figure 4.3 shows that claims on the government play a dominant role on the asset side. During the 2000/2001 financial crisis, net foreign assets became negative and the central bank supported the financial system with exceptional financing based on liquidity-providing open market operations and substantial purchases of government bonds, which can be mainly regarded as fiscal operations.[16] Thus, both net foreign assets and claims on the government are major autonomous factors on the asset side, which exceed currency in circulation and thereby put the Central Bank of Turkey into a debtor position.

On the liability side remunerated required reserves, reverse repos and interbank money market (IMM) transactions have been used as liquidity-absorbing instruments. The size of these sterilisation instruments has increased considerably since 2000. During the crisis, however, the central bank provided and absorbed liquidity by conducting both types of open market operations, which signals the malfunctioning of the interbank market during this period.

Egypt

The balance sheet structure of the Central Bank of Egypt is shown in the lower left panel of Figure 4.3. Although on the asset side foreign reserves have increased substantially, the dominant liquidity creating items are claims on the government, in particular in the form of government security holdings. Part of the large stock of government securities held on the central bank's balance sheet is due to outright purchases by the central bank on the primary market and can therefore be regarded as fiscal financing.[17]

The substantial increase in assets is matched by a substantial rise in liquidity-absorbing items on the liability side of the balance sheet. Required reserves and other central bank deposits of commercial banks have traditionally been the most important liquidity-absorbing instruments, but their relative size has decreased over time. Since 2003, sterilisation is increasingly conducted by OMOs, e.g. outright sales of bonds, deposit-taking auctions and – since 2005 – by selling debt instruments (certificates of deposit (CDs) and Central Bank of Egypt notes) to domestic banks.[18] Also the size of government deposits at the central bank has increased over time.

Morocco

The balance sheet of the Central Bank of Morocco is shown in the lower right panel of Figure 4.3. Given tight exchange rate stabilisation based on a currency basket and lively foreign exchange inflows, net foreign reserves have increased substantially since the year 2000 and are the main liquidity-providing autonomous factor.

The liquidity created by foreign reserve accumulation has been partially sterilised by small-scale OMOs, i.e. deposit-taking operations placed on so-called liquidity withdrawal accounts as well as required reserves included in the item 'banks' deposits'. Despite an aggregate liquidity surplus some banks conduct bilateral credit operations with the Bank of Morocco. Claims on the government consist mainly of advances although the size is smaller than claims on banks.

Jordan

Given a tight dollar peg and strong foreign exchange inflows Jordan has accumulated a large stock of foreign reserves on the asset side of the central bank balance sheet (upper left panel of Figure 4.4). Net foreign assets are therefore the main liquidity-providing autonomous factor on the asset side and exceed currency in circulation.[19]

In contrast to other central banks in the region, a large part of liquidity-absorbing transactions take place in open market operations, for instance by the sale of Certificates of Deposit (CDs). In addition required reserves have absorbed liquidity from the domestic money markets. Despite a liquidity surplus in the total domestic banking system, some banks conduct bilateral credit operations with the Central Bank of Jordan (a major share of claims on banks are reported as bail-out operations).

Syria

The Central Bank of Syria discloses little information on its balance sheet positions which are shown in the upper right panel of Figure 4.4. Since 1998 liquidity has

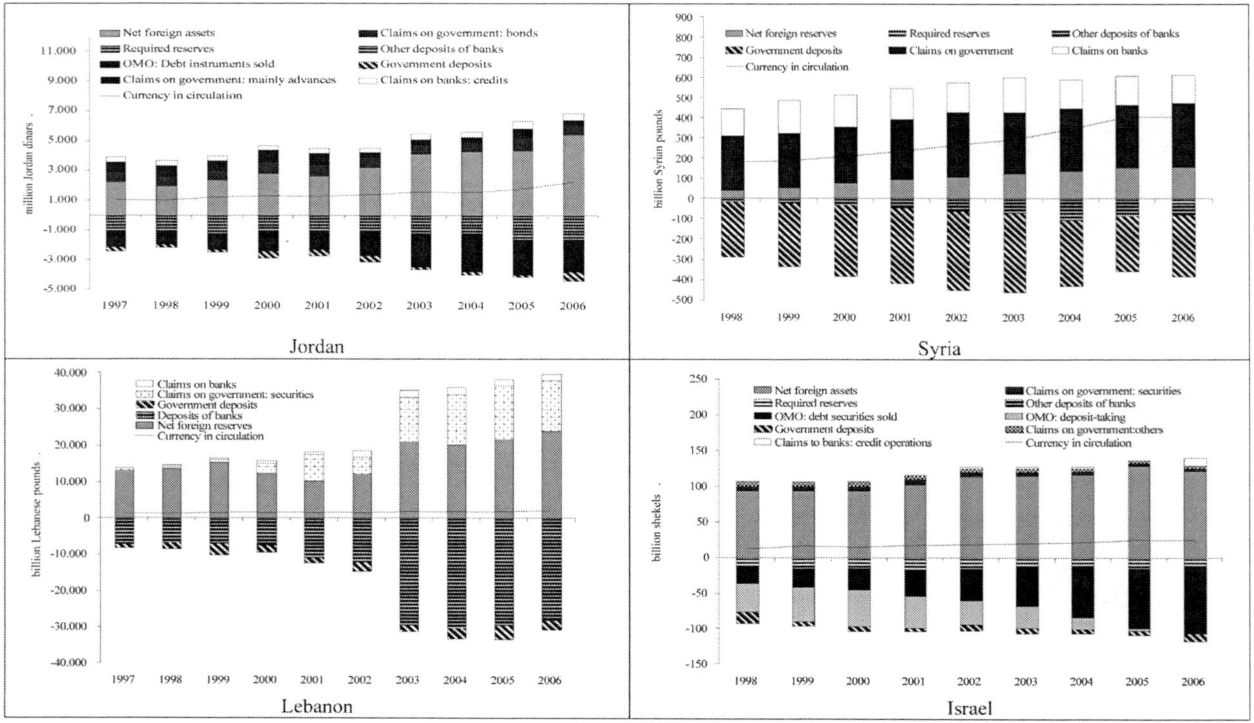

Figure 4.4 Central Bank balance sheets: Jordan, Syria, Lebanon, Israel.

Source: National Central Banks, IMF.

been created mainly by the accumulation of foreign reserves. Together with net foreign assets, claims on the government and on commercial banks can be regarded as autonomous factors on the asset side, however, they have not changed substantially. Furthermore, claims on the government on the asset side are matched by government deposits of similar size on the liability side. Sterilisation mainly takes place by minimum reserve holdings, which have increased over the sample period.

Lebanon

As shown in the lower left panel of Figure 4.4, the Banque du Liban reports an extremely large stock of foreign reserves in relation to currency in circulation. Due to a high degree of dollarisation the demand for domestic currency is comparatively low. Liquidity creation by either the accumulation of foreign reserves or purchases of government securities, the two most important autonomous factors on the asset side, increases the liquidity surplus in the domestic banking system.

The increase of net foreign assets and government securities in 2003 reflects the impact of the Paris II conference. The objective of Paris II was to seek support from the international community to alleviate the burden of the public debt and to reverse the macroeconomic and fiscal imbalances of the Lebanese economy. According to the Ministry of Finance the conference resulted in 10.1 billion dollars of grants and loans for the Lebanese government. 2.4 billion dollars were provided by seven lending countries, 3.6 billion dollars by commercial banks operating in Lebanon and 4.1 billion dollars from a Central Bank scheme,[20] which is reflected in the increase of government securities on the asset side of the central bank balance sheet.

In addition to the large official inflows related to Paris II, private capital inflows surged in 2003 and this contributed to the increase in net foreign assets on the central bank's balance sheet. Liquidity-absorbing items are included in the item bank deposits, of which the structure is not further disclosed. They include reserve requirements and presumably also certificates of deposit which the Banque du Liban uses to sterilise excess liquidity.

Israel

Due to the fact that the Bank of Israel has not intervened in the foreign exchange market since 1997, the level of net foreign assets has remained broadly unchanged. Nevertheless, foreign reserves remain the dominating autonomous factor on the asset side of the balance sheet as shown in the lower right panel of Figure 4.4. As in Lebanon, foreign reserves are very high compared to currency in circulation due to a high degree of dollarisation. The consequently low demand for domestic currency prevents the central bank escaping from its debtor situation, even though it does not create additional liquidity by foreign exchange intervention and only to a limited extent by credit operations with banks.[21]

Liquidity-absorbing open market operations consist of required reserves, deposit-taking auctions and debt securities sold, so-called *makam*. Debt security sales have become the dominating sterilisation instrument over the last few years. According to the Short-Term Loan Law 5744–1984 the government is authorised to issue bonds to be sold only to the Bank of Israel. Theoretically the Bank of Israel then buys and sells these bonds from and to the public to regulate liquidity. In practice, *makam* have been mainly used for soaking up excess liquidity. [22]

The government is obligated to deposit the entire proceeds of these bonds sales in the Bank of Israel and may not use the proceeds for anything apart from repaying the loan or paying the interest on it. The balance of *makam* shown in the balance sheet reflects the redemption value of bills held by the public *less* the balance of the discount not yet amortised (Bank of Israel, Financial Statements 2005).

3 Conclusions

The asymmetric incentive for exchange rate stabilisation in anchor currency countries and in emerging market countries is reflected in both the balance sheets of central banks and the monetary policy operations in each group of countries. While the European Central Bank and the Federal Reserve as creditor central banks provide liquidity based on different kinds of open market operations, the central banks of emerging market economies supply liquidity mainly by purchasing foreign assets and sometimes by increasing claims on the government due to fiscal financing. As the liquidity resulting from foreign exchange interventions (and fiscal operations) tends to be excessive with respect to the maintenance of price and/or financial stability, debtor central banks absorb liquidity partly by sterilisation. This implies an asymmetric causality in monetary policy making. In the balance sheet of a typical debtor central bank net foreign assets increase in the face of high foreign exchange inflows while on the liability side sterilisation instruments such as required reserves and liquidity-absorbing open market operations increase.

In the group of MENA countries the central banks are typically debtors to the domestic banking system. This is most evident in the central bank balance sheets of Jordan and Morocco. The central banks in oil exporting countries such as Algeria, Iran and Saudi Arabia as well as the central bank of Tunisia can be seen as another type of debtor central bank: they restrict liquidity increases due to foreign exchange inflows by placing these inflows in government deposits at the central bank. This kind of sterilisation requires close cooperation between the central bank and the government with respect to monetary policy targets. In Kuwait the sterilisation of oil revenues takes place partly via a sterilisation fund outside the central bank. In addition the central bank uses open market operations as sterilisation instruments.

Egypt, Iran, Lebanon, Syria and Turkey represent countries, in which – in addition to reserve accumulation – fiscal operations have contributed to the surplus liquidity which can be linked to sterilisation operations. Additionally, in Lebanon and Israel, the debtor position of the central bank is further enhanced due to high dollarisation and a correspondingly low demand for domestic currency. Even without creating additional liquidity by increasing autonomous factors on the asset side, it will therefore be difficult for these central banks to change their debtor position into a creditor position.

Notes

1 We thank Holger Zemanek for excellent research assistance and Michael Sturm as well as other workshop participants at the Mediterranean Research Meeting of the European University Institute in March 2007 for helpful comments. Any remaining errors are those of the authors. The findings, interpretations and conclusions do not necessarily represent the views of the Deutsche Bundesbank.

2 The Federal Reserve defines disorderly market conditions as rapid exchange rate changes as well as cases when the exchange rate does not reflect fundamental economic conditions (http://www.ny.frb.org/aboutthefed/fedpoint/fed44.html).

3 By contrast, in countries which are able to hold international debt and assets in domestic currencies such as the US and the euro area, exchange rate fluctuations leave the balance sheet of domestic banks and enterprises largely unaffected.

4 For a similar definition see ECB *Monthly Bulletin*, May 2002, p. 42.

5 Since the start of the monetary union in 1999, the Eurosystem has only intervened in the foreign exchange market in autumn 2000. There were three consecutive interventions aimed at strengthening the euro against the dollar.

6 Euro cash was introduced in January 2002. Since then, the stock of currency in circulation has been steadily increasing.

7 In line with this assumption, the Federal Reserve Bank of New York which is in charge of US foreign exchange intervention sterilises its foreign exchange intervention automatically, fully and instantaneously (Cross 1998: 93). The European Central Bank takes foreign exchange intervention into account within the monetary policy operations of the same maintenance period.

8 In general the central banks of emerging market economies and developing countries will prefer to hold the bonds of the large industrial countries rather than domestic government bonds, because US or euro area government bonds are less risky assets.

9 For an overview of monetary policy operations see Bindseil (2005).

10 These forms of market-based sterilisation operations are for instance widely used by the central banks in Central and Eastern Europe that intend to join the European Monetary Union and therefore have adopted market oriented principles.

11 It is for this reason that many national central banks in the Eurosystem prefer government deposits to be held at commercial banks and hold only low levels of government deposits in order to fulfil essential fiscal agent functions.

12 Egypt is a growing gas producer.

13 In Kuwait foreign reserves declined temporarily following the first Gulf war.

14 A positive side effect of this sterilisation operation is that such central bank bond sales contribute to develop a domestic money market.

15 The major share of direct advances is an advance to the state for Tunisia's capital subscription at the International Monetary Fund and the Arab Monetary Fund. A small part of the direct advances is restructured old public debt, on which the state pays preferential interest rates.

16 At the Central Bank of Turkey direct advances to the government were already banned in 1997. However, a major part of the position "claims on government: bonds" consists of public financing restructured during the crisis (Schobert 2006b). This portfolio mostly bears returns below market rates.

17 For example, the central bank finances cash deficits on government accounts at the central bank (Annual Report of the Central Bank of Egypt, 2002–2003, 32).

18 Since June 2005 the central bank has also implemented an interest rate corridor for the interbank market which has largely stabilised money market rates (see Annual Report of the Central Bank of Egypt, 2005–2006).

19 In comparison to the foreign reserves, other liquidity-providing items of the asset side of the balance sheet such as claims on the government and commercial banks are small and have hardly changed during the observation period. Claims on banks consist of advances and a special government bond. This non-interest bearing bond was issued by the Ministry of Finance to the order of the central bank in accordance to a special law in 1992 that deals with the settlement of extraordinary advances (Annual Report of the Bank of Jordan 2005, 122).

20 See www.forlebanon.net/bio.htm.

21 The small size of direct lending to banks also includes bail-out operations. Claims on the government mainly include a portfolio of tradable securities and long-term advances that were made until 1988.

22 On 28 Feb 2007 the Bank of Israel announced that it would now use makam as an active monetary tool. After more than a decade of gradually expanding the quantity of makam in order to establish it as a monetary instrument, the Bank of Israel will begin using makam for restoring or soaking up liquidity according to the circumstances (Bank of Israel 2007, Recent Economic Developments, 117).

References

Amuzegar, J. (2005) 'Iran's Oil Stabilisation Fund: A Misnomer'. *Middle East Economic Survey*, 48: 47.

Annual Reports and Financial Statements of Central Banks, various issues.

Bindseil, U. (2005) *Monetary Policy Implementation: Theory, Past and Present.* Oxford: Oxford University Press.

Chmelarova, V., and Schnabl, G. (2006) 'Exchange Rate Stabilisation in Developed and Underdeveloped Capital Markets'. *European Central Bank Working Paper* 636.

Cook, D., and Devereux, M. (2006) 'External Currency Pricing and the East Asian Crisis'. *Journal of International Economics*, 69: 37–63.

Cross, S. (1998) *All About the Foreign Exchange Market in the United States*. New York: Federal Reserve Bank of New York.

Eichengreen, B., and Hausmann, R. (1999) 'Exchange Rates and Financial Fragility'. *National Bureau of Economic Research Working Paper* 7418.

European Central Bank (2002) 'The Liquidity Management of the ECB'. *Monthly Bulletin*. May, 41–52.

European Central Bank (2007) *Review of the International Role of the Euro*. Frankfurt.

McKinnon, R. (1963) 'Optimum Currency Areas'. *American Economic Review*, 53: 717–25.

McKinnon, R., and Schnabl, G. (2004a) 'The East Asian Dollar Standard, Fear of Floating, and Original Sin'. *Review of Development Economics*, 8: 331–60.

McKinnon, R., and Schnabl, G. (2004b) 'A Return to Exchange Rate Stability in East Asia? Mitigating Conflicted Virtue'. *International Finance*, 7: 169–201.

Schobert, F. (2006a) 'Linking Financial Soundness and Independence of Central Banks – Central and Eastern Europe, Turkey and CIS Countries'. *Review of International Business and Finance*, 20: 239–55.

Schobert, F. (2006b) Why is Financial Strength Important for Central Banks? In L. Vinhas de Souza and O. Havrylyshyn (eds.), *Return to Growth in CIS Countries: Monetary Policy and the Macroeconomic Framework*. Berlin: Springer.

5 Central bank independence in a MENA transition economy

The experience of Algeria[1]

Abdallah Zouache and Mohamed-Cherif Ilmane

Introduction

The paradigm of time inconsistency (Kydland and Prescott, 1977) applied to the problem of monetary policy by Barro and Gordon (1983a) established the possibility of an inflationary bias. Devices have therefore been suggested in the literature to reduce this bias. Barro and Gordon (1983b) conclude that the best solution for the time-inconsistency problem consists of the introduction of fixed rules in monetary policy, that is, the authorities commit themselves to certain policy rules. Following the pioneering work by Rogoff (1985), the delegation of monetary policy making powers to independent central banks has been widely believed to bring about lower inflation. Since then, a number of studies have provided empirical support for this negative relationship between central bank independence and inflation for various samples of developed economies (Alesina and Summers, 1993). However, empirical evidence from developing countries has been less clear-cut (Fuhrer, 1997). Furthermore, there are few studies of the independence of the central banks of Middle East and North African (MENA) countries, and especially of the independence of the Bank of Algeria.

In 1996, the Arab Monetary Fund evaluated the degree of independence of eleven Arab central banks on the basis of the Cukierman (1992) scoring. The Bank of Algeria (score 0.4966) was ranked in fourth place after the Bank of Lebanon (0.603), the Monetary Agency of Saudi Arabia (0.502) and the Central Bank of Egypt (0.500) but before the Tunisian Central Bank (0.430) and the Moroccan Bank El-Maghrib (0.375). Accordingly, one could conclude from this study that the Bank of Algeria enjoyed considerable independence. However, in a more recent study by Gisolo (2009), the Bank of Algeria obtains a bad ranking as regards its independence. Gisolo concludes that Algeria 'shows a higher-than-expected medium-term inflation rate when compared to the legal independence enjoyed by its central bank' (p. 46). What is interesting is that Gisolo (p. 35) views Algeria as an '*anomaly*', a statement that derives according to him from the methodology he uses. In our opinion, Algeria does indeed deserve a special mention, but this is not because of the methodology used but because of its profile. In this sense, Gisolo's statement is very revealing of the case of Algeria. We would say that the experience of Algeria is *original* (to avoid the term 'schizophrenic') as a result of the profile of the country. A former socialist state, classified as a MENA country, an oil and gas producer in the same vein as the Gulf countries, Algeria is also a former French colony, with a colonial past that should be borne in mind when one analyses Algeria's economic and monetary organisation, and especially the statute and the role of its central bank.

This chapter analyses the evolution of the independence of the Bank of Algeria since the political independence of the country in 1962. In particular it examines the role of the central bank in the recent transition period after Algeria chose to abandon the Soviet model at the end of the eighties. The chapter then confirms two main results from the literature on the independence of central banks in developing countries: First, the attention that should be paid to the distinction between *de jure* and *de facto* independence, and second, the need to go further than quantitative measures of legal independence in order to fully understand the independence of central banks. The chapter is organised as follows. Section 1 reviews the lessons that can be drawn from the literature on central bank independence. Section 2 emphasises the role of the institutional legacy in understanding the autonomy of the Bank of Algeria. Section 3 analyses the evolution of the *de jure* and *de facto* independence of the Bank of Algeria since 1990. Section 4 concludes.

1 Does central bank independence matter in developing countries?

The academic literature has developed a broad consensus on the desirable framework for central bank independence. It is widely believed that a high level of central bank independence, coupled with some explicit mandate for the bank to restrain inflation, is an important institutional device to assure price stability. While central bank independence promotes price stability (Eijffinger and de Haan, 1996), it has no measurable impact on real economic performance (Alesina and Summers, 1993). The aim of this section is to draw the lessons from this literature for the issue of the independence of the Bank of Algeria. In particular, many empirical studies prove the limitations of a quantitative approach when one deals with developing countries.

Definitions and measures of central bank independence

The literature distinguishes between *legal* and *actual* independence. Legal independence refers to the legislation that governs the functioning of the central bank, especially with respect to its relationship with the government. Actual independence concerns the level of autonomy that this central bank enjoys with respect to the authority (prime minister or minister of finance, treasury). In a recent article, Cukierman (2007) prefers to use the terms *de jure* and *de facto* independence. *De jure* independence is derived from central bank charters and is seen as a proxy for *de facto* independence.

Grilli, Masciandaro, and Tabellini (1991) have focused on two key dimensions of independence: *political* independence and *economic* independence. Debelle and Fisher (1994) called these two aspects *goal* independence and *instrument* independence. Goal independence refers to the central bank's ability to determine the goals of policy without the direct influence of the fiscal authority. To defend its goals, however, a central bank must wield effective policy instruments. Instrument independence refers to the central bank's ability to adjust its policy tools freely in pursuit of the goals of monetary policy. A bank is independent with respect to its instruments if it is free to choose the means by which to achieve its goals. It is not independent if it requires government approval to use its policy instruments. The issue is then to determine whether central banks should have both forms of independence or if instrument independence is a sufficient criterion when one assesses the autonomy of central banks.

Since the pioneering attempt made by Bade and Parkin (1982), these definitions have produced several measures of central bank independence. The index of Grilli, Masciandaro, and Tabellini (1991) is based on factors such as whether or not the central bank governor and the board are appointed by the government, the length of their appointments, whether government representatives sit on the board of the bank, whether government approval is required for monetary policy decisions and whether the 'price stability' objective figures explicitly and prominently in the central bank statute. Generally, the combined score for both political and economic independence is employed as an indicator for legal independence. The Cukierman (1992) and Cukierman, Webb, and Neyapti (1992) index is based on four legal characteristics as described in a central bank's charter. First, a bank is viewed as more independent if the chief executive is appointed by the central bank board rather than by the prime minister or minister of finance, is not subject to dismissal, and has a long term of office. These aspects help insulate the central bank from political pressures. Second, independence is higher the greater the extent to which policy decisions are made independently of government involvement. Third, a central bank is more independent if its charter states that price stability is the sole or primary goal of monetary policy. Fourth, independence is greater if there are limitations on the government's ability to borrow from the central bank.

The challenge for developing countries

Although most studies on central bank independence are confined to industrial countries, several papers deal with developing countries. While standard indices of central bank independence are negatively associated with inflation in developed economies, this does not hold for developing economies (Fuhrer, 1997). The challenge raised by these results is that the legal central bank independence could be very different from actual independence in countries where the practice of monetary policy deviates from the letter of the law. In other words, even when the laws are quite explicit, actual practice may deviate from them. Accordingly, Cukierman (1992) argues that legal independence measures may be a better proxy for actual independence in industrial countries than in developing countries. As an alternative, Cukierman *et al.* (1992) developed a yardstick for central bank autonomy based on the actual average term of office of central bank governors in a number of countries from 1950 to 1989. This indicator is based on the presumption that a higher turnover of central bank governors indicates a lower level of independence, at least above some threshold, and that even if the central bank law is quite explicit, it may not be operational if a different tradition takes precedence.

Studies of the turnover rate as a proxy for central bank independence led to two conclusions (Eijffinger and de Haan, 1996). First, the turnover rate differs greatly across countries. Second, the mean and standard deviation of the turnover rate for developing countries are much higher than the corresponding measures for industrial countries. Consequently, although legal independence is seen as a good proxy for actual autonomy in industrial countries, proxies such as the turnover rate of the central bank governorship or the political vulnerability of the central bank should be used for developing countries.

Other scholars believe that more autonomy for central banks in transition countries will be insufficient to guarantee a permanently lower level of inflation (Eijffinger and de Haan, 1996); a principle also valid for developed countries (Posen, 1998). Fuhrer (1997) found 'no clear relationship … between central bank independence and any measures of economic performance, either inflation or real activity'. In the same vein, but for developed countries, Hayo and Hefeker (2001) argued that central bank independence is neither necessary nor sufficient for reaching monetary stability. Ismihan and Ozkan (2004) went further and argued that, in developing countries where inflationary finance was important and the productivity of investment was high, delegating monetary policymaking to an independent central bank might even harm inflation performance in the long term. Their argument is that lower contemporaneous inflation produced by an independent central bank reduces the financing available for public investment, which impacts unfavourably on the productive capacity of an economy, and hence on the scope for inflation reduction in the future.

It follows from these studies that existing indices of central bank independence are often incomplete and noisy indicators of actual independence. This does not mean that they are uninformative, but it does imply, as pointed out by Cukierman (2007), that their use should be supplemented by judgment of the problem under consideration. That proposition is particularly relevant for a country such as Algeria where the institutional context has been so varied and so important in the post-1962 period.

2 Institutional heritage and the independence of the Bank of Algeria

In our opinion, the experience of Algeria should not be considered without taking a look at the institutional framework in which the Bank of Algeria has been involved. This section emphasises that the Bank of Algeria has been *dependent* on institutional constraints. This institutional detour examines the peculiarities of the Algerian case, and asks whether Algeria should be considered as a transition economy or a MENA country.

The socialist legacy: the Bank of Algeria in a planned economy (1962–1990)

The literature on transition economics deals especially with the former East European countries and with the Russian case. Cukierman *et al.* (1992) consider certain East European economies but without including Algeria. Siklos (1994), Eijffinger and Van Keulen (1995), Loungani and Sheets (1997), Lybek (1999) and the synthesis of Cukierman *et al.* (1992) proposed a more elaborate approach which takes account of the peculiarities of Eastern Europe but again without considering Algeria. In fact, Algeria is not included in the group of transition economies which includes Central and Eastern European transition economies, the Baltic States and the Commonwealth of Independent States (e.g. United Nations *World Economic Survey*).

Nevertheless, economic studies from the international institutions consider that Algeria is facing a number of similar challenges, especially that of achieving the transition to a market economy in order to guarantee lasting growth (IMF, 2006; OECD, 2006). Furthermore, Algeria is very close to the path that Eastern Europe took since it was a socialist economy characterised by the planned organisation of economic activities, in the line of the Union of Soviet Socialist Republics (USSR). Thus, the adjustment to a more market-based economy means that Algeria has had to face similar issues to those faced by centrally planned economies. This section illustrates to what extent this part of Algeria's institutional past had an impact on the role of the central bank after the independence of the country.

Until 1967, the structure and the organisation of the Algerian economy, especially as regards the monetary and banking system, corresponded to the norms of a market economy. The choice of centrally planned command economy as a system for organising the development of the national economy was made in the first four-year plan, from 1970 to 1973. This system was the result of an ideological choice that considered that planning was more efficient than market coordination for developing the 'national economy'. This Soviet-type planning was formulated in physical terms. The financial side was 'reformed' in the 1971 finance law. The fundamental principles that governed the financing of planned investments were the following:

- The centralisation of internal and external financial resources at the level of the Treasury, including central bank advances whose limitation to 5 per cent of ordinary fiscal revenues by the 1962 banking law was replaced *sine die* by the 1965 complementary finance law;
- Those financial resources were to be used to finance long term planned investment *via* the banking system;
- Otherwise, investments would be financed by medium-term credits that were automatically re-discountable at the central bank;
- The obligation for public enterprises to keep their accounts at a single bank;
- The obligation imposed on those enterprises to make all their payments by banker's order.

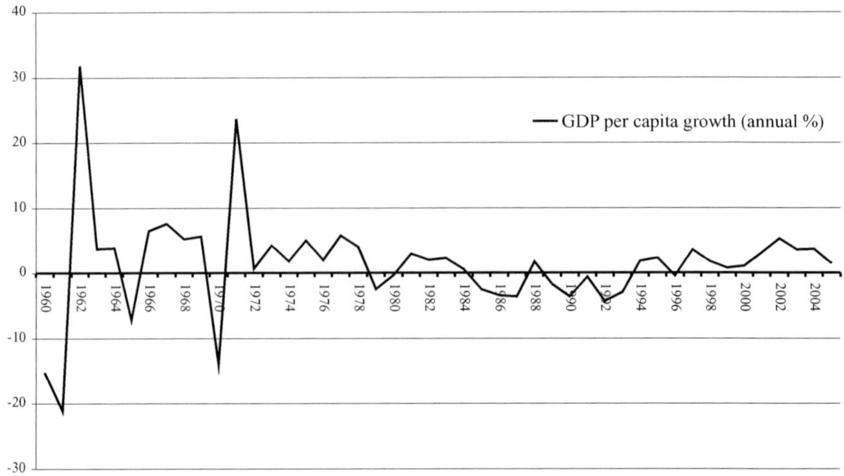

Figure 5.1 GDP per capita growth (annual %).

Source: World Bank Indicators.

This economic organisation led to huge investments that surely explain the good performance of the Algerian economy after independence (see Figure 5.1). But this scheme also had consequences for the independence of the Bank of Algeria through three dimensions of the monetary system: the organisation of the banking system, the function of money and the role of monetary policy, and the management of the exchange rate.

First of all, it must be noted that, given the planning mechanism, it was not obvious that there was an Algerian banking *system* as such. Once the plan was formulated and approved in physical terms, it was necessary to add the financial part. The first step (this was the role of the Treasury) was to centralise long-term external and internal resources which were then distributed by the public banks among the public enterprises in charge of planned investments. The second step was to call on the public banks to take charge of medium-term investments in the form of credits that were both legally and effectively re-discountable by the central bank. Banks also financed the working of public enterprises insofar as short-term credits were freely re-discountable by the central bank. One consequence of this system was that the Bank of Algeria had no autonomy as a lender of last resort. We can go further and assert that the Algerian banking system was close to the Soviet model of the Gosbank. There was no real hierarchy between the commercial banks and the Bank of Algeria so that the banking system constituted a one level system.

Of course, the aim of this financial and banking system was to control the realisation of planned investments by the banks. But, from a monetary point of view, it led to the introduction of a two-sided monetary circulation: bank money circulation between public enterprises and fiduciary circulation between households and private enterprises. As regards the household sector, the payment function was impeded by the structural insufficiency of aggregate supply: Kornai (1984) has

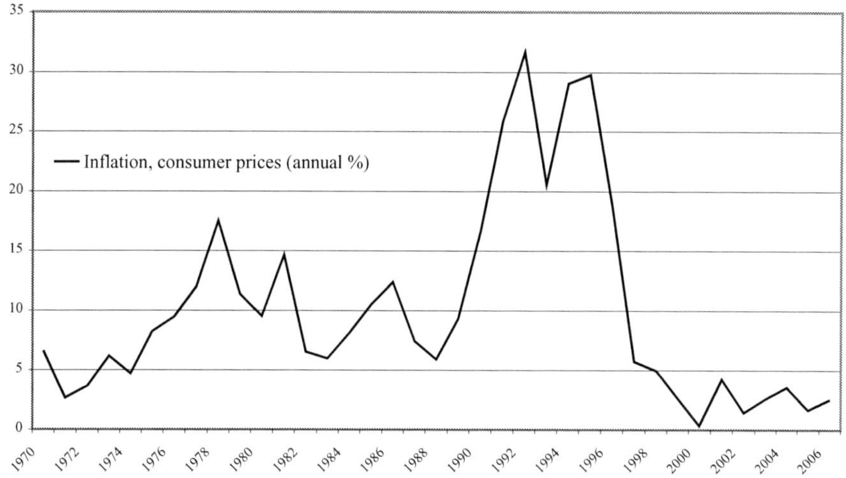

Figure 5.2 Inflation, consumer prices (annual %).

Source: World Bank Indicators.

shown how this kind of economic organisation leads to generalised shortage. The possession of means of payment gives no choice to the consumer, as is shown by the development of forced substitutions: forced saving, forced expenditure, an informal market, and so on.

Finally, money failed to perform its true role in the public sector as well as in the private and household sectors. This situation had direct consequences for the practice of monetary policy. Indeed, the aim of monetary policy was to control, via the manipulation of the dinar, the fulfilment of the plan. Monetary policy was meant to ensure that the monetary flows were in accordance with the real flows decided in the plan. One can even conclude that there was no monetary policy in this scheme. Accordingly, to talk about the independence of the Algerian central bank in this socialist system would be absurd.

Finally, the Bank of Algeria was also dependent on the planning system as regards its exchange rate policy. From January 1974, the exchange rate of the Algerian dinar was pegged to a basket of currencies in which the U.S. dollar was assigned a relatively large weight due to its importance in hydrocarbon export receipts and debt-service payments, with adjustments taking place from time to time. In 1986, Algeria's economy experienced the reverse oil shock, and the government responded to the dramatic erosion of export revenue by borrowing abroad and intensifying import restrictions. In parallel, the Bank of Algeria let the Algerian dinar depreciate against the basket by 31 per cent between 1986 and 1988 (Koranchelian, 2005). In 1988, the Bank of Algeria installed a system by which foreign exchange was allocated to the five public commercial banks within a framework of credit ceilings, which were consistent with balance of payments targets. The public banks in turn would allocate foreign exchange to their client public enterprises. This kind of exchange rate policy survived the liberalisation of the economy.

The question of independence was raised at the end of the eighties, after the collapse of the economy and the years of high inflation (see Figures 5.1 and 5.2). The upgrading of central bank independence and the creation of best-practice western-type central banks in the former socialist countries was part of a more general attempt by these countries to create the institutional framework needed for the orderly functioning of a market economy. The fact that many of these new central banks, and notably the Bank of Algeria, were granted substantial *de jure* independence was no doubt motivated by evidence from the industrial economies, suggesting that inflation and legal independence are negatively related.

Algeria as a MENA country: the Bank of Algeria in a 'capitalist' economy (1990–2005)

Being a transition economy, Algeria is nevertheless classified in the regional group of Middle East and North Africa countries, also referred to as MENA countries, whose composition straddles the Africa and Middle East regions (IMF, 2007). This group is defined as the Arab League countries plus the Islamic Republic of Iran. Algeria is also classified according to the following analytical criterion: the type of export earnings. On that basis it is viewed as a fuel country since its main exports are crude oil and natural gas. The role that the Bank of Algeria had in the 1990–2005 period is related to three institutional factors: the liberalisation of the economy, political events and the control that the IMF had in the 1990s on the finances of the country. Indeed, from 1990 to 2000, Algeria experienced many political and economic troubles and was even forced by the IMF to follow a structural adjustment programme between 1994 and 1998. Three sub-periods can be distinguished.

On the impact of political constraints: the independence of the Bank of Algeria at the time of the 'events' (1990–1993)

In this sub-period the political and social context – what Algerians discreetly call the events ('*les évènements*') but which was more like a civil war – and the low oil price undermined the degree of freedom of the authorities. Figure 5.3 shows that this sub-period was characterised by high inflation and unemployment combined with low growth. Inflation was caused, with a lag of up to twelve months, by an increasing budget deficit linked to an excessive growth of the money supply (M_2). As a consequence of this political context, the authorities, and notably the Bank of Algeria, were obliged to sustain public enterprises. That led to spending deficits that were financed through money creation. Monetary policy was accommodating in order to avoid a collapse of the banking system. The financing of the budget was made possible by the suspension of the law that limited the advances of the Bank of Algeria to the Treasury (see section 3).

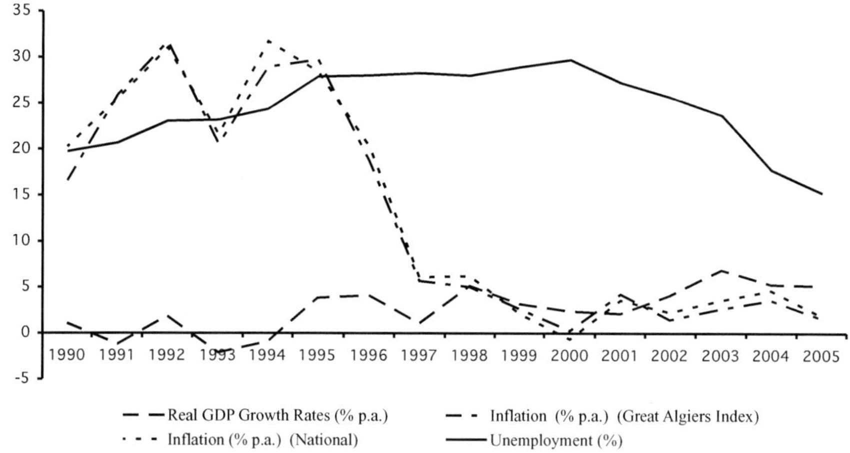

Figure 5.3 Inflation, growth and unemployment.

The dependence of the Bank of Algeria on the IMF: the impact of the adjustment programmes (1994–1998)

A ‘true’ monetary policy appears for the first time with the macroeconomic stabilisation programme (April 1994 to March 1995) and the structural adjustment programme (April 1995 to March 1998). However monetary policy and thus the Bank of Algeria were not independent. Monetary policy was a part of a broader ‘package’ – consisting of exchange rate policy, import liberalisation and the rescheduling of the Algerian debt – whose aim was to revive the transition process and to revitalise the Algerian economy. Indeed, at the end of 1993, the Algerian economy was in bad shape: recession, unemployment close to 30 per cent, a budget deficit equal to 8.7 per cent of GDP, a rapid growth of the money supply (+21 per cent), a deficit on the balance of trade exacerbated by a fall in the exchange reserves until they could cover only six weeks of imports, and a debt burden of 82 per cent of GDP. Within the context of the macroeconomic stabilisation programme, Algeria obtained a rescheduling of its external public debt at the Paris Club and of its external private debt at the London Club. Algeria also obtained multilateral loans from international institutions (IMF, World Bank, Arab Monetary Fund, etc.). Finally, the government drastically cut social expenditures and public investments.

Monetary policy was an appendage of this stabilisation programme. The aim was to lower the inflation rate. The trouble is that the Bank of Algeria did not have many instruments at its disposal. Without a secondary market for bonds, no open-market operations were possible. Instead, the Bank of Algeria used two techniques: credit by tender and the re-discount rate. This policy led to the following results. The rate of growth of the money supply (M_2) decreased from 21.5 per cent in 1993 to 10.5 per cent in 1995. The inflation rate (on the consumer price index for

Greater Algiers) increased from 20.5 per cent in 1993 to 29.8 per cent in 1995. The growth rate became positive and reached 3.9 per cent in 1995 as opposed to –2.2 per cent in 1993.

The structural adjustment programme, which operated from April 1995 to March 1998, followed the aims of the macroeconomic stabilisation programme: to promote growth by liberalising the economy (privatisation, reduction of tariffs, control of wages and decreases in investment expenditures). The first objective of monetary policy was to fight inflation. Under the supervision of the IMF, the Bank of Algeria ran a restrictive quantitative monetary policy limiting the growth of the money supply through the control of its internal assets. The policy was a success since the inflation rate decreased enormously from 30 per cent in 1995 to 5.7 per cent in 1997 (Greater Algiers index). On the other hand, the GDP growth rate declined to 1.2 per cent and the unemployment rate rose to 28 per cent. The tight Algerian monetary policy at this period, together with a strict fiscal policy and sustained by the rises of the oil price and of the exchange rate between the dinar and the dollar, led to a stabilisation of the price level during this period at the cost of high unemployment and low GDP growth.

The exchange rate regime was also brought within the control of the IMF. Under the structural adjustment programme, Algeria's exchange rate regime became in 1996 a managed float with no pre-announced path for the exchange rate. This floating exchange rate regime was established in several steps. From September 1994 to December 1995, the managed float regime was implemented through fixing sessions between the Bank of Algeria and the commercial banks. At the end of 1995, the Council of Money and Credit initiated an inter-bank foreign exchange market that was established in 1996. But this market has never really functioned, since forward transactions have not been made feasible. Accordingly, the Algerian dinar turned out to be a partially convertible currency: it is not fully convertible but it is commercially convertible, which means that any locally registered enterprise can import goods and pay by debit of its Algerian dinar account without prior approval from the Bank of Algeria. For payments of services, prior approval from the central bank is needed. This partial convertibility of the Algerian dinar enables the Bank of Algeria to monitor all international financial operations carried out by public and private banking institutions.

A political and economic context favourable to the independence of the Bank of Algeria: 2000/2001–2005

The factors that constrained the independence of the Bank of Algeria were relaxed in the 2000s: the 'events' came to an end, the dinar was more stable (against the US dollar) (see Figure 5.4), the oil price increased and that led to a positive balance of trade and a banking system with excess liquidity. Within this new context, it was possible for the Bank of Algeria to formulate and conduct an independent monetary policy. Since 2001, the single final objective has been price stability with an inflation target of 3 per cent. Algeria experienced stable and moderate inflation. In the tradition of the quantity theory, the inflation target was attained

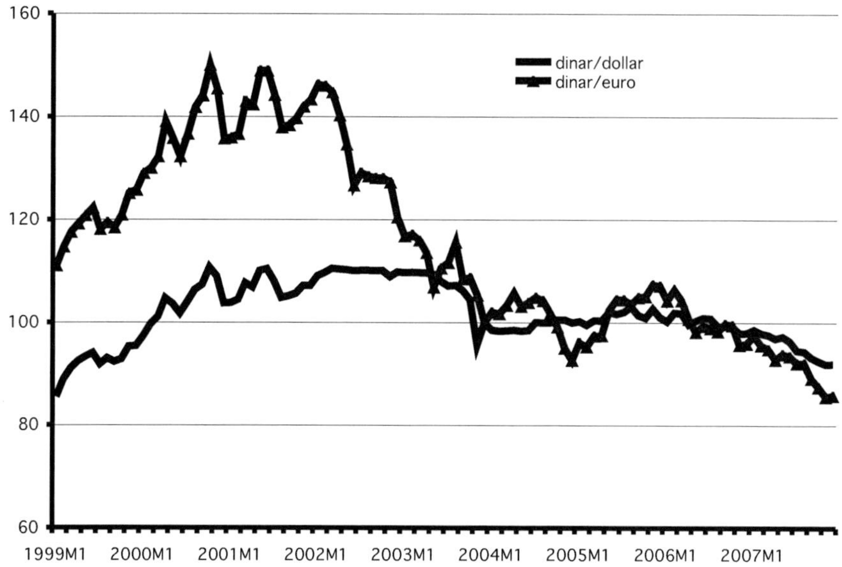

Figure 5.4 Exchange rate dinar/dollar and dinar/euro (base=100 at 31/12/2003).

Source: Bank of Algeria.

through two intermediate targets: the growth rates of money supply (M_2) and of credit supply (in other words credit rationing). Both targets have been controlled through mandatory reserves and the mopping up of bank liquidity. Furthermore, the authorities have aimed to maintain a stable real effective exchange rate against a basket of currencies weighted on the basis of the trade shares of Algeria's main trading partners so that Algeria anchors to the euro. The real effective exchange rate of the Algerian dinar was stabilised at the end of 2003 around the time-varying long-run equilibrium exchange rate (Koranchelian, 2005).

3 The evolution of the *de jure* and *de facto* independence of the Bank of Algeria

The evolution of the institutional constraints in Algeria reviewed in the former section helps to explain the evolution of the independence of the Bank of Algeria. Two periods can be distinguished. In the first period, from 1990 to 2003, the Bank of Algeria benefited from a legal framework – the 90–10 law relative to money and credit (LMC) promulgated on 14 April 1990 – which improved its legal independence compared to the socialist era, but the Bank did not enjoy a *de facto* independence, in particular because of the political context and the supervision of the IMF. In the second period, since 2003, the new ordinance led to a decrease of the legal independence of the Bank of Algeria. However, in practice, with the relaxation of the institutional constraints, the *de facto* independence increased.

De jure *and* de facto *independence from 1990 to 2003*

The transition process in the financial sphere was first legitimised through the 1990 law relative to money and credit (LMC) which was inspired by French monetary and financial arrangements. There is a general agreement that the LMC was a decisive step on the path of economic reforms that Algeria took at the end of the 1980s. We should nevertheless ask to what extent the LMC contributed to the transition toward a market economy in Algeria. In fact, the LMC was more than a law. It was an act providing a framework for a monetary programme since it not only codified existing practices but also established new monetary and banking rules whose aim was to introduce market mechanisms. What was the main influence of this law on the independence of the Bank of Algeria relative to the old socialist system? On the one hand it increased the *de jure* independence of the Bank of Algeria, but on the other hand it had little effect on its *de facto* independence.

Why the Bank of Algeria took the path towards de jure *independence*

First, the LMC cancelled the legal domination of public enterprises over public banks by suppressing (a) the obligation for a public enterprise to keep its accounts at a single bank, and (b) the automatic granting of credits to public enterprises by public banks. Furthermore, the granting of credit had to follow prudential rules, notably on the division of risks and the provision of funding.

Second, the LMC increased the autonomy of the central bank relatively to the Treasury. From the 1965 complementary finance law that suppressed the limitation of central bank advances to the Treasury, the budget deficit had been systematically monetized. At the end of 1989, the debt of the Treasury with regard to the central bank was equal to 110 billion dinars. At this date, the overall debt of the Treasury vis-à-vis the banking system represented 50 per cent of the internal public debt.

The LMC put an end to this situation through the following articles:

- Article 213 obliged the Treasury to repay its debt to the central bank over a period of fifteen years and according to a convention between both institutions.
- Article 78 restricted the impact of the annual public budget since it put an upper limit on central bank advances to the Treasury equal to 10 per cent of the ordinary fiscal revenues of the current fiscal year and set a maximum duration of 240 days. The whole of the advances has to be paid back before the end of the fiscal year.
- Article 77 put an upper limit on the amount of public assets that the central bank could hold in its portfolio to 20 per cent of the ordinary fiscal revenues of the current fiscal year.
- Article 80 obliged the central bank to keep in its National Girobank account (CCP) an amount of resources equivalent to its annual expected needs.
- Finally, article 93 established mandatory reserves which allowed the central bank to regulate banks' liquid assets so that the compulsory subscription of Treasury bonds by the banks no longer had any *raison d'être*.

Third, the LMC created a two-stage banking system. Having the monopoly of issue of the reserve currency (art. 4), the Bank of Algeria became a lender of last resort in a system where it was at the top of the hierarchy. No legal arrangement obliged it to furnish automatically to the banks the amounts of currency they desired. Furthermore, the LMC allocated to the central bank the design and the conduct of monetary policy (art. 55). The Bank of Algeria was also in charge of defining the prudential rules that banks and financial institutions should respect (art. 92). Finally, the LMC gave the central bank the possibility of controlling the hiring conditions of the banks and of the executive managers of financial institutions (arts. 95 and 125).

The LMC also created an institution in charge of supervising banks to ensure they respected the regulations: the Banking Commission. This is an autonomous institution composed of two judges (three since the 2003 law) and two persons who are known to be highly competent in the financial, banking and accounting domains, and chaired by the governor of the central bank. The sanctions go from public criticism to the withdrawal of licences or liquidation. The autonomy of the Commission was reinforced by the 2003 ordinance which confers the power of nominating the members of the Commission on the President of the Republic, whereas this had been the responsibility of the Prime Minister under the LMC.

For these reasons, one can conclude that the LMC gave a *de jure* independence to the Bank of Algeria. Here it is useful to consider four criteria that usually contribute to the definition of legal independence: how the managers are elected, how monetary policy is conducted, the role of price stability among the targets of monetary policy, and the link with the budgetary sphere.

The election of the managers

- The governor is nominated by a decree of the president of the Republic (1996 constitution) for a six–year term of office that can be renewed once. Legally, the governor cannot be fired except for medical reasons or for major errors. The same arrangements apply to the three vice-governors except for the duration of their term which is five years. Power over monetary matters resides in the Council of Money and Credit, which is composed of three external members without a fixed term and chosen by the Prime Minister, plus the governor and three vice-governors. Note that the external members also have a position at the central bank.

The conduct of monetary policy

- The question here is the role of the Council of Money and Credit (CMC). The LMC established this council (in its art. 44) to be in charge of the regulation of every banking activity but also of the definition of the instruments and intermediate objectives of monetary policy. The Council on Money and Credit is responsible for issuing licences and regulations. However, the law forces the government to consult the Bank of Algeria on every element of regulation linked to finance or money in general. And the governor and three vice-governors constitute a majority over the three external members nominated by the government.

The stability of prices

- There is a risk of conflict between the various objectives given to the central bank, especially in bad economic circumstances. The law does not establish the priority between the objectives, so that the central bank is free to choose the target it considers appropriate.

The budget deficit and monetary policy

- The LMC does not prohibit the financing of the public deficit but it sets limitations on the amount and duration of such financing.

However, an examination of the practice of monetary policy reveals that *de jure* independence was not a good proxy for the *de facto* independence of the Bank of Algeria in the 1990s.

From* de jure *to* de facto *independence in the 1990s

In theory, the relations between public banks and public enterprises were subject to contractual arrangements. But, in reality, the public banks continued to finance public enterprises and allowed them huge bank overdrafts. Those overdrafts plus charges were transformed into nonperforming assets. From 1991–1992, the Treasury habitually converted those bad claims into bonds. Up to the end of 2003, the former director of the Treasury reported that those conversion operations concerned 1100 billion dinars, that is approximately 15 billion US dollars (Kessali, 2005: 23). According to Kessali, at the end of 2003, the banks possessed 631 billions of dinars in treasury bonds corresponding to 20 per cent of their assets and providing them with one third of their profits.

In the same vein, the public banks did not respect the prudential rules. In 2003, the provisioning shortfall for the five largest public banks was 24 per cent. Three quarters of the provisioning shortfall was attributable to loans extended to major state enterprises, 14 per cent to private sector loans and the balance to smaller state enterprises (IMF, 2004). This situation obliged the Treasury either to re-capitalise those banks or to buy a part of their bad debts. It seems that the choice was made to repurchase 283 billion dinars of bad debts to public firms in financial difficulties (Banque d'Algérie, 2005b: 3). This constituted an offence under the new regulation and the banks should have been punished but the Banking Commission did nothing. Note that the private sector was not in a better condition. According to the IMF (2006), the checks made by the Bank of Algeria revealed that 40 per cent of credits attributed to public enterprises were nonperforming. The corresponding proportion for the private sector was 33 per cent at the end of 2003.

It seems that some entrepreneurs enjoyed certain facilities in seeking credits because of their personal relationships with political circles. Accordingly, some credits were given without any relationship to the size or the potential of the firms. For example, the firm Tonic Emballage obtained credits for an amount of more than 10 billion dinars that have never been reimbursed. The managers of the bank (BADR) and of the firms were subsequently arrested. The Bank of Algeria had not been able to reject these over-risky credits. In contrast, the Bank of Algeria punished private banks by withdrawing the licences of El Khalifa Bank, the Bank of Commerce and Industry (BCIA), the Union Bank (UB) and the Algerian Banking Company (CAB).

The independence of the Bank of Algeria has also been influenced by the political context and especially by the characters of the governor, the Prime Minister, the Minister of Finance and even the President who nominated these people. In Algeria, the political authorities can break the law for their own benefit whatever the social cost. But above all they put pressure on the Bank of Algeria. For instance, in 1992, the governor suffered a political dismissal by the High State Committee (HCE) which was designed to find a solution to the Algerian political conflict. At his first meeting with the managerial staff of the Bank of Algeria, the new governor declared that he had been nominated to ensure 'a mission for the head of government'. In article 172 of the finance law for 1993, the government suspended one of the arrangements of the LMC on the creation of money to finance the budget deficit. This article stated that 'despite the legal dispositions programmed otherwise, the ceiling at 31 December of the accumulated advances consented to the Treasury by the Bank of Algeria is fixed at one hundred and seventy billion dinars'. This legislative change made it possible for the government to raise the overall budget deficit from 12.2 billion dinars in 1992 to 100.6 billion in 1993, that is from 1.2 per cent of GDP to 8.7 per cent of GDP. At the same time, inflation increased from 20.5 per cent in 1993 to 29 per cent in 1994.

Finally, the predominance of the public banking sector – a legacy of the socialist planning system – weakened the economic independence of the Bank of Algeria, since it was not able to fully exert its supervision over the financial system for two reasons. First, it seemed to be inappropriate for the central bank to suspend the licence of a public bank. Second, when the financial system was illiquid, the Bank of Algeria was obliged to refinance it. Of course, this is its function as lender of last resort in the Algerian economy. But the real issue is that this lending was a substitute for structural measures that should have been imposed on the public sector. In other words, this last resort lending was not justified from a monetary point of view since it was a way of avoiding heavy restructuring in the public industrial sector. Such 'politically biased' financial behaviour is often the source of inflation in transition economies (Ilieva and Healey, 2001).

It thus seems that the legal independence of the Bank of Algeria, both economic and political, was, in practice, a fiction.

What has changed with the 2003 ordinance

The 2003 ordinance caused the *de jure* independence of the Bank of Algeria to shrink. At the same time, the practice of the Bank reveals that its *de facto* independence increased.

The LMC had asserted that

> the mission of the central bank is to create and maintain in the monetary, credit and exchange fields the most favourable conditions for an orderly development of the national economy, promoting the employment of all the productive resources of the country and, at the same time, guarding the internal and external stability of the currency.
>
> (LMC, art. 55, first paragraph)

This article raised the question of which goal was most important for the Bank of Algeria: there could be a dispute in the prioritisation of tasks, as between 'orderly development' and 'internal and external stability of the currency'. As for the target of currency stability, this is a standard objective for western central banks but, in this article, it seems not to be considered as a priority for the Bank of Algeria. We will see that this a priori difficulty has been resolved by the central bank itself.

Let it first be noted how this article was modified in ordinance 03-11. The first paragraph of article 35 of this ordinance amends significantly article 55 of the LMC:

> The mission of the Bank of Algeria is to create and maintain in the money, credit and exchange fields the most favourable conditions for a *rapid development* of the economy, at the same time guarding the internal and external stability of the currency.

This article introduced two main changes. First, the substitution of the adjective 'rapid' instead of 'orderly': this implies that the central bank should focus on the short or medium term rather than on the long term. Second, the suppression of the ambiguous expression: 'employment of all productive resources': does this mean that price stability became the only target as in many central banks? Does it imply that the central bank is supposed to be able to reach this target?

In fact, the modifications made to the LMC in 2001, then its abrogation and finally its replacement in 2003 have considerably reduced the legal independence of the Bank of Algeria for two main reasons.

The first reason is related to article 13 of ordinance 01-01 dated 27–12–2001 which cancelled the arrangements made in article 22 of the LMC relative to the mandates of the governor and of the vice-governors. Article 10 of the same ordinance added to the seven members of the Council of Money and Credit three new external members, turning the managers of the Bank of Algeria into a minority. Those members were two professors of economics and the general secretary of the Association of Banks and Financial Companies (ABEF). Here, it is important to remember that Algerian banks are mainly public banks under the control of the Minister of Finance.

The second reason derives from the 03-11 ordinance, especially article 46, according to which 'the Bank of Algeria is also authorised to consent exceptionally to the Treasury an advance exclusively aimed at the active management of the external public debt'. Clearly, this clause allowed the financing of the budget deficit. It is true that this possibility has not been used so far because of the budget surplus resulting from the favourable oil context. But the intention was clear. In the 2004 finance law, a line 'advances to the Bank of Algeria' had been added to the resources from the revenue regulation fund (FRR) which had been created following the rise in the oil price.

This fund had been designed to reduce the public debt and to protect public expenditures from fluctuations in the budget surplus due to unpredictable variations in the oil price. The 2006 finance law made the situation official. It allowed the financing of the Treasury deficit up to a limit of 740 billion dinars (10 billion US dollars). That means that if the resources from the FRR are insufficient, there remains the possibility of 'printing money'. What is revealing is that, even if the financial resources of the FRR are largely positive, and, despite its good financial situation (a surplus of 3244 billion dinars at the end of 2006), the Treasury called in the second half of 2006 for exceptional advances from the Bank of Algeria aimed at the reimbursement in advance of the re-scheduled debt (Bank of Algeria, 2007). In other words, a part of Algeria's external debt has been transformed into internal debt.

Nevertheless, a careful examination of the practice of monetary policy in Algeria shows the extent to which the Bank of Algeria has attained *de facto* independence.

From **de jure** *to* **de facto** *independence in the 2000s*

Two illustrative pieces of evidence are the focus of this section. The first concerns the interpretation of the law on the objectives of the Bank of Algeria. In response to a question on the independence of the Bank of Algeria posed by the Commission on 'Perspectives et Développement Economique et Social' of the Social and Economic National Council (CNES), the governor declared that:

> 'if we look at all the dimensions of the independence of a central bank, it appears that, except for the terms of office of the managers, the other elements defining the independence of the Bank of Algeria are fulfilled.'
>
> (Conseil National Economique et Sociale, 2005: 5)

What is interesting is the argument he refers to in the justification of his view:

> 'Although the objectives of the Bank of Algeria as they appear in the banking law go beyond that of price stability, in the documents published by the Bank of Algeria it is clearly indicated that the ultimate objective of its monetary policy is *price stability*.' (Governor's emphasis)

Indeed, in the 2002 and 2003 reports of the Bank of Algeria, we can read that:

> 'the ultimate objective of monetary policy is to maintain price stability, understood as a limited increase of the consumer price index'
>
> (Banque d'Algérie, 2002: 72 and 2003: 90)

The last report (Banque d'Algérie, 2004: 111) reformulates the objectives as follows:

> 'the ultimate objective of monetary policy is to maintain monetary stability through price stability, understood as a limited increase of the consumer price index'.

Furthermore, the Bank of Algeria has adopted a 'rule-approach' since 2003 in its conduct of monetary policy, targeting an inflation rate of 3 per cent in a medium-term perspective. Indeed, before 2003, the target was not clearly fixed. It was the 2003 report of the Bank of Algeria (2004: 115) that made this explicit a posteriori: 'the ultimate objective of monetary policy in the form of medium-term stability of prices, that is inflation below 3 %, has been achieved in 2003'.

It is thus interesting to note that, in principle, although the Bank of Algeria has no political independence since the choice of final objectives is a matter of the laws (see section 2), it took the liberty of selecting only one objective amongst those fixed in the law so that it has goal independence. Furthermore, the Bank of Algeria also has goal independence with respect to its exchange rate policy: it has decided to stabilise the dinar. The central bank influences the nominal exchange rate on the official market. Through its intervention, the Bank of Algeria adjusts periodically the nominal exchange rate so as to achieve its real exchange rate target (Koranchelian, 2005). In practice, the central bank is the counterparty of most transactions on the foreign exchange market, as a result of the combination of three factors (ibid.): first, hydrocarbon exports account for more than 95 per cent of total exports; second, by law, the foreign exchange receipts from hydrocarbon exports have to be converted into dinars directly at the central bank; third, capital account transactions are subject to strict controls.

The second piece of evidence, related to economic independence, relates to a problem provoked by ordinance 03-11, which the Bank of Algeria resolved in an 'illegal' manner. The problem arose from the abrogation by the ordinance of article 93 of the LMC which had established the principle of mandatory reserves. The Council of Money and Credit, which is in charge of defining the instruments of monetary policy, restored this principle in regulation 04-02 of 4 March 2004. This was possible because line c of article 62 of the 03-11 ordinance authorises the Council of Money and Credit to define the monetary instruments. However the instruments should be selected from among those suggested in the law. The Bank of Algeria, through the Council of Money and Credit, adopted a broad interpretation and included an instrument that was not even mentioned in the law. Furthermore, the working mechanism of mandatory reserves implies sanctions.

If the central bank cannot punish the banks, the principle of reserves has no real content. But ordinance 03-11 cannot give the possibility of sanctions to the Bank of Algeria for a principle that does not exist. Accordingly, regulation 02-04 of the Bank of Algeria could be qualified as unlawful. Nevertheless, the authorities have not reacted against it.

In view of these pieces of evidence, one can conclude that, since 2000–2001, the Bank of Algeria has been *de facto independent* without being *de jure independent* because in practice it has enjoyed goal and economic independence.

4 Conclusion

This chapter on the independence of the Bank of Algeria since 1962 has established two central points. The first is that, when one studies developing economies and especially transition economies, the distinction between *de jure* and *de facto* independence is crucial in assessing the independence of the central bank. Indeed, as regards the Bank of Algeria, we could at first glance conclude that it is dependent on the political authorities. Successive governments have made many efforts to cancel the process begun with the LMC in 1990 that gave some autonomy to the central bank. After several amendments, the final coup was the 11-03 ordinance promulgated by the President of the Republic, on 26 August 2003. This law abrogated and replaced the already-modified LMC and opened the path to the monetary financing of the budget deficit. Despite these political pressures, the Bank of Algeria has chosen to follow the suggestions of the IMF and of the central bank independence literature, that is to target a unique inflation rate in a public manner.

The second result is that institutional constraints, either economic or political, are often more important than the legal statutes, especially in a MENA country such as Algeria. After the socialist shortages came the hard times of the stabilisation and structural adjustment programmes, followed by dramatic political instability. Thanks to the rise of the oil price, the Bank of Algeria, with the approval of the IMF, succeeded in reaching a low inflation rate. This outcome was associated with a positive fiscal position. The latest forecast from the IMF (2007) expects an increase in the inflation rate that can be partially explained by the rise of the euro relative to the dollar. This raises the question of Algeria's policy of pegging to the euro rather than the dollar (see Adam and Cobham, 2009).

Note

1 The authors thank the participants at the Eighth Mediterranean Social and Political Research Meeting, March 2007, for their comments. They are particularly grateful to David Cobham and Ghassan Dibeh for their remarks and suggestions.

References

Adam, C., and Cobham, D. (2009) Alternative Exchange Rate Regimes for MENA Countries: Gravity Model Estimates of the Trade Effects, in D. Cobham and G. Dibeh (eds.), *Monetary Policy and Central Banking in the Middle East and North Africa* . Routledge: London.

Alesina A., and Summers L. (1993) 'Central Bank Independence and Macroeconomic Performance: Some Comparative Evidence'. *Journal of Money, Credit and Banking*, 25: 151–62.
Arab Monetary Fund (1996) 'Monetary Policies in the Arab Countries', *Collection Recherches et Discussions des Groupes de Travail*, No 2, Abu Dhabi. (in Arabic)
Bade, R., and Parkin, M. (1982) 'Central Bank Laws and Monetary Policy'. *Mimeo*, Department of Economics, University of Western Ontario.
Bank of Algeria (2002) *Rapport 2001: Évolution Économique et Monétaire en Algérie*, July.
Bank of Algeria (2003) *Rapport 2002: Évolution Économique et Monétaire en Algérie*, June.
Bank of Algeria (2004) *Rapport 2003: Évolution Économique et Monétaire en Algérie*, April.
Bank of Algeria (2005a) *Contribution de la Banque d'Algérie aux travaux de la Commission Perspectives de Développement Économique et Social du CNES*, May.
Bank of Algeria (2005b) *Rapport 2004: Évolution Économique et Monétaire en Algérie*, July.
Bank of Algeria (2006) *Rapport 2005: Évolution Économique et Monétaire en Algérie*, April.
Bank of Algeria (2007) 'Tendances Monétaires et Financières au second semestre de 2006'. *Bulletin de Conjoncture*, March.
Barro, R., and Gordon, D. (1983a) 'Rules, Discretion and Reputation in a Model of Monetary Policy'. *Journal of Monetary Economics*, 12: 101–21.
Barro, R., and Gordon, D. (1983b) 'A Positive Theory of Monetary Policy in a Natural Rate Model'. *Journal of Political Economy*, 91: 589–610.
Conseil National Economique et Social (2005) *Perspectives et Développement Economique et Social*. Algiers: Conseil National Economique et Social.
Cukierman, A. (1992) *Central Bank Strategy, Credibility, and Independence: Theory and Evidence*. Cambridge, Massachusetts: MIT Press.
Cukierman, A. (2007) De Jure, De Facto, and Desired Independence: The Bank of Israel as a Case Study, in N. Liviatan and H. Barkai (eds.), *The Bank of Israel, Vol. 2, Selected Topics in Israel's Monetary Policy*. Oxford: Oxford University Press.
Cukierman, A., Webb, S.B., and Neyapti, B. (1992) 'Measuring the Independence of Central Banks and its Effect on Policy Outcomes'. *World Bank Economic Review*, 6: 439–58.
Debelle, G., and S. Fischer. (1994) How Independent Should a Central Bank Be? in J.C. Fuhrer (ed.), *Goals, Guidelines, and Constraints Facing Policy Makers,* Boston: Federal Reserve Bank of Boston.
Eijffinger, S.C.W., and de Haan, J. (1996) 'The Political Economy of Central Bank Independence', *Princeton Studies in International Economics*, 19.
Eijffinger, S.C.W., and Van Keulen, M.V. (1995) 'Central Bank Independence in Another Eleven Countries', *Banco Nazionale del Lavoro Quarterly Review*, 192: 39–83.
Fuhrer, J.C. (1997) 'Central Bank Independence and Inflation Targeting: Monetary Policy Paradigms for the Next Millennium?', *New England Economic Review*, January–February, 19–36.
Gisolo, E. (2009) 'The Degree of Legal Independence of the Mediterranean Central Banks: International Comparison and Macroeconomic Implication', in D. Cobham and G. Dibeh (eds.), *Monetary Policy and Central Banking in the Middle East and North Africa*. Routledge: London.
Grilli, V., Masciandaro, D., and Tabellini, G. (1991) 'Political and Monetary Institutions and Public Financial Policies in the Industrial Countries'. *Economic Policy*, 13: 341–92.
Hayo, B. and Hefeker, C. (2001) 'Do We Really Need Central Bank Independence? A Critical Re-examination', *WWZ-Discussion Paper* 01/03, University of Basel, pp. 1–31.
Ilieva, I. and Healey, N.M. (2001) 'Measures and Patterns of Central Bank Independence in Transition Economies'. *Statistics in Transition*, 5: 151–66.

IMF (2004) 'Algeria: Financial System Stability Assessment'. *International Monetary Fund Country Report,* 04/138, May.
IMF (2006) 'Algeria: 2005 Article IV Consultation – Staff Report' *International Monetary Fund Country Report,* 06/93.
IMF (2007) *Globalization and Inequality*, World Economic and Financial Surveys.
IMF (2007) *World Economic Outlook*, Washington, DC: *International Monetary Fund.*
Ismihan M. and F.G. Ozkan (2004) 'Does Central Bank Independence Lower Inflation ?'. *Economic Letters*, 84: 305–09.
Kessali, B. (2005) 'Banques et Entreprises Publiques Financièrement Déstructurées'. *Strategica,* 3.
Koranchelian, T. (2005) 'The Equilibrium Real Exchange Rate in a Commodity Exporting Country: Algeria's Experience'. *International Monetary Fund Working Paper*, 05/135.
Kornai, J. (1984) *Socialisme et Économie de Pénurie.* Paris: Economica.
Kydland, F., and Prescott, E. (1977) 'Rules Rather Than Discretion: The Inconsistency of Optimal Plans'. *Journal of Political Economy*, 85: 473–90.
Loungani P. and Sheets, N. (1997) 'Central Bank Independence, Inflation and Growth in Transition Economies'. *Journal of Money, Credit and Banking*, 29: 381–99.
Lybek T. (1999) 'Central Bank Autonomy and Inflation and Output Performance in the Baltic States, Russia, and Other Countries of the Former Soviet Union'. *International Monetary Fund Working Paper*, 99/4.
Minister of Finance, Algeria (2004) *Rapport de Présentation de la Loi de Finances pour 2005. Année une du programme de consolidation de la croissance 2005–2009,* September. Algiers.
OECD (2006) 'Algeria'. *African Economic Outlook*, pp. 91–104.
Office National de Statistiques, (2005) *Indice des prix à la consommation:* http://www.ons.dz/ipc/Ev_g90-98.htm, 11/04/2005.
Posen, A. (1998) 'Central Bank Independence and Disinflationary Credibility: A Missing Link?'. *Oxford Economic Papers*, 50: 335–59.
Rogoff, K. (1985) 'The Optimal Degree of Commitment to an Intermediate Monetary Target'. *Quarterly Journal of Economics*, 100: 1169–1190.
Siklos P. (1994) Central Bank Independence in the Transitional Economies: a Preliminary Investigation of Hungary, Poland, the Czech and Slovak Republics, in J. Bonin and P. Szekely (eds.), *Development and Reform of Financial Systems in Central and Eastern Europe*, Edward Elgar, Cheltenham.

6 Inflation targeting and financial fragility in Tunisia[1]

Adel Boughrara, Mongi Boughzala and Hassouna Moussa

Introduction

Starting in the mid 1980s and following a period of acute balance of payments and internal imbalances, Tunisia has managed to achieve macroeconomic stability and to bring inflation down from over 10 per cent in 1984 to less than 3 per cent in 2005 thanks to the implementation of important trade, financial and monetary reforms. Recently, the government of Tunisia announced that it is preparing to adopt a monetary policy of inflation targeting (IT), after an indeterminate transition period, and to move to full liberalisation of capital mobility and full convertibility of the Tunisian Dinar (TND).

IT is a monetary policy whose fundamental goal is to keep the inflation rate (suitably defined) within a certain publicly announced band centred around a target level (Mishkin, 2002). The band allows the central bank some flexibility in responding to departures of the actual inflation rate from the target rate. Although the principle of IT is simple, the success of a central bank in implementing it requires certain preconditions to be realised. In Tunisia, many of these preconditions are not yet fulfilled. We shall argue below that the central bank of Tunisia lacks independence, the government lacks fiscal discipline, the exchange rate is not truly flexible, and the country lacks a strong and transparent financial system. Some of these preconditions are achievable gradually over a relatively short transition period. Others are not so easy to fulfil. Financial soundness is a major prerequisite, and it is a fact that the Tunisian financial system remains rather vulnerable. The banks, which dominate this system, remain fragile, and the severity of their non-performing loans (NPLs) problem undermines their effectiveness in performing their role as the most important channel of financial intermediation and transmission of monetary policy signals. Indeed, the success of IT requires a stronger banking system and a deeper financial market.

Moreover, since the early 1960s, Tunisian monetary policy has not had a definite objective, it has not always followed a clear strategy, and it has quite often deviated from its official targets. These anomalies are quite significant given that the successful implementation of IT depends in the first place on the government's ability and willingness to establish credible financial and monetary policies and to guarantee fiscal and monetary discipline. This situation suggests that Tunisia must undertake major reforms before it adopts a full fledged IT policy.[2] In this chapter, we shall describe the needed reforms and the consequences of the failure to implement them.

The rest of this chapter is organised in two sections. Section 1 briefly presents the preconditions required for the successful implementation of IT, examines the recent history of monetary policy and tries to assess to what extent the Tunisian financial and monetary system is ready for IT. Section 2 presents a fairly simple dynamic simulation model based on Tunisian data which takes into account the fragility of the Tunisian financial system. This model is used to simulate the functioning of IT under financial fragility and to show how IT may fail under the current circumstances. Section 3 concludes.

1 The readiness of the Tunisian monetary and financial system for inflation targeting

There is a consensus among economists and central bankers that in order to successfully implement IT, a country must fulfil a set of quite strong preconditions.[3] The most crucial of these may be divided into conditions regarding the efficiency and the role of the central bank and conditions regarding the financial system.

The central bank

The first fundamental precondition of IT is the independence, accountability and transparency of the central bank. The central bank must be independent in order to be able to adjust freely the instruments of its monetary policy. The concept of independence is often divided into goal and instrument independence (Debelle and Fischer, 1994). In the case of IT, only instrument independence is required since the inflation target is by definition the single goal of this kind of monetary policy. Who will set the exact target remains debatable. In many countries, it is jointly set by the central bank and the government. In this case, independence means that the central bank should have enough power and strength to resist any external pressure to deviate from the chosen objective. In particular, the central bank should be free and the public should believe that it is free to decide whether or not to finance a government budget deficit, solely in accordance with the requirements of its IT monetary policy. It follows that fiscal discipline is a pre-requisite for the credibility of the central bank's independence.

Accountability and transparency of the central bank are corollaries of the credibility of its independence. An independent central bank has to be accountable for its actions to the public concerning the successes and failures of its policy. The public must have the capacity, through its elected representatives, to control and ultimately punish incompetent policymakers in order to create better incentives for them to do their jobs well (Mishkin, 2002). Monetary policy decisions must also be communicated in a clear and regular manner to the public and particularly to financial markets and private economic decision-makers. Transparency should focus on the policy analysis and the operational objectives of the central bank in order to reduce the inflation bias and uncertainties in financial markets (Faust and Svensson, 2001). A transparent monetary policy means that policy decisions (usually changes in short-term interest rates) should not contradict the expectations of the market. Thereby, transparency lowers the cost of achieving the inflation target.[4]

In the case of Tunisia, there is serious doubt about the transparency, accountability and independence of its central bank (Banque Centrale de Tunisie, BCT). The lack of a clear performance indicator, the lack of independence from the executive branch of the government and the composition of its board compromise its independence and its credibility. The governor of the BCT is appointed by government decree and is responsible for the management of all the affairs of the bank. He is assisted by a board whose members are appointed by the government. Six of its ten members, including the governor and the vice governors, are government officers. The other four are chosen according to their professional experience, but also by the government. The composition of the board clearly gives the government a monopoly power over decision making. Given this institutional and governance framework, the BCT has only limited autonomy in terms of goals and instruments. In practice, the BCT is accountable only to the government, primarily to the head of state. The governor of the BCT has behaved as if he were a member of the government. There is only a vague notion of accountability of the BCT to the public, which emphasises responsible management of its affairs, and there are no explicit benchmarks to measure the BCT's performance in terms of the achievement of its goals.

As for the transparency of the BCT, there are indeed auditors whose role is to check the accounting practices of the central bank. The auditor general is empowered to make propositions to the board. Every year, he writes an annual report on the conduct of the bank's affairs for the minister of finance, but it is a routine auditing procedure unrelated to monetary policy and insufficient to anchor expectations. The Tunisian law 58-90 requires that the board publishes a short statement every month but the amount of information provided to the public concerning monetary policy in this statement has been meagre and limited to some vague comments on financial and monetary aggregates, prices, economic growth and exchange rates. The bank's decision about the interest rate that it will enforce in the money market during the following month is announced at the end of the statement but it rarely changes in response to changes in the economic indicators.

The soundness of the Tunisian financial system

The efficiency of the central bank depends on the degree of development of the country's financial markets and its stability. It has been shown that the most serious economic contractions arise when there is financial instability (Mishkin, 2002). To prevent financial instability, the BCT has tightly controlled interest rates, the amount and distribution of credit, and the financial system including banks. Such a practice and the lack of independence and accountability of the central bank have encouraged mismanagement of financial institutions and forced them to take excessive risk, making the system even more fragile.[5]

Banks that are badly managed, or are under stress for any reason, are likely to lobby the government for relief through any available channels and to undermine the functioning of monetary policy. Higher short term interest rates intended to reduce inflationary pressures are then likely to put fragile banks them under more stress and to hurt them more severely. The US experience in the 1980s with the crisis of the savings and loans associations and in the current year (2007–2008) with the sub-prime loan crisis shows that if a central bank decided to fight inflation, badly managed financial institutions would be put under severe stress and some of them would fail.

A fragile banking system may also be unable to deal with free capital mobility and exchange rate volatility since IT cannot succeed unless a flexible exchange rate regime is put in place and there should be only one main target of monetary policy. In the presence of free capital mobility, stabilisation of the exchange rate subordinates monetary policy to its requirements and may lead to intolerable deviations from the inflation target. This will destroy the credibility of the central bank's commitment to IT.[6]

The existence of a well developed financial system is also associated with a sound fiscal policy. There is a wide consensus among economists that fiscal dominance may threaten financial stability since it means that high pressures are put on the financial system and the central bank to finance the government budget deficit. Fiscal discipline is a main pillar for the credibility of the central bank's independence and the viability of the country's financial institutions, as it signifies that the central bank and the banks will not be forced eventually to finance government budget deficits by printing money as happened, for example, in Turkey in the 1990s.[7]

In Tunisia, the banking system remains the backbone of the financial system while the securities market is still small and securities constitute only a small portion of the financial system's assets. The number of firms listed on the Tunisian Stock Exchange (TSE) increased from 13 in 1990 to 45 in 2005. Despite a sharp increase in the volume of trading and capitalisation since the implementation of the 1989 and 1994 reforms, market capitalisation represented only 8.8 per cent of GDP in 2007 while the annual value of trading amounted to only 1 per cent of GDP, which is very small compared to other emerging markets. Moreover, the bond market is dominated by government securities, which represent over 85 per cent of the outstanding bond instruments, and the secondary market is in its infancy. Finally, non-bank financial institutions (insurance companies, pension funds, collective investment institutions and investment companies) play a relatively small role in the Tunisian economy. Their assets represent only 22 per cent of GDP.

The Tunisian banking system was composed of 14 commercial banks, 6 development banks and 8 offshore banks in 2006.[8] The commercial banks dominate with 64 per cent of the total assets of the financial institutions, and the state controlled banks dominate the banking sector (the state controls the three largest banks and more than half of the banking system's assets). The banking system remains inefficient, state dominated, and burdened by non-performing loans (NPLs), and the BCT has regularly met requests from the commercial banks for liquidity, thereby often missing its liquidity target. Because of its strategic importance for the government's economic development plan, the system has suffered from a lack of transparency and accountability.

Prior to 1995, the BCT and the ministry of finance in Tunisia controlled on behalf of the government almost every aspect of bank credit and management, and the banks were required to invest various proportions of their deposits in support of economic activity in various sectors that the government designated as priority sectors. In July 2001, the Tunisian government introduced a new banking law, Law 2001-65, intended to strengthen bank supervision and to help banks deal with the new economic and regulatory environment. The new law removed most of the previous qualitative and quantitative restrictions on bank lending, but the government imposed new restrictions to help it maintain its control of credit and interest rates.

Although one of the goals of these new regulations was to improve the quality of the banks' management and to insure that banks' balance sheets satisfy some of the core principles of the Basle Committee on Banking Supervision (Basle II), not all these principles are yet satisfied, in particular those regarding capital requirements and the independence of the supervisory and licensing body. Law 2001-65 invests the minister of finance with the authority to fix the minimum capital requirement and to license banks. It also requires the management of every bank to maintain the value of its assets after deflating them by appropriate risk factors above the total value of its liabilities, by an amount greater or equal to its minimum paid in capital. Article 21 of the 2001-65 law prohibits a bank from investing more than 10 per cent of own funds to acquire interest in a single non-financial business. It prohibits a bank from owning directly and/or indirectly more than a 30 per cent share of the capital of a non-financial institution and of engaging in businesses other than banking. However, Article 21 of the 2001-65 law allows a bank to own any share of the capital of another financial institution. Clearly, the goal of these restrictions is to enhance transparency and prudential management, while allowing room for mergers of banks and other financial institutions. According to principle 5 of Basle II, a merger or acquisition of any kind should be subject to approval by an independent supervisory body. Clearly, article 21 of the 2001-65 law is not consistent with this Basle II principle.

The Tunisian law 2001-65 invests the BCT with the power to obtain any information about any aspect of the financial situation of any credit institution. The BCT can request any credit institution to provide it with information on any of its activities or its financial position, and can also demand to examine the books of any credit institution on the spot and demand an audit of any bank by an outside auditing firm. One might think that the new law and these powers should have insured that every bank is transparent, endowed with a good risk management system, and thus profitable. Banks would then have a small and sustainable percentage of non-performing loans and adequate provisions to face any likely risk.

In fact, this is not the case as the statistics on non-performing loans reveal. The relatively high proportion of NPLs in Tunisian banks is due primarily to the fact that the central bank is not independent and it is not allowed to use all its legal powers and instruments to rigorously implement the existing regulation. It is also due to the fact that the regulations do not ensure that the banking system and the banks' managers have the right incentives to avoid non-performing loans, given that banks are shielded against the risk of non-performing loans granted to risky private and public borrowers, and the banks' managers are not rewarded, or penalised, according to their bank's performance.

The current arrangements for depositor protection also generate the wrong incentives and contribute to the accumulation of non-performing loans. It is a widely admitted principle that a proper protection of depositors is necessary to encourage saving and stimulate economic development. The government of Tunisia was aware of the need to protect depositors but it remained attached to what Japanese economists call the principle of the convoy system, which is derived from the military idea that all ships in a military convoy must support each other. The disadvantage of this principle is that it leads to a moral hazard situation where banks have less incentive to be prudent in their lending, and hence it leads to the accumulation of more bad loans.

The convoy system contributes to the fragility of the banking system because it leads the central bank, as the lender of last resort, to pay for the mismanagement of banks. Alternatively, if banks were subject to a risk-weighted fee for deposit insurance, there would be less moral hazard. Bank managers would be eager to be transparent and they would reduce their exposure to non-performing loans. This is important for the conduct of monetary policy under IT. We know that it is possible to safely abandon the convoy system; for instance, in 2001 the Turkish government abandoned it and introduced instead a system of deposit insurance financed by risk-based fees. At the present time, the convoy system remains well and alive in Tunisia and it accounts to some extent for the current fragility of its financial system.

Given the difference in their incentive systems, it is not surprising that public banks have a higher ratio of non-performing loans (24.3 per cent in 2002) than private banks (18 per cent). It is also not surprising that the public banks' provisions for NPLs remain low (44 per cent in 2002). This is consistent with the fact that the Tunisian Government has for a long time sought to encourage economic development by allowing the central bank to facilitate credits to finance public development programmes, often with little concern for the prudential requirements of lending by the Tunisian financial institutions.

Table 6.1 Non-performing loans in Tunisia (commercial banks)

	1993	*1996*	*1999*	*2000*	*2001*
Gross NPLs	3,503.0	3,601.3	2,949.8	3,082.0	2,949.8
of which state controlled banks	2,872.2	2518.9	2,063.2	2,155.7	2,063.2
As a % of gross claims	34.0	25.1	18.8	21.6	19.5
As a % of GDP	23.9	16.7	12.6	15.8	14.3

Source: IMF 2002, and own calculations.

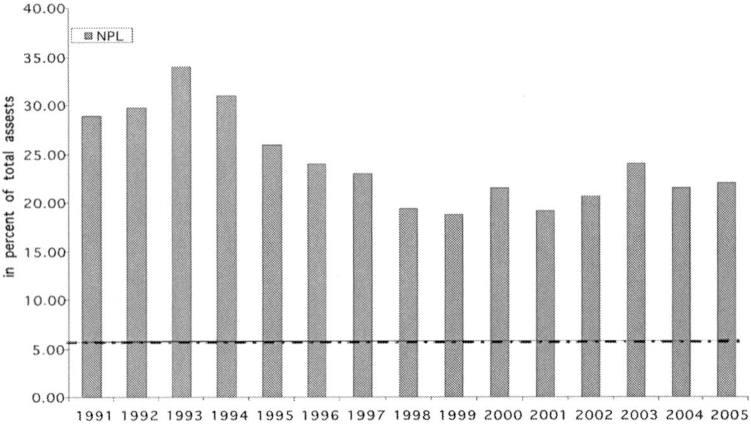

Figure 6.1 Non-Performing Loans in Tunisia.

Monetary and fiscal policies

Targeting broad money growth, in addition to pursuing a highly managed exchange rate regime, has long been the core of the BCT's monetary policy. Since the early 1990s Tunisia has followed a constant real effective exchange rate rule in an effort to index its nominal exchange rate to the domestic price level in order to protect the competitiveness of Tunisian producers. The BCT has interpreted this rule with some flexibility in order to smooth movements in the nominal exchange rate and to prevent it from serving as a nominal anchor.

This exchange rate policy has been quite successful. The absence of major terms of trade shocks and the maintenance of strict capital controls for residents and non-residents (except for foreign direct investors) have obviously facilitated the BCT's task.

Targeting money growth is, in principle, the main feature of the current monetary policy. The banking law provides the central bank with a variety of instruments but most of them are in fact intermediate instruments that serve to control the volume and distribution of credit and thus the money supply. The BCT's board is empowered by law to decide about the interest rate (the TAO[9]) applicable to the BCT's purchases and resales of securities, and to fix the amount of currency the BCT will inject or withdraw from the money market. Indeed, controlling and targeting the growth rate of the money supply has been the backbone of the BCT's policy over the last two decades. The setting of the money growth rate target has been based on the assumption of a constant velocity of money. Furthermore, the BCT has often published the intermediate targets months after schedule, which obviously weakens its credibility.

The main procedure for money control has been through competitive tenders over credit lines open to all banks for up to three months and renewable no more than twice. The BCT also makes shorter term advances to banks, overnight or up to one week, at a higher interest rate (one full point higher or 100 basis points).

The procedure for competitive tenders actually followed since the mid 1990s is such that the BCT maintains the previously applied interest rate and asks banks to specify only their demand for liquidity. This amounts to a *de facto* control of short term interest rates. Given that banks are quite dependent on its resources, the BCT usually satisfies their liquidity requests in order to keep interest rates stable. The BCT has also managed to exercise a quantitative control on the amount and distribution of total credit in the country. The point is that *in practice* the system has not systematically operated according to the strict rules of monetary targeting, and the targets have often been missed; the gap between the targeted value of M_2 (M3 since 2003) and the actual value exceeded the 2 per cent level more than 60 per cent of the time during the period 1987–2002 (see Figure 6.2). This gap exceeded 8 per cent during the years 1988, 1996 and 1999, which means that the BCT was not providing accurate guidance to private decision makers on which they could base their expectations (Boughrara, 2006).

The BCT's policy has in fact been driven more by the fear of financial system instability and by the government's economic development policy and its fiscal deficit than by the rules of its monetary policy. As a result of various contingencies and the government's need to meet the financial exigencies of its liabilities, the BCT had to meet requests for liquidity put forward indirectly by the government through the commercial banks, and hence to deviate from its money target. Banks had to supply unrestricted credits to meet government needs and private sector demands backed by the government authorities.

It is precisely for this reason that, although the BCT claims that the interest rates on credit are determined freely by the money market, it continues to control the level and distribution of credit indirectly and to link all interest rates to its 'Guiding rate'. Thus it is not surprising that the BCT has maintained interest rates constant over long periods.

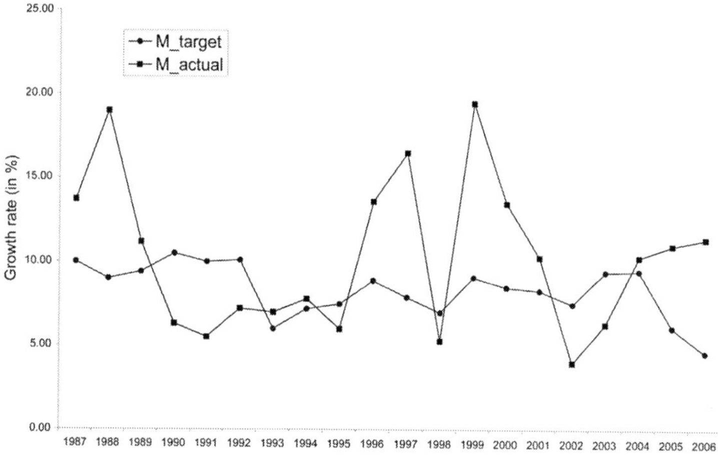

Figure 6.2 Actual and targeted monetary growth.

Moreover, it seems that BCT has in fact been more concerned about the exchange rate than about monetary targeting. Since it can't use a real exchange rate target and a money supply growth rate rule at the same time, the exchange rate targeting may dictate that it often misses the money growth rate target.

The BCT does not supply funds directly to the government. It may be argued that the fiscal reforms implemented during the 1990s established new rules and institutions that have contributed to the lowering of the inflation rate. Furthermore, the government has also adopted relatively more transparent and more market-based debt management instruments. Banks are no longer forced to invest a certain proportion of their deposits in government bonds. The government is now required to issue and sell new bonds on the open market to finance its deficit. These reforms led to the development of the government debt market and they were meant to create the right incentive for the government to master its deficit and to practice fiscal discipline.

However, these improvements did not mean that monetary policy had been completely freed from fiscal dominance and that the government now abided by the rules of fiscal discipline. A closer look at the indirect links between fiscal and monetary policies reveals that monetary policy remains subservient to fiscal policy and continues to accommodate the government's fiscal needs. This accommodation operates through several channels. One such channel is a tacit agreement that has prevailed at least since the mid–1980s, according to which every time the Ministry of Finance decides to issue and sell additional government bonds, the BCT systematically launches a competitive tender for a corresponding additional injection of liquidity in the money market.

In a growing economy, the independence of the monetary authority does not preclude it from increasing the money supply by purchasing government debt, and the point here is not so much to question the existence of a harmonisation procedure, which is desirable to some extent, but that the additional liquidity is large enough for all the banks to get the liquidity they need to buy the new government bonds with no increase in the money market interest rate as shown in Figure 6.4. As mentioned above, this explains in part why the monetary target

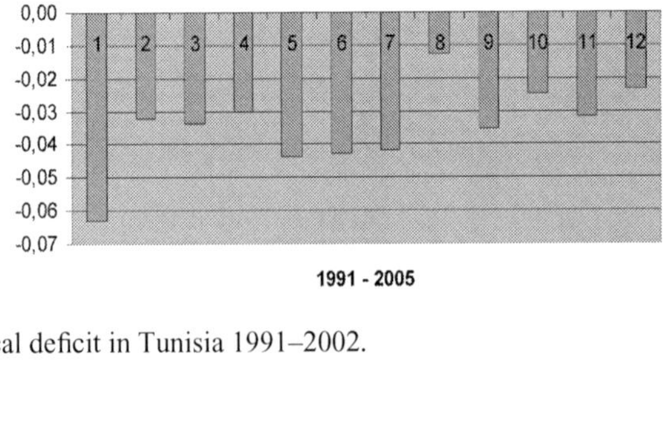

Figure 6.3 Fiscal deficit in Tunisia 1991–2002.

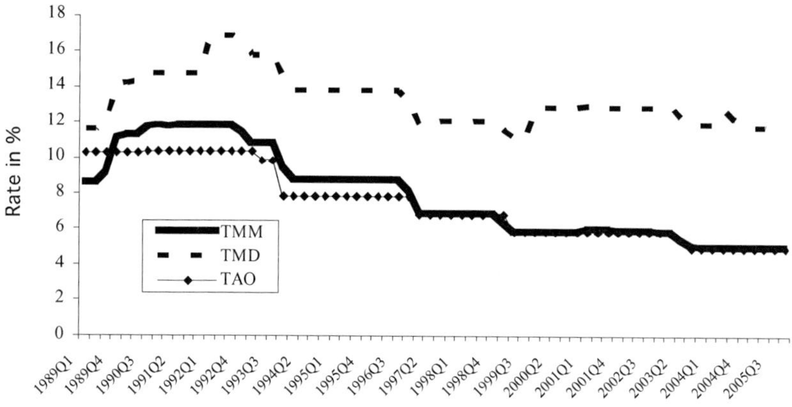

Figure 6.4 Main interest rates in Tunisia.

has often been missed. Figure 6.4 also shows clearly how all the major rates are rigidly linked to the TAO, the key BCT rate, including the average money market rate (TMM) and the maximum rate of bank overdraft, TMD. TMD may be taken as a proxy for the loan rate.

Direct coordination between fiscal policy and monetary policy is not the only mechanism leading to fiscal dominance. The government has carried important contingent liabilities in the form of arrears, especially during the 1980s and 1990s. The published fiscal deficit being calculated on the cash basis and not on the accrual basis, only completed transactions are accounted for and the arrears do not appear. In some years, these arrears built up and had to be settled through central bank financing.

For instance, between 1996 and 1999, as a result of important government arrears over almost a decade (debts that should have been paid to public enterprises), the BCT had to refinance these government commitments over a short period. Consequently M_2 grew well beyond its target, especially in 1999, despite the attempt of the BCT to drain the excess liquidity out of the system and to stabilise the money market rate. More recently, some measures have been taken to deal with this arrear issue and to avoid off-budget transactions. Significant progress has been achieved but the system does not seem totally immunised against this sort of risk yet.

2 Financial fragility and the effectiveness of inflation targeting: the analytical framework

Given the preponderance of the banking system in the Tunisian financial system, we may use the proportion of non-performing bank loans as an indicator of the financial fragility of the Tunisian economy. Obviously, the default risk of financial institutions depends on their rate of NPLs, given that the secondary market for government bonds is insignificant.

Our aim in this section is to present a fairly simple dynamic macroeconomic model that captures these important features. This model is used to simulate the impact of adopting IT. More precisely, we simulate under an IT regime the impact of an interest rate shock (increase) on NPLs, the demand for central bank liquidity and inflation. The outcome gives an assessment of the dependence of the banking system on the central bank and of the likelihood of a successful adoption (or failure) of IT.

The model is parsimonious and some of its equations have been deliberately simplified, hopefully with little cost in terms of the quality of the simulations. The purpose is not to provide accurate magnitudes for the aggregates that are of interest; the results merely illustrate the risks presented by an IT monetary policy under financial fragility.

The model

Let y_t be the aggregate supply or real GDP, y_t^n is potential output, and y_t^g is the output gap.[10,11] By definition

$$y_t = y_t^n + y_t^g \tag{1}$$

We compute the output gap by estimating the potential output y^n using the Hodrick-Prescott filter.[12]

Our main concern is to understand to what extent IT can operate successfully under the current Tunisian financial system and under various scenarios. We assume that the initial objective is to bring inflation down to a certain level. Then we consider different scenarios, some with favourable unexpected shocks and others with significant unexpected negative exogenous shocks. We also assume that these shocks are high enough to induce a significant drop in the rate of growth of real GDP and an increase in the rate of unemployment. In Tunisia, likely exogenous shocks are changes in the terms of trade or rainfall. External shocks are expected to become more likely and more severe in the near future as Tunisia opens up further both its trade and capital flows.

The second component of the model deals with the demand for and supply of loans. First, the interest rate structure is assumed to include two main rates: the central bank's main instrument, the interest rate (i_t), and the commercial banks' lending rate (R_t^L), the difference being the spread (s_t). The demand for bank loans is an increasing function of GDP (y_t) and a decreasing function of the interest rate $R_t^L = (i_t + s_t)$

$$L^d = L\left(y, R^L\right) \qquad \left(\partial L^d / \partial y\right) \geq 0 \text{ and } \left(\partial L^d / \partial i\right) \leq 0 \tag{2}$$

We assume that the interest rate channel of the monetary transmission mechanism operates through the demand for loans. The credit channel or the loan supply side may be operational too but we have not been able so far to provide a solid empirical proof of this. Above all, our interest is to investigate the dynamics generated when banks are willing to satisfy the demands for credits that have gone through their screening process, knowing that the central bank will support this strategy with more central bank credits when the firms' demand for credit increases, and vice-versa. Thus loan supply (L^S) is determined by loan demand, given the loan screening process followed by the banks:

$$L^s = L^d (y_t, i_t + s_t) \tag{3}$$

We are therefore implicitly assuming that the loan market equilibrium is not obtained through changes in R_t^L as a result of changes in the spread given i_t; which means that any change in the central bank rate (i_t) is fully (or almost fully) transmitted to the loan rate.

Given the high rate of NPLs, the aggregate loan supply granted to firms will be expressed as the sum of non-performing loans (NPL) and good quality loans (PL):

$$L^s = NPL + PL \tag{4}$$

As stressed in the beginning of this section, our emphasis will be on the dynamics of the NPLs as a measure of the performance of the banking sector. Thus, we model the share of non-performing loans in total loans as a function of contemporaneous and lagged macroeconomic variables such as economic growth, inflation, interest rates, the exchange rate, and deposits. A high rate of NPLs is, however, basically the outcome of poor risk management and signifies that not enough has been done to deal with the adverse selection and moral hazard problems linked to loan screening and management.

A fairly simple specification of the NPL dynamics could be expressed as follows:

$$NPL_t = f\left(y, y_t^g, a_t\right) \tag{5}$$

When output improves borrowers are less likely to default and NPLs should decrease; consequently, the sign of

$$\left(\partial NPL / \partial y^g\right)$$

is expected to be negative. Higher economic growth is expected to have a positive impact on the banks' asset quality and to lead to financial development. Either y or y^g could be used here; which one is omitted will be decided empirically. a_t stands for the banks' profit rate, which is a measure of their performance and a proxy for good management. So NPLs fall when a_t increases. When banks are managed better they operate a more efficient loan screening and monitoring process, and hence they allow for less NPLs. Nevertheless, the profit rate is a function of (or is correlated with) a set of variables:

$$a_t = g\left(R_{t-i}^L, \pi_{t-i}, D_{t-i}, CCB_{t-i}, NEER_{t-i}\right) \tag{6}$$

π is the inflation rate, D denotes deposits, CCB stands for credit obtained by banks from the central bank, and NEER is the nominal effective exchange rate. The lag i will be determined empirically. The profit rate does not necessarily increase when the loan rate increases since an increase of the (real) interest rate may worsen the banks' asset quality, leading to a higher rate of default. Arguably, following Stiglitz and Weiss (1981), this would be the outcome of imperfect and asymmetric information in the credit market leading banks to follow an adverse selection process. When the loan rate increases banks are led to select a larger share of riskier projects proposed by less 'honest' borrowers.

One might expect that the profit rate would decrease when the inflation rate increases because of the depreciation of the banks' assets; actually this is not certain since the effect of an increase in inflation depends on whether it was anticipated or not, how flexible lending rates are, and whether the increase signals general economic instability.

An increase in the nominal exchange rate is also likely to generate losses but this depends on the structure of the banks' assets and liabilities. Though the NEER variable seems to be an important transmission channel and a determinant of the NPL dynamics, the behavioural equation that describes its dynamics has not been integrated into the model for the sake of simplicity.[13] We may, however, consider an unexpected exogenous depreciation of the national currency and study its impact using this model. In general, when the currency goes into free fall, the banks may be rendered insolvent through a combination of the following channels: the sudden increase in the value (measured in domestic currency) of their foreign liabilities, the defaults on bank loans by domestic corporations bankrupted by the soaring of their external debts, and the defaults on bank loans by exporters who could not get short-term credit from their foreign suppliers of inputs.

Higher CCB indicates that a bank is under stress and is making fewer profits. Hence, the NPL equation, which describes how NPLs vary over time, becomes:[14]

$$NPL_t = \Psi\left(y_t, y_t^g, R_{t-i}^L, \pi_{t-i}, D_{t-i}, NEER_{t-i}, CCB_{t-i}\right) \tag{7}$$

From the profit function analysis, we may conclude that the derivative of the NPLs function with respect to the interest rate on loans is expected to be positive. A priori, its partial derivative with respect to inflation may be either positive or negative. As for the exchange rate, its effect depends on the composition of outstanding credit

$$\left(\partial NPL / \partial R^L\right)$$

(i.e., the size of unhedged positions and the share of borrowers whose business benefits from a given change in the exchange rate). In the case of Tunisia, we expect it to be negative.

Deposit supply, which appears in equation (7), is a function of output and the interest rate on deposits:

$$D^s = D\left(y, R^d\right) \tag{8}$$

With

$$R^d = (i_t - s_t^*),\ (\partial D/\partial y) \geq 0 \text{ and } \partial D^d/\partial R^L \geq 0$$

The variable s_t^* stands for the difference between R^d and i_t, and is different from s_t. As for the deposit demand, it is assumed to be equal to the households' supply (of deposits). The deposits market may reach equilibrium through movements in the deposit interest rate as a result of variations of the spread. Banks compete over deposits.

CCB is the amount of credit requested from the central bank and reflects the dependence of the banking system on the central bank. It is derived from the banks' balance-sheet, on the assumption that NPLs are worthless. The balance sheet links the sum of banks' liabilities (deposits plus loans from the central bank) to their assets (assets in stocks and securities B, reserves P and net loans, i.e. total minus NPLs), and may be written in the following form:

$$CCB + D = B + P + (L - NPL)$$

or equivalently:

$$CCB + D = B + P + L^*$$

with $L^* = L - NPL$;[15] which gives:

$$CCB = B + (L - NPL) + P - D \tag{9}$$

B stands for the banks' assets in stocks and securities and P denotes the amount of legal reserves. Because of the shallowness of the financial system and the absence of a viable secondary market for government securities, when banks lack liquidity or have excess liquidity they tend to turn to the central bank for relief. This dependency on central bank financing reflects their fragility.

To describe the inflation dynamics, various specifications, often of the Phillips curve type, may be considered: hybrid, forward-looking, backward-looking (Estrella, 2002; Svensson, 2002). The specification we have adopted in this paper is again a simple one:

$$\pi_t = \Pi\left(\pi_{t-i}, i_{t-i}, y_t^g, CCB_{t-i}, h_{t-i}\right) \tag{10}$$

where $(\partial\Pi/\partial i) \leq 0$, $(\partial\Pi/\partial y_t^g) \geq 0$; $(\partial\Pi/\partial CCB) \geq 0$ and $(\partial\Pi/\partial h0) \geq 0$

These assumptions say in particular that inflation might be brought about by the ability of the central bank to resist pressure coming from the banking system, expressed by the CCB level, and to other external pressures pushing it to supply more money, h_{t-i}. (h_{t-i}) is assumed to be a monetary shock generated by a past and persistent fiscal deficit. It is a proxy for fiscal pressure.

Simulations

The macroeconomic model described in the above section is allowed to work through its dynamic path from 1988:Q1 to 2005:Q3 to provide estimates of the endogenous variables in what we call the control or base run. Our main purpose is to simulate the impact of moving to an IT framework, while holding constant all the other exogenous conditions affecting the economy, notably those affecting inflation and NPLs.[16] We then change only the exogenous policy variable, under ceteris paribus conditions, and allow the model to run again through the same temporal path so as to yield a new set of estimates (the policy solution). The difference between the base run and the policy solution is attributed to the policy under consideration. The main idea behind this is to assess the soundness of the banking system and the efficiency of IT. Will the target be reached or missed? Would this interest rate destabilise the system? In particular, can the system reach its target even when important domestic or external shocks happen along the way? On the supply side, unexpected shocks linked to foreign trade or capital flows are assumed. Our primary focus in the simulation exercise has been put on the inflation and NPL dynamics.

The behavioural equations of the model have been estimated by the seemingly unrelated estimator of Zellner with data described in appendix 6.1 and the methodology in appendix 6.3. The result is summarised in table 6.2.

It is worth mentioning that some of the explanatory variables turned out to be statistically not significant, and hence have been dropped. The spread s_t has been proxied by the difference between the maximum rate on bank overdrafts, TMD, and the money market rate i. The behavioural equation describing the deposit supply dynamics was not reported because data on the spread s^*_t are not available. Therefore, $R^d_t = (i_t - s^*_t)$ could not be computed. Deposit dynamics are therefore assumed to be exogenous to the model. Our judgment is that this assumption will not affect substantially the simulation outcomes. Indeed, from the specification tests and the graphics (see appendix 6.2), the equation specification seems to be satisfactory since the structural model fits the data quite well. The simulated variables exhibit dynamics that are quite close to the actual series.

In the scenarios considered, we assume that the economy has just adopted an IT strategy with an inflation target around 2.5 per cent. We start the simulation exercise with inflation above the target inflation rate as observed at the end of 2001. Then, the central bank decides a large interest rate increase to lower inflation.

We consider an increase of the actual rate by either one or two percentage points decided in 2001:Q4. Formally, the dynamics of the simulated interest rate are as follows: $R^{sim}_t = R_t$ if t < 2001:Q4 and $R_t + x$ otherwise, with $x \in \{1, 2\}$. The simulation exercise has been run under two different assumption as regards the output gap, either the base run or a negative output shock occurring unexpectedly right after the interest rate increase. Will the economy and the financial system withstand this monetary decision and the negative supply shock?

The answer is given in table 6.3 where inflation and NPL dynamics are reported. Inflation is expressed in percentage points while NPLs are in log terms. Hence a

Table 6.2 Estimates of the behavioural equations

$$L_t = \underset{(1.447)}{0.098} + \underset{(17.597)}{0.811}\, L_{t-1} + \underset{(4.016)}{0.18}\, D_t + \underset{(2.741)}{0.013}\, REERt - \underset{(-1.795)}{0.01}\, i_{t-1}$$
$R^2 = 0.998$ DW=1.83

$$\pi_t = \underset{(-0.893)}{1.141} + \underset{(14.864)}{0.908}\, \pi_{t-1} - \underset{(-5.239)}{0.033}\, \pi_{t-3} + \underset{(4.224)}{4.233}\, \Delta REER_t + \underset{(3.453)}{0.312}\, y_{t-2}$$
$R^2 = 0.85$ DW=1.61

$$NPL_t = \underset{(-1.248)}{-0.225} + \underset{(3.026)}{0.043}\, CCB_{t-1} - \underset{(-2.550)}{0.035}\, CCB_{t-2} + \underset{(5.890)}{0.703}\, NPL_{t-1} + \underset{(3.20)}{0.312}\, NPL_{t-2} + \underset{(1.955)}{0.011}\, i_{t-6}$$
$R^2 = 0.990$ DW=2.04

Note: Numbers between parentheses are t-ratios.

change in this NPL measure gives their growth rate; for instance a change in NPLs from 8.4 to 8.5 means a growth rate equal to 0.1 or 10 per cent.

In table 6.3 the 'one–zero' column reports the results for the 1 per cent interest rate increase scenario without any output shock, the 'one–one' column reports the results for the 1 per cent interest rate increase scenario with a one standard deviation negative exogenous output shock (more exactly one standard deviation of the unanticipated component of the output); likewise for the 'two–zero' and the 'two–two' columns, which report respectively the results for a 2 per cent interest rate increase without and with a two standard deviation negative exogenous output shock. The supply shock happens right after the moment the BCT decides to increase its interest rate. Under the base run, if no action is taken, inflation starts increasing significantly in the third quarter of 2001 and reaches 3.7 per cent in the next quarter while the target is 2.5 per cent, and it would reach 4.5 per cent two years later after some fluctuations. Simultaneously, NPLs would be increasing steadily, at about 8 per cent per year (17 per cent over the two year period).[17]

It is clear that as a result of the central bank decision to raise the interest rate by one or two percent, if no negative output shock occurs, inflation is basically controlled quite rapidly, since it is brought back to around the 2.5 per cent target in about a year and stabilised. However, NPLs growth increases even more as it reaches about 25 per cent in the same two year period in both cases, which is a very high growth rate. Hence, even though the inflation target is reached the banking system becomes more fragile.

The outcome is more significant in the case where a negative output shock occurs. Here, NPLs grow a little faster than in the previous case, but more importantly the inflation target is missed. Inflation at first falls erratically and then starts to rise again; at the end of 2003, it is 2.8 per cent in the 'one–one' case and 2.78 per cent in the 'two–two' case. A larger interest rate increase is thus counter productive, so it does not help to use the interest rate lever more intensively.

Consequently, the simulation outcomes throw doubt on the effectiveness of IT under the present situation of the banking system. Because the system is too fragile, a negative supply shock will limit the effectiveness of IT. A similar failure of the IT policy may be obtained whenever the central bank finds itself under the obligation to create more high powered money or to satisfy any external pressure,

Table 6.3 The dynamics of inflation and Non-Performing Loans under the two scenarios

	interest rate	NPLs					Inflation				
		Base run	one-zero	one-one	two-zero	two-two	Base run	one-zero	one-one	two-zero	two-two
2000Q4	5.88	8.16					1.65				
2001Q1	6.06	8.21					1.15				
2001Q2	6.06	8.25					1.56				
2001Q3	6.06	8.28	8.39	8.34	8.35	8.32	2.53	3.16	3.22	3.15	3.22
2001Q4	5.96	8.21	8.40	8.36	8.36	8.33	3.70	3.17	3.21	3.15	3.23
2002Q1	5.94	8.27	8.43	8.39	8.38	8.35	3.80	3.33	3.46	3.32	3.48
2002Q2	5.94	8.28	8.45	8.41	8.40	8.37	3.26	2.94	3.14	2.93	3.15
2002Q3	5.95	8.34	8.43	8.40	8.37	8.35	2.04	2.68	2.99	2.66	2.99
2002Q4	5.91	8.28	8.44	8.42	8.38	8.36	2.00	2.63	3.12	2.63	3.12
2003Q1	5	8.28	8.47	8.44	8.40	8.38	1.40	2.05	2.46	2.05	2.46
2003Q2	5.44	8.34	8.47	8.45	8.42	8.40	2.07	2.21	2.60	2.21	2.60
2003Q3	5.1	8.37	8.51	8.49	8.46	8.44	3.43	2.38	2.74	2.39	2.73
2003Q4	5	8.38	8.51	8.49	8.47	8.45	4.50	2.56	2.80	2.56	2.78
2004Q1	5	8.47	8.56	8.54	8.53	8.51	4.74	2.55	2.68	2.54	2.67

Notes: The NPLs series are reported in log-level. The interest rate given is that for the base run.

for instance as a result of a high fiscal deficit that the government could not manage to finance otherwise.

3 Conclusion

The overall conclusion is that many reforms and actions remain to be undertaken before the final move to an IT framework, especially in terms of financial soundness, fiscal discipline and institutional and governance structure. Independence of the central bank remains a crucial condition. A deep transformation of the financial system is in fact necessary for the success of any sound monetary policy and IT is in any case not the only option for Tunisia. It is possible to make the banking system stand on its own feet in a reasonable period. The required reforms could be introduced in Tunisia but they are not costless in terms of institutional and political requirements, and they remain a political economy issue. It took Turkey a serious crisis to make the radical decision to switch to IT and to go through the required reforms after years of turbulence and unsound monetary policy. For the moment, the cost of doing so and the uncertainties linked to the transition to IT make this transition rather uncertain in Tunisia. Because the financial system is not yet ready for IT, it would be risky to move to IT soon. However, other countries' experiences (e.g. Turkey, Poland) show that it should not be excluded.

Notes

1 This work has benefited from a financial grant from the Economic Research Forum for which the authors are very grateful. The contents and recommendations do not necessarily reflect the views of the Economic Research Forum. The authors are thankful to Professors Ghassan Dibeh and David Cobham for their thorough review of and valuable comments on the manuscript.

2 The need to resolve these issues has been treated widely for emerging countries in general (Mishkin, 2004), but only recently for Tunisia (Boughrara, 2007), or for similar countries of the region.

3 See for instance, Masson *et al.* (1997); Taylor (2000); Mishkin (2002); Siklos (2002); Siklos and Abel (2002); Bernanke *et al.* (1999).
4 Nonetheless, Cukierman (2002 and 2007) and others argue that there should be a limit on the transparency requirement. Beyond a certain point, increased transparency may reduce the central bank's effectiveness and its ability to decide about trade-offs, such as those between less inflation and fighting a recession or stabilising the exchange rate. Some room for discretion must be left to the central bank even under IT.
5 More recently, the banking system has become excessively liquid and banks are becoming more risk averse.
6 According to Mishkin (2002, 2004), the exchange rate flexibility condition may even be weakened, and a trade-off between the inflation and exchange rate objectives may be considered within an adapted IT framework.
7 This has also happened elsewhere, for instance in Argentina, with the most recent episode occurring in 2001.
8 Some of the development banks have been transformed into commercial (universal) banks since 2006.
9 TAO stands for 'taux d'appel d'offre'.
10 All variables are expressed in term of the natural logarithms of the corresponding macroeconomic aggregate except for ratios, growth rates and the interest rate.
11 Alternatively, y_t^n may be interpreted as the government's output target.
12 An alternative way to compute the potential output could be the production function approach. In this approach, GDP is determined by the production factor inputs (capital and labour) and by the total factor productivity, or the efficiency with which these factors are used to generate output. We do not attempt, in this paper, to estimate potential output using such an approach because of the lack of reliable data. Other methods, such as the band-pass filter and regressions on polynomial trends, have been run but they provide very similar results to the Hodrick-Prescott filter. For more detailed analysis on output gap measures we refer to Almeida and Felix (2006) and Basistha and Nelson (2007).
13 Also because of a lack of data.
14 Seeing that there is no clear consensus about the specification of the equation describing the NPLs dynamics, we resort in practice to the 'general to specific' modeling approach (see for instance, Hendry and Richard, 1982), starting from a model including a maximum of variables with a maximum of lags and then simplifying it with regard to empirical data. It is worth noting that NPLs are considered in nominal terms even though some explanatory variables may be reported in real terms. The issue of which variable should be included in equation 7 is essentially an empirical issue.
15 Starting from an annual balance sheet we may write (i): $\Delta B + \Delta L^* + G$, where r is the average net income generated by the banks' assets, $r(B+L^*)$ the banks' total revenue and G total profit. Assuming that total revenue is entirely paid to the banks' owners as profits, we can write (ii): $r(B+L^*) = G$. Combining (i) and (ii) gives: $\Delta B + \Delta L^* + G = \Delta(D + CCB)$. Aggregating over time leads to: $CCB+D= B+L^* + P$ and to Eq.(9).
16 It is worth noting that when the ratio of non-performing loans to total assets, instead of the stock of NPLs, was considered, the simulation encountered numerical problems. We therefore preferred to simulate the future path of the log NPL stock under the scenarios considered. The issues of non-stationarity and cointegration have been kept for future research.
17 The dependent variables NPLs and L are considered in nominal terms.

References

Almeida, V., and Felix, R. (2006) 'Computing Potential Output and the Output Gap for the Portuguese Economy'. *Bank of Portugal Economic Bulletin*, Autumn 2006: 73–88.

Abeysinghe, T., and Ajaguru, G. (2004) 'Quarterly Real GDP Estimates for China and Asia with a Forecast Evaluation'. *Journal of Forecasting*, 23: 431–7.

Association Professionnelle Tunisienne des Banques et des Etablissements Financiers (2005) 'Evolution Des Comptes Du Bilan Durant La Période 1999/2003': http://www.apbt.org.tn/fr/htm/publications/bilans_des_banques.htm.

Bank Al Maghreb. *Annual Report*, various issues. Rabat, Morocco.

Banque Centrale de Tunisie (2005a) 'Surveillance Bancaire': http://www.bct.gov.tn/francais/politique/index.html.

Banque Centrale de Tunisie (2005b). 'Loi no 2001–65 du 10 juillet 2001, Relative aux Établissements de Crédit (1)': http://www.bct.gov.tn/francais/politique/index.html.

Basistha, A., and Nelson, C.R. (2007) 'New Measures of the Output Gap Based on the Forward-looking New Keynesian Phillips Curve'. *Journal of Monetary Economics*, 54: 498–511.

Bernanke, B.S., Laubach, T., Mishkin, F.S., and Posen, A.S. (1999) *Inflation Targeting: Lessons From the International Experience*. Princeton, New Jersey: Princeton University Press.

Bloem A.M., Dippelsman, R.J., and Maehle, N.O. (2001) 'Quarterly National Accounts Manual – Concepts, Data Sources, and Compilation': http//www.imf.org/external/pubs/ft/qna/2000/Textbook.

Boughrara, A. (2006) 'Are the Preconditions for the Monetary Targeting Strategy Gathered? Evidence From Tunisia'. *Indian Journal of Economics and Business*, 5: 89–105.

Boughrara, A. (2007) 'Can Tunisia Move to Inflation Targeting?' *Developing Economies*, 45: 27–62.

Cukierman, A. (2002) 'Are Contemporary Central Banks Transparent about Economic Models and Objectives and What Difference Does it Make?' *Federal Reserve Bank of St. Louis Review*, 84(4): 15–45.

Cukierman, A. (2007) 'The Limits to Transparency', forthcoming in Bohl, M., Siklos, P., Wohar, M. (eds.), *Frontiers in Central Banking*, Elsevier.

Debelle, G., and Fischer, F. (1994) How Independent Should a Central Bank Be? In J.C. Fuhrer, (ed.), *Goals, Guidelines and Constraints Facing Monetary Policy*. Boston: Federal Reserve Bank of Boston.

Estrella, A. (2002) 'Securitisation and the Efficacy of Monetary Policy', *Economic Policy Review*, 8: 243–255. New York: Federal Reserve Bank of New York.

Faust, J., and Svensson, L.A.O. (2001) 'Transparency and Credibility: Monetary Policy with Unobservable Goals'. *International Economic Review*, 42: 369–97.

Fischer, S. (1994) Modern Central Banking, in F. Capie, C. Goodhart, S. Fischer, and N. Schnadt (eds.), *The Future of Central Banking: The Tercentenary Celebration of the Bank of England*. Cambridge: Cambridge University Press.

Frain, J.C. (2004) 'A RATS Subroutine to Implement an Extended Chow-Lin Distribution/Interpolation Procedure'. *Central Bank and Financial Services Authority of Ireland Research Technical Paper* 2/RT/04.

Hendry, D.F., and Richard J.F. (1982) 'On the Formulation of Empirical Models in Dynamic Econometrics'. *Journal of Econometrics*, 20: 3–33.

IMF (2002) Tunisia: Financial System Stability Assessment. *International Monetary Fund, Country Report* 02/119.

Masson, P., Savastano, M. and Sharma, S. (1997) 'The Scope for Inflation Targeting in Developing Countries'. *International Monetary Fund Staff, Working Paper* 97/130., Washington, D.C.: International Monetary Fund.

Mishkin, F.S. (2002) 'Does Inflation Targeting Matter? Commentary'. *Federal Reserve Bank of St Louis Review*, 84: 149–53.

Mishkin, F.S. (2004) 'Can Inflation Targeting Work in Emerging Market Countries?'. Paper presented to a conference in honour of Guillermo Calvo, April. Washington: International Monetary Fund.

Siklos, P.L. (2002) *The Changing Face of Central Banking: Evolutionary Trends Since World War II*. Cambridge: Cambridge University Press.

Siklos, P.L., and Ábel, I. (2002) 'Is Hungary Ready for Inflation Targeting?' *Economic Systems*, 26: 309–33.
Stiglitz, J.E., and Weiss. A. (1981) 'Credit Rationing in Markets with Imperfect Information'. *American Economic Review*, 71: 393–410.
Svensson, L.E.O. (2002) 'Inflation Targeting: Should it Be Modeled as an Instrument Rule or a Targeting Rule?' *European Economic Review*, 46: 771–80.
Taylor, J.B. (2000) 'Using Monetary Policy Rules in Emerging Market Economies'. Paper presented at the 75th Anniversary Conference, Stabilisation and Monetary Policy: The International Experience, November 14–15. Bank of Mexico.

Appendix 6.1 Data description and sources

Variable	*Name*	*Source*
Consumer price index	CPI	IMF, IFS CD-ROM
Nominal effective exchange rate	NEER	IMF, IFS CD-ROM
Bank loans to households and firms	L	IMF, IFS CD-ROM
Real bank loans	BL	Computed as L/CPI
Short-run (nominal) interest rate	TMM	Central bank of Tunisia
Interest rate on deposits	RD	Central bank of Tunisia
Interest rate on loans	RL	Proxied by the maximum rate of bank overdraft (TMD)
Bank deposits	D	IMF, IFS CD-ROM
Real GDP	y_t	IMF, IFS CD-ROM
Non-performing loans	NPL	Proxied by frozen loans (Central bank of Tunisia)
Capital adequacy ratio	CR	Computed as CR= bank capital/total assets
Inflation rate	INFQ	Computed as Log(CPIt)-log(CPIt-4,)
Real effective exchange rate	REER	IFM, IFS CD-ROM
Credit from monetary authority	CCB	IMF, IFS CD-ROM
Reserves	RV	Central Bank of Tunisia

Note: All the variables are available on quarterly frequency except the real GDP which is available on an annual frequency. The Chow-Lin procedure has been used to generate quarterly figures. The basic idea here is to find some GDP-related quarterly series (notably the industrial production index) and develop a predictive equation by running a regression of annual GDP on annual related series. Then, the quarterly figures of the related series are used to predict the quarterly GDP figures, and adjusted to match the annual aggregates. This disaggregation procedure has been widely used in other works (see for instance, Abeysinghe and Ajaguru 2004; Frain, 2004; Bloem *et al.* 2001).

Appendix 6.2 Actual versus fitted variables: base run

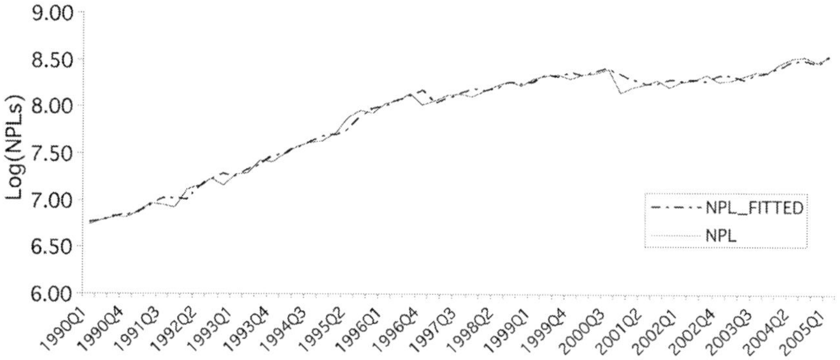

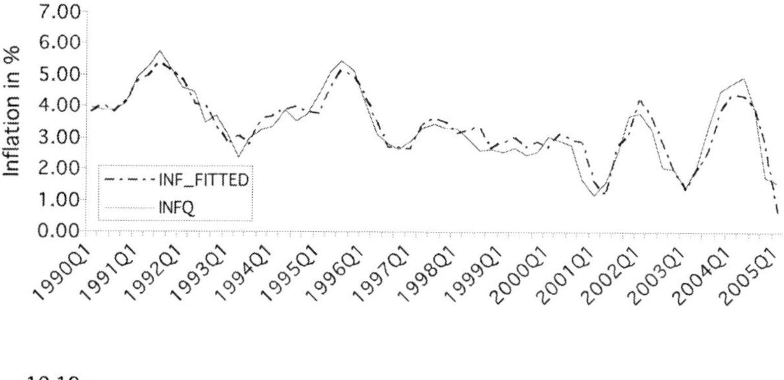

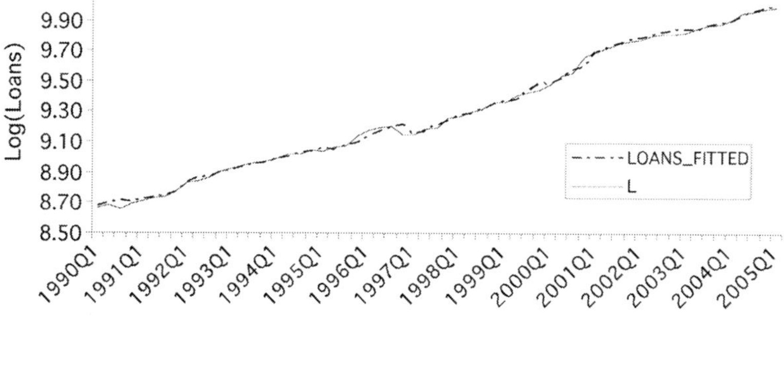

Appendix 6.3 Econometric estimation

The behavioural equations of the model have been estimated by the seemingly unrelated estimator of Zellner with data described in appendix 6.1. Each of the behavioural equations (equations Eq.(3), Eq.(7) and Eq.(10)) could be written in the following form:

$$Y_i = X_i\beta_i + u_i \tag{C1}$$

Y_i is a T×1 vector of observations on the ith dependent variable, X_i is a T×k_i matrix with rank k_i, of observations on k_i independent variables, β is a k_i×1 vector of regressions coefficients and u_i is a T×1 vector of random error terms, each with a mean of zero. The system of behavioural equations could be written as:

$$\begin{bmatrix} Y_1 \\ Y_2 \\ Y_3 \end{bmatrix} = \begin{bmatrix} X_1 & 0 & 0 \\ 0 & X2 & 0 \\ 0 & 0 & X_3 \end{bmatrix} \begin{bmatrix} \beta_1 \\ \beta_2 \\ \beta_3 \end{bmatrix} + \begin{bmatrix} u_1 \\ u_2 \\ u_3 \end{bmatrix} \tag{C2}$$

Or more compactly, as:

$$Y = X\beta + U \tag{C3}$$

Where $Y = [Y_1', Y_2', Y_3']'$, $\beta = [\beta_1', \beta_2', \beta_3']'$, $U = [u_1', u_2', u_3']'$ and X stands for the block diagonal matrix on the right hand side of equation (C2). The T×1 vector U in equation (C3) is assumed to have the following variance-covariance matrix:

$$\Omega = \begin{bmatrix} \sigma_{11} & \sigma_{12} & \sigma_{13} \\ \sigma_{21} & \sigma_{22} & \sigma_{23} \\ \sigma_{31} & \sigma_{32} & \sigma_{33} \end{bmatrix} \otimes I_T = \Sigma \otimes I_T \tag{C4}$$

Where IT is a unit matrix of order T×T and $\sigma_{ij}=E(u_{it}u_{jt})$ for t=1,2,…,T and i,j=1,2,…,3. Having at hand the set of the above regression equations, the regression coefficients are therefore estimated simultaneously by applying Aitken's generalised least-squares to the whole system of equations. The best linear unbiased estimator by this method takes the form:

$$\hat{\beta} = \left(W' \left(\Sigma^{-1} \otimes I_T \right)^{-1} W' \right)^{-1} \left(W' \left(\Sigma^{-1} \otimes I_T \right)^{-1} Y \right) \quad \text{(C5)}$$

While the variance-covariance matrix of the estimator is given by:

$$\text{VarW'IW'} \left(\hat{\beta} \right) = \left(\quad \left(\Sigma^{-1} \otimes {}_T \right)^{-1} \quad \right)^{-1}$$

This estimation procedure yields coefficient estimators at least asymptotically more efficient than single equation least-squares estimators.

Part II

Monetary policy and exchange rate regimes

7 Alternative exchange rate regimes for MENA countries

Gravity model estimates of the trade effects[1]

Christopher Adam and David Cobham

Introduction

Most Middle East and North African (MENA) countries peg their currencies more or less tightly to the US dollar, and have done so for many years. The historical origins of these practices probably lie in the relative underdevelopment at that time of financial institutions and markets in MENA countries and the dominance of the dollar as the main numéraire in the post-Bretton Woods era, indeed the lack of any real alternative numéraire, and possibly also in the debatable argument that it was better to peg to the dollar since the dollar was the currency of the oil market.

Some observers have pressed for greater flexibility in MENA exchange rates (Jbili and Kramarenko, 2003). On the other hand, with the creation of the European Monetary Union, there is now a real alternative numéraire and anchor for MENA countries in the form of the euro. Empirical gravity models suggest that the choice of exchange rate regime may have important implications for the volume of trade between countries. Rose (2000) initiated a vigorous debate by reporting estimates indicating that currency unions in particular had substantial trade-promoting effects. This prompted a substantial increase in the amount of literature in this area in which he and others tried to eliminate or at least reduce the very large positive effects he had found in his original work (see Baldwin and Taglioni, 2006, for a comprehensive survey). However, this debate has been concerned not just with empirical results but also with theoretical and methodological matters, in particular how to correctly account for the effect of changes in bilateral exchange rate regimes on trade with third countries (see, for example, Anderson and van Wincoop, 2003, 2004; Feenstra, 2004; Baier and Bergstrand, 2006; Carrère, 2006; Mélitz, 2007).

Some attention has also been directed towards the effects on trade of exchange rate regimes other than currency unions. Fritz-Krockow and Jurzyk (2004) investigated the trade-enhancing effects of fixed pegs for Caribbean countries. Klein and Shambaugh (2004) estimated the effects of direct and indirect pegs in a wider model. Adam and Cobham (2007a) estimated the effects of a full menu of exchange rate regimes which distinguishes free floats, managed floats (with and without a specific reference) and hard pegs as well as currency unions (and currency boards) and identifies when currencies are anchored on the same or different (or no) reference currencies. All of these researchers have found that at least some other exchange rate regimes have positive effects on trade, albeit smaller than those of currency unions.

In this chapter we draw on our contributions to this debate to consider the implications for MENA trade flows of alternative exchange rate regimes which include a hard peg to the dollar, dollarisation, a hard peg to the euro and euroisation. Thus the regression results on which the simulations reported in the chapter are based are taken from Adam and Cobham (2007b). In that paper we carried out a detailed assessment of alternative techniques of allowing for multilateral trade resistance, within the framework of the Baier and Bergstrand (2006) methodology. The model is estimated on data up to 2004 for a sample of some 175 countries, which means that it includes six years of European Monetary Union in addition to the small country (*plus* United States) currency unions which weigh heavily in Rose's (2002) sample. Our findings suggest that most MENA countries would have higher trade if they switched from anchoring on the dollar to anchoring on the euro.[2]

Section 1 explains the basic methodology and data. Section 2 explains the menu of exchange rate regimes considered. Section 3 presents the basic estimate of the trade equation, which is used for the simulations presented in Section 4. Section 5 concludes.

1 Methodology and data

In the modern version of the empirical gravity model trade flows between countries are determined not only by the conventional Newtonian factors of economic mass and distance, but also by the ratio of 'bilateral' to 'multilateral' trade resistance. Bilateral trade resistance (BTR) is the size of the barriers to trade between countries i and j, while multilateral trade resistance (MTR) refers to the barriers which each of i and j face in their trade with *all* their trading partners (including domestic or internal trade).

For example, trade between France and Italy depends on how costly it is for each to trade with the other relative to the costs involved for each of them in trading with other countries. Hence a reduction in the bilateral trade barrier between France and a third country such as the United Kingdom would reduce France's multilateral trade resistance (MTR). Although the bilateral trade barrier between France and Italy is unaffected, the fall in France's MTR caused by the decline in the UK–France bilateral barrier leads to a diversion of bilateral trade away from France–Italy trade and towards France–UK trade. Moreover, as Baier and Bergstrand (2006) show, there is a further (smaller) effect which operates in the opposite direction: the fall in France's MTR generates a (small) fall in the average of all countries' MTRs, which they call world trade resistance (WTR), and this encourages international trade instead of internal or domestic trade. The consequence of the reduction in the France–UK BTR for trade between France and Italy is the net of the bilateral trade diversion effect away from France–Italy trade and towards France–UK trade and the smaller multilateral trade creation effect away from internal France–France trade towards France's trade with all its international trading partners including Italy.

A formal gravity model

We use a model developed by Anderson and van Wincoop (2003) in which each country i = 1 … n produces a single good and consumes a constant elasticity of substitution composite defined over all *n* goods, including home production.[3] For the moment, we suppress any dynamic aspects so that the model describes trade flows across a single time period. All countries trade with each other, but because of natural and other barriers, cross-border trade is costly. Utility maximization by each country, subject to its budget constraint, the structure of trade costs and the set of market clearing conditions for each good, leads to the following equation for bilateral trade between countries *i* and *j*

$$F_{ij} = \frac{y_i y_j}{y^W}\left(\frac{t_{ij}}{P_i P_j}\right)^{1-\sigma} \tag{1}$$

where F_{ij} denotes the volume of trade between countries *i* and *j*, y_i and y_j are their respective total expenditures (proxied by Gross Domestic Product (GDP)), and y^W is global GDP. Bilateral trade resistance is denoted by t_{ij} which represents the gross mark-up in country *j* of country *i's* good over its domestic producer price: trade resistance is assumed to be symmetric so that $t_{ij} = t_{ji}$. P_i and P_j are the constant elasticity of substitution (CES) consumer price indices for *i* and *j* respectively and are defined as

$$P_i = \left[\sum_j \left(\beta_j p_j t_{ji}\right)^{1-\sigma}\right]^{1/(1-\sigma)} \quad \text{and} \quad P_j = \left[\sum_i \left(\beta_i p_i t_{ij}\right)^{1-\sigma}\right]^{1/(1-\sigma)} \tag{2}$$

where $\beta_j^{1-\sigma} = \theta_{ij}$ denotes the share of country *j* in country *i's* consumption. Anderson and van Wincoop (2003) refer to P_i and P_j as 'multilateral trade resistance' since each is a function of that country's full set of bilateral trade resistance terms (including internal trade resistance, t_{ii}, which is normalised to unity). Finally, σ is the elasticity of substitution between all goods (assumed to be greater than one so that, for example, an increase in bilateral trade costs has a negative effect on bilateral trade flows).

Bilateral trade resistance is defined as a function of a vector of continuous variables, including some measure of distance and population (where the latter reflects the ease of domestic rather than international trade), and a set of binary indicator variables reflecting, for example, whether two countries have a common border, the nature of their prior and existing colonial relations, and whether they have some particular trade or exchange rate arrangement. The detailed classification of *de facto* bilateral exchange rate arrangements used in this paper is explained in section 2. For the moment we note that each bilateral exchange rate regime, h=1…l can be denoted by an indicator variable $D_{ij}^h = 1$ if the bilateral regime between countries i and j is h, and zero otherwise. Combining these three groups of variables we specify the bilateral trade cost function as

$$\ln t_{ij} = \delta_1 \ln d_{ij} + \delta_2 \ln(pop_i . pop_j) + \boldsymbol{\alpha}\mathbf{b}_{ij} + \sum_{h=1}^{l} \gamma^h D_{ij}^h + v_{ij} \tag{3}$$

where d denotes a measure of distance, pop is population and **b** is the vector of indicator variables reflecting other barriers to trade. Taking logs of (1) and substituting from (3), we obtain the following estimating equation for the gravity model:

$$\ln(F_{ij}) = \beta_0 + \beta_1 \ln(y_i . y_j) + \delta_1(1-\sigma)\ln d_{ij} + \delta_2(1-\sigma)\ln(pop_i . pop_j)$$
$$+(1-\sigma)\boldsymbol{\alpha}\mathbf{b}_{ij} + (1-\sigma)\sum_{h=1}^{l} \gamma^h D_{ij} + \ln(P_i)^{\sigma-1} + \ln(P_j)^{\sigma-1} + (1-\sigma)\varepsilon_{ij} \tag{4}$$

where the constant term β_0 represents world GDP, and the error term ε_{ij} is a composite of the stochastic error in (1) and the residual term in the trade cost function (2).[4]

Estimating the gravity model

In our work we exploit a large panel data set. Equation (4) is correctly specified for estimation only in the case of a single cross section of data – as is done by Anderson and van Wincoop (2003) – so we first need to index equation (1) and the trade cost function (3) by time. Next, empirical estimation of this model has to take account of the fact that P_i and P_j are not directly observable. Three approaches have been developed to address this problem. First, Anderson and van Wincoop (2003) solve for P_i and P_j in terms of the observable determinants of the trade barrier (equation (3)) and then estimate (1) using a customised non-linear estimation technique designed for their particular model. Although this approach is feasible for the model with which Anderson and van Wincoop (2003) work, where both the number of observations and the number of variables are relatively limited, and where the model is estimated on a single cross-section only, it becomes infeasible in our case where (see below) our regression includes a vector of 11 control variables covering countries' geographical and cultural features, colonial relationships and trade arrangements, and 30 indicator variables for the different exchange rate regimes, and is estimated over an unbalanced panel of 165 countries over 32 years.

A second, widely-used and less cumbersome, alternative, adopted by Rose and van Wincoop (2001) and Mélitz (e.g. 2007) amongst others, is to proxy the multilateral terms by country-specific fixed effects. The multilateral trade resistance terms are therefore replaced by a vector of N country-specific indicator variables C_i and C_j, each taking the value of 1 for trade flows between i and j, and zero otherwise. The coefficients on these indicators ($\kappa_i = \ln(P_i)^{(1-\sigma)}$ and $\kappa_j = \ln(P_j)^{(1-\sigma)}$) measure the common element in each country's trade with every other country, which is precisely the notion of multilateral trade resistance.

As Feenstra (2004) and others make clear, OLS estimation of (4) under this modification generates consistent estimates of multilateral trade resistance. However, some elements of the multilateral trade resistance terms vary over time, notably exchange rate arrangements. It follows that proxying for the unobserved MTR by using only country-specific dummy variables controls only for the *average over time* of multilateral trade resistance and not the time-varying component. The time-varying component becomes part of the equation error and hence represents a potential source of bias if it is correlated with the variables of interest. Since the time-varying component of multilateral trade resistance – that is, the evolution of the vector of pair-wise exchange rate regimes – is necessarily correlated with the vector of bilateral exchange rate regimes, this bias is highly likely to be present. It is therefore essential to allow for the relevant time variation in the multilateral trade resistance terms. In principle, country fixed effects could be interacted with time to remove this source of bias, but this would entail adding an additional NT regressors (over 5,000 in this case) to the model, rendering estimation difficult if not impossible. But even if it were feasible to estimate the model in this fashion, it would still not allow us to compute the specific variation in the MTR terms which we need in order to simulate the consequences for trade of varying one or more than one country's exchange rate regime.

Third, Baier and Bergstrand (2006) have proposed the use of a first-order Taylor series expansion to approximate the multilateral price resistance terms. This makes it possible to separate out the different terms in the P_i and P_j functions and use OLS rather than Anderson and van Wincoop's non-linear estimation, and they show that (in some cases at least) the bias involved is small. As discussed above, their approximation also introduces a third term, in addition to the two countries' multilateral trade resistance, which they call 'world trade resistance', and which is a function of the multilateral trade resistance faced by every country in the world.

In Adam and Cobham (2007b) we have experimented with a number of variations on the Baier and Bergstrand technique, including both equal and GDP-based weights, and with the addition of either country fixed effects (CFEs) or country pair fixed effects (CPFEs), in models which exclude and include exchange rate regimes. We argue there that the best equation is that which uses GDP weights and includes, as separate regressors, CFEs designed to pick up any country-specific effects which are not captured elsewhere.

In the Baier and Bergstrand approach, each element of the trade cost function is defined to reflect its contribution to the bilateral and multilateral trade resistance. Hence for any variable, x_{ijt}, which is defined on a country-pair basis (by year), its contribution to overall trade between i and j consists of three components: a direct impact on bilateral trade, x_{ijt}; an effect operating through the impact on the multilateral trade resistance of country i and country j defined as

$$\sum_j \theta_{jt} x_{ijt}$$

for country i and

$$\sum_i \theta_{it} x_{ijt}$$

for country *j* respectively; and a final effect from the impact on world trade resistance, defined as

$$\sum_i \sum_j \theta_{it} \theta_{jt} x_{ijt} \, ,$$

where θ_{it} denotes country *i's* share in world GDP at time *t*.

Collecting these terms, our modified estimating equation takes the form

$$\begin{aligned} \ln(F_{ijt}) = {} & \beta_0 + \beta_1 \ln(y_{it}.y_{jt}) + \tilde{\mathbf{a}}\left[\mathbf{b}_{ijt} - \left(\sum_j \theta_{jt}\mathbf{b}_{ijt} + \sum_i \theta_{it}\mathbf{b}_{ijt}\right) + \sum_j \sum_i \theta_{jt}\theta_{it}\mathbf{b}_{ijt}\right. \\ & + \sum_{h=1}^{l-1} \tilde{\gamma}^h \left[D^h_{ijt} - \left(\sum_j \theta_{jt} D^h_{ijt} + \sum_i \theta_{it} D^h_{ijt}\right) + \sum_j \sum_i \theta_{jt}\theta_{it} D^h_{ijt}\right] \\ & + \sum_{t=1}^{T-i} \lambda_t yr_t + \delta_i C_i + \delta_j C_j + \varepsilon_{ijt} \end{aligned} \tag{5}$$

where the **b** vector now includes the log of distance and the log product of population as well as the other indicator variables, and the C terms introduce country-specific fixed effects, which we showed in Adam and Cobham (2007b) improved the fit of the equation. This equation can be estimated by ordinary least squares. Given that the data are defined on a country-pair by year basis we report, and base our inference on, standard errors which are robust to both arbitrary heteroscedasticity and potential intra-group correlation.

Equation (5) is estimated on a slightly modified and extended version of the data set placed in the public domain by Rose (2003). In addition to adding our own classification of exchange rate regimes (see below), we also use data provided to us by Mélitz (2003, 2007) which measures the distance between each country's most populous city (as the centre of gravity for economic activity), rather than as the distance between the geographic centres as recorded by Rose (2003).[5]

Rose's data set consists of annual data from 1948 to 1999 for 175 countries.[6] We exclude the Bretton Woods era[7] but also extend the sample beyond 1999 so that our full sample runs from 1973 to 2004.[8] By extending the data up to 2004 (the last year for which relatively complete trade data are available) we are able to include six years of post-European Monetary Union (EMU) data and thus to increase significantly the proportion of trade flows occurring in the context of currency union arrangements.

2 Exchange rate regimes

In this paper we use the Reinhart and Rogoff (2004) classification of exchange rate regimes, which is one of several classifications that focus on the exchange rate policies governments operate rather than on how they themselves describe their policies (see also Levy-Yeyati and Sturzenegger, 2005; Bailliu, Lafrance and Perrault, 2003; Shambaugh, 2004).

Reinhart and Rogoff (2004) classify most of the countries in our sample in terms of 15 different regimes,[9] and we have filled in the gaps ourselves for the other countries.[10] They classify countries on an individual basis, but for use in a gravity model the classification has to be by country pairs and our interest is in differences between regimes in terms of exchange rate uncertainty and transactions costs. We therefore start by aggregating Reinhart and Rogoff's 15 categories into six: currency union/currency board; peg; managed float with a reference currency; managed float without a reference (where we include currencies managed with

Table 7.1 Classification of exchange rate regimes

R&R fine code	*R&R description*	*New classification*
1	No separate legal tender	Currency board or currency union
2	Currency board arrangement or	
2	Pre-announced peg	
3	Pre-announced horizontal band that is narrower than or equal to +/–2%	Currency peg
4	*De facto* peg	
5	Pre-announced crawling peg	
6	Pre-announced crawling band that is narrower than or equal to +/–2%	
7	*De facto* crawling peg	Managed floating with a reference currency
8	*De facto* crawling band that is narrower than or equal to +/–2%	
9	Pre-announced crawling band that is wider than or equal to +/–2%	
10	*De facto* crawling band that is narrower than or equal to +/–5%	Managed floating (without a reference currency)
11	Moving band that is narrower than or equal to +/–2% (i.e. allows for both appreciation and depreciation over time)	
12	Managed floating	
13	Freely floating	Freely floating
14	Freely falling	Freely falling
15	Dual market in which parallel market data is missing	[allocated elsewhere]

Sources: Reinhart and Rogoff (2004); text.

Table 7.2 Classification and distribution of exchange rate regimes by country pair

Description of exchange rate regime by country pair	*Dummy variable*	*Per cent of Total*
both countries use the same currency in a currency union and/or as the anchor for a currency board	SAMECU	1.3
one country is in a currency union/currency board for which the other country's currency is the anchor	ANCHORCU	0.8
both countries are in currency unions or operate currency boards, but with different anchors	DIFFCU	1.1
one country is in a currency union/currency board with an anchor to which the other pegs	SAMECUPEG	0.9
one country is in currency union/currency board with one anchor while the other pegs to different anchor	DIFFCUPEG	3.4
both countries peg to the same currency	SAMEPEG	1.8
one country is pegging to the other country's currency	ANCHORPEG	0.4
both countries peg but to different anchors	DIFFPEG	1.3
one currency is in currency union/board with anchor with reference to which the other is managed	SAMECUREF	3.0
one currency is in currency union/board with anchor other than reference to which the other is managed	DIFFCUREF	6.5
one country is pegged to the currency with reference to which the other's currency is managed	SAMEPEGREF	5.3
one country is pegged to a currency other than that with reference to which the other's is managed	DIFFPEGREF	5.8
both countries have managed floats with the same reference currency	SAMEREF	4.7
one country is managing its float with reference to the currency of the other	ANCHORREF	0.7
both countries are managing their floats, but with different reference currencies	DIFFREF	5.4
one country is in currency union/board, the other has a managed float with no specified reference currency	CUMAN	6.2
one country pegs, the other has a managed float with no specified reference currency	PEGMAN	6.7
both countries have managed floats, one with and one without a specified reference currency	REFMAN	13.1
both countries have managed floats, with unspecified reference currencies	MANMAN [default regime]	4.5
one country is in a currency union/currency board, the other has a floating currency	CUFLOAT	2.1
one country pegs, the other has a floating currency	PEGFLOAT	1.5
one country is managing its currency with a specific reference, the other has a floating currency	REFFLOAT	3.2

Description of exchange rate regime by country pair	*Dummy variable*	*Per cent of Total*
one country is managing its currency without a specific reference, the other has a floating currency	MANFLOAT	2.5
one country is in currency union/board, the other's currency is freely falling	CUFALL	2.6
one country pegs, the other's currency is freely falling	PEGFALL	3.0
one country has a managed float with a specified reference, the other's currency is freely falling	REFFALL	5.9
one country has a managed float with no reference, the other's currency is freely falling	MANFALL	3.7
both countries' currencies are freely falling	FALLFALL	1.0
one country has a floating currency, the other's currency is freely falling	FALLFLOAT	1.1
both countries have a flexible exchange rate	FLOATFLOAT	0.4
Total Observations		183,692

only a rather loose relationship to the reference currency, in line with Reinhart and Rogoff's 'fine codes'); free fall; and free float. This involves separating their second category ('currency board arrangement or pre-announced peg') into hard pegs, such as the peg of sterling to the dollar between 1951 and 1971, and currency boards, such as those operated in many colonies, in Africa and elsewhere, prior to independence in the late 1950s or 1960s.[11] We have also allocated the very small number of cases of Reinhart and Rogoff's category 15 ('dual market in which parallel market data are missing') into one or other of our five categories. Table 7.1 shows the correspondence between their 15 and our six categories.

Next, we define a vector of 29 mutually exclusive 0–1 dummy variables to identify exchange rate regimes on a country-pair basis. We distinguish between regimes such as (a) two countries use the same currency in a currency union and/or as the anchor for a currency board (dummy variable SAMECU = 1), in which case there is zero uncertainty and near-zero transactions costs involved in trade between them; (b) two countries peg to the same currency (SAMEPEG = 1), in which case there is some uncertainty and definite transactions costs; (c) both countries' exchange rates float but are managed with reference to the same anchor currency (SAMEMANREF = 1), in which case there is more uncertainty and probably higher transactions costs (from wider spreads); (d) cases where one country has a pegged and another a managed currency (without a specific reference currency) (PEGMAN = 1); (e) cases where one currency is in a currency union and the other is freely falling (CUFALL = 1), and so on.

Table 7.2 gives the full specification, together with the distribution of observations

Table 7.3 MENA country exchange rate regimes

Country	*Reinhart-Rogoff latest (end-2001)*	*Major changes since R&R*	*Classification for 2003*
Algeria	*de facto* crawling band around €, band width +/– 2%	—	managed float on euro
Bahrain	not in R&R; data suggest $ peg with zero band width	—	peg to US dollar
Egypt	*de facto* peg to $/multiple rates	float announced January 2003, but still managed	managed float on dollar
Iran	managed float/dual market (official rate pegged to $)	2002 free fall, from 2003 managed float	managed float
Iraq	managed float 1982–98, nothing in R&R after 1998	currency reform 2003–4; managed float w.r.t. $?	managed float on dollar
Jordan	*de facto* peg to $	—	peg to dollar
Kuwait	*de facto* moving peg to $ (official peg to basket)	—	managed float on dollar
Lebanon	*de facto* peg to $	—	peg to dollar
Libya	managed float on $ 1986–98, then dual market (but band width and official regime unchanged)	—	managed float on dollar
Morocco	moving band around €, band width +/– 2%, officially peg to basket	—	managed float on euro
Oman	not in R&R; data suggest $ peg with zero band width	—	peg to dollar
Qatar	not in R&R; data suggest $ peg with zero band width	—	peg to dollar
Saudi Arabia	*de facto* peg to $, official peg to SDR	—	peg to dollar
Sudan	not in R&R; data suggest relative stability against $	—	free float
Syria	*de facto* crawling band around $/parallel market; multiple rates, official rates pegged to $	—	managed float on dollar
Tunisia	*de facto* crawling band around €, band width +/– 2%	—	managed float on euro
Turkey	(2001) freely falling/freely floating	free float from 2003	free float
UAE	not in R&R; data suggest $ peg with zero band width	—	peg to dollar

Country	*Reinhart-Rogoff latest (end-2001)*	*Major changes since R&R*	*Classification for 2003*
Yemen	not in R&R; data suggest relative stability against $ from 1997	—	managed float

Sources: Reinhart, C., and Rogoff, K. (2004); text.

across regimes.[12] The default exchange rate regime in the regression is where both countries have a managed float without a reference currency (MANMAN = 1).[13]

The exchange rate regimes currently operated by the MENA countries are set out in Table 7.3.[14] There is a heavy predominance of US dollar pegs: the six Gulf Cooperation Council countries peg to the dollar, either less (Kuwait, Saudi Arabia) or more tightly (Bahrain, Oman, Qatar, United Arab Emirates); Jordan and Lebanon have *de facto* pegs to the dollar; Egypt, Iraq, Sudan and Yemen have managed floats on the dollar; and Syria has the official rates (among its various multiple exchange rates) pegged to the dollar. The Maghreb countries, Algeria, Morocco and Tunisia, have managed floats on the euro; Iran has a managed float without a clear reference currency; and Turkey has a free float.

Before we proceed to estimation we need to set out our prior expectations for these various dummies. Given the existing literature on the effect of currency unions within gravity models, we expect countries in the same currency union/currency board to have significantly higher trade than those in the default regime, so that (the coefficient on) SAMECU should be positive. We expect that countries which peg to the same currency should also have somewhat higher trade, *ceteris paribus*, since the exchange rate uncertainty is less than in the default regime but there are significant transactions costs; so SAMEPEG should be positive but smaller than SAMECU. In the same vein countries which manage their currencies with reference to the same currency should experience a limited improvement in external trade (relative to the default regime), so that SAMEMANREF would be positive but smaller again. On the other hand, when two countries both have freely falling currencies, we would expect their trade to be less than that in the default situation (when both currencies operate a managed float without a reference currency), so that FALLFALL should be negative.

For exchange rate regimes which cross categories or involve different anchors, pegs or reference currencies, however, it is necessary to be more precise. In particular, we can distinguish three different effects:

1 a change in the bilateral exchange rate regime between two countries which reduces uncertainty and transactions costs will tend to increase the trade between them: this is a positive direct effect analogous to a 'trade creation' effect;
2 this may be partially offset if one country replaces trade with the other by trade with a third country with which it now has a 'closer' exchange rate regime: this is a (negative) substitution effect loosely analogous to a 'trade diversion' effect;

3 the change in exchange rate regime may also affect trade positively via an indirect reduction in transactions costs in the case where the producers of a country which trades with more than one user of a single currency, or with more than one country that pegs to the same vehicle currency, can now economise on working balances in the single or (to a lesser extent) the vehicle currency; this is a positive indirect effect.

For example, where one country is in a currency union/currency board with an anchor to which the other pegs, the common anchor/peg should reduce uncertainty (relative to the default regime) and insofar as it trades with other members of the union the pegging country should be able to economise on working balances, both of which effects would increase trade; on the other hand, the country in the currency union may substitute trade with its currency union partner(s) for trade with the same-peg country, which would reduce trade.

Thus, with positive direct and indirect effects but a negative substitution effect, the sign of SAMECUPEG is not clear a priori. Similarly, where two countries peg to different currencies, the existence of pegs may enable both countries to economise on working balances in the vehicle currencies, but there may be substitution effects in favour of trade with same-peg countries. So, with a zero direct effect (because the two anchor currencies are floating against each other), a positive indirect effect and a negative substitution effect, the sign of DIFFPEG is also not clear a priori.

3 The estimation result

Table 7.4 presents the result of estimating our preferred equation. The coefficients on the basic regressors – the log product of real GDP, log product of population and log distance – accord reasonably well with theory, with cross-border trade increasing in the log-product of GDP and decreasing in the log product of population and the log of distance between countries.[15] The coefficients on the other control variables are comparable to those found elsewhere in the literature, and the country-dummies and the time-dummies are each jointly significant. The exchange rate regime coefficients are jointly and strongly significant, with the F-test decisively rejecting the null hypothesis that the effects are zero, while 22 out of the 29 estimated exchange rate regime coefficients are individually significant. The only regimes that have an insignificant impact on bilateral trade relative to the MANMAN default regime are DIFFCUPEG, CUMAN, PEGMAN, CUFALL, PEGFALL, MANFALL and FALLFALL.

Since these coefficients measure the difference between the specific exchange rate regime and the default category they are not directly comparable with estimates from studies where the default regime is different. Thus, for example, while our estimate of the effect of SAMECU (of 0.96) is above the corresponding point estimate (of 0.86) by Rose and van Wincoop (2001), the two coefficients measure different things: our estimate measures the (average) impact of two countries which had previously maintained managed floats without reference currencies

Table 7.4 The full model with MTRs and CFEs

Dependent Variable: Log bilateral trade (constant US dollars)

Pooled OLS Estimation. Sample: 1973–2004 [unbalanced panel]

	estimate	*t-statistic*[a]
Constant	–26.96	–52.77
Basic variables		
log product real GDP	1.24	68.80
log product population	–0.30	–13.80
log distance	–1.27	–48.53
Standard controls		
log product area	–0.12	–8.83
landlocked	–0.60	–14.15
island	–0.06	–1.20
common language	0.38	8.08
common border	0.49	3.97
common colony	0.54	7.58
current colony	1.53	5.70
ever colony	1.00	8.38
common country	–0.56	–0.43
regional trade agreement	0.95	4.67
GSP preferences	0.45	10.06
Exchange rate effects		
SAMECU	0.96	6.54
ANCHORCU	0.37	2.42
DIFFCU	0.35	2.47
SAMECUPEG	0.56	4.04
DIFFCUPEG	0.15	1.88
SAMEPEG	0.33	3.50
ANCHORPEG	0.31	1.96
DIFFPEG	0.21	2.41
SAMECUREF	0.53	6.03
ANCHORREF	0.39	2.81
DIFFCUREF	0.18	2.48
SAMEPEGREF	0.34	4.85
DIFFPEGREF	0.16	2.61

(*continued*)

	estimate	*t-statistic*[a]
SAMEREF	0.38	5.60
DIFFREF	0.21	3.39
REFMAN	0.16	2.99
CUMAN	0.04	0.56
PEGMAN	0.02	0.38
MANMAN	0.00	
CUFLOAT	0.22	2.61
PEGFLOAT	0.50	5.73
REFFLOAT	0.36	4.99
MANFLOAT	0.30	3.98
CUFALL	0.05	0.52
PEGFALL	–0.09	–1.14
REFFALL	0.24	3.90
MANFALL	–0.08	–1.16
FALLFALL	–0.13	–1.21
FALLFLOAT	0.33	3.19
FLOATFLOAT	0.44	3.32
year dummies	Yes	
country dummies	Yes	
MTRs (weights)	Yes	(GDP)
Adjusted R^2	0.703	
F[Year dummy effects=0][b]	69.46	[0.000]
F[country dummy effects=0][b]	18.06	[0.000]
F[Exchange rate dummy effects=0][c]	7.1	[0.000]
No. observations	183692	

Notes:

a t-statistics are heteroscedastic and autocorrelation robust

b F-test against joint significance of year and country dummies (probability in brackets).

c F-test against joint significance of exchange rate dummies (probability in brackets).

both joining the same currency union, whereas Rose and van Wincoop's (2001) estimate measures the effect of two countries joining the same currency union from a starting position represented by the *average* of all other exchange rate arrangements. Hence, the true difference between the two estimates is substantial.[16] Nonetheless, our estimate is surprisingly large, suggesting that if two countries currently on managed floats were to join a common currency union, the reduction in the bilateral trade barrier would, *ceteris paribus*, increase trade flows between them by 160 per cent.[17] However, this interpretation is not correct since the change in this particular bilateral exchange rate arrangement alters the multilateral trade resistance for each country (as well as for each country's other trading partners), which will reduce the estimated effect.

An alternative presentation of these results is shown in Figure 7.1, which plots the 95 per cent confidence intervals around the point estimates for each of the regime coefficients, arranged in descending order. It makes clear, for example, that much the largest coefficient is that for SAMECU, which offers some support for Rose's (2000) initial intuition, and this is significantly different from SAMECUPEG and SAMEPEG, while SAMECUPEG is greater than but not significantly different from SAMEPEG. Similarly DIFFCU is higher than DIFFPEG and than DIFFCUPEG, but none of these are significantly different from each other. At the other end MANFALL, PEGFALL and FALLFALL are all negative, though not significantly below the default regime (MANMAN), while CUFALL, CUMAN and PEGMAN are positive but not significant. In between there is a range of regimes with coefficients between 0.15 and 0.56, nearly all significantly different from zero but some more precisely defined than others.[18]

One way of summarising the effect of the exchange rate regimes is to take (unweighted) averages of the coefficients for each type of regime in association with itself and each other regime (ignoring DIFF– and ANCHOR– coefficients): for example, the average of SAMECU, SAMECUPEG, SAMECUREF, CUMAN, CUFLOAT and CUFALL is 0.39, while the corresponding average for the PEG regimes is 0.28, that for the REF regimes is 0.33, that for the MAN regimes is 0.07, that for the FALL regimes is 0.05, and that for the FLOAT regimes is 0.36. Our prior expectation was that the REF regimes would have smaller positive effects on trade than the PEG regimes; the fact that the comparison goes (slightly) the other way may suggest that the distinction Reinhart and Rogoff make between their coarse

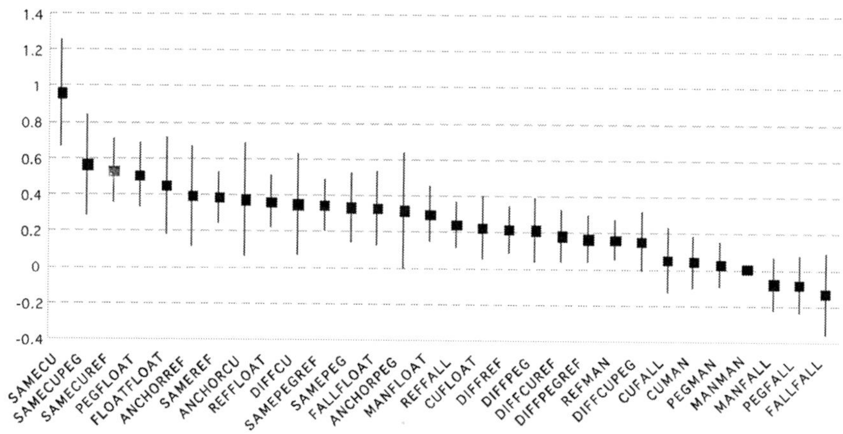

Figure 7.1 Exchange rate regime coefficients, point estimates and 95% confidence intervals Default Category MANMAN=0.

codes 2(peg)–4 and 5–9 is not really watertight. We also would have expected a larger difference between the MAN regimes and the FALL regimes. The FLOAT regimes, it should be noted, are relatively small categories (see Table 7.2) which are dominated by a small number of developed countries (three quarters of the observations involve one or more of the US, Australia, Japan and pre-EMU Germany).

Two further points can be made on the relative magnitudes of the coefficients. First, except in the case where the other currency is floating there seems to be no significant trade diversion from membership of a currency union (since SAMECUPEG and SAMECUREF are clearly positive), a result which has also been obtained in more general terms by other researchers, e.g. Micco *et al.* (2003). This implies that the direct and indirect effects of currency union membership significantly outweigh the substitution effect. Second, the patterns for regimes where the currencies/anchors/references are different are slightly less clear but quite intuitive. DIFFCU, DIFFCUPEG, DIFFPEG, DIFFPEGMAN and DIFFCUMAN are smaller in magnitude than the corresponding 'SAME' estimates, and all except DIFFCUPEG are significantly greater than zero. This provides strong empirical support for the claim that while membership of different currency unions, or maintaining a hard peg or managing a currency with respect to different reference currencies, has a weaker trade-promoting effect than if countries linked to the same currency, some of these arrangements nonetheless have positive effects on trade.

In general, our estimates suggest that there is a graduated effect by which greater exchange rate fixity and lower transactions costs encourage trade. The effect of currency unions on trade, on which the literature has concentrated, turns out to be strong, but other regimes which imply more uncertainty and larger transactions costs than in a currency union, but less than in the default regime of a double managed float, also promote trade.

In addition, the possible trade-diverting effect of 'closer' exchange rate regimes – the second of the three effects identified above – seems to be outweighed by the two trade-promoting effects. This is surely the obvious explanation for the positive and significant results for the DIFFCU regime: the direct effect of this regime (relative to the default) cannot be large since the unions are floating against each other, the substitution effect on trade must be negative, but the indirect effect on transactions costs must be positive and could be large, particularly in cases where the two unions are themselves large and the two countries trade widely with members of the other union. This argument would also help to explain the positive estimates for the other DIFF- regimes.

4 Simulation results

In this section we first show the existing trade patterns for MENA countries, and then present the results of simulations for different exchange rate regimes. We consider the following scenarios: 1) each MENA country pegs to the US dollar while all other MENA countries retain their existing exchange rate regime; 2) each MENA country pegs to the euro while all other MENA countries retain their existing regime; 3) each MENA country dollarises, that is, sets up a currency

Table 7.5 Baseline trade volumes and shares 2003

	Trade US$ m	*Geographical Distribution (% shares)*										
		US	*US bloc*	*Eurozone*	*Euro bloc*	*Other Europe*	*Latin America*	*Asia*	*Africa*	*Canada Australia New Zealand*	*MENA*	*Other*
Turkey	307.09	6.60	0.49	43.77	6.64	6.61	1.11	8.21	2.13	0.83	6.41	17.20
Bahrain	22.21	11.70	0.71	13.65	2.20	4.95	0.04	21.46	2.64	2.81	39.40	0.43
Jordan	25.58	12.80	1.60	16.58	3.97	2.88	2.43	18.74	1.12	1.48	22.33	16.07
Kuwait	80.44	14.79	0.79	14.91	1.42	4.96	0.67	53.84	0.44	2.04	5.60	0.55
Lebanon	23.47	5.17	0.90	43.70	6.51	4.70	1.36	11.42	0.41	0.68	19.31	5.84
Oman	47.10	5.73	0.44	6.47	1.37	4.33	0.55	63.27	2.48	1.57	12.87	0.90
Qatar	65.77	3.60	0.14	9.43	0.83	3.79	0.19	59.16	14.51	1.08	7.14	0.14
Saudi Arabia	357.74	18.39	0.46	19.33	2.03	3.78	1.69	39.49	3.39	2.49	8.34	0.59
Syria	34.87	4.12	0.20	45.74	6.10	1.91	1.87	11.14	0.91	0.77	20.82	6.41
UAE	253.55	4.77	2.79	15.93	2.43	4.67	0.73	51.26	2.41	2.55	7.94	4.51
Egypt	77.50	14.94	0.85	33.19	4.05	6.02	3.96	16.67	2.38	1.91	11.18	4.84
Yemen	22.10	3.50	0.87	7.85	0.93	1.96	–	55.95	0.58	1.43	23.82	3.11
Algeria	123.10	12.57	0.20	55.26	7.80	1.70	4.00	5.10	0.23	4.91	6.29	1.95
Morocco	64.10	3.78	0.10	63.60	3.06	6.45	2.86	7.62	1.58	0.98	6.55	3.42
Tunisia	52.82	1.57	0.10	75.58	3.11	2.65	1.34	3.66	4.25	0.57	4.83	2.33
TOTAL	1557.45											

board on the dollar, while all other MENA countries retain their existing regime; 4) each MENA country euroises, that is, sets up a currency board on the euro, while all other MENA countries retain their existing regime; 5) all MENA countries together peg to the dollar; 6) all MENA countries together peg to the euro; 7) all MENA countries together form a monetary union which is pegged to the dollar; and 8) all MENA countries together form a monetary union which is pegged to the euro.

The existing trade patterns for each of the MENA countries[19] in 2003 are shown in Table 7.5, which gives the volume of a country's trade, and the percentage of its trade with each of a number of blocs, the latter defined primarily with reference to the currency of the bloc concerned: we distinguish between the (rest of the) MENA countries; the US; the hard US dollar bloc (countries which have a currency union with or a currency board on the dollar); the eurozone; the euro bloc (countries which have hard pegs to the euro or manage their currencies with reference to the euro);[20] other European countries; other Latin American countries; Asian countries (excluding MENA); African countries (excluding MENA); Canada, Australia and New Zealand; and Other (all countries not elsewhere included).

Four points should be noted. First, every country has more trade with the Eurozone than with the US (and more with the Eurozone + Euro bloc than with the US + US bloc), but the size of the differences varies widely as between, for example, Tunisia on the one hand and Bahrain on the other. Second, some oil-exporters have large shares of trade (typically oil exports) with Asia. Third, most MENA countries have relatively low shares of trade with other MENA countries: only Bahrain, Jordan, Syria and Yemen do more than 20 per cent of their trade with other MENA countries, while Turkey, Kuwait, Qatar, Saudi Arabia, the UAE and the Maghreb countries do less than 10 per cent. And fourth, a small number of countries have large shares with 'Other'; for Turkey and Jordan much of this is trade with Israel.[21]

Table 7.6 presents a summary of the results of the various simulations, and Tables 7–14 in the Appendix give more detail. The simulations for each country are relative to its exchange rate regime as of 2003, as set out in Table 7.3. For each, the trade volumes and shares were generated by (i) assuming the country concerned switched its exchange rate regime in the way indicated (without, in the individual experiments, and with, in the regional experiments, the other MENA countries doing the same), (ii) re-computing the vector of pair-wise dummy variables describing that country's bilateral exchange rate regime with each of its partners (in other words the new D_{ij} vector), (iii) calculating the percentage change in trade volumes implied by the change in the D_{ij} vector arising from the change in the three components of the overall exchange rate effect identified in equation (5), that is, the direct effect, the multilateral trade resistance effect for each country, and the corresponding implied change in world trade resistance, and (iv) applying the changes under (ii) and (iii) to the actual trade patterns of each country as of 2003.[22] Applying these changes to the actual trade patterns means that the simulations retain any idiosyncratic country-pair features of trade which are not explicitly included in the model.

Table 7.6 Summary of exchange rate experiments

Country	ACTUAL TOTAL TRADE 2003	ACTUAL TRADE SHARE 2003	Individual experiments: % growth in trade				Regional experiments: % growth in trade			
			Peg US$ [1] (table 7.7)	*Peg Euro* [2] (table 7.8)	*MU US$* [3] (table 7.9)	*MU Euro* [4] (table 7.10)	*All Peg $* [5] (table 7.11)	*All Peg €* [6] (table 7.12)	*All MU $* [7] (table 7.13)	*All MU €* [8] (table 7.14)
Turkey	307.1	19.7	–9.86%	10.82%	2.34%	40.42%	–9.54%	11.29%	3.7%	3.1%
Bahrain	22.2	1.4	0.0%	3.3%	12.5%	5.5%	0.2%	7.8%	34.8%	32.3%
Jordan	25.6	1.6	0.0%	7.1%	14.7%	13.6%	2.0%	9.2%	23.1%	18.5%
Kuwait	80.4	5.2	–0.4%	4.1%	5.6%	5.2%	–0.1%	4.7%	2.7%	–3.5%
Lebanon	23.5	1.5	0.0%	20.6%	14.2%	50.6%	–0.2%	22.2%	24.4%	24.6%
Oman	47.1	3.0	0.0%	–3.4%	9.5%	–6.0%	0.1%	–1.9%	7.6%	0.6%
Qatar	65.8	4.2	0.0%	0.2%	2.5%	–1.0%	0.0%	1.0%	1.1%	–3.1%
Saudi A	357.7	23.0	0.0%	11.1%	3.3%	13.1%	0.2%	11.7%	5.8%	1.8%
Syria	34.9	2.2	–1.3%	20.3%	10.6%	50.2%	–2.2%	20.6%	24.1%	24.6%
UAE	253.6	16.3	0.0%	4.5%	4.0%	7.8%	0.3%	5.3%	3.0%	–0.3%
Egypt	77.5	5.0	–2.1%	15.2%	7.3%	32.6%	–2.2%	15.6%	12.5%	10.2%
Yemen	22.1	1.4	25.3%	18.0%	46.7%	18.0%	24.9%	21.0%	50.6%	40.7%
Algeria	123.1	7.9	–19.5%	1.5%	–10.1%	25.6%	–20.1%	1.0%	–5.7%	–6.7%

(*continued*)

Country	ACTUAL TOTAL TRADE 2003	ACTUAL TRADE SHARE 2003	Individual experiments: % growth in trade				Regional experiments: % growth in trade			
			Peg US$	*Peg Euro*	*MU US$*	*MU Euro*	*All Peg $*	*All Peg €*	*All MU $*	*All MU €*
			[1]	*[2]*	*[3]*	*[4]*	*[5]*	*[6]*	*[7]*	*[8]*
			(table 7.7)	*(table 7.8)*	*(table 7.9)*	*(table 7.10)*	*(table 7.11)*	*(table 7.12)*	*(table 7.13)*	*(table 7.14)*
Morocco	64.1	4.1	–19.5%	1.8%	–7.5%	32.5%	–19.5%	2.1%	–4.4%	–4.7%
Tunisia	52.8	3.4	–23.1%	2.3%	–10.6%	40.1%	–23.2%	2.2%	–8.2%	–7.8%
TOTAL	1557.5	100.0								
Mean growth in trade (unweighted)			–3.4%	7.8%	7.0%	21.9%	–3.3%	8.9%	11.7%	8.7%
Weighted growth in trade [group experiments]							–4.8%	8.4%	5.2%	2.5%
Weighted growth in trade [individual experiments][a]			– 4.8%	7.7%	3.0%	21.1%				

Notes:
a Calculated as a share-weighted growth rate. But since each row of the individual experiments is independent (i.e. it is assumed all other countries maintain their baseline exchange rate regimes), the weighted growth rate is strictly meaningless.

Table 7.6 shows the growth in trade for each country under each of the experiments, with the three rows at the bottom indicating the unweighted average growth of trade in each experiment, the weighted average growth in trade for the regional experiments and the weighted average growth for the individual experiments (but note that for the individual experiments the numbers are the average of the effect for each country of its 'own' experiment, which strictly speaking has no meaning; the point is merely to suggest the overall effects of the different experiments in the different columns). It is convenient to discuss the results by pairs of columns where each pair refers to a similar type of exchange rate regime on (a) the (US) dollar and (b) the euro.

For the unilateral pegs (columns 1 and 2 of Table 7.6), nearly every country in the sample is projected to have higher trade if it pegs to the euro than if it pegs to the dollar; the only exceptions are Oman and Yemen. For some countries the difference is large – over 20 per cent for Turkey, Lebanon, Syria and the Maghreb countries – while for others like Qatar it is trivial. On average, pegging to the dollar results in a 3–5 per cent fall in trade, and pegging to the euro seems to make trade some 8 per cent higher than in the baseline (2003) case. These results reflect both the initial trade patterns and the changes in exchange rate regimes. In the case of Turkey, for example, a peg to the euro means that Turkey's exchange rate regime with the eurozone countries (which covers 44 per cent of Turkey's trade, see Table 7.5) goes from CUFLOAT (0.22, see Table 7.4) to SAMECUPEG (0.56), while its regime with China goes from PEGFLOAT (0.50) to DIFFCUPEG (0.15). On the other hand a peg to the dollar would mean DIFFCUPEG (0.15) vis-à-vis the eurozone and SAMEPEG (0.33) vis-à-vis China. In the case of Oman, a peg to the dollar indicates the existing situation, while a peg to the euro means the exchange rate regime with eurozone countries goes from DIFFCUPEG (0.15) to SAMEPEG (0.33), while its regime with China goes from SAMEPEG (0.33) to DIFFPEG (0.21). China is part of Asia, which accounts for 8 per cent of Turkey's trade but 63 per cent of Oman's.

For unilateral currency boards (columns 3 and 4 of Table 7.4), nine countries are projected to have higher trade under a currency board on the euro, but six do better under a currency board on the dollar. The latter include four oil-exporters – Bahrain and Oman, for which the difference is large, and Kuwait and Qatar for which it is small – together with Jordan and Yemen. The averages suggest countries benefit from a currency board on the dollar but benefit much more – some 14 to 18 per cent more – from a currency board on the euro.

For the joint pegs (columns 5 and 6 of Table 7.4), the pattern is similar to that for the unilateral pegs: all countries are expected to have higher trade under the joint peg to the euro than under the joint peg to the dollar, except Oman and Yemen. Most countries do only a little better under a joint peg to the euro than under a unilateral peg to the euro: this presumably reflects the low level of intra-MENA trade. The average effects of the dollar pegs are very close to those for the unilateral effects, those for the euro pegs are a little higher.

On the other hand, for the monetary unions pegged to the dollar or the euro (columns 7 and 8 of Table 7.4), most countries are projected to have higher trade under a union pegged to the dollar than under one pegged to the euro. The exceptions are Lebanon, Syria and Tunisia, but in none of these cases is the difference more than 1 per cent, whereas for countries like Jordan, Kuwait, Oman and Yemen the difference in the opposite direction is over 5 per cent. In addition, for some countries such as Bahrain the effect of a monetary union (with either peg) is much higher than the effect of a unilateral peg or a currency board, while for others such as Turkey the effect is lower. On average, forming a monetary union pegged to the euro raises trade by 2.5 per cent (weighted) or 8.7 per cent (unweighted), but a monetary union pegged to the US dollar raises trade by 5.2 per cent (weighted) or 11.7 per cent (unweighted).

Finally, if we identify the exchange rate regime which gives the highest level of trade for each country, it turns out that nine countries do best under a unilateral currency board on the euro: Turkey, Lebanon, Saudi Arabia, Syria, UAE, Egypt, Algeria, Morocco and Tunisia. Three do better under a unilateral currency board on the dollar: Kuwait, Oman and Qatar. And three do better under a joint monetary union pegged to the dollar: Bahrain, Jordan and Yemen.

There are two points that should be noted in connection with these results. First, for those countries which have large oil exports the gravity model as used here may not be appropriate. The model underpinning the estimating equations presented at the beginning of this chapter strictly applies to cases where each country produces its own differentiated product, or each country produces one differentiated product within each product class. But oil is essentially homogeneous (allowing for some differences in sulphur content etc.) and is produced only in a limited number of countries. These points imply that variations in trade costs due, for example, to changes in exchange rate regimes should not be expected to have major effects on the pattern of trade in oil. In that case the results derived here overestimate the effects on oil exporters' trade of their exchange rate regimes, notably in their trade with other Asian countries that peg to or manage on the dollar. Second, it is possible that this effect is compounded by a potential bias in the Reinhart and Rogoff (2003b) classification of exchange rate regimes, which appears to give priority to a currency's relation to the dollar except for currencies which are obviously and publicly related to the euro. Cobham (2007) has shown that if the identification is based on currencies' actual movements against the dollar or the euro, fewer countries genuinely anchor on the dollar than those identified as such by Reinhart and Rogoff.

5 Conclusions

In this paper we have estimated a gravity model of trade with a full menu of bilateral exchange rate regimes using the Baier and Begrstrand (2006) method to take account of multilateral trade resistance (and the corresponding world trade resistance). Our estimates of the effects on trade of different exchange rate regimes are broadly plausible, in both their absolute magnitudes and the relativities between them. In general the estimates suggest a graduated effect of exchange rate regimes on trade, in line with the size of transactions costs and uncertainty under each regime.

This approach enables us to carry out simulations of the effects of changes in a country's exchange rate regime on its trade, allowing properly for the implied change in each country's multilateral resistance and in world resistance, as well as the direct change in bilateral resistance. We have produced preliminary estimates here for the effects on MENA countries of changing their existing exchange rate arrangements towards pegs or stronger attachments to the US dollar or the euro, both when one country changes its regime on its own and when all MENA countries do it together. These estimates suggest that for most MENA countries their trade would be higher if they anchored on the euro rather than on the dollar. We obtained different results for some countries; these were typically oil-exporters (for which the underlying assumptions of the gravity model may be inapplicable) and/or countries with a large share of trade with Asian countries (which in 2003 were in many cases pegged to the dollar).

However, we should re-emphasise that the impact of the exchange rate regime upon a country's trade is in any case not the only criterion to be used in choosing regimes. Countries need to consider a range of other issues including (at least) the price and exchange rate stability of the proposed anchors in themselves, the cyclical convergence or divergence between the country and the anchor economy and the country's own ability to operate monetary and fiscal policy in a coherent and disciplined manner.

Notes

1 We are grateful to Mauro Caselli for some excellent research assistance.

2 Lahrèche-Révil and Milgram (2006) used a gravity model to investigate the trade patterns of some MENA countries (Algeria, Morocco and Tunisia; Turkey, Egypt and Israel), using measures of exchange rate volatility as regressors and contrasting these countries with the new member states of the European Union. They use a more conventional gravity model specification, with time and country fixed effects. Our sample of countries is much larger than theirs, we consider a larger number of MENA countries, and we use explicit exchange rate regimes rather than exchange rate volatility.

3 Anderson and van Wincoop (2004) derive comparable results for a model in which each country produces a product within each product class.

4 Notice, also, that the theory underpinning equation (1) implies $\beta_1 = 1$.

5 Across the sample as a whole this modification makes little difference, but there are obvious cases where it does. In Canada, for example, economic activity is concentrated close to the border with the US while the geographic centre is much further north, and in a number of Middle Eastern and African countries the geographic centre is determined by large areas of economically empty desert while economic activity is concentrated on the shores of a sea or a river which may be far from the geographic centre of the country.

6 The main sources for the data are International Monetary Fund (IMF) and World Bank publications and the CIA's *World Factbook*. See Rose (2003) for further details.

7 In the Bretton Woods period many developing countries – particularly those in Africa and the Caribbean – were colonies with exchange rate regimes imposed by their colonial masters. The currency unions and hard peg regimes that proliferated under such arrangements were also associated with relatively low tariff barriers as the result of systems of 'imperial preference'. The pre-1973 period therefore provides a much less suitable field for testing the effect of exchange rate regimes on trade than the later years when former colonies had become free to choose their own regime and tariffs and where non-tariff barriers generally were much lower (Rose, 2003).

8 In practice we updated the data from 1997 in order to correct an error in the Rose (2003) data arising from a change in base year for the GDP deflator.

9 Monthly data is provided in Reinhart and Rogoff (2003b).

10 Countries not covered in Reinhart and Rogoff but included in the dataset are: Afghanistan, Angola, Aruba, Bahamas, Bahrain, Bangladesh, Barbados, Belize, Bermuda, Bhutan, Brunei, Cambodia, Cape Verde, Comoros, Djibouti, Fiji, Kiribati, Maldives, Mozambique, Namibia, Oman, Papua New Guinea, Qatar, Rwanda, Samoa, Sao Tome, Seychelles, Sierra Leone, Solomon Islands, Somalia, Sudan, Syria, Tonga, Trinidad and Tobago, United Arab Emirates, Vanuatu, Vietnam, Yemen, Zimbabwe (before 1980). We used individual country webpages and world exchange rate arrangements tables from the IMF's website, supplemented by the *CIA World Factbook* and examination of basic exchange rate data. The Reinhart and Rogoff data go up to 2001 only, so we have extended the series relying largely on what they give for the final years of their sample and on International Financial Statistics (IFS) data on exchange rates for 2002–2004.

11 In general the distinction is clear-cut, but for a range of ex-colonies it was necessary to make judgments about the transition from currency boards to hard pegs, and for that purpose the information given in Page (1993) was very useful.

12 The classification used here is the same as that in Adam and Cobham (2007a), except that here we distinguish the cases where two countries are, respectively, in the same currency union, or pegged to the same anchor currency, or managing their currencies with respect to the same reference currency, from the cases where one country is in a currency union which uses the currency of the other as its anchor (ANCHORCU), or one country is pegged to the currency of the other (ANCHORPEG), or one country is managing its currency with respect to the currency of the other (ANCHORREF).

13 In our dataset each country has (for each year) a code indicating its unilateral exchange rate regime: currency union/currency board, hard peg, managed float, free float or free fall. It also has codes indicating the currency which it is using in a currency union/board, if any; the currency to which it is pegged, if any; and the currency with reference to which it manages its float, if any. Thus for each country there are four unilateral codes; the eight codes for a pair of countries determine the bilateral exchange rate regime between them.

14 We follow the widespread convention whereby Israel is not included in the MENA group although geographically it would appear that it should be, partly because including Israel would raise issues of what kind of relations should be assumed between it and the Arab countries (and Iran). The possible peace dividend, in terms of the trade effects of a full normalisation of relations between Israel and its neighbours, together with the creation of an independent Palestinian state, would be the subject of a separate paper. In the simulation results presented in Table 7.3 Israel figures in the 'Other' group.

15 The relatively large value of the income elasticity of trade relative to the theoretical prior of one may reflect the calculation of the dependent variable as the log of average bi-directional trade rather than the average of log bi-directional trade (Baldwin and Taglioni, 2006).

16 In addition it should be noted that our SAMECU variable differs from Rose's strict currency union dummy insofar as (a) SAMECU is 1 but Rose's *custrict* is 0 where two countries each have (institutionally separate) currency unions or currency board arrangements with the same anchor currency, eg Argentina and Hong Kong in the 1990s, and (b) SAMECU is 0 and *custrict* is 1 in some post-independence years when, according to Reinhart and Rogoff and other sources, some of the colonial currency board arrangements became pegs rather than currency boards.

17 The marginal effect is $\exp(\tilde{\gamma}^{h}) - 1 = \exp(0.96) - 1$.

18 The regimes with large confidence intervals are typically those where the number of observations (see Table 7.2) is relatively small, e.g. the ANCHOR regimes.

19 We do not include Iraq, whose recent trade pattern reflects the unusual circumstances of the US occupation and the prolonged period of trade sanctions against Iraq before

that, so that its recent trade patterns are unlikely to provide a sensible base for forecasts of future trade. Nor do we include Iran or Sudan, since their current trade patterns are heavily distorted by US sanctions, which we have not allowed for at this stage in our work, or Libya, for which data is not available.

20 The reason for the asymmetry in our definitions of the US dollar bloc and the eurozone bloc is the assumption that pegging to, or managing with reference to, the eurozone represents a clear choice about the particular anchor, while pegging or managing with reference to the dollar sometimes reflects a choice about the regime in general (given the lack of an alternative numéraire before 1999) rather than the anchor. There are also geographical considerations which favour separate identification of, for example, Latin America (other than the dollarised countries) and Asia.

21 Jordan's trade with Israel (which is classified as a managed float on the dollar) is heavily dependent on a tariff subsidy offered by the US for joint production. There is also a similar but smaller effect for Egypt.

22 We use 2003 rather than 2004, the latest year for which we have data, (presented in Table 7.3) because the dataset is less complete in the final year.

References

Adam, C., and Cobham, D. (2007a) 'Exchange Rate Regimes and Trade'. *Manchester School*, 75(s1): 44–63.

Adam, C., and Cobham, D. (2007b) 'Modelling Multilateral Trade Resistance in Gravity Models with Exchange Rate Regimes'. Mimeo, Oxford University and Heriot-Watt University.

Anderson, J., and van Wincoop, E. (2003) 'Gravity with Gravitas: a Solution to the Border Puzzle'. *American Economic Review*, 93: 170–92.

Anderson, J., and van Wincoop, E. (2004) 'Trade Costs'. *Journal of Economic Literature*, 42: 691–751.

Baier, S., and Bergstrand, J. (2006) '*Bonus Vetus* OLS: A Simple Approach for Addressing the "Border-Puzzle" and Other Gravity Issues'. Mimeo, Clemson University and University of Notre Dame.

Bailliu, J., Lafrance, R., and Perrault, J-F. (2003) 'Does Exchange Rate Policy Matter for Growth?' *International Finance*, 6: 381–414.

Baldwin, R., and Taglioni, D. (2006) 'Gravity for Dummies and Dummies for Gravity Equations'. National Bureau of Economic Research, Working Paper 12516.

Carrère, C. (2006) 'Revisiting the Effects of Regional Trade Agreements on Trade Flows with Proper Specification of the Gravity Model'. *European Economic Review*, 50: 223–47.

Cobham, D. (2007) 'Euro Versus Dollar: Who Goes with Which?'. Mimeo, Heriot-Watt University.

Feenstra, R. (2004) *Advanced International Trade: Theory and Evidence*. Princeton: Princeton University Press.

Fritz-Krockow, B., and Jurzyk, E. (2004) 'Will you Buy My Peg? The Credibility of a Fixed Exchange Rate Regime as a Determinant of Bilateral Trade'. International Monetary Fund.Working Paper 04/165, Washington DC.

Jbili, A., and V. Kramarenko (2003) 'Choosing Exchange Rate Regimes in the Middle East and North Africa'. *International Monetary Fund:* http://www.imf.org/external/pubs/cat/longres.cfm?sk=16585.0

Klein, M., and Shambaugh, J. (2004) 'Fixed Exchange Rates and Trade'. National Bureau of Economic Research Working Paper 10696.

Lahrèche-Révil, A., and Milgram, J. (2006) 'Exchange-rate Policies and Trade in the MENA Countries'. *Mimeo*, University of Granada.

Levy-Yeyati E., and Sturzenegger, F. (2005) 'Classifying Exchange Rate Regimes: Deeds vs. Words'. *European Economic Review*, 49: 1603–35.

Mélitz, J. (2003) 'Distance, Trade, Political Association and a Common Currency'. Mimeo, University of Strathclyde (revised version of 'Geography, Trade and Currency Union', *Centre for Economic Policy Research Discussion Paper* 2987).
Mélitz, J. (2007) 'North, South and Distance in the Gravity Model'. *European Economic Review*, 51: 971–91.
Micco, A., Stein, E., and Ordoñez, G. (2003) 'The Currency Union Effect on Trade: Early Evidence from EMU'. *Economic Policy*, 18: 315–356.
Page, S. (ed.) (1993) *Monetary Policy in Developing Countries*. London: Routledge.
Reinhart, C., and Rogoff, K. (2003a) 'Background Material': http:// www.wam.umd.edu/~creinhar/papers.htm.
Reinhart, C., and Rogoff, K. (2003b) 'Monthly Classification, 1946–2001': http:// www.wam.umd.edu/~creinhar/papers.htm.
Reinhart, C., and Rogoff, K. (2004) 'The Modern History of Exchange Rate Arrangements: a Reinterpretation'. *Quarterly Journal of Economics*, 119: 1–48.
Rose, A. (2000) 'One Market, One Money: Estimating the Effect of Common Currencies on Trade'. *Economic Policy*, 15: 7–45.
Rose, A. (2003) 'Which International Institutions Promote International Trade?' *Centre for Economic Policy Research Discussion Paper* 3764.
Rose, A., and van Wincoop, E. (2001) 'National Money as a Barrier to International Trade: the Real Case for Currency Union'. *American Economic Review*, 91: 386–90.
Shambaugh, J. (2004) 'The Effects of Fixed Exchange Rates on Monetary Policy'. *Quarterly Journal of Economics*, 119: 301–52.

Data definitions

Data definitions:	
F	the average value of real bilateral trade (constant US dollars)
d	the great circle distance between most populous cities (standard miles)
y	real GDP (constant US dollars)
pop	the population of the country
Basic elements of **b**:	
Area	the area of the country (square kilometres)
Lang	a dummy with value 1 if the two countries have the same language, and 0 otherwise
ComBord	a dummy variable with value 1 if the two countries have a common border
Landl	the number of landlocked countries in the pair (0,1 or 2)
Island	the number of countries in the pair which are islands (0,1 or 2)
Comcol	a dummy with value 1 if i and j were ever colonies after 1945 with same coloniser, and 0 otherwise
Colony	a dummy with value 1 if i ever colonised j or vice versa
Curcol	a dummy with value 1 if i and j are colonies at time t
ComNat	a dummy with value 1 if i and j are part of the same nation at time t
Regional	a dummy with value 1 if i and j belong to the same regional trade agreement at time t
GSP	a dummy with value 1 if i extended a GSP concession to j at time t or vice versa
$\{yr_t\}$	a set of time fixed effects
$\{C_i\}$	a set of country fixed effects

Data sources:

a Data on variables from F above to GSP taken from Rose, A. (2003) and extended by the authors from 1998 to 2004, except for data on distance, most of which was given to us by Jacques Melitz. Data on exchange rate regimes constructed by us, see section 3 above.

Appendix 7.1

Table 7.7 Each country pegs unilaterally to US dollar

		Geographical Distribution (% shares)										
	% change over baseline	*US*	*US bloc*	*Eurozone*	*Euro bloc*	*Other Europe*	*Latin America*	*Asia*	*Africa*	*Canada Australia New Zealand*	*MENA*	*Other*
Turkey	–9.86%	6.45	0.75	45.48	6.03	5.60	1.09	8.75	2.24	0.81	6.17	16.63
Bahrain	0.0%	11.71	0.71	13.65	2.20	4.95	0.04	21.47	2.64	2.81	39.38	0.43
Jordan	0.0%	12.56	1.57	16.27	3.89	2.83	2.38	18.39	1.10	1.45	21.89	17.67
Kuwait	–0.4%	13.78	0.82	14.60	1.40	4.34	0.62	55.76	0.48	2.21	5.51	0.49
Lebanon	0.0%	5.18	0.90	43.70	6.51	4.70	1.36	11.42	0.41	0.68	19.30	5.84
Oman	0.0%	5.74	0.44	6.47	1.37	4.33	0.55	63.28	2.48	1.57	12.86	0.90
Qatar	0.0%	3.60	0.14	9.43	0.83	3.80	0.19	59.16	14.50	1.08	7.13	0.14
Saudi Arabia	0.0%	18.41	0.46	19.32	2.03	3.78	1.69	39.49	3.39	2.49	8.34	0.59
Syria	–1.3%	3.88	0.21	45.23	6.02	1.69	1.99	11.59	0.95	0.69	21.86	5.90
UAE	0.0%	4.78	2.79	15.93	2.43	4.67	0.73	51.27	2.40	2.55	7.94	4.51
Egypt	–2.1%	14.18	0.90	33.11	4.02	5.36	4.06	17.88	2.48	1.89	11.57	4.56
Yemen	25.3%	2.84	1.16	7.01	0.74	1.60	–	57.06	0.51	1.34	24.82	2.91
Algeria	–19.5%	14.92	0.36	47.41	6.94	1.84	4.51	7.36	0.32	5.35	8.57	2.43
Morocco	–19.5%	4.49	0.18	54.61	3.00	6.98	3.28	10.98	2.10	1.08	8.98	4.30
Tunisia	–23.1%	1.96	0.19	67.93	3.20	3.01	1.80	5.49	6.27	0.66	6.50	3.00
Total												
Weighted	–3.4%											
Unweighted	–4.8%											

Table 7.8 Each country pegs unilaterally to euro

		Geographical Distribution (% shares)										
	% change over baseline	*US*	*US bloc*	*Eurozone*	*Euro bloc*	*Other Europe*	*Latin America*	*Asia*	*Africa*	*Canada Australia New Zealand*	*MENA*	*Other*
Turkey	10.82%	6.34	0.41	55.47	5.78	4.55	0.84	6.63	1.65	0.66	4.86	12.82
Bahrain	3.3%	13.69	0.46	19.81	2.51	4.79	0.04	19.31	2.34	2.72	33.93	0.42
Jordan	7.1%	14.45	1.00	23.24	4.37	2.69	2.25	16.05	1.00	1.38	18.74	14.83
Kuwait	4.1%	15.92	0.52	20.94	1.57	4.15	0.59	48.37	0.46	2.12	4.89	0.47
Lebanon	20.6%	5.19	0.50	54.39	6.31	3.90	1.12	8.70	0.33	0.57	14.39	4.61
Oman	–3.4%	7.17	0.30	10.04	1.66	4.48	0.56	58.81	2.56	1.63	11.84	0.93
Qatar	0.2%	4.34	0.10	14.11	0.98	3.79	0.18	54.51	14.47	1.07	6.31	0.14
Saudi Arabia	11.1%	20.03	0.28	26.10	2.16	3.41	1.51	33.73	3.05	2.25	6.98	0.51
Syria	20.3%	3.84	0.12	55.59	5.80	1.39	1.62	8.72	0.70	0.57	16.92	4.74
UAE	4.5%	5.52	1.78	22.88	2.75	4.47	0.69	46.06	2.27	2.44	6.92	4.20
Egypt	15.2%	14.55	0.51	42.17	3.99	4.55	3.42	14.09	2.04	1.61	9.36	3.70
Yemen	18.0%	3.64	0.82	11.16	0.94	1.69	–	53.77	0.54	1.42	23.37	2.64
Algeria	1.5%	14.29	0.19	56.36	5.73	1.46	3.57	5.47	0.23	4.24	6.68	1.78
Morocco	1.8%	4.29	0.10	64.76	2.72	5.52	2.57	7.89	1.48	0.85	6.71	3.11
Tunisia	2.3%	1.78	0.09	76.52	2.77	2.26	1.33	3.77	3.97	0.50	4.92	2.09
Total												
Weighted	7.7%											
Unweighted	7.83%											

Table 7.9 Each country unilaterally introduces currency union on US dollar

		Geographical Distribution (% shares)										
	% change over baseline	*US*	*US bloc*	*Eurozone*	*Euro bloc*	*Other Europe*	*Latin America*	*Asia*	*Africa*	*Canada Australia New Zealand*	*MENA*	*Other*
Turkey	2.34%	6.01	0.98	48.48	5.38	5.01	0.99	7.81	2.12	0.64	6.33	16.26
Bahrain	12.5%	11.01	0.94	14.68	1.96	4.47	0.05	18.65	2.51	2.00	43.35	0.39
Jordan	14.7%	11.82	2.08	17.51	3.47	2.56	1.76	17.35	0.88	1.11	23.20	18.27
Kuwait	5.6%	13.75	1.15	16.66	1.31	4.15	0.56	54.04	0.36	1.69	5.87	0.47
Lebanon	14.2%	4.80	1.17	46.37	5.75	4.19	1.13	10.79	0.36	0.55	19.57	5.31
Oman	9.5%	5.54	0.60	7.15	1.25	4.02	0.48	62.41	1.89	1.23	14.60	0.84
Qatar	2.5%	3.72	0.21	11.13	0.81	3.76	0.19	56.21	14.31	0.91	8.63	0.14
Saudi Arabia	3.3%	18.88	0.67	22.67	1.99	3.73	1.65	35.89	2.66	2.08	9.17	0.63
Syria	10.6%	3.66	0.28	48.84	5.36	1.53	1.50	11.08	0.86	0.61	20.61	5.64
UAE	4.0%	4.86	4.00	18.55	2.35	4.57	0.70	47.30	2.14	2.03	8.92	4.58
Egypt	7.3%	13.69	1.22	36.56	3.70	4.97	3.29	16.69	2.07	1.57	11.65	4.60
Yemen	46.7%	2.57	1.47	7.24	0.64	1.39	–	56.91	0.39	0.93	25.51	2.94
Algeria	–10.1%	14.14	0.49	51.38	7.24	1.67	3.93	6.65	0.29	4.84	6.95	2.43
Morocco	–7.5%	4.14	0.24	57.51	2.73	6.18	2.82	10.39	2.02	0.94	8.83	4.21
Tunisia	–10.6%	1.78	0.24	70.67	2.87	2.63	1.37	5.01	6.41	0.57	5.56	2.90
Total												
Weighted	3.0%											
Unweighted	7.0%											

Table 7.10 Each country unilaterally introduces currency union on euro

		Geographical Distribution (% shares)										
	% change over baseline	*US*	*US bloc*	*Eurozone*	*Euro bloc*	*Other Europe*	*Latin America*	*Asia*	*Africa*	*Canada Australia New Zealand*	*MENA*	*Other*
Turkey	40.42%	3.78	0.39	65.13	5.52	3.66	0.63	4.52	1.24	0.47	4.05	10.60
Bahrain	5.5%	10.13	0.54	28.86	2.98	4.77	0.04	16.32	2.21	2.13	31.60	0.41
Jordan	13.6%	10.30	1.14	32.59	4.99	2.58	1.75	13.49	0.80	1.12	16.91	14.33
Kuwait	5.2%	11.91	0.63	30.83	1.89	4.17	0.56	42.91	0.36	1.69	4.57	0.48
Lebanon	50.6%	3.14	0.48	64.79	6.15	3.17	0.85	6.19	0.25	0.42	10.97	3.60
Oman	–6.0%	5.58	0.38	15.37	2.08	4.69	0.53	55.26	2.20	1.43	11.50	0.97
Qatar	–1.0%	3.32	0.12	21.25	1.20	3.90	0.19	48.04	14.83	0.94	6.07	0.14
Saudi Arabia	13.1%	14.87	0.33	38.15	2.57	3.40	1.49	27.81	2.42	1.90	6.54	0.52
Syria	50.2%	2.32	0.11	66.28	5.65	1.13	1.09	6.25	0.51	0.45	12.23	3.97
UAE	7.8%	4.05	2.09	33.02	3.23	4.41	0.65	38.09	2.01	1.96	6.32	4.17
Egypt	32.6%	9.55	0.54	54.50	4.20	4.02	2.62	10.62	1.55	1.27	7.73	3.39
Yemen	18.0%	2.75	0.99	16.60	1.13	1.72	–	50.44	0.49	1.16	22.02	2.68
Algeria	25.6%	8.73	0.19	67.78	5.70	1.20	2.81	3.77	0.17	3.46	4.71	1.48
Morocco	32.5%	2.49	0.09	74.04	2.53	4.32	1.92	5.45	1.11	0.65	4.94	2.45
Tunisia	40.1%	0.98	0.08	83.16	2.46	1.68	0.85	2.45	2.92	0.36	3.46	1.59
Total												
Weighted	21.1%											
Unweighted	21.9%											

Table 7.11 All countries peg to US dollar

	% change over baseline	*Geographical Distribution (% shares)*										
		US	*US bloc*	*Eurozone*	*Euro bloc*	*Other Europe*	*Latin America*	*Asia*	*Africa*	*Canada Australia New Zealand*	*MENA*	*Other*
Turkey	–9.54%	6.42	0.75	45.31	6.01	5.58	1.09	8.72	2.23	0.81	6.51	16.57
Bahrain	0.2%	11.69	0.71	13.63	2.19	4.94	0.04	21.42	2.64	2.81	39.50	0.43
Jordan	2.0%	12.57	1.57	16.28	3.89	2.83	2.38	18.40	1.10	1.45	21.84	17.69
Kuwait	–0.1%	13.74	0.82	14.56	1.40	4.32	0.62	55.60	0.48	2.21	5.77	0.49
Lebanon	–0.2%	5.20	0.90	43.85	6.53	4.71	1.37	11.45	0.41	0.69	19.03	5.86
Oman	0.1%	5.74	0.44	6.47	1.37	4.33	0.55	63.27	2.48	1.57	12.88	0.90
Qatar	0.0%	3.60	0.14	9.43	0.83	3.80	0.19	59.16	14.51	1.08	7.12	0.14
Saudi Arabia	0.2%	18.40	0.46	19.31	2.03	3.78	1.69	39.46	3.39	2.49	8.39	0.59
Syria	–2.2%	3.91	0.22	45.65	6.08	1.71	2.01	11.69	0.95	0.70	21.13	5.96
UAE	0.3%	4.77	2.79	15.91	2.43	4.67	0.73	51.20	2.40	2.55	8.05	4.50
Egypt	–2.2%	14.18	0.90	33.12	4.03	5.36	4.06	17.88	2.48	1.89	11.53	4.56
Yemen	24.9%	2.85	1.16	7.04	0.75	1.60	–	57.27	0.51	1.34	24.55	2.92
Algeria	–20.1%	15.02	0.37	47.73	6.99	1.85	4.54	7.41	0.32	5.39	7.94	2.44
Morocco	–19.5%	4.50	0.18	54.63	3.00	6.99	3.28	10.98	2.10	1.08	8.95	4.30
Tunisia	–23.2%	1.96	0.19	67.98	3.20	3.01	1.80	5.49	6.27	0.66	6.43	3.00
Total												
Weighted	–4.8%											
Unweighted	–3.3%											

Table 7.12 All countries peg to Euro

		Geographical Distribution (% shares)										
	% change over baseline	*US*	*US bloc*	*Eurozone*	*Euro bloc*	*Other Europe*	*Latin America*	*Asia*	*Africa*	*Canada Australia New Zealand*	*MENA*	*Other*
Turkey	11.29%	6.30	0.41	55.21	5.76	4.54	0.84	6.60	1.64	0.66	5.28	12.76
Bahrain	7.8%	13.11	0.44	18.98	2.41	4.59	0.03	18.51	2.24	2.61	36.67	0.40
Jordan	9.2%	14.15	0.98	22.77	4.28	2.64	2.21	15.74	0.98	1.36	20.35	14.54
Kuwait	4.7%	15.81	0.52	20.81	1.56	4.12	0.59	48.07	0.45	2.10	5.50	0.47
Lebanon	22.2%	5.12	0.49	53.67	6.23	3.85	1.11	8.58	0.32	0.56	15.52	4.55
Oman	–1.9%	7.06	0.30	9.89	1.64	4.42	0.55	57.97	2.53	1.61	13.12	0.92
Qatar	1.0%	4.31	0.09	14.00	0.97	3.76	0.18	54.09	14.35	1.06	7.04	0.14
Saudi Arabia	11.7%	19.90	0.28	25.96	2.14	3.39	1.51	33.55	3.03	2.23	7.51	0.51
Syria	20.6%	3.83	0.12	55.46	5.79	1.38	1.62	8.71	0.70	0.56	17.11	4.73
UAE	5.3%	5.48	1.77	22.70	2.73	4.44	0.69	45.71	2.26	2.42	7.65	4.16
Egypt	15.6%	14.48	0.51	42.00	3.98	4.54	3.41	14.03	2.03	1.60	9.74	3.69
Yemen	21.0%	3.55	0.80	10.88	0.91	1.65	–	52.43	0.53	1.39	25.29	2.57
Algeria	1.0%	14.34	0.19	56.61	5.75	1.47	3.59	5.49	0.23	4.26	6.28	1.79
Morocco	2.1%	4.27	0.10	64.52	2.71	5.50	2.56	7.86	1.48	0.85	7.04	3.10
Tunisia	2.2%	1.78	0.09	76.58	2.78	2.26	1.34	3.77	3.98	0.50	4.83	2.09
Total												
Weighted	8.4%											
Unweighted	8.9%											

Table 7.13 All countries form monetary union pegged to US dollar

		Geographical Distribution (% shares)										
	% change over baseline	*US*	*US bloc*	*Eurozone*	*Euro bloc*	*Other Europe*	*Latin America*	*Asia*	*Africa*	*Canada Australia New Zealand*	*MENA*	*Other*
Turkey	3.67%	6.30	0.41	55.21	5.76	4.54	0.84	6.60	1.64	0.66	5.28	12.76
Bahrain	34.8%	13.11	0.44	18.98	2.41	4.59	0.03	18.51	2.24	2.61	36.67	0.40
Jordan	23.1%	14.15	0.98	22.77	4.28	2.64	2.21	15.74	0.98	1.36	20.35	14.54
Kuwait	2.7%	15.81	0.52	20.81	1.56	4.12	0.59	48.07	0.45	2.10	5.50	0.47
Lebanon	24.4%	5.12	0.49	53.67	6.23	3.85	1.11	8.58	0.32	0.56	15.52	4.55
Oman	7.6%	7.06	0.30	9.89	1.64	4.42	0.55	57.97	2.53	1.61	13.12	0.92
Qatar	1.1%	4.31	0.09	14.00	0.97	3.76	0.18	54.09	14.35	1.06	7.04	0.14
Saudi Arabia	5.8%	19.90	0.28	25.96	2.14	3.39	1.51	33.55	3.03	2.23	7.51	0.51
Syria	24.1%	3.83	0.12	55.46	5.79	1.38	1.62	8.71	0.70	0.56	17.11	4.73
UAE	3.0%	5.48	1.77	22.70	2.73	4.44	0.69	45.71	2.26	2.42	7.65	4.16
Egypt	12.5%	14.48	0.51	42.00	3.98	4.54	3.41	14.03	2.03	1.60	9.74	3.69
Yemen	50.6%	3.55	0.80	10.88	0.91	1.65	–	52.43	0.53	1.39	25.29	2.57
Algeria	–5.7%	14.34	0.19	56.61	5.75	1.47	3.59	5.49	0.23	4.26	6.28	1.79
Morocco	–4.4%	4.27	0.10	64.52	2.71	5.50	2.56	7.86	1.48	0.85	7.04	3.10
Tunisia	–8.2%	1.78	0.09	76.58	2.78	2.26	1.34	3.77	3.98	0.50	4.83	2.09
Total												
Weighted	5.2%											
Unweighted	11.7%											

Table 7.14 All countries form monetary union pegged to euro

		Geographical Distribution (% shares)										
	% change over baseline	*US*	*US bloc*	*Eurozone*	*Euro bloc*	*Other Europe*	*Latin America*	*Asia*	*Africa*	*Canada Australia New Zealand*	*MENA*	*Other*
Turkey	3.07%	5.2	0.5	49.4	6.2	5.0	0.9	6.2	1.7	0.6	10.7	13.7
Bahrain	32.3%	8.1	0.4	12.8	2.0	3.8	0.0	13.0	1.8	1.7	56.0	0.3
Jordan	18.5%	9.9	1.1	17.4	3.9	2.5	1.7	12.9	0.8	1.1	35.2	13.6
Kuwait	–3.5%	13.0	0.7	18.7	1.7	4.6	0.6	46.8	0.4	1.8	11.2	0.5
Lebanon	24.6%	3.8	0.6	43.6	6.2	3.8	1.0	7.5	0.3	0.5	28.5	4.2
Oman	0.6%	5.2	0.4	8.0	1.6	4.4	0.5	51.7	2.1	1.3	24.0	0.9
Qatar	–3.1%	3.4	0.1	12.1	1.0	4.0	0.2	49.1	15.2	1.0	13.8	0.1
Saudi Arabia	1.8%	16.5	0.4	23.6	2.4	3.8	1.7	30.9	2.7	2.1	15.4	0.6
Syria	24.6%	2.8	0.1	44.5	5.6	1.4	1.3	7.5	0.6	0.5	31.1	4.5
UAE	–0.3%	4.4	2.3	19.9	2.9	4.8	0.7	41.2	2.2	2.1	15.2	4.5
Egypt	10.2%	11.5	0.6	36.5	4.2	4.8	3.2	12.8	1.9	1.5	19.2	3.8
Yemen	40.7%	2.3	0.8	7.8	0.8	1.4	–	42.4	0.4	1.0	40.8	2.3
Algeria	–6.7%	11.8	0.3	50.8	7.1	1.6	3.8	5.1	0.2	4.7	12.7	1.9
Morocco	–4.7%	3.5	0.1	57.2	3.0	6.0	2.7	7.6	1.5	0.9	14.1	3.3
Tunisia	–7.8%	1.5	0.1	70.3	3.2	2.5	1.3	3.7	4.4	0.6	10.0	2.3
Total												
Weighted	2.5%											
Unweighted	8.7%											

8 Exchange rate arrangements and price stability in MENA countries

Elias El-Achkar and Wassim Shahin

Introduction

This study aims to examine for the MENA region the impact of the behaviour of exchange rates and the nature of the *de facto* exchange rate arrangement on price stability. Several MENA countries have explicitly or *de facto* adopted conventional fixed peg arrangements for many reasons related to the external sector and macroeconomic discipline including price stability. To this end, the paper studies the impact of changes in exchange rates and exchange rate policies on inflation in eighteen MENA countries from 1975 to 2005 using empirical testing methods. The issue we investigate is the extent to which pegged exchange rate arrangements succeeded in achieving price stability, which is different from the many studies investigating the links between import prices and domestic prices. We build on the international literature which addresses the evaluation of pegged exchange rate regimes across the world and the studies analysing exchange rate policies in MENA countries. We hope to contribute to the literature on whether the majority of MENA countries that have adopted pegged exchange rate arrangements were able to achieve stable and low inflation rates as a result of such policies. Determining the cost of these policies as well as the choice of exchange rate regimes are beyond the scope of the current analysis.

The empirical methodology used in the paper consists of running multi-country pooled time series estimation. Annual data over the last thirty years is used to investigate the behaviour of inflation rates under *de facto* parities in MENA countries and to test whether changes in the exchange rates and the nature of the exchange rate regime are likely to contribute to changes in the inflation rates. The equation specification is dictated by theory and influenced by data availability.

The findings reached show that the actual behaviour of the exchange rate along with other monetary policy variables is significant in terms of the impact on inflation rates. Our results also did not find any significant difference between various *de facto* exchange rate arrangements when it comes to the effect on inflation rates, as the exchange rate dummy was shown to be insignificant. This implies that for the countries in our sample and the period considered, the choice of the adopted exchange rate regime is not significant. These findings are not always in line with some of the results reached in the literature on pegged exchange rate arrangements around the world, which show in some cases that inflation is lower and more stable under fixed exchange rate regimes or in others that a relationship appears between fixed exchange rate regimes and inflation when long pegs are considered.

On the other hand, our results coincide with some findings on industrial countries which show that there is no significant link between exchange rate regimes and inflation irrespective of the period of the peg, or those on some emerging markets which show that the exchange rate regime does not have a systematic effect on inflation. However, the results on the significance of the exchange rate variable rather than the regime dummy may imply that the dummy variable is too simple or too weak in this data set. The significance of the exchange rate variable itself which measures the effect of actual exchange rates could possibly indicate that exchange rate regimes matter. In this case, the present results might be less out of line with some results in the literature.

The first section of this chapter reviews the literature which examines the impact of pegged exchange rate arrangements in MENA countries on several economic variables and the success of the choice of exchange rate regimes adopted in these countries. In addition, this section reviews the results of the empirical studies conducted on the relationship between the nature of the exchange rate regime and price stability, using world samples. Section 2 discusses the past and current *de facto* and *de jure* exchange rate classification in the eighteen MENA countries considered. The third section develops the testing methodology. Section 4 highlights the empirical results obtained while section 5 contains some concluding remarks on the policy implications.

1 Literature review

This section starts by briefly reviewing that part of the relevant literature which evaluates the experience of selected MENA countries with various exchange rate arrangements. Then we evaluate the findings of some of the studies dealing with the link between exchange rate arrangements and inflation across the world, and build our model and testing methodology partly on these studies.

The literature on the performance of some MENA countries under different exchange rate arrangements is largely of two types. The first relied on empirical methodology to address the impact of chosen regimes on the economy in terms of economic growth (Domac and Shabsigh, 1999, Bailliu, Lafrance and Perrault 2003) and manufacturing and export competitiveness (Nabli and Veganzones-Varoudakis, 2002). Specifically, Domac and Shabsigh (1999) examined the effect of real exchange rate misalignment on economic growth in Egypt, Jordan, Morocco and Tunisia in the 1970s and 1980s. During this period, the four countries adopted exchange rate policies motivated by the need to protect the external balance from external shocks and expansionary domestic policy. The results reached confirmed the adverse effects of this misalignment on growth using all the measures of misalignment adopted in endogenous growth models. Bailliu, Lafrance and Perrault (2003) estimated the impact of exchange rate arrangements on growth using a panel data set of 60 countries between 1973 and 1998.

The evidence obtained suggested that pegged, intermediate (crawling pegs or target zones) and flexible exchange rate regimes affect economic growth positively when there is a monetary policy anchor. In the absence of an anchor, intermediate and flexible exchange rate regimes are detrimental for growth. The results indicate that it is the presence of a monetary policy anchor rather than the type of exchange rate regime that affect economic growth.

Nabli and Veganzones-Varoudakis (2002) addressed the impact of overvaluation in ten selected MENA countries on economic activity in the 1970s and 1980s using the competitiveness of manufactured exports as a case in point. The results show that manufactured exports were negatively affected by overvaluation. However, when some countries reduced their exchange rate misalignment in the 1990s, their manufactured exports increased, in line with the findings in the international literature.

The second type of studies addressed the choice of exchange rate regimes (Karam, 2001; Jbili and Karamarenko, 2003; Bhattacharya, 2003; Kamar, 2004). The issues considered centred around the major question of whether and under what conditions MENA countries should float, peg, or follow a somehow more flexible system. These studies also addressed the viability of policies of exchange rate cooperation. They dealt with different sets of countries using different methodologies to reach similar results; in many cases on countries common to the various sets. Bhattacharya (2003) for example, suggests that perhaps the most sensible conclusion for Lebanon and Jordan at this stage is to adopt a fixed exchange rate regime, given the lack of evidence on real wage and relative price flexibility and the difficulty of finding a substitute for the exchange rate as the nominal anchor for Lebanon. Using a different method of analysis, Jbili and Karamarenko (2003) also reach the conclusion that the choice of a flexible exchange rate regime is not clear-cut for Lebanon and Jordan and more of a long-term nature. The transition to a more flexible exchange rate arrangement raises the issue of what conditions these countries need to meet.

The present paper falls under the first type of studies as it examines the impact of fixed exchange rate arrangements on price stability. The choice of exchange rate addressed in the second type is beyond the scope of this study. However, this paper differentiates itself from the existing studies on MENA countries in that it builds on the international literature reviewed next, which has examined the impact of pegged exchange rate arrangements on price stability. In addition, this paper draws on a large sample of eighteen MENA countries for a period extending from 1975 to 2005. This period has witnessed changes in exchange rate arrangements in most countries over the years.

Several studies have examined the impact of exchange rate regimes on macroeconomic discipline. The analysis is confined to three of these studies that are the most relevant in this instance. The first study, by Ghosh, Gulde, Ostry and Wolf (1997), uses data covering nine regime types for 136 countries over the period 1960–1990 to examine the relationships between the nature of the exchange rate regime and inflation and economic growth. The authors note that casual observations show that the pegged exchange rate regimes are largely concentrated in the low inflation period of the 1960s whereas the flexible regime observations are more pronounced in the higher inflation periods of the 1970s and 1980s. Then they examine the causality of these results by empirically testing the significance of money growth, output growth, interest rates and several exchange rate regime dummies on inflation using various alternative methods. The results show that inflation is lower and more stable under pegged exchange rate arrangements than under floating regimes. Money growth rates and output growth are highly significant whereas the interest rate term is insignificant.

The second study by Levy-Yeyati and Sturzenegger (2001) examines the impact of exchange rate regimes on inflation, real interest rates, nominal money growth and output growth. The sample used covers 1925 annual observations for 154 countries over the period 1973–1999. Given that many of these countries exhibit extraordinarily high inflation, the authors concentrated the analysis on the medians which are less affected by extreme values. The reasoning behind the analysis was based on the assumption that the exchange rate regime affects inflation directly through lower inflation expectations and indirectly through the disciplinary effects on changes in the rate of growth of money. The authors found that for industrial countries there is no significant link between exchange rate regimes and inflation irrespective of the length of the period of the peg. However, for non-industrial economies a robust link between fixed exchange rate regimes and inflation appears only when long pegs or pegs that have been in place for at least five consecutive years are considered. Short lived pegs appear even to be inferior to floats when it comes to achieving lower inflation rates. The results on inflation of the other explanatory variables such as money growth, real Gross Domestic Product (GDP) growth, lagged inflation and interest rates are all significant and of the expected signs.

The third study by Husain, Mody and Rogoff (2005) draws on the new data and advances in exchange rate regime classification developed in Reinhart and Rogoff (2004) to examine exchange rate regime durability and performance in developing and advanced economies. The results suggest that for developing economies with little access to international capital markets, pegged exchange rate regimes deliver relatively low inflation and high exchange rate durability. As countries become more financially developed, they gain from moving to more flexible exchange rate regimes and achieve higher growth without higher inflation. However, for emerging markets, the exchange rate regime does not seem to have a systematic effect on inflation and growth.

2 Exchange rate regime classification in MENA countries

This section is divided into two parts. The first summarises various exchange rate classifications adopted by the International Monetary Fund (IMF) from 1975 until the present. The second part examines the exchange rate policies adopted by various MENA countries in terms of evolution and performance.

The IMF exchange rate classification

From 1975 through to 1998 the IMF classified members' exchange rate arrangements under three main categories: pegged (against a single currency or a currency composite), limited flexibility vis-à-vis a single currency or group of currencies, and more flexible, including other managed and independently floating. This grouping was based on members' official notifications or declarations to the IMF about their exchange rate policies and flexibility when they first became members and after any changes in their arrangements. This is well known in the literature as the *de jure* classification which has its own advantages and disadvantages.

One of the benefits is that there are 24 years of data and very wide country coverage, which allows many empirical studies on exchange rate regimes to rely upon this database in testing hypotheses and lending empirical support for a specific argument. A main shortcoming is that what countries are officially claiming to be doing (*de jure*) may differ largely from what they are actually pursuing (*de facto*). This reduces the transparency of the exchange rate policy undertaken and makes effective tracking, surveillance and analysis of the evolution and performance of the exchange rate regime for research and policy implications difficult and perhaps less accurate or even biased. There are many reasons often cited for this behaviour, including to avoid possible exchange rate speculation and attacks on the domestic currency under certain circumstances or to avoid the political cost associated with one or more desired devaluations and perhaps to preserve export competitiveness under an announced peg (Bubula and Otker-Robe, 2002).

To address the *de jure* classification shortcomings, the IMF introduced in 1999 a new classification system based on what countries are doing in reality, that is, based on the actual, *de facto*, policies. This new system ranks exchange rate regimes on the basis of the different degrees of flexibility of the arrangement and distinguishes among the many forms of pegged regimes from the more rigid to the more soft, in order to better assess the implications of the choice of the exchange rate regime for the degree of independence of monetary policy (IMF, 2000). The 1999 IMF nomenclature, still in use, identified the following exchange rate regimes: (1) exchange arrangements with no separate legal tender, (2) currency board arrangements, (3) conventional fixed-peg arrangements, (4) pegged exchange rates within horizontal bands, (5) crawling pegs, (6) exchange rates within crawling bands, (7) managed floating with no pre-determined path for the exchange rate, and (8) independent floating.[1]

The improvement made in the classification system was partly induced by the literature which focused on the need to analyse *de facto* policies. This also motivated many researchers to go back in time and construct a historical database on *de facto* regimes for a large number of countries. The studies that came before or after the 1999 IMF classification used either this or a broadly similar classification for going back in time for updating (such as Reinhart and Rogoff, 2004; Bubula and Otker-Robe, 2002), or a largely modified classification, or new definitions and categories (Levy-Yeyati, and Sturzenegger, 2005; Ghosh, Gulde, Ostry, and Wolf, 1997). The latter were based either on quantitative measures such as the variability of the exchange rate, international reserves, and the level of foreign exchange intervention or on a combination of quantitative and qualitative analysis.[2] The purpose of these studies has been to overcome the limited usefulness of the IMF's new classification for empirical analysis or to address perceived shortcomings with a view to examining whether certain opinions on exchange rate regimes hold.

Exchange rate regimes in MENA countries: evolution and performance

In this paper, we rely on the IMF exchange rate regime classification which was revised in 1999, to identify *de jure* and *de facto* exchange rate policies in the MENA region and study the linkages between pegged regimes and inflation in this group of countries. This is because the IMF has access to a wide range of credible sources of information ranging from the bilateral discussions and technical assistance offered to member countries, to IMF country desk economists and their reports on observed exchange rate behaviour. Table 8.1 summarises the evolution of *de jure* policies from the 1970s till 1998 and the *de facto* policies from 1990 until 2005 of most MENA countries. The sources of information are IMF *Annual Reports* (various countries), and the study done by Bubula and Otker-Robe (2002) which constructed a database on *de facto* exchange rate regime classification from 1990 until 2001 for almost all IMF member countries, using the IMF nomenclature adopted in 1999.

Gulf Co-operation Council (GCC) countries

The *de facto* classification of exchange rate regimes in Bahrain, Oman, Qatar, Saudi Arabia and the United Arab Emirates (UAE) has been conventional fixed peg arrangements against a single currency, at least since 1990 (given data availability). The Kuwaiti *de facto* regime was a conventional fixed peg arrangement against a composite from 1990 and perhaps earlier until 2001, when it became a conventional fixed peg arrangement against a single currency. The *de jure* classification (ending in 1998), based on the official declarations of country authorities to the IMF, classified the Oman and Kuwait exchange rate arrangements as pegged to the US dollar and to a currency composite respectively. The *de jure* exchange rate arrangements of Bahrain, Qatar, Saudi Arabia, and the United Arab Emirates were categorised as showing limited flexibility vis-à-vis a single currency (the US dollar).

As for performance, the period average exchange rate per US dollar has been fixed since 1981 in Bahrain, Qatar and UAE at 0.376, 3.64, and 3.67 respectively. The exchange rate against the US dollar was maintained in Oman at 0.35 from 1975 until 1985 and then at 0.38 from 1986 until the present, whereas it has been stable at 3.75 in Saudi Arabia since 1987. Before that date, the Saudi Riyal fluctuated within a range of +/– 4 per cent. The largest currency appreciation of the Kuwaiti Dinar against the US dollar was around 4 per cent in 1987 and the largest depreciation was close to 5 per cent in 1989. These facts explain the very low exchange rate volatility or strong currency stability in the GCC countries for the period 1975–2005, as evidenced by the means and medians of exchange rate changes displayed in Table 8.2.

Table 8.1 Exchange rate arrangements of MENA countries

	Officially announced (de jure)	*Actual arrangement (de facto)*
GCC		
Bahrain	Limited flexibility vis-à-vis a single currency	Classified under Other Conventional Fixed Peg Arrangements where the country pegs its currency at a fixed rate to a major currency or a basket of currencies and where the exchange rate fluctuates within a narrow margin of at most +/– 1% around a central rate. The peg is against a single currency
Kuwait	Pegged against a currency composite	Classified under Other Conventional Fixed Peg Arrangements. The peg was against a composite until 2001 but changed later to peg against a single currency
Oman	Pegged against a single currency	Classified under Other Conventional Fixed Peg Arrangements. The peg is against a single currency
Qatar	Limited flexibility vis-à-vis a single currency	Classified under Other Conventional Fixed Peg Arrangements. The peg is against a single currency
Saudi Arabia	Limited flexibility vis-à-vis a single currency	Classified under Other Conventional Fixed Peg Arrangements. The peg is against a single currency
UAE	Limited flexibility vis-à-vis a single currency	Classified under Other Conventional Fixed Peg Arrangements. The peg is against a single currency
North Africa		
Algeria	Managed floating	From 1994 classified under Managed floating with no pre-announced path for exchange rate. From 1990 until 1993, conventional fixed peg against a composite
Egypt	Managed floating	From 2002 classified under Managed floating with no pre-announced path for exchange rate. The same classification applies to 1999–2000. Classified under Pegged exchange rates within horizontal bands (1991–96, 2001) where the value of the currency is maintained within margins of fluctuation around a formal or *de facto* fixed peg that are wider than +/– 1% around a central rate. Much earlier classified under Other Conventional Fixed Peg Arrangements (1990, 1997, 1998) with the peg being against a single currency

	Officially announced (de jure)	*Actual arrangement (de facto)*
Libya	Domestic currency pegged to SDR	From 2001 classified under Other Conventional Fixed Peg Arrangements with the peg being against a composite. Earlier classified under Pegged exchange rates within horizontal bands
Morocco	Domestic currency pegged to a currency composite other than the SDR	Classified under Other Conventional Fixed Peg Arrangements. The peg is against a composite
Tunisia	Managed floating	Classified under Managed floating with no pre-announced path for exchange rate (2000–2001, 2005). Classified under Crawling pegs (1990–1999, 2002–2004) where the currency is adjusted periodically in small amounts at a fixed, pre-announced rate
Other MENA		
Yemen	Independently floating	From 1996 classified under Independently floating. A conventional fixed peg arrangement against a single currency existed from 1990–1995
Jordan	Currency pegged to a currency composite	Classified under Other Conventional Fixed Peg Arrangements. The peg is against a single currency starting 1995 and against a composite from 1990–1994
Lebanon	Independently floating	From 1998 classified under Other Conventional Fixed Peg Arrangements. The peg is against a single currency. A crawling peg regime existed 1993–1997 following a managed floating regime with no predetermined path for the exchange rate from 1990–1992
Syria	Domestic currency pegged to USD	Classified under Other Conventional Fixed Peg Arrangements. The peg is against a single currency
Turkey	Managed floating	From 2001 classified under Independently floating. Earlier classified under Crawling pegs
Cyprus	Currency pegged to a currency composite	Classified under Pegged exchange rates within horizontal bands since 1993. A conventional fixed peg arrangement against a composite existed in 1990–1991
Iran	Managed floating	Starting 2002, classified under Managed floating with no predetermined path for the exchange rate. Earlier classified under Other Conventional Fixed Peg Arrangements. The peg is against a single currency from 1993–2001 compared to against a composite from 1990–1992

Table 8.2 Exchange rates, money growth and inflation

	Bahrain	*Kuwait*	*Oman*	*Qatar*	*Saudi Arabia*	*UAE*
Exchange rates[a] %						
Mean	–0.16	0.01	0.31	–0.29	0.18	–0.25
Median	0.00	0.28	0.00	0.00	0.00	0.00
Money Growth %						
Mean	12.83	10.53	11.14	12.10	15.16	11.29
Median	7.85	6.32	7.22	10.68	7.26	9.04
Inflation %						
Mean	3.51	2.81	1.82	4.28	2.91	5.29
Median	1.48	2.53	0.93	2.96	0.59	4.40
No of observations	31	31	28	29	31	29

	Algeria	*Egypt*	*Libya*	*Morocco*	*Tunisia*
Exchange rates[a] %					
Mean	11.24	11.20	6.04	2.78	3.89
Median	4.36	0.00	0.00	1.03	3.61
Money Growth %					
Mean	17.96	19.95	9.87	12.72	12.86
Median	17.35	19.34	6.50	12.23	13.44
Inflation %					
Mean	11.23	11.63	5.39	5.69	6.01
Median	9.32	11.26	5.51	5.74	6.17
No of observations	31	31	31	31	31

	Yemen	*Jordan*	*Lebanon*	*Syria*	*Turkey*	*Cyprus*	*Iran*
Exchange rates[a] %							
Mean	30.09	3.02	36.69	6.19	48.80	1.13	78.64
Median	4.13	0.00	1.67	0.00	46.32	0.74	0.17
Money Growth %							
Mean	20.09	14.21	41.69	18.74	66.26	13.02	25.62
Median	17.50	15.00	23.59	18.96	50.51	13.36	24.44

	Yemen	Jordan	Lebanon	Syria	Turkey	Cyprus	Iran
Inflation %							
Mean	21.14	6.22	43.75	11.60	53.55	5.06	19.95
Median	12.24	3.85	18.60	9.29	54.40	4.14	18.19
No of observations	15	31	31	31	31	31	28

Notes: Annual changes in the period average exchange rate against the USD. A positive sign indicates a depreciation.

North Africa

The *de facto* regimes of Morocco and Libya have been conventional fixed peg arrangements against a composite at least since 1990 and 2001 respectively. Earlier, the Libyan exchange rate arrangement was a pegged exchange rate within horizontal bands. In Algeria, the arrangement was a conventional fixed peg against a composite until 1993. From 1994 the regime is classified as managed floating with no pre-determined path for the exchange rate. From 1990 until 1999 Tunisia had a crawling peg classification which was changed to managed floating with no pre-determined path for the exchange rate from 2000 until 2001, and changed back to a crawling peg from 2002 until 2004. In 2005, Tunisia went back to a managed floating regime with no pre-determined path for the exchange rate. The *de facto* exchange rate policies in Egypt fluctuated between a conventional fixed peg arrangement against a single currency (1990, 1997, 1998), pegged exchange rate within horizontal bands (1991–1996, 2001), and managed floating with no pre-determined path for the exchange rate (1999, 2000, 2002-2005). The *de jure* classification showed that the exchange rate regimes in Libya and Morocco have been pegged to a currency composite (SDR for Libya and another composite for Morocco). However the exchange rate has been maintained within margins of +/– 47 per cent for Libya compared to +/– 3 per cent for Morocco. The arrangements in Algeria, Egypt and Tunisia have been classified as managed floating. It should be noted that both Libya and Egypt operated exchange rate arrangements involving more than one market and that the classification reported in the text is the one maintained in the major market.

In both Morocco and Tunisia, the largest currency depreciations took place in 1981 with the period average exchange rates per US dollar falling by 31 per cent and 23 per cent respectively. In the rest of the period under study, changes in the exchange rate were low to moderate, which contributed to relatively low volatility with fluctuations not exceeding an annual average of 3 to 4 per cent respectively. The large currency depreciation of 106 per cent against the US dollar in Algeria in 1991, together with less sharp depreciations in other years, resulted in a high currency volatility as seen in Table 8.2. In Libya, the exchange rate was fixed at 0.2959 against the US dollar from 1975 until 1985. The largest currency depreciation occurred in 2002 with the currency losing 86 per cent of its value against the US dollar. As for Egypt, the exchange rate was fixed to the US dollar at 0.39 from 1975 until 1978, at 0.7 from 1979 until 1988, and at 3.39 from 1994 until 1998. In other years, the exchange rate varied with the largest annual depreciation (82 per cent) taking place in 1990.

Other MENA countries

The *de facto* exchange rate regime in Syria has been a conventional fixed peg arrangement against a single currency at least since 1990. Jordan had a conventional fixed peg arrangement against a composite from 1990 until 1994 then moved to a conventional fixed peg arrangement against a single currency. Lebanon had a managed floating regime with no predetermined path for the exchange rate from 1990 until 1992, then experienced a crawling peg regime from 1993 until 1997. A conventional fixed peg arrangement against a single currency was then adopted from 1998 until the present.

In 1990 and 1991, Cyprus had a conventional fixed peg arrangement against a composite, which was changed in 1993 to pegged exchange rates within horizontal bands. Iran also had a conventional fixed peg arrangement against a composite from 1990 until 1992 before moving to a conventional fixed peg arrangement against a single currency from 1993 until 2001. Since 2002 the *de facto* exchange rate regime for Iran has been a managed float with no pre-determined path for the exchange rate. From 1990 until 2000, Turkey had a crawling peg which was changed in 2001 to an independently floating regime. Finally, Yemen had a conventional fixed peg arrangement against a single currency from 1990 until 1995. An independently floating regime was adopted in 1996 and was replaced by a managed float in 1999 and 2000 only. The *de jure* classification for this group of countries consisted of a pegged arrangement against a single currency for Syria, and against a composite for Jordan and Cyprus; a managed float for Iran and Turkey; and an independent float for Lebanon and Yemen. It should be noted that both Syria and Iran maintained exchange rate arrangements involving more than one market throughout the period under study and up until 2001, and that the classification reported in the text is that maintained in the major market.

In Syria the average exchange rate per USD was fixed at 3.93 from 1976 until 1987 and then at 11.23 from 1988 until 2005. Therefore a single currency depreciation of 186 per cent occurred in 1988 and caused the discrepancy between the mean annual depreciation (6.2) and the median (0). Jordan also had low exchange rate volatility, with the average exchange rate per USD being fixed at 0.709 from 1996 until 2005. Earlier, in 1989, the largest currency depreciation was 54 per cent. As a result, the mean annual depreciation was 3 per cent for the period 1975–2005 compared to a median of 0. In Yemen, the exchange rate per USD was fixed at 12.01 from 1990 until 1994. In 1995, a major currency depreciation of 240 per cent took place, followed by two years of large but less intense depreciations. This contributed to a mean drop of 30 per cent for the period 1990–2005 compared to a median of 4 per cent. As for Lebanon, the period average exchange rate per USD has been fixed since 2000 at 1507.5. The period 1984 until 1992 was characterised by large annual currency depreciation with the largest being of 485 per cent in 1987. This resulted in a mean depreciation of 37 per cent and a median of 2 per cent.

Unlike Turkey and Iran, Cyprus enjoyed relatively low exchange rate variability for the period 1975–2005. Its largest currency depreciation was 19 per cent in 1981 and its largest appreciation was 15.5 per cent in both 1986 and 2003. For the period under study, Cyprus had a mean annual depreciation of 1.3 per cent and a median of 0.7 per cent. Iran's exchange rate depreciated sharply in 1993 with the period average exchange rate per USD falling by 1834 per cent in that year. The Iranian currency also dropped by 294 per cent in 2002. Otherwise, exchange rate movements were low to moderate and this resulted in a mean annual depreciation of 79 per cent for the period 1975–2005 and a median of 0.2 per cent. As for Turkey, high exchange rate volatility marked the period from 1978 until 2002, with the largest currency depreciations against the USD occurring in 1994 (170 per cent) and 1980 (144 per cent). Thus the mean annual depreciation (49 per cent) was close to the median (46 per cent).

3 Testing methodology

Our methodology is in line with the models used in the international literature that has addressed the impact of exchange rate regimes on macroeconomic variables (Husain, Mody and Rogoff, 2005; Levy-Yeyati and Sturzenegger, 2001; Ghosh, Gulde and Wolf, 1998; Ghosh *et al*, 1997; Edwards and Losada, 1994). The resulting empirical specification is represented by:

$$INFL_{it} = a_0 + a_1\ INFL_{it-1} + a_2\ RGDP_{it} + a_3\ INT_{it} + a_4\ M_{2it} + a_5\ EXR_{it} + a_6\ REG_{it} + U_{it}$$

where i stands for the ith country and t for the *t*th time period and where:

INFL = the inflation rate measured as the annual percentage change in the Consumer price index.

RGDP = rate of growth of real GDP;

INT= nominal interest rate (deposit rate);

M_2= the rate of growth of broad money (money + quasi money);

EXR = annual percent change in the period average exchange rate against the US dollar;

REG_t= a dummy that takes the value of 1 when an observation is classified as a pegged regime and 0 when it is classified as managed or independently floating;

U = error term.

The exchange rate change variable (EXR) was not included in the previous studies reviewed as they used exchange rate dummies to examine the link between the nature of the exchange rate regime and price stability. However, it was decided when examining the raw data that *de facto* exchange rate arrangements were not necessarily always successful in maintaining the value of the exchange rate specified by the arrangement. In addition, *de facto* exchange rate pegs were changed regularly for many countries in the sample over the period of study.

It was decided to examine the effect of this variable on inflation in the absence of regime dummies and also in their presence, as we wanted to study this relationship irrespective of the nature of the exchange rate regime. The exchange rate regime dummy is included to capture the effects of the exchange rate regimes on inflation through channels other than those passing via the growth of broad money M_2. The inflation rate is also regressed on the lagged inflation rate ($INFL_{t-1}$) to control for the effect of past inflation on current inflation expectations. Dropping foreign inflation from the empirical testing specification is motivated by the fact that changes in this variable should be captured and absorbed by the exchange rate changes examined in the various runs.

As far as the dependent variable is concerned, as Table 8.2 shows, some countries exhibit high and even hyper-inflation in one or more years, which means that there are countries that could be outliers with respect to this exogenous variable used in the econometric model. We therefore had the choice of either eliminating these countries or retaining them by using the relevant best known statistical techniques to adjust for the outliers. As the first choice implies losing many observations, it was decided to utilise the second option, employing the following steps. We first estimated the model and examined the results before we deleted any outliers. Then we deleted data points that we thought were producing extreme biases and ran the model again to compare the results. We also attempted to run the model by making the assumption in case of high or hyper-inflation that any inflation rate which is, for example, above 100 per cent could be rounded down to 100 per cent. An alternative was to use the log of inflation rather than inflation itself to smoothen sharp changes or fluctuations in the inflation rate.

Our sample consists of annual observations for 18 MENA countries over the period 1975–2005. The empirical investigation was limited to this specific period because of data availability and our interest in examining relatively recent inflation behaviour and linkages. The period considered, provides a large or at least acceptable number of annual observations, with a dataset consisting of 31 observations per country and thus a total of 578 observations as a whole. However, missing or interrupted data for one or more years concerning one or more variables resulted in fewer observations, depending on the specifications. To illustrate, data availability with regard to the dependent variable was limited to 29 observations for the period studied (1975-2005) in two countries (Qatar and UAE) and to 28 observations in Oman and to no more than 16 observations in Yemen.

Data availability regarding one of our explanatory variables (interest rates) varied across countries over the period in question and that was another reason for having an even smaller number of observations (smaller sample) in one of the regressions. There are also other issues, related to experimentation with different lags and to regime dummies which were available only from 1990 to 2005, which influenced the specifications and the number of observations as was discussed in section 2. The main sources of our data are the IMF *International Financial Statistics* CD-ROM and the *World Economic Outlook* databases for INFL and RGDP, the IMF *International Financial Statistics* CD-ROM for INT, M_2 , and EXR, the IMF *Annual Reports* and Bubula and Okter-Robe (2002) for exchange rate arrangement dummies. In very rare cases, and when necessary to supply missing data, we relied on central bank bulletins and reports of the countries in question. The list of sample countries is presented in Table 8.1.

4 Empirical results

The findings of our econometric investigation are displayed in Table 8.3 which reports the results of five different specifications depending on which explanatory variables are used in the regression equation and the time period.

In the first specification in column 1, we exclude the exchange rate regime dummy to examine the impact of exchange rate changes on inflation in the absence of this variable. The second specification in column 2 includes the exchange rate dummy variable but leaves out the exchange rate variable to test the link between the nature of the exchange rate regime and inflation. The third regression in column 3 includes all the explanatory variables mentioned above.

The results reported in Table 8.3 show that changes in the exchange rates are significant in both the specifications that include the dependant variable of inflation (columns 1 and 3). The exchange rate regime dummy is not significant in either of the specifications that include the dependent variable of inflation (columns 2 and 3). Most importantly, the dummy does not have an independent effect on inflation in column 3 when all the other macroeconomic variables are controlled for in comparison to the significant effect of the exchange rate variable.

This could indicate that no significant difference between various *de facto* exchange rate arrangements exists as far as inflation is concerned, supporting the idea that the actual behaviour of the exchange rate under the strong commitment to the peg is the one to bring the benefit in terms of lower inflation in emerging economies. It is also consistent with the cases of many industrial countries where price stability has been achieved irrespective of the nature of their exchange rate regimes. However, the results could possibly imply that the dummy variable is too simple or too weak in this data set. The significance of the exchange rate change (EXR) variable which measures the real impact of exchange rates may indicate that exchange rate regimes do matter. In this case, the present results may be less out of line with some results in the literature.

Therefore, this paper addresses not only the issue of successful versus unsuccessful exchange rate pegs and arrangements, but also the significance, if any, of the impact of these arrangements on price stability. The findings on the insignificance of the exchange rate dummies do not coincide with some of the results reached in the literature on pegged exchange rate arrangements, particularly the study reviewed earlier by Ghosh *et al.* (1997) which showed that inflation is lower and more stable under fixed exchange rate regimes. The results also do not coincide with the findings in the study by Levy-Yeyati and Sturzenegger (2001) which showed that a relationship appears between fixed exchange rate regimes and inflation when long pegs are considered. However, our results are in line with some findings on industrial countries which indicate that there is no significant link between exchange rate regimes and inflation irrespective of the period of the peg (Levy-Yeyati and Sturzenegger, 2001) and some findings on emerging markets which show that the exchange rate regime does not seem to have a systematic effect on inflation (Husain, Mody and Rogoff, 2005). In addition, the latter study found that pegged exchange rate regimes seem to deliver low inflation rates with these rates remaining low as countries move to more flexible ones.

The results of the present study also show that in the three specifications in columns 1, 2 and 3 of Table 8.3 the coefficients for growth in broad money are all highly significant and of the expected sign. Lagged inflation is also significant in the first specification and highly significant in the other two. This is largely consistent with the theory linking money to prices and past inflation to current inflationary expectations. The interest rate and real GDP growth variables, however, are insignificant. It is worth mentioning that even if we exclude from the sample high inflation observations with annual inflation rates above 100 percent to reduce the influence of outliers, the findings remain the same in terms of the significance of various variables.

Contemporaneous explanatory variables (except lagged inflation) were initially used but the significance of the growth in the broad money variable in the first specification was substantially improved when it was lagged by one period. We conducted hypothesis testing with contemporaneous variables in an attempt to know the speed at which changes in the explanatory variables were translated into higher prices. The standard errors reported are corrected for heteroscedasticity and serial correlation and some of the diagnostic tests to assess the goodness of fit of the model are reported in the notes beneath the table.

Subsequently, two separate data analyses were conducted. The first was designed to disaggregate the specification in column 1 of Table 8.3 into two sub-periods, 1975–1989 and 1990–2005, in order to examine the relationship before and after the new data on exchange rate classification became available. The results, reported in columns 4 and 5 of Table 8.3, are in line with the initial results of the study in terms of the significance of various variables. However, the variable representing the percentage change in the exchange rate (EXR) is more significant in column 4 (1975–1989) than in column 5 (1990–2005).

The opposite holds true for the growth rate of the money variable. This could be attributed to the fact that the first period witnessed more exchange rate volatility (as discussed in section 2) than did the second period where many countries adopted more pegged-type exchange rate arrangements. The volatility in exchange rates could have helped the authorities to maintain stronger control over money supply growth, causing inflation to move more with the exchange rate rather than money supply behaviour.

Table 8.3 Macroeconomic variables associated with inflation

	Specification (1)	*Specification (2)*	*Specification (3)*	*Specification (4)*	*Specification (5)*
Real GDP growth (RGDP)	–0.016 (0.100)	–0.054 (0.079)	–0.022 (0.083)	–0.090 (0.112)	0.056 (0.075)
Growth rate in money and Quasi money (M_2)	0.176*** (0.053)	0.403*** (0.121)	0.361*** (0.104)	0.141** (0.062)	0.362*** (0.120)
Percent changes in the exchange rate (EXR)	0.636*** (0.174)		0.108*** (0.040)	0.277*** (0.098)	0.139** (0.057)
Interest rate (INT)	0.014 (0.200)	0.102 (0.195)	0.058 (0.179)	–0.133 (0.203)	0.146 (0.182)
Lagged inflation (INFL – 1)	0.145* (0.086)	0.446*** (0.134)	0.427*** (0.125)	0.399*** (0.153)	0.351*** (0.120)
Regime dummy (REG)		–0.556 (1.247)	–0.185 (1.047)		
Time period	1975–2005	1975–2005	1975–2005	1975–1989	1990–2005
Number of observations	395	226	226	169	213
Cross sections	17	16	16	15	16
R-squared	0.814	0.913	0.922	0.830	0.920
F-statistic	340.00***	461.40***	429.63***	87.27***	479.19***
Akaike Info Criterion	8.056	6.319	6.222	7.257	6.189
Durbin-Watson stat	2.016	2.065	2.039	2.027	2.053

Notes:

a Standard errors are in parentheses.

b One, two and three asterisks indicate significance levels of 10, 5 and 1 per cent respectively. Dependent variable is inflation.

The second analysis was to separate the group of countries into the three classifications described in Table 8.3 and run pooled data regressions individually on the three separate sub-samples: GCC (six countries), North Africa (five countries), and other MENA (seven countries). The influence of the exchange rate regime dummy on inflation remained insignificant across the three sub-samples whereas the exchange rate variable remained significant. The results concerning the other explanatory variables remained the same in terms of significance.

5 Conclusion

The impact of exchange rate arrangements on some economic variables in selected MENA countries has been addressed in the literature dealing with exchange rate regimes. Studies have also examined the choice of exchange rate regimes by considering the conditions under which MENA countries should float, peg, or follow a more flexible system. These countries have pursued various *de facto* exchange rate arrangements over the period of study within each country where different regimes were used historically and across the chosen sample. Similarly, some countries have implemented *de facto* exchange rate arrangements that deviate from officially announced ones. The current study differentiates itself from existing ones by attempting to examine the impact of the behaviour of exchange rates and of the exchange rate regimes on price stability in a selected group of eighteen MENA countries for a period extending from 1975 to 2005, pooling time-series and cross-sectional data in a pooled regression framework.

The results of the present study show that the actual behaviour of the exchange rate along with other monetary variables such as the rate of growth of money and lagged inflation are significant in terms of their impact on inflation rates. Our results also did not find any significant difference between various *de facto* exchange rate arrangements, which implies that for the countries in our sample and the period considered the choice of the adopted exchange rate regime is not significant. The results concerning all variables remained the same in terms of significance after we disaggregated the period into two sub-periods and after we separated the group of countries into the three classifications described in Table 8.3 and ran pooled data regressions individually on the three separate sub-samples: GCC (six countries), North Africa (five countries), and other MENA (seven countries).

These findings do not coincide with some of the results reached in the literature on pegged exchange rate arrangements around the world, which show in some studies that inflation is lower and more stable under fixed exchange rate regimes or in others that a relationship appears between fixed exchange rate regimes and inflation when long pegs are considered.

On the other hand, our results are in line with some findings on industrial countries according to which there is no significant link between exchange rate regimes and inflation irrespective of the period of the peg and with studies on some emerging markets according to which the exchange rate regime does not have a systematic effect on inflation. However, the results on the significance of the exchange rate variable rather than the regime dummy may imply that the dummy variable is too simple or too weak in this data set.

The significance of the exchange rate change variable which measures the effect of actual exchange rates could possibly indicate that exchange rate regimes matter. In this case, the present results may be less out of line with the results in the literature. Finally, we should note that recommendations on the choice of the exchange rate regime to be adopted in various MENA countries are beyond the scope of the current study.

Notes

1 See any IMF annual report starting from the year 2000 for an explanation of the different categories.
2 See Bubula and Otker-Robe (2002) for a discussion on the limitations associated with a classification based purely on quantitative analysis.

References

Bailliu, J., Lafrance, R., and Perrault, J-F. (2003) 'Does Exchange Rate Policy Matter for Growth?'. *International Finance*, 63: 381–414.

Bhattacharya, R. (2003) 'Exchange Rate Regime Considerations for Jordan and Lebanon'. International Monetary Fund Working Paper 03/137.

Bubula, A., and Otker-Robe, I. (2002) 'The Evolution of Exchange Rate Regimes Since 1990: Evidence from De Facto Policies'. *International Monetary Fund Working Paper* 02/155.

Domac, I., and Shabsigh, G. (1999) 'Real Exchange Rate Behaviour and Economic Growth: Evidence from Egypt, Jordan, Morocco, and Tunisia' International Monetary Fund Working Paper 99/40.

Edwards, S., and Losada, F. (1994) 'Fixed Exchange Rates, Inflation and Macroeconomic Discipline'. National Bureau of Economic Research Working Paper 4661.

Ghosh, A., Gulde, A-M., and Wolf, H. (1998) 'Currency Boards: The Ultimate Fix?' International Monetary Fund Working Paper 98/8.

Ghosh, A., Gulde, A-M., Ostry, J., and Wolf, H. (1997) 'Does the Nominal Exchange Rate Regime Matter?' National Bureau of Economic Research Working Paper 5874.

Husain, A., Mody, A., and Rogoff, K. (2005) 'Exchange Rate Regime Durability and Performance in Developing versus Advanced Economies'. *Journal of Monetary Economics*, 52: 35–64.

International Monetary Fund *Annual Reports*, various issues.

International Monetary Fund *International Financial Statistics*, CD-ROM.

International Monetary Fund *World Economic Outlook*, Database.

Jbili, A., and Kramarenko, V. (2003) 'Should MENA Countries Float or Peg?' *Finance and Development*, 40(1): 30–33.

Kamar, B. (2004) 'De Facto Exchange Rate Policies in the MENA Region: Toward Deeper Cooperation'. Paper presented at the 11th Annual Conference of the Economic Research Forum, December 16–18, Beirut, Lebanon.

Karam, P. (2001) 'Exchange Rate Policies in Arab Countries: Assessment and Recommendations'. Arab Monetary Fund, December.

Levy-Yehati, E. and Sturzenegger, F. (2000) 'Classifying Exchange Rate Regimes: Deeds vs Words' *European Economic Review*, 49, 1603-35

Levy-Yehati, E., and Sturzenegger, F. (2001) 'Exchange Rate Regimes and Economic Performance'. *International Monetary Fund Staff Papers*, 47: 62–98.

Nabli, M., and Veganzones-Varoudakis, M-A. (2002) 'Exchange Rate Regime and Competitiveness of Manufactured Exports: The Case of MENA Countries'. MENA Working Paper 207, World Bank.

Reinhart, C., and Rogoff, K. (2004) 'The Modern History of Exchange Rate Arrangements: A Reinterpretation'. *The Quarterly Journal of Economics*, 94: 1–48.

9 Exchange rate regimes for small countries

An application to the Maghreb countries

Chrysost Bangaké, Jean-Baptiste Desquilbet and Nabil Jedlane

Introduction

The choice of exchange rate regime for small countries is a question which is attracting increasing attention. The interest in this topic has been reinforced by the unfortunate experiences of some emerging market countries in recent years in managing their exchange rates. Recent experience may seem to favour freely floating exchange rates or hard pegs, but economists have held different and changing views on the choice of exchange rate regimes. At the beginning of the 1960s,[1] the literature stressed the effects of shocks on the domestic economy as the crucial criterion. According to this approach, the choice between flexible or fixed exchange rate regimes depends on the nature and sources of the shocks which affect the domestic economy. The main result of these studies was to indicate the superiority of the flexible exchange rate regime if the economy faces primarily real shocks such as fluctuations in national aggregate demand. However, when the economy faces nominal shocks, for example to money demand, a fixed exchange rate is preferable. Edwards and Levy-Yeyati (2003) and Broda (2004) confirm this point of view, which contrasts with the argument supported by the cycle school to the effect that there is no significant difference between exchange rate regimes.[2]

Furthermore, the contribution of Barro and Gordon (1983a, 1983b) allowed the issue of exchange rate regime choice to be related in a new perspective to the credibility of the policymaker. Barro and Gordon (1983a, 1983b) tackle the case of a central bank which uses discretionary monetary policy to generate surprise inflation in order to reduce unemployment. They show that with rational expectations the result would be higher inflation but the same unemployment because people adjust their inflationary expectations in a way that eliminates any consistent pattern of surprises. The only way to protect against this time-inconsistency is to institute a commitment mechanism which ties the hands of the monetary authorities. In this configuration, a fixed exchange rate regime could provide a clear nominal anchor and help to establish a stabilisation programme (Guillaume and Stasavage, 2000).

Since the middle of the 1990s, theoretical and empirical studies have made it possible to refine the debate on the choice of exchange rate regimes. On the one hand, the banking and currency crises in Asia and Latin America have reinforced the support for exchange rate regimes at each end of the spectrum – either a pure free floating rate or a strongly fixed rate (Calvo and Reinhart, 2002; Masson, 2001; Fischer, 2001; Razin and Rubinstein, 2006). In this perspective, Razin and Rubinstein have shown that the influence of currency regimes on the overall macroeconomic performance depends on the likelihood of sudden stops of capital flows. Thus countries with a low probability of crisis can benefit from an exchange rate peg and capital market liberalisation. Countries with an intermediate level of crisis probability might benefit from a more flexible exchange rate regime and some controls on capital flows. Thus, there is no universally optimal regime.[3]

On the other hand, recent theoretical literature has analysed exchange rate regimes in a general equilibrium model with nominal rigidities (Bayoumi, 1994; Obstfeld and Rogoff, 1995; Ricci, 1997; Corsetti and Pesenti, 2001). Our model is part of this tradition insofar as it draws on the study of Ricci (1997) on Optimum Currency Area (OCA) theory. However, while these studies focus on a two-country theoretical model, our study introduces a three-country model with two small countries (1 and 2) and a large one (3). The main results show that the choice of exchange rate regime for a small country depends on its economic features, the nature of the shocks it faces, the degree of monetary policy autonomy, the nature of the large country shocks and finally the type of fixed exchange regime considered.

In the Maghreb countries, the recent call of the Union of Maghreb Banks in November 2007 (Maghreb Arabe Press, 2007) to create a single money for the Maghreb has provoked some doubts concerning such a project and has renewed interest in the question of the appropriate exchange rate regimes for the Maghreb countries. It is clear that the successful launch of the euro has stimulated interest in other regions. Monetary union is seen as a way of reinforcing regional cohesion and demonstrating a commitment to regional solidarity.

It is useful to point out that the main motives for monetary integration in Maghreb countries come from the desire to reinforce the integration of the real economies of the region and concerns with macroeconomic stability, economic growth, and historical and cultural links (Bangaké, Belhadj, and Jedlane, 2007). However, the European monetary union experience shows how long the road really is. If the objective of monetary integration seems well founded, it is clear that the structural differences among Maghreb countries could inhibit progress toward monetary integration. In particular, Maghreb countries face different shocks, so that the choice of exchange rate regimes is complex and needs to be carefully examined.

That is the purpose of this chapter, to examine the optimal exchange rate regime for Maghreb countries. It starts in section 1 by assessing the brief economic background of these countries, particularly Algeria, Morocco and Tunisia.[4] Section 2 then considers a three-country theoretical model which extends the two-country model by Ricci (1997) in order to analyse different kinds of fixed or flexible exchange rate regimes. While section 3 examines shocks and adjustments, section 4 presents an evaluation of the exchange rate regime. Finally section 5 concludes with a broader look at the external arrangements that might be appropriate for Maghreb countries.

1 Brief economic background of Algeria, Morocco and Tunisia

In this section, we present a brief synopsis of the economies of Algeria, Morocco and Tunisia. The purpose is to provide the reader with background information on the three countries. We provide basic macroeconomic indicators on trade links, the evolution of the exchange rate, budget balance and other main economic indicators. Although promoting trade in the Maghreb region is an explicit objective of the various national authorities, internal trade remains quite low (see tables 9.1 and 9.2 which show bilateral trade between pairs of countries).

As table 9.1 shows, the trade among the three Maghreb countries (Algeria, Morocco, and Tunisia) is still low. For example, exports from Algeria to Morocco or Tunisia do not exceed 1 per cent of Algeria's total exports, at 0.72 per cent and 0.43 per cent respectively. These values are still low when bilateral trade is normalised by Gross Domestic Product (GDP). On the import side, the relationships are the same. Although the Maghreb countries are beginning to reap the benefits of trade liberalisation (for example, Moroccan imports from Algeria exceed 1 per cent of its total imports) trade among them is still modest. This situation could be explained by a high tariff protection averaging nearly 20 per cent in the region, roughly 10 percentage points above the world average (Allain and Loko, 2007).

However, tables 9.1 and 9.2 also identify the non-negligible trade flows between the Maghreb countries and the European Union. Trade with the European Union

Table 9.1 Maghreb exports: Intra-regional and with the European Union, averages, 1996–2005

	Bilateral Trade[a] *as a share of total exports (%)*	*Bilateral Trade*[a] *as a share of GDP (%)*
Algeria		
Exports to Morocco	0.72	0.23
Exports to Tunisia	0.43	0.13
Exports to EU	61.41	19.58
Morocco		
Exports to Algeria	0.26	0.04
Exports to Tunisia	0.69	0.12
Exports to EU	69.29	13.74
Tunisia		
Exports to Algeria	1.09	0.35
Exports to Morocco	0.67	0.21
Exports to EU	80.43	26.00

Source: IMF, Direction of Trade Statistics database.

Notes:
a Bilateral trade is calculated by averaging exports from country 1 to country 2 over 1996–2005.

Table 9.2 Maghreb imports: Intra-regional and with the European Union, averages, 1996–2005

	Bilateral Trade[a] as a share of total imports (%)	*Bilateral Trade[a] as a share of GDP (%)*
Algeria		
Imports from Morocco	0.15	0.03
Imports from Tunisia	0.55	0.11
Imports from EU	61.03	12.27
Morocco		
Imports from Algeria	1.25	0.41
Imports from Tunisia	0.34	0.11
Imports from EU	56.69	18.41
Tunisia		
Imports from Algeria	0.90	0.40
Imports from Morocco	0.58	0.26
Imports from EU	72.26	32.63

Source: IMF, Direction of Trade Statistics database.

Notes:
a Bilateral trade is calculated by averaging imports of 1 from 2 over 1996–2005.

exceeds 61 per cent, 69 per cent and 80 per cent of total exports respectively in Algeria, Morocco and Tunisia. On the import side, the situation is the same. The European Union is an important destination for Maghreb countries' exports and source for their imports. Substantial trade with the European Union could involve an important policy choice for these countries, for example whether to peg or not to the euro.

What are the Maghreb countries' experiences with independent currency regimes over the last 10 years? The objective of the analysis here is twofold. First, and most importantly, Maghreb countries currently involved in proposals to form a monetary union, particularly an Arab Maghreb Union (Masson and Patillo, 2004), have to evaluate the potential desirability of such arrangements against the costs and benefits of the alternative, which is the continued use of independent currencies, in either a flexible or a fixed rate system. Second, by highlighting periods or situations during which exchange rate management became a key macroeconomic instrument, some important policy choices are drawn for Maghreb exchange rate regimes.

Note that we use first the official classifications published by the International Monetary Fund (IMF) (2006), which are *de jure* or based on countries' self-reporting of their regime. Then, an alternative classification scheme based on observed behaviour, provided by Levy-Yeyati and Sturzenegger (2005) and Reinhart and Rogoff (2004), is used.

As table 9.3 shows, according to the *de jure* classification, while Algeria and

Table 9.3 Evolution of the exchange rate regimes in the Maghreb countries, 1996–2006

			Exchange arrangement		
Country	*Currency*	*Article VIII Acceptance date*[a]	*IMF classification*[b]	*Levy-Yeyati & Sturzenegger*[c]	*Reinhart & Rogoff*[d]
Algeria	Algerian dinar	Sep-97	1996–2006 **MF**	1996–1997 **IN** 1996–2001 **FL**	1996–2001 **2**
Morocco	Dirham	Jan-93	1996–2006 **P**	–	1996–2001 **3**
Tunisia	Tunisian dinar	Jan-93	1996–1998 **MF** 1999 **CP** 2000–2001 **MF** 2002–2004 **CP** 2005–2006 **MF**	1996 **IN** 1997 **FL** 1998 **FX** 1999–2001 **IN**	1996–2001 **2**

Notes and Sources:

a Acceptance of article VIII of the IMF's Articles of Agreement commits a country to currency convertibility for international payments for goods and services.

b IMF classification, 1996–2006:
NL Exchange arrangements with o separate legal tender
CB Currency Board Arrangement
P Conventional pegged arrangement
BH Pegged exchange rate within horizontal bands
CP Crawling peg
BC Crawling band
MF Managed floating with no preannounced path for the exchange rate
IF Independently floating

c Levy-Yeyati, E., and Sturzenegger, F., (2005) 1996–2001:
FL Float
IN Intermediate (dirty; dirty/crawling peg)
FX Fix

d Reinhart, C., and Rogoff, K. (2004) 1996–2001:
Fixed
Crawling peg or band
Managed floating/wide crawling band/moving band
Freely floating
Freely falling.

Tunisia had managed floating with no pre-announced path for the exchange rate in 2006, Morocco was classified as having a conventional pegged arrangement, more precisely a peg to a basket of currencies. The successful launch of the euro has further significant repercussions for the evolution of the exchange rate regime in Morocco. For example, the weight of the euro in the basket of currencies is 80 per cent while the US dollar represents 20 per cent as of 2006 (Jedlane, 2006). In the period 1996–2006, Tunisia practiced either managed floating or a crawling peg.

When we consider the *de facto* classification according to Levy-Yeyati and Sturzenegger (2005) or the Reinhart and Rogoff (2004) classification, there appears to be some ''*fear of floating*''. For example, while the *de jure* classification identifies Tunisia as a managed floating regime in 1998, an alternative classification based on observed behaviour suggests a fixed exchange rate regime.[5]

Table 9.4 Average performance of Maghreb countries under different regimes 1996–2006[a]

Performance indicator	*Algeria Managed float (1996–2006)*	*Morocco Conventional pegged (1996–2006)*	*Tunisia under managed floating (1996–1998, 2000–2001, 2005–2006)*	*Tunisia under crawling peg (1999, 2002–2004)*
Exchange rate				
Exchange rate volatility	0.013	0.017	0.018	0.017
Real GDP				
Growth	3.80	4.0	5.0	4.6
Per capita growth	2.10	2.8	3.7	3.5
Percent change in				
Terms of Trade	7.6	–1.8	0.5	0.0
REER	–1.5	0.0	–2.1	–0.8
Inflation	4.1	1.7	2.9	3.0
Budget balance as percent GDP	4.89	–3.02	–4.08	–2.95

Note:

a IMF classification (*de jure* classification) used to identify exchange rate regime periods. Regimes classified as managed floating or independently floating are termed *flexible*.

How did the exchange rate systems of the Maghreb countries perform in terms of key macroeconomic indicators in the period 1996–2006? Table 9.4 summarises the average performance of the Maghreb countries during their periods of flexibility (managed floating) as well as crawling peg or conventional pegged arrangements.

In general, flexible exchange rate systems (managed floating) have been associated with favourable macroeconomic effects in Algeria and Tunisia. Growth in real GDP is higher on average (see table 9.4 where real GDP is 3.80 per cent in Algeria and 5.0 per cent in Tunisia). Table 9.4 also indicates that the Real Effective Exchange Rates (REERs) have depreciated on average during these countries' flexible periods. In general this depreciation was accompanied by an improvement of the terms of trade (by 7.6 per cent in Algeria and 0.5 per cent in Tunisia). Furthermore, in Algeria and Tunisia managed floating has contributed to moderate inflation (4.1 per cent in Algeria and 2.9 per cent in Tunisia). However, the situation concerning the budget balance is mixed. While the budget balance has been in surplus in Algeria, probably due to oil exports, on average the fiscal deficit of Tunisia under managed floating has been around 4.1 per cent.

The countries' experiences with fixed or adjustable pegs are somewhat different in terms of economic performance. While growth in both real GDP and real GDP per capita is higher on average in Morocco and Tunisia during basket peg and crawling peg systems (see table 9.4), other performance indicators are mixed. In Morocco, basket pegs were associated with low inflation (1.7 per cent), a deterioration in the terms of trade (–1.7 per cent) and a fiscal deficit of around 3 per cent. In Tunisia some macroeconomic indicators improved in the crawling peg period. The fiscal deficit is somewhat lower than in the managed floating period and the depreciation of the REER is –0.8 per cent compared to –2.1 per cent under the managed float.

2 The model

We develop a three-country theoretical model extending the two-country model by Ricci (1997), which allows for analyses of different kinds of fixed or flexible exchange rate regimes. The theoretical model is based on a Ricardian model of free trade, with specialised economies each producing one traded and one non-traded good. The analysis is static and ignores the existence and accumulation of capital. Labour is fully mobile between sectors within the same country but immobile between countries. Money is taken into account through standard Cambridge equations. Inflation occurs whenever the demand for goods rises above full capacity, unemployment whenever the demand for goods falls below full capacity. Exchange rates are determined by trade balance equilibrium in flexible exchange rate regimes, whereas any kind of fixed exchange regime puts some constraints on the money supply.

Markets for goods

The traded goods denoted A, B and C and non-traded goods N_1, N_2 and N_3 are produced respectively by countries 1, 2 and 3. The three countries are endowed with fixed quantities of labour, denoted L_1, L_2 and L_3. Production functions exhibit constant returns to scale, which is consistent with complete specialisation.

Supplies of goods are given by

$$A^s = \theta_A L_A \quad B^s = \theta_B L_B \quad C^s = \theta_C L_C \quad N_1^s = \theta_{N1} L_{N1} \quad N_2^s = \theta_{N2} L_{N2} \quad N_3^s = \theta_{N3} L_{N3}$$

$$L_A + L_{N1} \leq L_1 \quad L_B + L_{N2} \leq L_2 \quad L_C + L_{N3} \leq L_3$$

where θ_i and L_i denote respectively the average (and marginal) labour productivity and the employment level in sector i.

Firms behave competitively. The zero-profit condition in each sector implies that the real wage is equal to labour productivity

$$\frac{W_1}{P_A} = \theta_A \quad \frac{W_1}{P_{N1}} = \theta_{N1} \quad \frac{W_2}{P_B} = \theta_B \quad \frac{W_2}{P_{N2}} = \theta_{N2} \quad \frac{W_3}{P_C} = \theta_C \quad \frac{W_3}{P_{N3}} = \theta_{N3}$$

where w_1, w_2 and w_3 are nominal wages in countries 1, 2 and 3, respectively, and P_i is the price of goods in sector i (in the currency of the employers' or producers' country).

Consumers have Cobb–Douglas preferences over the three traded goods (A, B and

C) and their home country non-traded good (N_1 or N_2 or N_3). Preferences are assumed to differ in the three countries in order to investigate the effects of the degree of openness and of the symmetry of shocks on the desirability of a currency union.

The representative consumer k of country 1 maximises the following utility function

$$U_i = A_k^{\alpha_1} B_k^{\beta_1} C_k^{\gamma_1} N_{1k}^{1-\alpha_1-\beta_1-\gamma_1}$$

subject to the budget constraint

$$P_A A_k + \frac{P_B}{e_1}\tau_1 B_k + P_C e_3 \tau_3 C_k + P_{N1} N_{1k} = Y_k$$

Likewise, the representative consumer m of country 2 maximises

$$U_m = A_m^{\alpha_2} B_m^{\beta_2} C_m^{\gamma_2} N_{2m}^{1-\alpha_2-\beta_2-\gamma_2}$$

subject to

$$P_A e_1 \tau_1 A_m + P_B B_m + P_C e_2 \tau_2 C_m + P_{N2} N_{2m} = Y_m$$

and the representative consumer n of country 3 maximises

$$U_n = A_n^{\alpha_3} B_n^{\beta_3} C_n^{\gamma_3} N_n^{1-\alpha_3-\beta_3-\gamma_3}$$

subject to

$$\frac{P_A}{e_3}\tau_3 A_n + \frac{P_B}{e_2}\tau_2 B_n + P_C C_n + P_{N3} N_{3j} = Y_n$$

where e_1, e_2 and e_3 are respectively the nominal exchange rates between countries 1 and 2, countries 2 and 3 and countries 1 and 3. The parameters τ_1, τ_2 and τ_3 (>1) indicate the presence of Samuelson's iceberg-type transactions costs between countries 1 and 2, countries 2 and 3 and countries 1 and 3 respectively. The consumer needs to buy τ units of foreign goods to consume 1 unit. In a currency union $\tau = e = 1$, and the transactions costs disappear.

Y_1, Y_2 and Y_3 are the respective nominal incomes of countries 1, 2 and 3. In the absence of dividends paid to workers, wages constitute the only source of income. The nominal incomes are therefore equal to wages multiplied by the amount of labour:

$$Y_1 = W_1(L_A + L_{N1}) \leq W_1 L_1 \quad Y_2 = W_2(L_B + L_{N2}) \leq W_2 L_2 \quad Y_3 = W_3(L_C + L_{N3}) \leq W_3 L_3$$

where the equalities hold in full employment equilibria.

The income of the representative consumer in country *i* is simply Y_i / L_i.

Solving for the optimal consumption by representative consumers and computing for total consumption of goods yields:

$$A^d = \alpha_1 \frac{Y_1}{P_A} + \alpha_2 \frac{Y_2}{P_A e_1} + \alpha_3 \frac{Y_3 e_3}{P_A}$$

$$B^d = \beta_1 \frac{Y_1 e_1}{P_B} + \beta_2 \frac{Y_2}{P_B} + \beta_3 \frac{Y_3 e_2}{P_B}$$

$$C^d = \gamma_1 \frac{Y_1}{P_C e_3} + \gamma_2 \frac{Y_2}{P_C e_2} + \gamma_3 \frac{Y_3}{P_C}$$

$$N_1^d = (1-\alpha_1 - \beta_1 - \gamma_1) \frac{Y_1}{P_{N_1}}$$

$$N_2^d = (1-\alpha_2 - \beta_2 - \gamma_2) \frac{Y_2}{P_{N_2}}$$

$$N_3^d = (1-\alpha_3 - \beta_3 - \gamma_3) \frac{Y_3}{P_{N_3}}$$

Preference parameter α_i measures the share of country A's traded good in country i's consumption. The same interpretation holds for the other preference parameters.

Prices are assumed to be flexible. Equilibrium in each sector yields:

$$A = \alpha_1 \frac{Y_1}{P_A} + \alpha_2 \frac{Y_2}{P_A e_1} + \alpha_3 \frac{Y_3 e_3}{P_A} = \theta_A L_A$$

$$B = \beta_1 \frac{Y_1 e_1}{P_B} + \beta_2 \frac{Y_2}{P_B} + \beta_3 \frac{Y_3 e_2}{P_B} = \theta_B L_B$$

$$C = \gamma_1 \frac{Y_1}{P_C e_3} + \gamma_2 \frac{Y_2}{P_C e_2} + \gamma_3 \frac{Y_3}{P_C} = \theta_C L_C$$

$$N_1 = (1-\alpha_1 - \beta_1 - \gamma_1) \frac{Y_1}{P_{N_1}} = \theta_{N_1} L_{N_1}$$

$$N_2 = (1-\alpha_2 - \beta_2 - \gamma_2) \frac{Y_2}{P_{N_2}} = \theta_{N_2} L_{N_2}$$

$$N_3 = (1-\alpha_3 - \beta_3 - \gamma_3) \frac{Y_3}{P_{N_3}} = \theta_{N_3} L_{N_3}$$

Money, prices and exchange rates

Money is introduced by assuming a standard Cambridge equation, with a constant velocity.

Money market equilibrium in country *i* is hence assumed to be represented by

$$V_i M_i = Y_i$$

where M_i and V_i represent respectively money supply and velocity in country i.

Trade balance equilibrium is reached through nominal exchange rate adjustment in flexible exchange rate regimes. Trade balance equilibrium in countries 1, 2 and 3 respectively is given by

$$\alpha_2 . \frac{Y_2}{e_1} + \alpha_3\, e_3\, Y_3 - (\gamma_1 + \beta_1) Y_1 = 0$$

$$\beta_1\, e_1\, Y_1 + \beta_3\, e_2 Y_3 - (\alpha_2 + \gamma_2)\; Y_2 = 0$$

$$\gamma_1\, \frac{Y_1}{e_3} + \gamma_2\, \frac{Y_2}{e_2} - (\alpha_3 + \beta_3) . Y_3 = 0$$

Goods market equilibrium and trade balance yield the equilibrium prices of goods:

$$P_A = \frac{(\alpha_1 + \beta_1 + \gamma_1) Y_1}{\theta_A L_A};\; P_B = \frac{(\alpha_2 + \beta_2 + \gamma_2) Y_2}{\theta_B L_B};\; P_C = \frac{(\alpha_3 + \beta_3 + \gamma_3) Y_3}{\theta_C L_C}$$

Money market equilibrium and trade balance yield the equilibrium level of exchange rates in a flexible exchange rate regime:

$$e_1 = \frac{\alpha_2 \beta_3 + \alpha_3 (\alpha_2 + \gamma_2)}{\alpha_3 \beta_1 + \beta_3 (\beta_1 + \gamma_1)} \frac{V_2 M_2}{V_1 M_1} = s_1 \frac{V_2 M_2}{V_1 M_1}$$

$$e_2 = \frac{\gamma_2 \beta_1 + \gamma_1 (\alpha_2 + \gamma_2)}{\alpha_3 \beta_1 + \beta_3 (\beta_1 + \gamma_1)} \frac{V_2 M_2}{V_3 M_3} = s_2 \frac{V_2 M_2}{V_3 M_3}$$

$$e_3 = \frac{\gamma_2 \beta_1 + \gamma_1 (\alpha_2 + \gamma_2)}{\alpha_2 \beta_3 + \alpha_3 (\alpha_2 + \gamma_2)} \frac{V_1 M_1}{V_3 M_3} = s_3 \frac{V_1 M_1}{V_3 M_3}$$

Shocks

Preferences and monetary parameters are subject to shocks before consumers and firms make their optimal choice. Their percentage changes (denoted ^) are distributed as truncated normals, whose means, variances are in brackets:

$$\hat{\alpha}_i \sim N(0, \sigma_{\alpha_i})$$

$$\hat{\beta}_i \sim N(0, \sigma_{\beta_i})$$

$$\hat{\gamma}_i \sim N(0, \sigma_{\gamma_i})$$

$$\hat{V}_i \sim N(0, \sigma_{V_i})$$

Initial equilibrium

Firms' behaviour

Firms behave competitively and face a labour supply curve which is infinitely elastic at the given wage until full employment is reached. National employment cannot rise above full employment. Hence, after the resolution of uncertainty, domestic and foreign firms maximise profits subject to, respectively

$$w_1 = w_{S1} \;;\; L_A + L_{N1} \leq L_1$$

$$w_2 = w_{S2} \;;\; L_B + L_{N2} \leq L_2$$

$$w_3 = w_{S3} \;;\; L_C + L_{N3} \leq L_3$$

When the initial equilibrium is disturbed by an increase in demand for the goods of one country, firms in that country find it optimal to raise price, as they cannot hire more workers to produce more. When demand for the goods of one country goes down, in order to avoid losses (due to fixed wages), firms of that country will reduce employment until their aggregate output equals aggregate demand at the marginal cost pricing.

Uncertainty and the timing of actions

Uncertainty arises from goods demand and monetary shocks. We assume that the world is initially in full employment equilibrium. The corresponding wages are respectively w_1, w_2 and w_3.

Before the uncertainty is resolved, nominal wages are set at levels, w_{s1}, w_{s2} and w_{s3} which are above the equilibrium wages w_1, w_2 and w_3. Such an assumption introduces nominal rigidities and allows for the incorporation of an inflationary bias as in Barro and Gordon (1983a, 1983b).

After the resolution of uncertainty, with wages given, unexpected demand and monetary shocks appear, and firms choose the competitively optimal employment under the constraint that the equilibrium wages are given by

$$\hat{W}_i = \hat{M}_i + \hat{V}_i \text{ if } \hat{M}_i + \hat{V}_i \geq E(\hat{M}_i)$$

$$\hat{W}_i = E(\hat{M}_i) \text{ i } \hat{M}_i + \hat{V}_i \leq E(\hat{M}_i) \quad \text{(downwards nominal rigidity of wages).}$$

where $\hat{V}_i$, $\hat{M}_i$, $\hat{W}_i$ and $\hat{W}_{si}$ denote respectively the growth rates of the money velocity, money stock, wages and minimum wage of country i, and E ($\hat{M}_i$) = μ where μ_i is the inflation target of the monetary authorities in country i. The equilibrium price is given by

$$P_i = \frac{V_i . M_i}{\theta_i . L_i}$$

with $E(\theta i) = 0$.

Economic policy objectives

We define the *economic policy objectives* with respect to inflation and unemployment in order to measure the net benefits that are expected to arise from different exchange rate regimes. For example, OCA theory proposes that the benefits of participating in a single currency result from the difference between the gains from the adoption of the single currency and the adjustment costs in terms of inflation and unemployment. The economic policy objectives for inflation and unemployment used here are similar to the monetary authority's loss function used in macroeconomics since Barro and Gordon (1983a and 1983b). The square terms in our specification are superfluous because no trade-off exists between inflation and unemployment.

The economic policy objectives of country i are assumed to be

$$H^i = E\left(u^i + \lambda^i \pi^i + CT^i\right)$$

where E is the expectation operator, $u^i > 0$ is the unemployment rate, π^i is the inflation rate. In contrast with Ricci (1997), where the inflation rate is measured by the change in GDP-deflator, we assume that the inflation target is the increase in traded good prices. Although this is a strong hypothesis, it allows us to make the analysis more tractable. λ is the relative weight the authority assigns to inflation versus employment. The *economic policy objectives* are measured as a percentage of the labour force; as a consequence, transactions costs and unemployment have the same weight.

Transaction costs

As specified in the model of Ricci (1997), the transaction costs are meant to represent all the additional deadweight and efficiency losses implied by multiple currencies. Due to the Samuelson's iceberg assumption, paying transaction costs is like wasting hours of work.

$$CT = (\beta_1 + \gamma_1)Y_1 - \left(\frac{\beta_1}{\tau_1} + \frac{\gamma_1}{\tau_3}\right)Y_1$$

Country 1 spends $(\beta_1+\gamma_1)Y_1$ on foreign goods, but its citizens effectively consume

$$\frac{\beta_1 Y_1}{\tau_1} + \frac{\gamma_1 Y_1}{\tau_3}$$

the difference being due to the transaction costs. In equilibrium, $Y_1 = W_1 L_1$. The transaction costs faced by country 1 are calculated as the difference between the amount demanded and the amount consumed, as a percentage of the working population.

3 Shocks and adjustment

We analyse the consequences of the short run adjustment to shocks for unemployment and inflation, under different exchange rate regimes. Relative to Ricci, a larger array of possible exchange rate regimes is considered:

- a flexible exchange rate regime, in which all countries float against each other;
- a fixed exchange rate regime of the Bretton-Woods type (BW, Fix1) where the large country (Country 3) retains monetary autonomy;
- a fixed exchange rate regime of the European Monetary System type (EMS, Fix2): the two countries peg their bilateral exchange rate, one of them acting as the follower and the other being the leader;
- a monetary union between the two small countries (countries 1 and 2) which floats against the large country;
- an explicit euroisation of the small countries which form a *de facto* monetary union with the large country and import its monetary policy.

Unless otherwise specified, changes of variables are calculated from the initial equilibrium and are expressed in percentage terms.

Flexible exchange regime (Flex)

Under the flexible exchange rate regime, the money stock is exogenous (the money supply is controlled by the monetary authorities, $\hat{M} = \mu$), and the adjustment of the trade balance is due to the variation of the exchange rate. Given the hypotheses of a minimum wage ($\hat{W}_i = E(\hat{M}_i)$ if $\hat{M}_i + \hat{V}_i \leq E(\hat{M}_i)$) and maximum limit to labour supply, we can obtain the level of anticipated inflation and domestic unemployment.

Inflation

$$\pi_A = \hat{W}_1 - \hat{\theta}_A \Rightarrow \quad \pi_A = \mu_1 + \hat{V}_1 - \hat{\theta}_A \qquad \text{if } \hat{V}_1 \geq 0$$

$$\pi_A = \mu_1 - \theta_A \qquad \text{if } \hat{V}_1 < 0$$

$$E(\pi_A) = \iint \pi_A\left(\hat{V}_1, \hat{\theta}_A\right) f_v\left(\hat{V}_1\right) f_\theta\left(\hat{\theta}_A\right) d\hat{V}_1 d\hat{\theta}_A$$

$$E(\pi_A) = \frac{\sigma_{V_1}}{\sqrt{2\pi}} + \mu_1$$

Unemployment

$$E(u_1) = \frac{\sigma_{V_j}}{\sqrt{2\pi}}$$

Fixed exchange rate regime of the BW type (Fix1): the large country retains monetary autonomy

The money supply is fixed in country 3 ($\hat{M}_3 = \mu_3$). Given that shocks can create an imbalance in the goods market, the two countries (1 and 2) must adjust. As the exchange rate is fixed, the adjustment takes place through the money supply:

$$\hat{M}_1 = \mu_3 - \hat{s}_3 + \hat{V}_3 - \hat{V}_1$$

hence

Inflation

$$E(\pi_A) = \mu_3 + \frac{\sqrt{\hat{V}_3^2 + \hat{s}_3^2}}{\sqrt{2\pi}}$$

Unemployment

$$E(u_j) = \frac{\sqrt{\hat{V}_3^2 + \hat{s}_3^2}}{\sqrt{2\pi}}$$

Fixed exchange rate regime of EMS type: floating against the large country

Countries 1 and 2 agree on a fixed bilateral exchange rate system which floats against the currency of the large country, and imposes a coordinated monetary policy. We denote by $\bar{\mu} = \xi\mu_1 + (1-\xi)\mu_2$ the common monetary rule, where ξ is the degree of autonomy of country 1's monetary policy. In the case where $\xi = 1$, country 1 retains full monetary autonomy in the bilateral system, and country 2 has to keep the bilateral exchange rate fixed. Otherwise $\xi = 0$, and country 2 sets the course of monetary policy, which country 1 has to follow. Under this assumption:

$$\hat{M}_1 = \xi\mu_1 + (1-\xi)(\mu_2 + \hat{s}_1 + \hat{V}_2 - \hat{V}_1) = \bar{\mu} + (1-\xi)(\hat{s}_1 + \hat{V}_2 - \hat{V}_1)$$

$$\hat{M}_2 = \xi(\mu_1 - \hat{s}_1 - \hat{V}_2 + \hat{V}_1) + (1 - \xi)\mu_2 = \overline{\mu} + \xi(\hat{s}_1 - \hat{V}_2 + \hat{V}_1)$$

and

$$E(\pi_A) = \overline{\mu} + \frac{\sqrt{(1-\xi)^2\left(\sigma_{\hat{s}_1}^2 + \sigma_{\hat{V}_2}^2\right) + \xi^2\sigma_{\hat{V}_1}^2}}{\sqrt{2\pi}}$$

$$E(u_j) = \frac{\sqrt{(1-\xi)^2\left(\sigma_{\hat{s}_1}^2 + \sigma_{\hat{V}_2}^2\right) + \xi^2\sigma_{\hat{V}_1}^2}}{\sqrt{2\pi}}$$

Monetary Union between countries 1 and 2 (MU): floating against the large country.

In this case, inflation and unemployment for country 1 are same as in the EMS regime. The difference between the two regimes results from transaction costs.

4 Evaluation of exchange rate regimes: a cost-benefit analysis

We define the net benefits (NB) for the home country as the difference between the expected losses under the different regimes enumerated above. Such expected losses are evaluated through the economic policy objectives defined in section 1. So under the different regimes the net benefits are:

$$NB_{FIX1/FLEX} = \lambda(u_1 - u_3) + (\lambda + 1)\left(\frac{\sigma_{\hat{V}_1} - \sqrt{\sigma_{\hat{s}_3}^2 + \sigma_{\hat{V}_3}^2}}{\sqrt{2\pi}}\right)$$

$$NB_{FIX2/FLEX} = \lambda(u_1 - \overline{u}) + (\lambda + 1)\left(\frac{\sigma_{\hat{V}_1} - \sqrt{(1-\xi)^2\left(\sigma_{\hat{s}_1}^2 + \sigma_{\hat{V}_2}^2\right) + \xi^2\sigma_{\hat{V}_1}^2}}{\sqrt{2\pi}}\right)$$

$$NB_{MU/FLEX} = \lambda(u_1 - \overline{u}) + (\lambda + 1)\left(\frac{\sigma_{\hat{V}_1} - \sqrt{(1-\xi)^2\left(\sigma_{\hat{s}_1}^2 + \sigma_{\hat{V}_2}^2\right) + \xi^2\sigma_{\hat{V}_1}^2}}{\sqrt{2\pi}}\right) + \beta_1 r_1$$

$$NB_{FIX1/FIX2} = \lambda(\overline{u} - u_3) + (\lambda + 1)\left(\frac{\sqrt{(1-\xi)^2\left(\sigma_{\hat{s}_1}^2 + \sigma_{\hat{V}_2}^2\right) + \xi^2\sigma_{V_{21}}^2}}{\sqrt{2\pi}} - \frac{\sqrt{\sigma_{\hat{s}_3}^2 + \sigma_{\hat{V}_3}^2}}{\sqrt{2\pi}}\right)$$

$$NB_{MU/Fix1} = \lambda(u_3 - \overline{u}) + (\lambda + 1)\frac{\sqrt{\sigma_{\hat{s}_3}^2 + \sigma_{\hat{V}_3}^2} - \sqrt{(1-\xi)\left(\sigma_{\hat{s}_1}^2 + \sigma_{\hat{V}_2}^2\right) + \xi^2\sigma_{\hat{V}_1}^2}}{\sqrt{2\pi}} + \beta_1 r_1$$

$$NB_{MU/Fix2} = \beta_1 r_1$$

The adjustment costs component

We discuss the net benefits resulting from the adjustment costs in terms of inflation and unemployment. Regimes are compared according to their ability to reduce inflation, to stabilise monetary and real shocks and to economise on transaction costs:

$$NB_{MU/FLEX} = \frac{(\lambda+1)}{\sqrt{2\pi}}\left(\sigma_{\hat{V}_1} - \sqrt{(1-\xi^2)(\sigma^2_{\hat{s}_1} + \sigma^2_{\hat{V}_2}) + \xi^2\sigma^2_{\hat{V}_1}}\right)$$

NB $_{MU/FLEX}> 0$ if the following condition is satisfied:

$$\sigma^2_{\hat{V}_1} > (1-\xi)^2(\sigma^2_{\hat{S}_1} + \sigma^2_{\hat{V}_2}) + \xi^2\sigma^2_{\hat{V}_1}$$

Under the flexible regime, the variability of nominal domestic income of country 1 is due only to domestic monetary shocks ($\sigma_{\hat{y}_1} = \sigma_{\hat{V}_1}$). In a monetary union between two small countries 1 and 2, the variability of nominal domestic income is due to monetary and real shocks:

$$\sigma^2_{\hat{y}_1} = (1-\xi)^2(\sigma^2_{\hat{S}_1} + \sigma^2_{\hat{V}_2}) + \xi^2\sigma^2_{\hat{V}_1}$$

Besides, this component rises with the relative weight λ assigned to inflation by the authority. The more the home country (country 1) is autonomous the more the stability of its economy depends upon its monetary shocks and the less upon the monetary shocks of country 2, because it is the home country's monetary policy which is followed by the central bank. To make this point clearer, we find it useful to discuss two cases in more depth.

If the home country is fully autonomous ($\xi = 1$), the effects of monetary union on this country disappear whereas country 2 bears all the losses. The difference between monetary union and the flexible regime results from the fact that in a currency union the monetary authority relinquishes the exchange rate as an internal instrument of adjustment to deal with real shocks but it also imports the monetary stability (or instability) of the other member of the monetary union. However, if country 1 retains the independence of its monetary policy under the currency union, its situation is the same as in the flexible regime and therefore NB $_{MU/FLEX}= 0$

However, if country 1 acts as a follower i.e. depends fully on country 2 (ξ=0), the net benefit component is:

$$NB_{MU/FLEX} = \frac{(\lambda+1)}{\sqrt{2\pi}}\left(\sigma_{\hat{V}_1} - \sqrt{(\sigma^2_{\hat{s}_1} + \sigma^2_{\hat{V}_2})}\right)$$

In this case, in contrast to country 2 where the net benefit from the participation in a currency union is zero, that of the home country is positive if

$$\sigma^2_{\hat{V}_1} > \left(\sigma^2_{\hat{S}_1} + \sigma^2_{\hat{V}_2}\right)$$

The home country gains from the creation of a currency union if its monetary instability is higher than the monetary shocks transmitted by the other small country and the real shock from the home country.

Our interpretation of this component is different from that of Ricci (1997) because he takes into account the degree of openness in the transmission of shocks, while our analysis centres on the degree of monetary autonomy in the currency union.

Monetary shocks

If real shocks are absent or subject to full adjustment, the adjustment cost component due to monetary shocks is given by

$$NB_{MU/FLEX} = \frac{(\lambda+1)}{\sqrt{2\pi}}\left(\sigma_{\hat{V}_1} - \sqrt{\left(1-\xi^2\right)\sigma^2_{\hat{V}_2} + \xi^2\sigma^2_{\hat{V}_1}}\right)$$

This component is positive if the following condition is satisfied:

$$\sigma^2_{\hat{V}_1} > \frac{(1-\xi)}{(1+\xi)}\sigma^2_{\hat{V}_2}$$

If country 1 is fully autonomous, it is not affected by the creation of a monetary union compared to the flexible exchange rate regime. However, if is fully dependent on country 2, the net benefit component is positive if $\sigma^2_{\hat{V}_1} > \sigma^2_{\hat{V}_2}$. In this case, our interpretation is the same as that of Ricci (1997) for the case when monetary shocks are positively correlated across the countries of a monetary union. Therefore, the country with higher monetary instability would gain stability from the creation of a currency union. In contrast to Ricci (1997), McKinnon's (1963) argument on openness is not brought into question.

The comparison between monetary union and Fix1 allows us to define under what conditions it is advantageous to anchor the domestic currency on an international currency. Indeed, when the home country belongs in a monetary union and its exchange rate is anchored to the large country, the stability of its economy depends on the variability of real and monetary shocks for the large country ($\sigma^2_{\hat{y}_1} = \sigma^2_{\hat{s}_3} + \sigma^2_{\hat{v}_3}$). The home country would gain from monetary union if

$$(1-\xi)^2\left(\sigma^2_{\hat{s}_1} + \sigma^2_{\hat{V}_2}\right) + \xi^2\sigma^2_{\hat{V}_1} > \sigma^2_{\hat{S}_3} + \sigma^2_{\hat{V}_3}$$

Indeed,

$$NB_{MU/Fix} = \frac{(\lambda+1)}{\sqrt{2\pi}}\left(\sqrt{\sigma^2_{\hat{S}_3} + \sigma^2_{\hat{V}_3}} - \sqrt{\left(1-\xi^2\right)\left(\sigma^2_{\hat{S}_1} + \sigma^2_{\hat{V}_2}\right) + \xi^2\sigma^2_{\hat{V}_1}}\right)$$

If country 1 is fully autonomous ($\xi = 1$), the net benefit component is positive if $\sigma^2_{\hat{v}_1} > \sigma^2_{\hat{v}_3}$. By anchoring its currency on that of the large country, the home country would gain monetary stability from a monetary union.

The Maghreb countries have been advised by the IMF and World Bank to establish flexible exchange rate regimes. This would enable them to redefine their monetary policy frameworks so as to control inflation. Besides, the data available shows that money velocity in Morocco and Tunisia is relatively stable. However, money demand could be unstable after the reform of the financial sector because of financial liberalisation (Jbili and Kramarenko, 2003).

Real shocks

If we neglect monetary shocks, the creation of a monetary union or the institution of a fixed exchange rate regime of the Bretton Woods type, relative to a flexible exchange rate regime, would generate costs. This confirms that a flexible exchange rate regime is a real shock absorber.

$$NB_{MU/FLEX} = -\frac{(\lambda - 1)}{\sqrt{2\pi}}(1-\xi)\sigma_{\hat{s}_1}$$

$$NB_{FIX1/FLEX} = -\frac{(\lambda - 1)}{\sqrt{2\pi}}\sigma_{\hat{s}_3}$$

In a currency union this negative component diminishes with the degree of monetary autonomy (ξ) and rises with the variance of the trade shocks of the home country ($\sigma_{\hat{s}_1}$). In the Bretton Woods fixed regime, the negative component rises with the variance of the shocks of the large country:

$\sigma_{\hat{s}_1}$ increases with the variance of the trade shocks σ_{α_2}, σ_{α_3}, σ_{β_1}, σ_{β_3}, σ_{γ_1} and σ_{γ_2}, increases with $\sigma_{\alpha_2\alpha_3}$, $\sigma_{\beta_3\beta_1}$, $\sigma_{\beta_3\gamma_1}$, $\sigma_{\beta_3\gamma_2}$, $\sigma_{\beta_1\gamma_1}$, $\sigma_{\gamma_1\gamma_2}$, and $\sigma_{\beta_1\gamma_2}$, but decreases with $\sigma_{\alpha_2\beta_3}$, $\sigma_{\alpha_2\beta_1}$, $\sigma_{\gamma_1\alpha_2}$, $\sigma_{\alpha_3\beta_3}$, $\sigma_{\beta_1\alpha_1}$, $\sigma_{\alpha_3\gamma_1}$ and $\sigma_{\alpha_3\gamma_2}$. $\sigma_{\hat{s}_3}$ increases with the variance of the trade shocks σ_{α_2}, σ_{α_3}, σ_{β_1}, σ_{β_3}, σ_{γ_1}, and σ_{γ_2}, increases with $\sigma_{\alpha_2\alpha_3}$, $\sigma_{\alpha_2\beta_3}$, $\sigma_{\gamma_2\alpha_2}$, $\sigma_{\beta_1\gamma_2}$, $\sigma_{\beta_1\gamma_1}$, $\sigma_{\gamma_1\gamma_2}$, and $\sigma_{\alpha_3\beta_3}$, and decreases with $\sigma_{\alpha_2\beta_1}$, $\sigma_{\gamma_1\alpha_2}$, $\sigma_{\alpha_3\gamma_2}$, $\sigma_{\beta_3\gamma_2}$, $\sigma_{\alpha_3\beta_1}$, $\sigma_{\alpha_3\gamma_1}$, $\sigma_{\beta_3\beta_1}$ and $\sigma_{\beta_3\gamma_1}$.

If $(1 - \xi)\ \sigma_{\hat{s}_1} > \sigma_{\hat{s}_3}$, it is beneficial for the home country to peg its bilateral exchange rate to the other small country and to the large country:

$$NB_{FIX/FLEX} - NB_{MU/FLEX} = NB_{FIX1/MU} = \frac{(\lambda + 1)}{\sqrt{2\pi}}\left[(1-\xi)\sigma_{\hat{S}_1} - \sigma_{\hat{S}_3}\right]$$

If country 1 is fully autonomous in terms of monetary policy in the currency union, its net benefit is zero:

$$NB_{MU/FLEX} = 0$$

This result confirms the argument that countries facing asymmetric real shocks would have high costs if they renounced the exchange rate as an instrument of adjustment. The flexible exchange rate regime would be a shock absorber with $\sigma_{\hat{y}_1} = 0$ in comparison with fixed exchange rate regimes:

in the monetary union case $\sigma_{\hat{y}_1} = (1 - \xi)\, \sigma_{\hat{s}_1}$

in the Fix 1 case $\sigma_{\hat{y}_1} = \sigma_{\hat{s}_3}$

In addition, our result illustrates well the (n-1) problem because in a monetary union the country with monetary policy autonomy ensures the stability of its own economy even in the presence of real shocks: $\sigma_{\hat{y}_1} = 0$.

On the other hand, if the real shocks were perfectly and positively correlated, and had equal standard deviations, in contrast to Ricci's (1997) result, the adjustment would imply an additional cost of a monetary union relative to a flexible exchange rate regime, although the negative component does not depend on $\sigma_{\alpha_2\beta_1}$ and $\sigma_{\gamma_1\gamma_2}$.

In the case of the Maghreb countries, there is a positive correlation between real shocks (Darrat and Pennathur, 2002; Horvath and Grabowski, 1997) and therefore the monetary union would be more advantageous than pegging to the euro, at least for Morocco where the correlation is not strong vis-à-vis European countries (IMF, 2006). Even in the presence of this positive correlation between real shocks in the Maghreb countries, a flexible exchange rate regime would be more advantageous than a monetary union if these countries faced asymmetric real shocks. However, a flexible exchange rate regime could create a monetary instability which would have a negative effect on growth and trade.

The inflationary bias component

The component of the net benefits due to the existence of an inflationary bias is given by

$$NB_{MU/FLEX} = \lambda(1 - \xi)(\mu_1 - \mu_2) = \lambda(\mu_1 - \bar{\mu})$$

This component indicates a net benefit for country 1 if the union chooses an average rate of growth of money supply which is lower than that of country 1, in other words if $\mu_1 > \bar{\mu}$, where $\bar{\mu}$ is the monetary rule in the monetary union.

This component rises with λ, the relative weight assigned by the authority to inflation, and diminishes with ξ, the degree of monetary policy autonomy. That is, the more country 1 is autonomous the lower is the gain. If country 1 is fully autonomous ($\xi = 1$), the net benefit from participation in monetary union disappears.

In what conditions should the monetary union authority anchor its single currency on that of the large country? If the monetary rule $\bar{\mu}$ in the currency union is higher than the average rate of growth of money supply of country 3 (μ_3) or if it is difficult to find a monetary rule in the currency union, it is advantageous to anchor the single currency to that of the large country. This is the case of the CFA franc zone which has pegged its exchange rate to the French franc and then the euro, and imported credibility from the Bank of France and then the European Central Bank:

$$NB_{FIX/MU} = \lambda(\bar{\mu} - \mu_3)$$

If country 1 is fully independent, the benefit from adopting Fix 1 compared to a monetary union or a flexible exchange rate regime is the same:

$$NB_{FIX1/MU} = NB_{FIX1/FLEX} = \lambda(\mu_1 - \mu_3)$$

Indeed, in the case of a flexible exchange rate regime, the monetary policy is independent. So country 1's net benefit is positive if the average rate of growth of money supply is higher than that of the large country.

As in Ricci 1997), the analysis of the inflationary bias component confirms the advantage of a nominal anchor which permits the reduction of inflation: the advantage of tying one's hands. Indeed, if the objective of low inflation announced by the monetary authority is not time-consistent, the high inflation country can reduce its inflation by pegging its exchange rate to a low inflation currency. This means that the monetary authorities anchor the exchange rate irrevocably. This is the case of regimes which fix the exchange rate by legal action, that is exchange rate unions (Bordo and Jonung, 2003), and gain from the credibility of the nominal anchor via what Willett (2000) calls a 'credibility effect'. Otherwise, the pressure to maintain a fixed exchange rate imposes an anti-inflationary bias on monetary policy which Willett refers to as a 'disciplinary effect'. It involves limits on the monetary financing of the deficit on the one hand, and on the lax refinancing of the banking sector by the central bank on the other (Combes and Veyrune, 2004).

The exchange rate union category includes currency unions, dollarisation and currency boards. The difference between intermediate exchange rate regimes and exchange rate unions could be explained by the introduction of the probability of devaluation. This is one possible extension of the model.

For the Maghreb countries, the low inflation reduces the net benefits of anchoring their currencies to the euro. The low inflation is due to their careful monetary policy, price controls, the low level of investment demand and domestic consumption and the stability of their currencies against the euro and the US dollar in the case of Morocco. Algeria and Tunisia have adopted flexible exchange rate regimes since 1994 and 2000 respectively.

However, the Maghreb countries are exposed to inflationary risks. In Algeria, inflation could rise because of increases in oil receipts and wages. In the case of Morocco, inflation could result from economic growth, while in Tunisia it could arise from inflows of capital (IMF, 2006).

Transactions costs

As in Ricci (1997), the transaction costs are a proxy for the deadweight and efficiency losses associated with the existence of multiple currencies:

$$NB_{MU/FIX2} = \beta_1 r_1$$

The net benefit of country 1 from participation in a monetary union with country 2 compared to one of the other exchange rate regimes increases with β_1, the share of country 2-made traded goods in country 1's aggregate demand.

In terms of transaction costs, it would not be advantageous for the Maghreb countries to form a monetary union because of the low level of their trade linkages (Tables 9.1 and 9.2). On the other hand, a currency union with the euro area would be beneficial because that is their main trade partner. In addition, the endogeneity theory (Frankel and Rose, 1998; Rose, 2002) shows that monetary union could increase the trade links and therefore increase the net benefit of the participating countries.

The net benefit from participation of the three countries in a monetary union compared to the case where only the two small countries participate in the union increases with γ_1. The net benefit compared to other exchange rate regimes (Fix1, Fix2, Flex) increases with $(\beta_1+\gamma_1)$, where γ_1 represents the share of country 3-made traded goods in country 1's aggregate demand.

5 Conclusion

This chapter has investigated the theory of optimal regimes for small countries in the way we think appropriate for countries such as the Maghreb countries. We develop a three-country theoretical model with two small countries and a large one and a wide array of fixed exchange rate regimes is considered (EMS or Bretton Woods). Some of the results described have already been discussed extensively in the OCA literature. We would like to underline other points which stem from our model.

The net benefits that country 1 expects from its participation in a monetary union compared to a flexible exchange rate regime increase with the difference between the inflationary bias of the domestic authority and the inflationary bias of the authority of the monetary union, and with the variability of domestic monetary shocks, as parts of these shocks are transmitted to the other small country within a monetary union. The net benefits decrease with the variability of domestic real shocks and the variability of the monetary shocks of the other small country in the monetary union.

The net benefits that one country expects from a Bretton Woods type fixed exchange rate regime compared to a flexible exchange rate regime increase with the difference between the inflationary bias of the domestic authority and that of the authority of the large country and with the variance of domestic monetary shocks. The benefits decrease with the variance of the monetary and real shocks of the large country.

The net benefits that country 1 expects from a Bretton Woods type fixed exchange rate regime compared to a monetary union increase with the difference between the inflationary bias of the authority of the monetary union and that of the large country, and with the variance of the domestic real shocks and monetary shocks of the members of the monetary union. These benefits decrease with the variance of the monetary and real shocks of the large country.

Furthermore, if the real shocks were perfectly and positively correlated, and had equal standard deviations, in contrast to Ricci's (1997) result, the adjustment would imply an additional cost in a monetary union in comparison with a flexible exchange rate regime.

Finally, the effect of monetary union on one country when it acts as a leader in setting monetary policy is lower than that on a follower country. Indeed, when the leader country sets its monetary policy based on its own inflation objective, then the net benefits in terms of inflationary bias disappear; in the case of monetary or real shocks, the benefit from participation in a monetary union is zero.

Let us briefly apply this framework to the Maghreb countries. The interesting question about the Maghreb Countries is to know if they should link their currencies to the euro or form a monetary union between them that may or may not peg to the euro zone. We could distinguish two cases. If the motivation for the future monetary union is to stimulate real integration, we think that the benefits of monetary union would be weak because the trade flows between the Maghreb countries are low. Bangaké *et al.* (2007) have tested the Frankel and Rose (1998) relation for the Maghreb countries in the period 1980–2003; they found no evidence to support optimum currency area endogeneity in the Maghreb countries. Furthermore, using moving six-year correlations, they found that real shocks are not correlated between the Maghreb countries.

If the objective of the Maghreb countries is to pursue macroeconomic stability, a collective peg to the euro is appropriate because of their substantial trade links with the European Union.[6] The Maghreb could import credibility from the European Central Bank (ECB). However, if the Maghreb countries continue to face real shocks, a flexible exchange rate could be a real shock absorber.

Several extensions to the work presented here would be of great interest: in particular, the analysis of optimal monetary policy and of its interaction with fiscal policy, and the addition of a fourth country (two small countries and two large countries) in order to investigate what type of anchor currency should be chosen (US dollar or euro).

Notes

1 See Mundell (1963).
2 Baxter and Stockman (1989), Flood and Rose (1995) and Sopraseuth (2003) find no difference between exchange rate regimes in terms of macroeconomic performance. There is a disconnection between exchange rate volatility and macroeconomic fundamentals.
3 Frankel (1999), Mussa, Masson, Swoboda, Jadresic, Mauro and Berg (2000).
4 The Maghreb countries are a group of five countries: Algeria, Libya, Mauritania, Morocco and Tunisia. However, in this paper we focus on three countries (Algeria, Morocco and Tunisia).
5 Levy-Yeyati and Sturzenegger (2005).
6 Cobham and Robson (1994) analysed monetary integration in Africa, suggesting that if African countries peg their currencies to the European Currency Unit (ECU), they could avoid any problems of asymmetries and inequalities.

References

Allain, L., and Loko, B. (2007) 'Fresh Impetus Toward Maghreb Integration'. *International Monetary Fund Survey* 07/2007.

Bangaké, C., Belhadj, A., and Jedlane, N. (2007) 'Towards Maghreb Monetary Unification: What does the Theory and History Tell Us?' *Savings and Development*, forthcoming.

Barro, R., and Gordon, D. (1983a) 'A Positive Theory of Monetary Policy in a Natural-Rate Model'. *Journal of Political Economy*, 91: 589–610.
Barro, R., and Gordon, D. (1983b) 'Rules, Discretion and Reputation in a Model of Monetary Policy'. *Journal of Monetary Economics*, 12: 101–21.
Baxter, M., and Stockman, A.C. (1989) 'Business Cycles and the Exchange Rate System: Some International Evidence'. *Journal of Monetary Economics*, 23: 377–400.
Bayoumi, T. (1994) 'A Formal Model of Optimum Currency Areas'. *International Monetary Fund Staff Papers*, 41: 537–54.
Bordo, M.D., and Jonung, L. (2003) '*The Future of EMU: What Does the History of Monetary Unions Tell Us*?' in F. Capie and G. Woods (eds.) *Monetary Unions: Theory, History, Public Choice*. London: Routledge.
Broda, C. (2004) 'Terms of Trade and Exchange Rate Regimes in Developing Countries'. *Journal of International Economics*, 63: 31–58.
Calvo, G.A., and Reinhart, C.M. (2002) 'Fear of Floating'. *Quarterly Journal of Economics*, 117: 379–408.
Cobham, D., and Robson, P. (1994) 'Monetary Integration in Africa: a Deliberately European Perspective'. *World Development*, 22: 285–99.
Combes, J.L., and Veyrune, R. (2004) 'Effet de Discipline et Effet de Crédibilité de l'Ancrage Nominal'. *Revue d'Economie Financière*, 75: 55–69.
Corsetti, G., and Pesenti, P. (2001) 'Welfare and Macroeconomic Interdependence'. *Quarterly Journal of Economics*, 116: 421–46.
Darrat, A.F., and Pennathur, A. (2002) 'Are the Arab Maghreb Countries Really Integratable? Some Evidence from the Theory of Cointegrated Systems'. *Review of Financial Economics*, 1: 79–90.
Edwards, S., and Levy-Yeyati, E. (2003) 'Flexible Exchange Rate As Shock Absorbers'. *European Economic Review*, 49: 2079–2105.
Fischer, S. (2001) 'Exchange Rate Regimes: Is the Bipolar View Correct?' *Journal of Economic Perspectives*, 15: 3–24.
Flood, R.P., and Rose, A.K. (1995) 'Fixing Exchange Rates: A Virtual Quest for Fundamentals'. *Journal of Monetary Economics*, 36: 3–37.
Frankel, J.A. (1999) 'No Single Currency Regime is Right for all Countries or at all Times'. *Princeton Essays in International Finance* 215.
Frankel, J.A., and Rose, A.K. (1998) 'The Endogeneity of the Optimum Currency Area Criteria'. *Economic Journal*, 41: 753–60.
Guillaume, D., and Stasavage, D. (2000) 'Improving Policy Credibility: Is there a Case for African Monetary Unions?'. *World Development*, 8: 1391–407.
Horvath, J., and Grabowski, R. (1997) 'Prospects of African Integration in Light of the Theory of Optimum Currency Areas'. *Journal of Economic Integration*, 1: 1–25.
IMF (2006) 'Morocco: Selected Issues and Statistical Appendix'. *International Monetary Fund Country Report* 05/419.
Jbili, A., and Kramarenko, V. (2003) 'Should MENA Countries Float or Peg?'. *Finance and Development*, 40(1): 30–33.
Jedlane, N. (2005) 'Des Caisses d'Émission au Maghreb?'. Paper presented at the International Conference 'l'Europe et le Maroc: dix ans après le Processus de Barcelone'. Madrid: Centro de Estudios de Cooperación al Desarrollo (CECOD).
Jedlane, N. (2006) 'Unification Monétaire et Caisses d'Émission au Maghreb'. Paper presented at the Congrès IDEAL 'L'intégration africaine, quelle stratégie pour quelle insertion dans l'économie mondiale?' Lille: Université Catholique de Lille.
Levy-Yeyati, E., and Sturzenegger, F., (2005) 'Classifying Exchange Rate Regimes: Deeds vs Words'. *European Economic Review*, 49: 1603–35.
McKinnon, R. (1963) 'Optimum Currency Areas'. *American Economic Review*, 53: 717–25.
Maghreb Arabe Presse (2007) 'L'Union des Banques Maghrébines Appelle à la Monnaie Unique', 16 November 2007.

Masson, P. (2001) 'Exchange Rate Regime Transitions'. *Journal of Development Economics*, 64: 571–86.

Masson, P., and Patillo, C. (2004) *The Monetary Geography of Africa.* Washington D.C.: Brookings Institution.

Mundell, R. (1963) 'Capital Mobility and Stabilisation Policy under Fixed and Flexible Exchange Rates'. *Canadian Journal of Economics and Political Science*, 29: 475–85.

Mussa, M., Masson, P.R., Swoboda, A.K., Jadresic, E., Mauro, P., and Berg, A. (2000) 'Exchange Rate Regimes in an Increasingly Integrated World Economy'. International Monetary Fund Occasional Paper 193.

Obstfeld, M., and Rogoff, K. (1995) 'Exchange Rate Dynamics Redux'. *Journal of Political Economy*, 103: 624–60.

Razin, A., and Rubinstein, Y. (2006) 'Evaluation of Currency Regimes: The Unique Role of Sudden Stops'. *Economic Policy*, 45: 119–52.

Reinhart, C., and Rogoff, K. (2004) 'The Modern History of Exchange Rate Arrangements: a Reinterpretation'. *Quarterly Journal of Economics*, 119: 1–48.

Ricci, L.A (1997) 'Un Modèle Simple de Zone Monétaire Optimale'. *Economie et Prévision*, 2: 1–19.

Rose, A. (2002) 'One Money, One Market: Estimating the Effect of Common Currencies on Trade'. *Economic Policy*, 15: 745–60.

Sopraseuth, T. (2003) 'Exchange Rate Regimes and International Business Cycles'. *Review of Economic Dynamics*, 6: 339–61.

Willett, T. (2000) 'International Financial Markets as Sources of Crises or Discipline: The Too Much, Too Late Hypothesis'. *Essays in International Finance,* 218: 1–48.

10 Estimating central bank behaviour in emerging markets

The case of Turkey[1]

Ozan Hatipoglu and C. Emre Alper

Introduction

After the adoption of floating exchange rate regimes, several emerging markets decided to switch to an inflation-targeting framework which entailed explicit medium-term quantitative targets for inflation that their central banks had publicly declared.[2] However, even after switching to inflation targeting, an emerging market central bank (EMCB) has reasons to care about exchange rate movements and their effects on the financial account balance. Firstly, due to the observed high degree of asset and liability dollarisation and shallow financial markets, emerging markets are more susceptible to sudden capital account reversals, and an EMCB is more likely to actively respond to sudden movements in exchange rates when compared with, for example, the Federal Reserve or the Bank of England. Secondly, central banks in countries that depend heavily on exports for their economic welfare may be more inclined to bow to political pressure to adjust their exchange rates. An upcoming election, for instance, may compound that pressure.

From a policy point of view, the effect of exchange rate volatility is more than just a side concern for an EMCB adopting inflation targeting. Exchange rate movements may affect inflation expectations, since such movements generally affect the price of imported goods and are reflected in the consumer price index (Allsopp, Kara and Nelson, 2006).[3] They may also affect the output gap by affecting employment decisions simply by changing the marginal rate of substitution between labour and capital, where the latter consists partially of imported inputs. Given the possibility that both inflation and the output gap are implicitly embedded in such a policy rule as the one used by Clarida, Galí and Gertler (2000), an emerging market central bank may choose to intervene pre-emptively to correct for unexpected deviations in the exchange rate.

From an empirical point of view, if a central bank commits to price stability in a forward-looking manner, then the estimation of future policy inputs, such as expected inflation, becomes crucial for ensuring that the policy rule can be implemented. Since exchange rate movements are important in determining future price levels due to the exchange rate pass-through to domestic prices, a model must successfully capture the link between exchange rate movements and expected inflation. While previous empirical studies report a decline in exchange rate pass-through after the adoption of an inflation-targeting regime, the pass-through effect will always be a force to reckon with so long as the emphasis of policy remains inflation targeting.[4] This is especially true given the observation that emerging markets are generally characterised by high public debt and dollarisation, which complicates the role of exchange rates in monetary policy.[5] Sargent and Wallace (1981) within a closed economy framework argue that high public debt and exogenously given public deficits will eventually cause monetary policy to be dominated by fiscal concerns. For a small highly indebted open economy, increasing the policy rate as a response to a perceived increase in inflation and currency depreciation may cause the rates on government debt to increase, which in turn may increase the default risk and may lead to further currency depreciation.

We analyse the reaction function of the Central Bank of Turkey (CBT) in the post-2001 floating exchange rate period, using a multivariate structural model with time-dependent parameters and regime shocks. Using Turkey as a case study is appealing in several respects. First, since the full capital account liberalisation at the end of the 1990s, Turkey has experienced high inflation, lax fiscal policies and episodes of sudden capital account reversal and high exchange rate volatility; the latest was in May 2006, almost five years after Turkey switched to inflation targeting.[6] Second, because of Turkey's concerns over export performance as well as the high degree of asset and liability dollarisation, sustained appreciation of the domestic currency, partly due to improvements in the global liquidity conditions in the post 2001 period, has put pressure on the CBT to make adjustments ever since the adoption of inflation targeting in 2002, regardless of whether such adjustments were aligned with the implied policy rule or not. Finally, although the initial phases of inflation targeting have been successful, CBT has overshot its target for the last two years by at least four percentage points, raising questions about what role exchange rates play in the CBT's reaction function and about how the CBT updates its inflation target following an exchange rate crisis.[7]

An increase in the volatility of exchange rates may not only induce pre-emptive adjustments by EMCBs, but also lead to regime shifts or structural breaks in the reaction function. In an inflation-targeting regime the monetary authority has to consider its own credibility when implementing an explicitly announced rule. Although inflation targeting as a policy increases the transparency and credibility of monetary policy, an EMCB may initially lack institutional credibility, which could cause the monetary authority to shift regimes more frequently. Other issues associated with EMCBs also require special attention. For instance, a higher frequency of governor appointments might lead to more frequent structural breaks in the reaction function of an EMCB. Such shifts cannot be represented by the class of linear Taylor rules suggested for developed countries. Estimating a Taylor rule for the purpose of describing policymaker behaviour in this case would require appropriate modelling of such policy shifts.

Another important issue is that the standard Taylor rules incorrectly assume that the policymaker has perfect information about the current actual output gap, which is not necessarily the case, a point forcefully made by Orphanides and van Norden (2005). For this reason, accurate measurement of the potential output – in other words, the productive capacity of the economy – is crucial. A serious mismeasurement of the output gap may lead to an activist stabilisation policy that achieves undesired outcomes. The absence of statistical sophistication and the relatively large informal sector in emerging economies mean that potential output is more likely to be mismeasured by an EMCB compared to a central bank in a developed country. Given the fact that potential output is at least partially determined by the available imported machinery, exchange rates play a further role in determining the output gap. Such issues make it more challenging to model and predict the reactions of EMCBs.

In this chapter, an empirical nonlinear state-space model is presented that addresses the concerns mentioned above. We start with a benchmark model that includes exchange rates as an input to the rule, along with the inflation gap and the output gap. We employ a dual extended Kalman filter (DEKF) technique to estimate simultaneously both time varying parameters (random coefficients) and unobserved variables, such as expected inflation and potential output. This technique allows us to track changes in central bank behaviour over time. We estimate several augmented Taylor rules for the Turkish economy in the post-2001 period and we find positively significant coefficients for the output gap and the inflation gap and an insignificant negative coefficient for the exchange rate gap. We also report that the Central Bank of Turkey has given relatively more importance to the inflation gap than to either the output gap or the exchange rate gap in determining interest rates, though this did not happen immediately after the switch. We compare our model with existing models of smooth adjustment as well as with linear models that treat exchange rates as an input to the rule. While our model does not offer an accurate measurement of potential output, it offers an empirical advantage. Specifically, it produces a larger set of information that can be utilised for the optimal estimation of the output gap as it pertains to the estimation of the reaction function.

There are several articles that include exchange rates in the Taylor Rule, albeit without any consideration of the operational framework of the monetary authority in developing countries.[8] Taylor (2001) argues that rules that respond directly to exchange rates do not perform better than those that respond indirectly. Edwards (2006) examines the role of the exchange rate in Taylor rules and finds that it has a significant coefficient for most inflation-targeting countries. Our analysis extends that of Edwards (2006) in that we incorporate the effect of exchange rates both in the measurement of the output gap and in the estimation of expected inflation, both of which are inputs to the policy rule. We also compare this new rule to those of Edwards (2006) and previous researchers who have used exchange rates as exogenous inputs. We find that incorporating the effects of exchange rates into the rule gives a better description of CBT behaviour in the period after 2001.

Engel and West (2005) and Mark (2005) study open-economy Taylor rules that include exchange rates, but their aim is to evaluate the effect of such a rule on the time-series properties of exchange rates. In a developing country framework, De Gregorio, Tokman, and Valdés (2005) study the case of Chile and argue that if the effects of the exchange rate changes are already incorporated in calculations of the output and inflation gaps, there is no need to give an independent role to the exchange rate in the policy rule. This approach is followed in the present paper, even though there is room for the EMCB to intervene pre-emptively and directly when the inflation and output gaps are slow to respond to changes in the exchange rate. On the other hand, our work differs from that of De Gregorio *et al.* (2005) in how we estimate unobservables and how we incorporate exchange rates into the model, which is explained in more detail in the next section.

One major difficulty in estimating a Taylor rule is measuring potential output as a determinant of the output gap. Basic procedures such as Hodrick-Prescott (HP) filters and quadratic detrending methods are widely used, while the Kalman filter and its extended version have also been recently employed. While HP filters perform well when estimating potential output in developed economies, where output is less volatile, they are poorly suited to emerging market economies, which are more prone to outside shocks and therefore show wider variation in their trend indicators. The Kalman filter algorithm, on the other hand, has several advantages over traditional filters.[9] These merits have been documented by Ozbek and Ozlale (2005), who use a univariate extended Kalman filter to provide potential output estimates for Turkey. Orphanides and van Norden (2005) calculate the potential output using a univariate Kalman filter, whereas we use a multivariate one.[10] Similarly, Bueno (2005) looks at the hidden states in the policy rule in a Markov switching model using a multivariate Kalman filter, but without including exchange rates as a determinant of the policy rule.

Another major issue is estimating potential output correctly when it is affected by movements in exchange rates. By employing a multivariate structural version of the filter one can capture such effects and utilise more of the available information to estimate the output trend. We can introduce time-varying parameters, which allow us to track the changes in the central bank's behaviour after its switch to the inflation-targeting regime. Finally, the state-space setup allows us to evaluate the Taylor rule using a multivariate structural model that incorporates the joint estimation of all important unobserved variables – such as potential output – into one complete model.

The aim of this chapter is to explain the behaviour of an EMCB with the available information at hand. Therefore, it does not address the issue of real-time measurement of potential output as suggested by Orphanides (2003b). The methodology that we employ provides recursive optimal forecasts of the potential output at each point in time, which approximates the level of information available to an EMCB when it makes policy decisions.

In the next section, we describe the model. In section 2 we present the data and our estimation results. Section 3 concludes.

1 The empirical model

Both theoretical and empirical studies have shown that the exchange rate has an indirect role in inflation targeting because it affects both expected inflation and the output gap. Therefore, such effects may already be embedded in a forward-looking

Taylor rule that considers the exchange rate as an input to the rule. In this respect, one possibility is to include in the original rule the deviations of the real exchange rate from the trend instead of including the nominal or the real exchange rate as a separate term in the rule. A zero real exchange rate gap can be considered to be consistent both with a zero inflation gap and a zero output gap. Another possibility is to model the effects of nominal exchange rate changes on inflation expectations separately, by treating inflation expectations as an unobserved variable. Both approaches are different from the one used in Clarida *et al.* (1998) and in subsequent papers mentioned above, all of which use exchange rates as exogenous linear inputs to the policy rule. The problem of accurately estimating future inflation is more difficult in the case of developing countries such as Turkey. Our results suggest that it is more appropriate to use the second approach because it captures the role of exchange rates in a way that more closely resembles the behaviour of an EMCB in an inflation-targeting regime. In other words, the exchange rate matters to the extent that it affects future inflation and output gaps. This approach is also useful in the sense that it prevents an EMCB from responding both to depreciation and a higher expected future inflation, given that the latter already includes effects of the former. However, when there is a delayed response between changes in the exchange rate and the inflation or output gaps, the EMCB may choose to respond immediately to changes in the exchange rate to control the pass-through effect on the inflation and output gaps. This pre-emptive intervention by the central bank is suggested by Edwards (2006), who argues that the exact reaction function will be country-specific and dependent on pass-through elasticities. For the Turkish case, Kara and Öğünç (2005) provide evidence that the pass-through effect is relatively high, which might justify looking at the effect of exchange rates on expected future inflation separately, as opposed to including exchange rates explicitly in a Taylor rule that already includes expected future inflation in its inflation gap component.[11]

Ample evidence in the literature indicates that rules with lagged policy rates have better predictive power over those without interest rate smoothing (Rudebusch, 2006). While this may reflect monetary policy inertia, there may also be persistent influences on central bank behaviour that cannot be explained by smooth adjustment of interest rates. In fact, the distinction between interest rate smoothing and persistent influences on the EMCB is even more blurred in emerging markets pursuing inflation targeting, because the central bank may be subject to political pressures as well as to sustained periods of currency depreciation or appreciation. In order to control for such effects, we experimented with the inclusion of a lagged interest rate term in the Taylor rule as suggested by Rudebusch (2006), as well as a time-varying intercept term to capture regime shifts and other external factors.

We assume that the central bank follows a Taylor Rule in a forward-looking manner in order to control inflation.[12] We started with a baseline model in which the EMCB responds to inflation gaps, output gaps, and some external factors like foreign interest rates or real exchange rate gaps. We took the nominal over-night interbank interest rate as the policy rate, and made several implicit assumptions. First, the response of the central bank is immediate, that is we assumed the EMCB does not smooth changes in the interest rate, thus eliminating the need for a lagged term in the rule. Second, we assumed that the EMCB is concerned only with the economic environment and we do not allow for systematic changes in the EMCB's behaviour, whether triggered by an internal mechanism or by political influence.

Hence the first baseline model can be written as:

$$i_t = \alpha + \beta(\pi^e_{t,t+1} - \pi^*_{t,t+1}) + \gamma(y_t - y^*_t) + \delta q_t + \varepsilon_t \tag{1}$$

where i_t is the policy rate, $\pi^*_{t,t+1}$ is the target level of the inflation rate as announced by the central bank, $\pi^e_{t,t+1}$ is the inflation at t+1 as expected at time t, y_t is the actual output, y^*_t is the unobserved potential output, q_t represents external factors, such as the real exchange rate gap or foreign interest rate.

We then relax the assumption that the EMCB does not smooth its policy rate and estimate the following equation.

$$i_t = \alpha + \rho i_{t-1} + \beta(\pi^e_{t,t+1} - \pi^*_{t,t+1}) + \gamma(y_t - y^*_t) + \delta q_t + \varepsilon_t \tag{2}$$

We further relax the above assumptions by allowing for systematic changes in the EMCB's behaviour. We also allow for time-variable coefficients and regime switches. We further assume that the central bank responds to changes in exchange rates with the goal of controlling inflation. In other words, changes in the exchange rate affect the expected inflation in the reaction function. In this setup, the expected inflation is not directly observable by the central bank but can be inferred in a way that is consistent with the state of the economy as described by the model. This leads to the following specification:

$$i_t = \alpha_t + \rho_t i_{t-1} + \beta_t(\pi^e_{t,t+1} - \pi^*_t) + \gamma_t(y_t - y^*_t) + \delta q_t + \varepsilon_t \tag{3}$$

$$\alpha_t = \lambda_1 + \lambda_2 \alpha_{t-1} + \xi_t \tag{4}$$

$$\pi^e_{t,t+1} = a\pi_t + b\Delta s_t + c\Delta s_{t-1} + \zeta_t \tag{5}$$

$$y^*_t = y^*_{t-1} + \phi_{t-1} + \omega_t \tag{6}$$

$$\phi_t = (1 - \eta_t)\phi_0 + \eta_t \phi_{t-1} + \vartheta_t \tag{7}$$

$$y_t = y^*_t + x_t \tag{8}$$

$$x_t = \tau_{1,t} x_{t-1} + \tau_{2,t} r_t + \tau_{3,t} q_t + \tau_{4,t} \pi_t + \psi_t \tag{9}$$

where Δs_t is the change in nominal exchange rate from the previous period, ϕ_t is the potential output growth rate or the trend output growth rate, η_t is the persistence of the deviations from the trend output, x_t is the output gap, r_t and is the real rate. Finally α_t, β_t, γ_t, η_t, $\tau_{1,t}$, $\tau_{2,t}$, $\tau_{3,t}$ and $\tau_{4,t}$ are random coefficients and ε_t, ξ_t, ζ_t, ω_t, ϑ_t and ψ_t represent shocks to the system, which are assumed to be *i.i.d.* with zero mean and constant variances.

Equation (3) is the augmented Taylor rule we adopted in our estimations and represents our baseline model. The EMCB responds to changes in deviations of the expected inflation from its target, as described by the term ($\pi^e_{t,t+1} - \pi^*_t$), to changes in actual output from its potential level, as described by the term ($y_t - y^*_t$) and to an external factor, q_t, such as the deviation of the real exchange rate from its trend or the foreign interest rate. The inclusion of the lagged dependent variable, i_{t-1}, reflects the inertia in monetary policy or smooth adjustments to the policy rate. The variable intercept term, α_t , represents regime shocks or noisy information faced by the central bank as emphasised by Orphanides (2003a). The policy follows an AR(1) process if the output gap and inflation gap are both zero and there is no noisy information about the state of the economy as it is perceived by the EMCB.

We extend the model to a state-space setup by adding the following equations. Equation (4) describes the evolution of the noisy information faced by the EMCB. Equation (5) expresses the dynamics of inflationary expectations, π^e_t, both through inflation persistence and exchange rate pass-through calculated by the marginal effect of past nominal exchange rates, s_{t-1} and s_{t-2}. Equation (6) describes the evolution of potential output as in Aguiar and Gopinath (2004) and Sarkaya, Öğunç, Ece, Kara, and Özlale (2005). We specify a flexible random walk with a drift model where growth rate of the output trend, ϕ_t, is time-variable. We argue that in developing countries the trend of potential output is more prone to external shocks and may depend on productivity and labour force participation. Aguiar and Gopinath (2004) show that business-cycles in emerging markets occur because there are frequent changes in economic policies that cause shocks to the growth rate of the trend. Given the vulnerability of the emerging markets to such volatile shocks we adopt a stochastic model for the trend as in Sarkaya *et al.* (2005), where shocks are permanent and the persistence of the growth rate, η_t, can be specified *a priori*. This is given in equation (7), where the potential growth rate exhibits an AR(1) process with η_t representing the persistence of the deviations from the long-run growth rate ϕ_o. Equation (8) is the decomposition of the actual output into potential output and the output gap. The above model can be expressed in state-space form in the following way:

$$W_{t+1} = A_t W_t + B_t U_t + u_{t+1} \tag{10}$$

$$Y_t = C_t W_t + D_t V_t + v_t \tag{11}$$

where Y_t is an $n \times 1$ vector of observed variables, U_t and V_t are $k \times 1$ and $j \times 1$ vectors of predetermined or exogenous variables. A_t, B_t, C_t and D_t are time-variable coefficient matrices. W_t is a $r \times 1$ vector of unobserved state variables. We then estimate the unobserved components in a state-space setup using Kalman filtering methods.[13]

The above model is first estimated using the Standard Kalman Filter (SKF) algorithm. SKF is useful when the coefficient matrices are time invariant. The algorithm involves estimating the state-space model given by (10) and (11) in a recursive manner in two distinct steps: update and measurement. In the update step, the unobserved state variables, W_t are estimated by using information on observed signal variables, U_t, and previously estimated state variables, W_{t-1}. Using a maximum likelihood algorithm *a priori* estimates of the state variables, $\hat{W}_t^-$, and the *a priori* estimate of the error covariance, $\hat{P}_t^-$, are obtained. Once a state vector is estimated, it is measured by a signal vector Y_t in the measurement step by controlling for other exogenous variables V_t. The error covariance matrix associated with the measurement error is used along with the estimated coefficient matrices, $\hat{C}$ and $\hat{D}$, and the predicted covariance matrix from the update step, P_t^-, to produce the correction term, or the `Kalman gain'. This correction is used to refine the *a priori* estimates of $\hat{W}_t^-$ and $\hat{P}_t^-$ and to transform them into *a posteriori* estimates $\hat{W}_t^+$ and $\hat{P}$. In the next update step, new *a priori* estimates of $\hat{W}_{t+1}^-$ and $\hat{P}_{t+1}^-$ are found by utilising the a posteriori estimates, $\hat{W}_t^+$ and $\hat{P}_t^+$, from the last step and the process repeats itself.

After a switch to a new monetary policy regime, there is a period during which the agents, including the central bank, adjust to the new environment. In this respect, allowing the parameters to vary allows us to explore how central banks adapt to an inflation-targeting regime. In econometric terms this extension is not straightforward. If one allows for time-variable parameters the model becomes nonlinear in state variables and it is no longer appropriate to apply the SKF. Normally, non-linearity would be handled easily by applying the Extended Kalman Filter (EKF). But, since both parameters and the state variables are presented in multiplicative form, EKF by itself is insufficient to linearise the system, because of the filter's recursive structure.

To summarise briefly, each state estimate requires the full knowledge of the coordinates at which the linearisation should take place. One also needs other state estimates, such as estimates of the unknown parameters, in order to specify the coordinates. To address this problem, we propose a Dual Extended Kalman filter (DEKF) which applies a linear approximation algorithm to the SKF at the last step in state variables and parameters. It does so by using two separate extended Kalman filters, one for signal estimation and another for model estimation. One EKF generates state estimates by utilising a priori state estimates and a priori parameter estimates, while the other EKF generates parameter estimates by utilising a priori state estimates.[14] DEKF has several advantages to the simple EKF, as described in Haykin (2000).

Data and estimation

We use the simple monthly average of the daily overnight interbank borrowing rate set by the Turkish Central Bank as the policy rate for the sample period from January 2002 through to July 2007. Inflation is defined as the logarithmic difference of the annual seasonally adjusted CPI. Output is taken to be the natural logarithm of seasonally adjusted real Gross Domestic Product (GDP). The real exchange rate is based on CPI and taken from the CBT's web-site along with the real rates. The nominal exchange rate is a basket of the euro and the dollar with equal weights.

Our estimation consists of several steps. First we estimate the baseline model with constant parameters where we experiment with several candidates for q_t. Next

Table 10.1 Baseline and extended model estimates

	Baseline(1)	*Baseline(2)*	*Baseline(3)*	*Baseline(4)*	*Extended (SKF)*	*Extended (DEKF)*
Inflation gap	1.821 (0.422)	1.92 (2.04)	1.112 (0.438)	1.660 (0.551)	1.004 (0.401)	1.062 (0.373)
Output gap	0.047 (0.199)	0.012 (0.233)	0.048 (0.089)	0.198 (0.267)	0.051 (0.021)	0.055 (0.314)
Real exchange rate	–0.022 (0.071)	0.131 (0.187)				
Real exchange rate gap			–0.062 (0.091)		–0.051 (0.052)	–0.044 (0.131)
Foreign interest rate				–0.078 (0.055)		
Lagged interest rate		0.911 (0.132)	0.838 (0.114)	0.677 (0.252)	0.861 (0.156)	0.733 (0.128)
Mean square error	18.76	11.56	12.34	11.77	1.837	1.653

Notes: Standard errors in parenthesis except EKF where MSE is reported. In EKF the parameter value is reported at the last observation.

we estimate the multivariate structural model with constant coefficients using SKF, again experimenting with several candidates for q_t and several initial conditions. Finally, we estimate the complete model with time-variable parameters using DEKF. One candidate we experimented with for q_t is the real exchange rate as put forward by Taylor (2001). Another is the real exchange rate gap where the gap is measured by a deviation from its Hodrick-Prescott (HP) trend. We also included the US federal funds rate as in Adam *et al.* (2005).

We estimated the above model for the period between the first month of 2002 and seventh month of 2007. The results are selectively reported in Table 10.1 which presents the best results we were able to obtain using the above methodology, where we define best as having the lowest mean squared error.[15] The baseline models refer to the estimation of equation (1), where each gap is calculated using a HP filter and coefficients are time-invariant. The coefficients of the output gap and the inflation gap are positive and significant. The latter is greater than one, which reflects the aggressive monetary policy employed by the CBT during the inflation-targeting period. The coefficient of the exchange rate gap is insignificant and negative. Introducing the lagged interest rate improves the fit of the model. This is expected, since the CBT smoothed the interest rate movements, except for the one-time hike in May 2006 as shown in Figure 10.1.

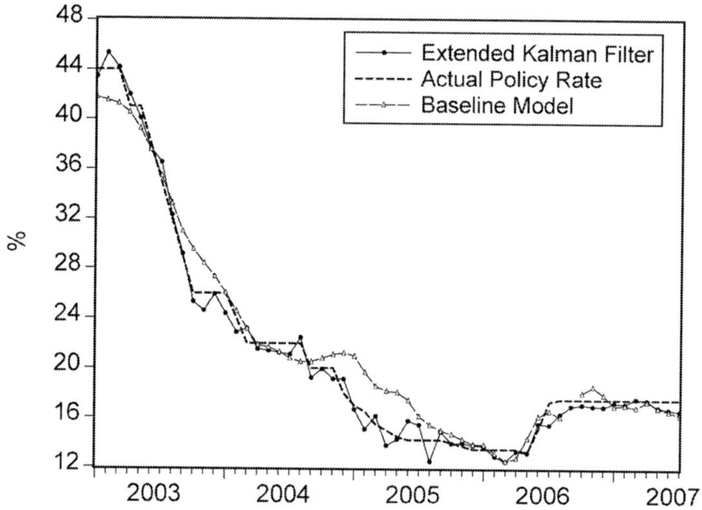

Figure 10.1 Actual versus fitted rates.

The last two columns show the results we obtained using the extended model. Here, we report the estimated coefficients obtained at the last step of the recursive algorithm which corresponds to the last observation. They are similar to the baseline model, except that the extended model fits the data considerably better. The estimation exercise using the constant coefficient model with SKF results in a positive and significant coefficient for both the inflation gap and the output gap, and a negative and insignificant coefficient for the exchange rate gap. By employing the random coefficient model with DEKF we obtain similar results. This is shown in the last column. We present the results we obtained by letting $q_t = 0$ in equation (3), where the exchange rates and the foreign interest rate are not considered exogenous policy inputs. All of the coefficient estimates are the estimates at the last observation of the sample period.[16] While the coefficient of the inflation gap turns out to be positive for each step of the estimation, the coefficient of the output gap is insignificant. The coefficient of the exchange rate is negative and insignificant at the last step.

To show how the baseline model and the extended model compare in describing the CBT's response, we present the actual overnight rates and the fitted rates in Figure 10.1.[17] The extended model with constant coefficients performs better than the baseline one. In particular, there are sustained periods during which the implied rule overestimates or underestimates the actual rates. To recap, we found that an empirical Taylor rule with variable policy parameters and regime shocks explains the CBT behaviour after 2001 better than the baseline model or the extended model with constant coefficients.

In Figure 10.2, we trace the CBT response over time. The figure shows the evolution of the coefficients of the inflation gap and the exchange rate gap obtained by the recursive estimation. The figure shows the behaviour of the CBT after it switched to inflation targeting. Reading Figure 10.2 requires caution: the initial

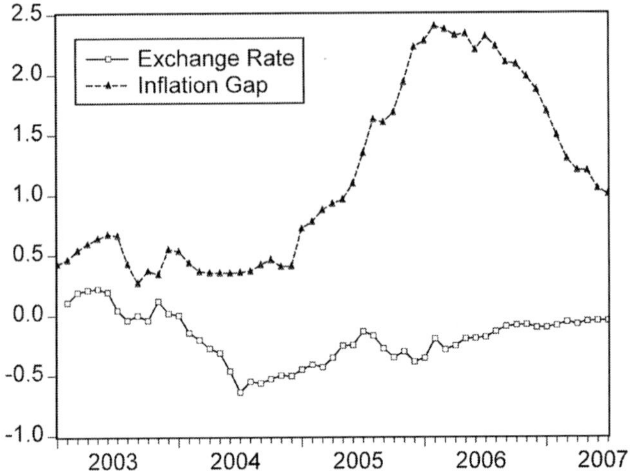

Figure 10.2 Central bank behaviour.

estimates in the sample period are produced with few observations and have no statistical significance. Therefore, we choose to comment about the last half of the sample only. According to the figure, the CBT has always given more weight to the inflation gap than to the exchange rate, although the relative weights have varied.

The inflation gap has become more important over the course of the inflation-targeting period, which reflects the fact that the CBT was initially more concerned with fiscal dominance and lack of credibility. Because of the high initial level of foreign currency denominated Turkish debt and thereby high default risk , an increase in the rates as a response to high inflation would have contributed to a real depreciation by making domestic debt lest attractive. Under such a scenario reducing inflation requires fiscal discipline rather than monetary adjustments. On the other hand, the relative importance of the inflation gap subsequently diminished towards the end of our sample, which may explain the overshooting observed in the last 1.5 years.

Conclusion

In this paper, we proposed a model to estimate the reaction function for an inflation-targeting emerging market central bank of a highly dollarised economy during a floating exchange rate period. It is not immediately clear from the previous literature whether the exchange rate should be considered separately within the Taylor rule for open economies. If the output gap and the inflation gap carry enough information to describe the state of the economy, then there is no need to include the exchange rate because any information it contains will already be captured in these two statistics. However, since the latter include unobservables such as potential output and inflationary expectations, the current and future values of which are at least partially determined by exchange rates, one can improve the estimates by utilising the information provided by exchange rate movements. Our model incorporates the effects of exchange rate movements on inflationary expectations and the output gap in a state-space setup. We introduce time-varying parameters and regime shifts to describe changes in EMCB behaviour. We use the model to estimate the CBT reaction function in the post-2001 period. When regime shifts are taken into account, the extended model predicts the CBT's behaviour better than the standard Taylor rule. We find that the CBT has responded to inflation more aggressively over time, reflecting its initial concerns about fiscal dominance. We also find that the CBT has mostly ignored the movements in exchange rates during the inflation-targeting period, in line with the classical definition of inflation targeting.

From an econometric point of view, it is better to consider the exchange rate as part of the environment of monetary policy for the EMCB rather than an exogenous input for the implied rule. This is important in several ways. First, including exchange rates in the rule might create bias in the estimates as its effects on the policy rate might already be captured by both expected and observed inflation as well as the output gap. Second, one might suppose that the central bank might respond independently to changes in the exchange rate. However, in this case modelling and estimating an exchange rate target independent of the inflation target might require strict assumptions on the central bank's behaviour.

While further study is needed to understand the general role of exchange rates in describing EMCB behaviour, we recognise that the role of exchange rates in monetary policy is largely an empirical and country-specific issue, as suggested by Edwards (2006). An exercise using real-time output gaps instead of forecasts provided by the algorithm in this chapter might provide more insight into the observed outcomes of monetary policy. The model presented here could be useful in studying central bank behaviour in other emerging market economies subject to similar shocks, such as Egypt, where the central bank is on the verge of adopting an inflation-targeting regime.

Notes

1 We are grateful to Oya Pinar Ardic, David Cobham, Ghassan Dibeh, Burcay Erus, Refik Erzan, Douglas Pearce and participants at the 2007 Mediterranean Research meeting as well as the 2008 Middle East Economic Association (MEEA) annual conference for many helpful comments. We are also grateful for financial support by the Scientific & Technological Research Council of Turkey (TUBITAK), project number 10K297. Alper acknowledges financial support from TUBA-GEBIP (Turkish Academy of Sciences – Young Scientists Scholarship Program). The usual disclaimer applies.

2 In particular, Brazil, Chile, Columbia, Mexico, Peru, South Africa, Thailand, and Turkey switched to inflation-targeting frameworks following their adoption of floating exchange rate regimes.

3 The correlation between CPI inflation and nominal exchange rate changes is not always strong, however. See Allsopp *et al.* (2006) for a study on the U.K. In general, low income countries are expected to show a stronger correlation between the exchange rate and domestic prices, because the relative share of the non-tradable services sector is lower compared to the share in developed economies.

4 Edwards (2006) reports declines in exchange rate pass-through for Australia, Canada, Brazil, Chile, Israel, South Korea, and Mexico. Kara *et al.* (2005) find the same result for Turkey in the post-2001 period.

5 Several empirical studies report that exchange rate volatility and high inflation leads to dollarisation. On the other hand, reverse causality is also possible. Akçay *et al.* (1997) report that a higher degree of dollarisation leads to higher levels of exchange rate uncertainty in Turkey.

6 For a brief review of the financial crises that Turkey faced in the aftermath of the 1989 capital account liberalisation, see Alper and Öniş (2003).

7 Turkey adopted implicit inflation targeting in 2002 and open inflation targeting in 2006. During the period of implicit inflation targeting, partly due to favourable global liquidity conditions, annual inflation rate fell to single digits.

8 See Clarida *et al.* (1998) and Edwards (2006) on developed economies.

9 First, unlike the HP filter or other detrending methods, the Kalman filter allows for greater volatility in the trend component and more flexibility in modeling the trend. This is especially crucial for emerging market economies and it has been one of the main criticisms of the HP filter, which produces too 'smooth' a trend for such economies. Second, by including all possible variables in the estimation of potential output, the Kalman filter utilises more information in the estimation of potential output, which results in lower forecast errors. Thirdly, the Kalman filter is not plagued by the problem of incorrectly estimating the trend at the end of the sample period.

10 In the univariate version, the only information source is the current real GDP.

11 For instance, in March 2006, the Central Bank of Turkey increased the interest rate by 16.5 per cent, or 425 basis points, from 13.25 per cent to 17.5 per cent in response to a sudden currency depreciation.

12 Lawrence and Rostagno (2001) show that monetary policy operated according to the Taylor rule may inject additional volatility into the economy if it ignores the money growth rate. We ignore the money growth rate on the following grounds. First, a single interest rate policy can be supported by various money growth rules. Second, in an inflation-targeting framework, money growth is important to the extent that it can forecast future inflation, but there is little evidence that it can forecast this.

13 The specification of these matrices can be found in the Appendix.

14 See Appendix for a brief description of the DEKF we employ in this estimation.

15 All other estimation results are available from the authors.

16 The Bayesian recursive estimation also requires specification of the initial conditions for all state variables, including the random coefficients. For the potential output, we chose the actual value at the beginning of the sample. For the expected inflation, we used a fitted value from Equation (5). For the random coefficients, we started with the fitted values we obtain from the baseline model. We further experimented with a considerably large set of arbitrary initial conditions. These results are also available from the authors.

17 Unlike Clarida *et al.* (2000), we tested our model's fit by comparing the actual rates with the fitted rates instead of by comparing actual target rates with fitted target rates. Clarida *et al.* (2000) implicitly assume that central banks continuously adjust their target rates. This is a valid exercise for a central bank which pursues implicit inflation targeting but for an emerging market's central bank operating in an open economy inflation-targeting framework, credibility requires that target rates are set well in advance and therefore it is reasonable to expect little volatility in target rates.

References

Adam, C., Cobham, D., and E. Girardin, E. (2005) 'Monetary Frameworks and Institutional Constraints: UK Monetary Policy Reaction Functions,1985–2003'. *Oxford Bulletin of Economics and Statistics*, 20: 497–516.

Aguiar, M., and Gopinath, G. (2004) 'Emerging Market Business Cycles: The Cycle is the Trend'. National Bureau of Economic Research Working Paper 10734.

Alper, C.E., and Öniş, Z. (2003) 'Financial Globalisation, the Democratic Deficit and Recurrent Crises in Emerging Markets: the Turkish Experience in the Aftermath of

Capital Account Liberalisation'. *Emerging Markets Finance and Trade*, 39: 5–26.

Allsopp C., Kara, A., and Nelson, E. (2006) 'United Kingdom Inflation Targeting and the Exchange Rate'. *Economic Journal*, 116: 232–44.

Bueno, R. (2005) 'Taylor Rule with Hidden States' Working Paper. Chicago: University of Chicago.

Clarida, R., Gali, J., and Gertler, M. (1998) 'Monetary Policy Rules in Practice: Some International Evidence'. *European Economic Review*, 42: 1033–67.

Clarida, R., Gali, J., and Gertler, M. (2000) 'Monetary Policy Rules and Macroeconomic Stability: Evidence and Some Theory'. *Quarterly Journal of Economics*, 115: 147–180.

De Gregorio, J., Tokman, A., and Valdés, R. (2005) 'Tipo de Cambio Flexible con Metas de Inflación en Chile: Experiencia y Temas de Interés'. *Economic Policy Papers* 14. Chile: Central Bank of Chile.

Edwards, S. (2006) 'The Relationship Between Exchange Rates and Inflation Targeting Revisited'. National Bureau of Economic Research Working Paper. 12163.

Engel, C., and West, K.D. (2005) 'Exchange Rates and Fundamentals'. *Journal of Political Economy*, 113: 485–517.

Haykin, S. (2001) *Kalman Filtering and Neural Networks*. Hoboken, New Jersey: Wiley.

Kara, H., and Öğünç, F. (2005) 'Exchange Rate Pass Through in Turkey: It is Slow, but is it Really Low?' Central Bank of Turkey Working Paper 05/10, Ankara.

Kara, H., Tuğer, H.K., Özlale, Ü., Tuğer, B., Yavuz, D., and Yücel, E. (2005) 'Exchange Rate Pass Through in Turkey: Has it Changed and to What Extent?' Central Bank of Turkey Working Paper 05/04, Ankara.

Lawrence, J.C., and Rostagno, M. (2001) 'Money Growth Monitoring and The Taylor Rule'. National Bureau of Economic Research Working Paper 8539.

Mark, N.C. (2005) 'Changing Monetary Policy Rules, Learning, and Real Exchange Rate Dynamics'. National Bureau of Economic Research Working Paper 11061.

Orphanides, A. (2003a) 'Monetary Policy Evaluation with Noisy Information'. *Journal of Monetary Economics*, 50: 605–31.

Orphanides, A. (2003b) 'The Quest for Prosperity without Inflation'. *Journal of Monetary Economics*, 50: 983–1022.

Orphanides, A., and van Norden, S. (2005) 'The Reliability of Inflation Forecasts Based on Output Gap Estimates in Real Time'. *Journal of Money, Credit and Banking*, 37: 583–601.

Ozbek, L., and Özlale, L. (2005) 'Employing the Extended Kalman Filter in Measuring the Output Gap'. *Journal of Economic Dynamics and Control,* 29: 1611–22.

Rudebusch, G.D. (2006) 'Monetary Policy Inertia: Fact or Fiction?' *International Journal of Central Banking*, 2: 85–135.

Sargent, T.J., and Wallace N. (1981) 'Some Unpleasant Monetarist Arithmetic'. *Federal Reserve Bank of Minneapolis Quarterly Review*, 5: 1–17.

Sarkaya Ç., Öğünç F., Ece, D., Kara, H., and Özlale, U. (2005) 'Estimating Output Gap for the Turkish Economy'. Central Bank of Turkey Research Department Working Paper 05/03, Ankara.

Taylor, J.B. (2001) 'The Role of the Exchange Rate in Monetary-Policy Rules'. *American Economic Review*, 91(2): 263–67.

Appendix 10.1

While estimating the state-space model, in addition to Equations (3–9) we use a random-walk specification for the parameters. The detailed exposition of Kalman filtering theory can be found in Haykin (2001). We present here the modifications and the specifications of state-space matrices, as well as the computational algorithm employed.

The state-space matrices are specified as follows.

$$W_t^T = \begin{bmatrix} \alpha_t & \pi^e_{t,t+1} & y_t^* & \phi_t & x_t & \beta_t & \gamma_t & \rho_t & \eta_t & \tau_{1,t} & \tau_{2,t} & \tau_{3,t} \end{bmatrix}$$

$$Y_t^T = \begin{bmatrix} i_t & y_t \end{bmatrix}$$

$$U_t^T = \begin{bmatrix} \pi^*_{t,t+1} & i_{t-1} & 1 & \pi_{t-1} & \Delta s_t & \Delta s_{t-1} & 1 & -\phi_0 & \eta_t & 1 & r_t & q_t & \pi_t \end{bmatrix}$$

where T denotes the transpose of a matrix. The parameters are collected in the following matrices:

Except for the single cell $A(3, 4) = 1$, A_t is a 13 × 13 diagonal matrix with the diagonal elements as follows:

$$A_t = Diag\{\lambda_2, 0, 1, \eta_t, \theta_{1,t}, 1, 1, 1, 1, 1, 1, 1, 1\}$$

B_t is a 13 × 13 matrix of zeros with the following exceptions: $B(1, 3) = \lambda_1$, $B(2, 4) = a$, $B(2, 5) = b$, $B(2, 6) = c$, $B(4, 7) = -\phi_0$, $B(4, 8) = \eta_t$, $B(5, 8) = \tau_{2,t}$, $B(5, 9) = \tau_{3,t}$, $B(5, 10) = \tau_{4,t}$

$$C_t = \begin{bmatrix} 1 & \beta_t & 0 & 0 & \gamma_t & 0 & 0 & 0 & 0 & 0 & 0 & 0 & 0 \\ 0 & 0 & 1 & 0 & 1 & 0 & 0 & 0 & 0 & 0 & 0 & 0 & 0 & 0 \end{bmatrix}$$

$$D_t = \begin{bmatrix} -\beta_t & \rho_t & 0 & 0 & 0 & 0 & 0 & 0 & 0 & 0 & 0 & 0 & 0 \\ 0 & 0 & 0 & 0 & 0 & 0 & 0 & 0 & 0 & 0 & 0 & 0 & 0 & 0 \end{bmatrix}$$

The unobserved state variables and parameters are initialised by:

$$\widehat{i_0} = E(i) \quad \sum a = E\left[(i - \widehat{i_0})\,(i - \widehat{i_0})^T\right] \qquad \text{for } i = A, B, C, D$$

$$\widehat{W_0} = E(W) \quad \sum w = E\left[(W - \widehat{W_0})\,(W - \widehat{W_0})^T\right]$$

where E denotes the expectations operator and Σi is the covariance matrix for random variable vector i. In the simulation, we used values obtained from the baseline model including those obtained from an HP filter. Two separate, non-linear filters provide their estimates by running concurrently for both the parameters and the state variables. The state filter takes a priori state estimates and a priori parameter estimates to produce a current state estimate. The current state estimate is then updated by using the measurement taken on observed variables to produce the a posteriori state estimate. The parameter filter, on the other hand, takes the a priori state estimates to produce a current parameter estimate, then updates it using the current state estimate and the measurement taken on observed variables. In both filters, the time update and the measurement update steps are run using extended Kalman filtering methods.

11 A common currency for Middle Eastern and North African countries?

Lessons from the European Monetary Union[1]

Sergio Rossi

Introduction

The string of financial crises that have occurred over the last decade or so in emerging economies around the world points to the importance of stabilising the exchange rates of local currencies in the current international monetary and financial environment characterised by free markets, capital account liberalisation, and an increasing regionalisation of international trade as well as capital flows – as is captured by gravity models that explain trade as well as foreign direct investment (FDI) mainly by geographic proximity. In this framework, as Cohen (1998, 2002) and McKinnon (2004) observe, exchange rate volatility between key currencies like the US dollar and the euro has increased significantly in recent years. The same may be argued with respect to international capital flows, which have become more volatile, especially at the short-term end of the spectrum (see Stiglitz, 2004). Clearly, volatile capital flows and exchange rates are at present two major sources of financial instability (and crises) to which countries not engaged in regional monetary integration are exposed. Middle Eastern and North African (MENA) countries are a case in point in this regard.

MENA countries have gradually opened up their current and capital accounts since the 1980s, although a number of them maintain some restrictions on the foreign ownership of assets and repatriation of earnings (Creane, Goyal, Mobarak and Sab, 2004). Exchange rate regimes in this region range from currency board arrangements to free floats, with intermediate regimes such as managed floats. In fact, the majority of MENA countries have adopted exchange rate arrangements more by inertia than as a result of a comprehensive macroeconomic analysis of alternative exchange rate regimes. The majority of these countries peg their currencies to the US dollar, although both their trade and financial flows are stronger with the European Union (EU) than the US economy, owing largely to geographic proximity and a long historical record of extensive commercial and financial flows across the Mediterranean Sea. Looking ahead, the Euro–Mediterranean Agreements (EMAs) signed between the EU and the partner countries in the so-called Barcelona Process (which aims at setting up a free-trade area between the EU and a number of Mediterranean countries by 2010)[2] are likely to increase the number as well as the amount of both trade and financial flows across the

Mediterranean Sea. International capital flows may thereby represent a serious threat to financial stability for MENA countries, if the exchange rate arrangements adopted by these countries are not appropriate to control this situation.

This chapter considers the array of alternative exchange rate regimes that are available today, from hard pegs to floating rates, all of which have the potential to lead to financial instability and turmoil. It then proposes an alternative exchange rate arrangement, which MENA countries might adopt as a preliminary, instrumental step in order to converge and thus adopt a single currency along a more gradual, and less costly, path than the path the EU countries followed to achieve monetary union at the turn of the century. In doing so, this chapter points out some lessons to be learned from the European Monetary Union (EMU) experience for the monetary integration of MENA countries. Its aim is to elaborate on the institutional as well as structural features required for regional monetary integration, before MENA countries move on to the more demanding process (both in economic and political terms) of monetary union.

Section 1 focuses on the situation in MENA countries over the recent past, notably with respect to the convergence criteria enshrined in the Maastricht Treaty for the EMU, noting that the extensive country heterogeneity in the MENA region suggests the design of a more elaborate path to monetary union than the EMU path. The second section considers the array of alternative exchange rate regimes available today, pointing out that all these regimes have a number of drawbacks that make them a second best solution to monetary integration, which differs from monetary union in the sense that the former does not require the abandoning of local currencies. In light of this, the third section sets out a strategy to introduce a common currency rather than a single currency for (selected) MENA countries, particularly for those countries having an increasing number of commercial and/or financial ties between each other as well as with respect to the EU, which is their major trading and financial partner. The final section concludes.

1 Economic performance in MENA countries: some stylised facts and figures

The MENA region is very heterogeneous in terms of population and economic conditions. The most highly populated countries are Iran and Egypt – in each of which there are nearly 70 million inhabitants – whilst eight countries have a population of less than five million. MENA countries are also very different with regard to income levels and political structures. In 2006, for instance, per capita nominal income ranged from 693 US dollars in Yemen to more than 63,000 US dollars in Qatar, with an average per capita income level of 9,879 US dollars. This heterogeneity in income levels does not really help in reducing the differences in measured unemployment rates within the region. As a matter of fact, widely differing unemployment rates between MENA countries lead to migration pressure both within this region and from it to the EU-15, where the per capita income level is well above the MENA level (with the notable exception of Israel and some small oil-producing countries). Growth performance in the MENA region is rather diverse, too, but generally higher than in the EU, although not so high as in the most dynamic emerging market economies around the world.

As regards the level and evolution of nominal variables, notably those concerning the criteria for adoption of a single currency in EMU, a number of MENA countries are characterised by a rather stable monetary environment over the period 2001–2006. In most countries, stability-oriented monetary policies contributed to a reduction in the measured rate of (Consumer Prices Index (CPI)) inflation. Nevertheless, in several MENA countries the fiscal deficit of the general government sector was high, and sometimes increasing, with respect to Gross Domestic Product (GDP). Public deficits in the MENA region deteriorated over the first six years of the new millennium. Accordingly, public debts also increased with respect to GDP over the same period of time. Indeed, a number of authorities in the region acknowledged the need to carry out processes of fiscal and institutional reforms over the next few years, in an attempt to enhance their growth potential and attractiveness for FDI within a stable monetary environment (Sturm and Gurtner, 2007).

As regards political structures and political integration, which are both crucial for the success and durability of monetary union, the MENA region seems far from having the political requirements to form a single-currency area. In the Bretton Woods epoch, Arab countries had a political will to cooperate in exchange-rate policy issues. In 1945, 22 Arab countries agreed notably to launch a single currency that they labelled the 'Arab dinar.' Much more recently, the Islamic Development Bank – which was set up in 1973 and covers 56 countries, including several MENA countries – called for the creation of a 'golden dinar' as a common means of payment for its member countries. At the time of writing, only the Gulf Cooperation Council (GCC) countries are still pursuing their efforts to adopt a single currency (pegged to the US dollar) by 2010. Of course, the Arab League (consisting of 22 countries) provides a regional framework for political and economic integration in the region, and in particular for monetary cooperation through the Arab Monetary Fund. 'However, the Arab framework does not include Iran or, of course, Israel, two major players in the region, and suffers from a lack of political coherence' (Mazzaferro, Mehl, Sturm, Thimann and Winkler, 2002: 13). In short, there is currently no impetus for Arab political integration; nor, in fact, for North African political union. Now, it is by way of contrast widely acknowledged that the primary driving force behind EMU was the determination of several EU member country governments to adopt a single European currency before the end of the twentieth century – despite a lack of fiscal discipline as measured by the Maastricht parameters and required by the original Stability and Growth Pact as well as by the European Central Bank (see Eichengreen and Bayoumi, 1999).

In the second half of the 1990s the first-round EMU member countries converged nominally on measured inflation rates, interest rates, and the general government position in relation to GDP, but they did not show the same progress towards real convergence, measured with respect to the annual growth rates of real GDP, per capita income levels, unemployment rates, and output gaps. 'This was the major omission of the Maastricht Treaty, which is preoccupied by "nominal" as opposed to "real" convergence' (Bayoumi, Eichengreen and Mauro, 2000: 144). This situation has not changed much since the euro changeover in 1999. As empirical evidence shows, within the euro area real variables did not converge over the first eight years of monetary union (see Rossi, 2006).

Now, if within a single currency area real convergence is insufficient, it is extremely difficult for the single monetary policy to do justice, at the same time, to the needs of all its member countries. The differences in terms of both economic structure and performance between these countries are likely to bring about tensions in monetary policy decision making. In a nutshell, the one-size-fits-all interest rate policy oriented towards the needs of the single currency area as a whole might be hampered by extensive country heterogeneity as regards real magnitudes. Further, with heterogeneous cross-country responses the single monetary policy could induce idiosyncratic business cycles across the single currency area (see Suardi, 2001).

As a result, the economic divergences across that area might increase, thus slowing down the speed of the convergence process rather than doing the opposite. Also, if the supranational monetary authority in charge of the single monetary policy felt obliged to intervene in an attempt to counteract a major shock in one of its member countries, it might in fact increase the cyclical divergence between its members, and thus hinder the synchronisation of the business cycle across the whole area. If such divergences arise, as they do within Euroland, they can only be addressed by those economic policies that remain in the competence of national governments, such as fiscal and structural policies. In fact, as Sturm and Siegfried (2005: 71) point out in this regard:

> monetary union ultimately results in the transfer of sovereignty from the national to the supranational level in monetary affairs and, to some extent, needs to be accompanied by constraints for government budgets, which are areas widely regarded as being at the core of national sovereignty.

In this connection, the governments of MENA countries have to ask themselves whether they are ready (in economic as well as in political terms) to centralise monetary policy decisions at a supranational level – which requires the establishment of a supranational decision-making body to which they will transfer a significant part of their national sovereignty – and to accept and bear the burden of limiting this sovereignty in other important areas of their economic policy such as fiscal policy, which in a monetary union has to operate under tighter constraints in order to avoid strategic forms of behaviour by individual countries which have the same currency.

This set of questions, with which MENA governments will be confronted as soon as they start a discussion on the option of entering a process leading their countries to monetary union, goes along with the choice of an exchange rate arrangement to provide the financial stability that is required for them to adopt the same currency at the end of the process for monetary union. In fact, these countries need an exchange rate system that helps them accelerate convergence, in real as well as in nominal terms, without imposing on them too many binding constraints over too short a horizon, which might harm rather than help their efforts towards both economic convergence and financial stability (see Kenen and Meade, 2003). As Angeloni, Flad and Mongelli (2005: 29) point out in this respect:

> On the one hand, a high degree of exchange rate flexibility may reduce the burden on policy-makers, freeing up room for manoeuvre that can be used to attain domestic policy targets. On the other hand, excessive exchange rate volatility may be a hindrance to the convergence process itself, by undermining the effort to stabilise market expectations. Striking the correct balance can be particularly complex.

This challenge is elaborated on in the next section.

2 Exchange rate arrangements, trade, and financial stability

The South-Eastern neighbouring countries of the E(M)U appear very heterogeneous as well as fragmented, in spite of more than ten years of preferential relationships under the umbrella of the Barcelona Process (see Lahrèche-Révil and Milgram, 2006). Despite the efforts to promote intra-regional trade between MENA countries, intra-MENA trade remains low (Dennis, 2006: 3). Even between the GCC countries, which are aiming to adopt monetary union with a single currency by 2010, intra-regional trade is very modest. In 2005, for instance, trade between GCC members accounted for only 8.1 per cent of all GCC exports and 8.9 per cent of total imports, according to the data provided by the Islamic Development Bank.[3] This figure is substantially smaller than what could be observed in the same year within the euro area (where more than fifty per cent of trade was intra-euro-area trade). This might suggest that the macroeconomic benefits of adopting a single currency for the GCC countries will not be as high as those (expected) for EMU, even considering that monetary union might generate trade and financial flows endogenously – as argued by Frankel and Rose (2002). In fact, as Adam and Cobham (2007: 61) point out in the conclusions of their analysis:

> The basic results confirm the importance of currency unions in encouraging trade between countries, but ... they also indicate that some regimes other than currency unions are significantly more pro-trade than flexible exchange rates: there is a graduated positive effect on trade as uncertainty and transactions costs are reduced.

Clearly, any exchange rate arrangement that reduces uncertainty and transactions costs on the foreign exchange market is a better regime than a free float. Indeed, floating exchange rates tend towards volatility, which raises the exchange rate risk premium and thereby decreases potential capital inflows (in the form of FDI) to the detriment of the economic development of the countries adopting this exchange rate strategy. Exchange rate volatility (measured by the standard deviation in nominal exchange rates) tends also to reduce trade growth and decreases the level of trade considerably (see Anderton and Skudelny, 2001). Intermediate exchange rate regimes, like a crawling peg (or band) or a managed float, however, are not a better solution, because they can provoke financial instability within countries where capital movements to and from the rest of the world have been set free as a result of financial liberalisation. As a matter of fact, neither crawling pegs nor floating exchange rates can protect banks against panic by those foreign creditors who hold short-term claims denominated in foreign currency. Indeed, managing their currencies' exchange rates might prove to be too costly for countries that are directly hit by a speculative attack. This holds also for those neighbouring countries that are hit by negative spillovers. As a result, intermediate exchange rate arrangements can provide only limited protection against financial instability.

With regard to the current set of exchange rate arrangements adopted by MENA countries, the most probable strategy for the near future is for them (all) to peg their local currencies to the same anchor (which should be the euro rather than the US dollar, as noted above), in order for them to develop their trade and financial integration and eventually euroise their economies or adopt their own single currency, to be pegged to the euro. As the 1994–1995 Mexican crisis has shown, however:

> emerging markets with weak banking systems and heavy dependence on foreign capital should not peg their exchange rates. When banks run into trouble, a government seeking to maintain an exchange rate peg will have limited ability to inject credit into the banking system; since currency traders know that the authorities will find themselves between a rock and a hard place, banking problems inevitably spill over into the foreign exchange market. (Eichengreen and Bayoumi, 1999: 355)

A similar reasoning holds for fixed exchange rates, hard pegs, and currency boards: all these arrangements entail the risk of inflexibility and can give rise to economic costs for a country if it is likely to face asymmetric shocks with respect to the currency area to which it is linked (see Eichengreen and Bayoumi, 1999). Tying the hands of the monetary authorities and abolishing the risk of exchange rate volatility is thus not enough to dispose of the idiosyncrasies in countries that can jeopardise their progress towards adopting a single currency. Euroising the MENA economies would also be a problematic strategy, owing to the drawbacks of such an exchange rate regime as regards the lack of a lender of last resort and the loss of monetary sovereignty that goes along with the decision to give up the national currency.

All in all, the choice of the exchange rate regime is still an open question, which asks what kind of exchange rate arrangement the MENA countries should implement, if they want to achieve regional monetary integration without increasing the risks of financial instability and the potential for a currency crisis. To be sure, exchange rate stability is important for attracting FDI, which is crucial for the

Euro–Mediterranean partnership as it will enhance trade and technology transfers between the two shores of the Mediterranean Sea. However, as the MENA region is also characterised, so far, by significant political turmoil, foreign investors might be reluctant to invest in this region, so that the exchange rates of the local currencies could be subjected to volatile capital flows, which would entail some risks of speculative attacks. This calls for regional monetary integration before too long, but of a form which sets up an international financial institution able to direct capital flows towards this region, particularly towards those MENA countries that are most in need of them and into which (private) capital would not otherwise flow.[4]

This issue is addressed in the next section, which puts forward an alternative exchange rate system aiming at financial stability and economic growth (including through important FDI flows).

3 A new framework for regional monetary integration

To date, MENA countries are not popular locations for FDI. This situation constrains growth and global supply in all this region. Despite efforts to provide a framework of price stability, finding the right balance between monetary and exchange rate policies is a challenging task for most MENA central banks, and some countries have recently tried to focus more strongly on domestic goals, in particular price stability developments, to the detriment of exchange rate stability. Exchange rate strategies, however, are crucial for attracting FDI and eventually also for monetary stability. These strategies concern both the level of the real exchange rate (which determines the competitiveness of a country) and the risks associated with the nominal exchange rate (that is, the volatility of the exchange rate). Both determine foreign investment decisions, because hedging is generally not possible for FDI.

In this section, we argue that the exchange rate strategy of the MENA countries should not be designed within a bilateral framework, but ought to be the result of some kind of multilateral agreement, analogous to the multilateral agreement that in 1950 led to the creation of the European Payments Union (EPU). In this regard, the presence of many competing emerging economies within the Euro–Mediterranean area has to be taken into account. Indeed, MENA countries could increase their long-term attractiveness for FDI by choosing the proper mixture between low uncertainty on the nominal exchange rates of their currencies and differentiation with the exchange rate arrangements of several central and Eastern European countries, which became popular locations for FDI when they joined the EU in May 2004. If so, then what is the appropriate exchange rate arrangement for MENA countries considered as a whole?

The answer this section provides to the above question combines the macroeconomic benefits of exchange rate stability with the flexibility offered by an exchange rate that can be adjusted over time by a multilateral decision of the countries concerned. To be sure, for all the MENA countries a certain degree of exchange rate flexibility will remain necessary in the near future. As the Deutsche Bundesbank (2001: 24) observes, 'sufficiently flexible exchange rates would facilitate the catching-up process, in conformity with stability. They safeguard the requisite monetary room for manoeuvre.' In this respect, even a small open economy will be able to implement fiscal and monetary policies oriented to its domestic needs, and this even in the case of an extremely high degree of capital mobility, as long as the country controls its own currency and avoids entering a single currency area or dollarising its economic space.[5]

In light of the risks of speculative attacks on the foreign exchange market pointed out above, MENA countries need, in particular, an exchange rate arrangement by which they can prevent the destabilising effects on their own economies of trade integration and international financial liberalisation. This reform requires an agreement between MENA countries to set up an international settlement institution, in order for this multilateral institution to record and to finalise payments between participating nations. In this respect, the EPU experience (1950–1958) provides some interesting features which are worth discussing in order to avoid the shortcomings that led to its dissolution (see Kaplan and Schleiminger, 1989). Indeed, as Triffin (1978: 15) explains:

> The EPU agreement was a remarkably clean and simple document, embodying sweeping and precise commitments of a revolutionary nature, which overnight drastically shifted the whole structure of intra-European payments from a bilateral to a multilateral basis.

EPU member countries used the Bank for International Settlements (BIS) as their settlement agent, to which they sent their bilateral payment orders once per month through their national central banks. These bilateral positions were cleared to give rise to a net multilateral debt or credit position of each country towards the BIS, which labelled all positions in its own unit of account, equal to 0.88867088 grammes of gold, which, at that time, corresponded to the gold value of a US dollar (Bank for International Settlements, 1951: 225). The problem with the EPU, which led to its dissolution, was related to the settlement of the net position that each member country had with respect to the Union (Gros and Thygesen, 1992: 6). Once the initial credit that each country participating in the EPU received upon its creation was spent, '[t]he payment of any net increase in debt to the Union had to be made partly in gold or dollars, and partly through an extension of credit with the Union' (Coffey and Presley, 1971: 15). The obligation, introduced in 1955, for debtor countries to pay with gold at least three quarters of their debt to the Union made international settlements problematic, as debtor countries were running out of precious metals. This made it more and more difficult for the EPU to settle with gold its debt to creditor countries, leading participating countries to bring the multilateral settlement agreement to an end in December 1958.

From the viewpoint of monetary integration, the undisputed achievement of the EPU was the multilateral character it gave to international settlements, whose accounting devices were provided by the BIS acting as a settlement agent. In fact, the demise of the EPU was due to the lack of a settlement institution between participating countries, as the BIS was merely recording all multilateral positions with its own unit of account, instead of issuing its own means of final payment for the settlement of international debts. In short, the problem with the EPU was the political unwillingness to transform the BIS from a settlement agent (merely keeping the books) into a settlement institution at the international level, allowing it to issue a truly international money in order for the multilateral debt and credit positions to be finally paid.[6] Clearly, no current or capital account deficit can be settled with a unit of account: an international means of final payment is needed for that purpose.[7]

Let us call 'MENA Settlement Institution' (MENA-SI) the proposed international settlement institution for MENA countries, and label as 'MENA dinar' the monetary unit in which this institution will record the settlement of a participating country's transactions with the rest of the world. As in modern domestic settlement systems, let us consider that the international settlement system we propose in this section works with a real-time gross-settlement protocol (RTGS), whereby each payment across borders is settled in MENA dinars between the countries involved, in order for them to be final in the Goodhart (1989) sense noted above.

In the proposed settlement system, any cross-border transactions concerning a MENA country will be finally settled in national currency within each of the countries concerned, and in the international monetary unit (dubbed 'MENA dinar') between them. In practice, the proposed exchange rate arrangement for MENA countries requires the introduction of a monetary–institutional structure between them, through which any commercial or financial imports are finally paid in local monies as far as residents (that is to say, importers and exporters) are concerned, whilst these same transactions are finally paid in MENA dinars as far as countries are concerned as a whole (that is, as the set of their residents). If so, then any importer pays using his/her national currency and any exporter is finally paid in his/her own local currency, through the relevant banking systems. This requires setting up in every country which participates in this international settlement system an institution that acts as a catalyst in any international payments resulting from (large-value) cross-border transactions on either goods or financial markets. Indeed, this institution might simply be an international book-keeping department of the relevant national central bank, as its task will be merely to record cross-border settlements in such a way that within the relevant country all payments are finalised using the national currency as a means of payment, whilst between any two participating countries all payments are finalised through the emission of MENA dinars as a vehicle for those goods or financial assets that move beyond a country's borders.

Three stylised cases can be singled out to illustrate the working of the proposed arrangement. They are considered separately here, through three simple numerical examples, to convey an illustrative picture of the exchange rate arrangement that we put forward in this section for the monetary integration of countries in the MENA region.

Payments between two MENA countries

Suppose that a MENA country, say Algeria, imports today from another MENA country, say Tunisia, goods worth 500 billion Algerian dinars (DZD) or, equivalently, 10 billion Tunisian dinars (TND) (assuming an exchange rate of 50 DZD for 1 TND). The Algerian importer is invoiced in Tunisian dinars by the exporter. Today, s/he may pay for these imports by writing a cheque on a bank account in Tunisian dinars, or by buying the necessary amount of Tunisian dinars on the foreign exchange market. Some other payment arrangement might be conceived, of course, but in any case there is an exchange rate risk as the DZD/TND exchange rate floats. If the new exchange rate arrangement were implemented along the lines proposed in this section, then the Algerian importer would pay for his/her imports in local currency, whilst the Tunisian exporter would be paid in his/her own local currency, at an exchange rate that is kept stable by the working of the international settlement system headed by the MENA-SI.

Indeed, any commercial items imported by a country's resident will have to be paid for with an equivalent export of securities, which in fact are goods in their financial representation.[8] In practice, this means that whenever an agent imports (exports) goods from (to) abroad, another agent, including the state, has to sell (buy) financial assets to (from) the partner country. To be sure, logic requires that each country must finance its foreign deficit eventually, which means that it must pay for its commercial imports by an equivalent amount of exports of real goods, services, or securities.[9] If so, then each demand for a currency is, simultaneously, a supply of the same currency and for the same amount, demand and supply being expressed here by the same country, defined as the set of its residents, acting simultaneously on both commercial and financial markets across borders.

Let us elaborate on this, to show how a country, say Algeria, can exert a demand for DZD on the securities market while it exerts a supply of DZD, and for the same amount, on the market for produced goods and services – which it imports from Tunisia in our stylised case.

In Algeria, a sum of 500 billion DZD is disposed of by the local importer, who obtains goods or services in exchange for it. In Tunisia, on the other hand, the exporter of goods or services is paid with an amount of 10 billion TND, which defines an identically equivalent purchasing power with respect to the value exported to Algeria. If so, the relevant entries in the proposed settlement system are shown with number 1 in Table 11.1 (entries are in billions of the relevant monetary unit).

In this system, the Algerian importer asks the bank (say, Bank B1) to pay a sum of 500 billion DZD to his/her foreign correspondent in Tunisia. In order to do this, Bank B1 will have to get in touch with its home-country central bank, whose international department will have to ask the MENA-SI to provide the amount of MENA dinars that are necessary in order for the final settlement to take place between the two countries involved (let us suppose an exchange rate of 50 DZD for 1 MENA dinar). As a result, Algeria is debited with an amount of 10 billion MENA dinars, a sum that is credited to Tunisia, through the relevant central banks.

Now, to avoid a net demand for MENA dinars, hence also a net demand for Tunisian dinars, on the foreign exchange market – as this would affect the relevant

Table 11.1 The result of an international settlement for intra-MENA trade

Central bank of Algeria			
Domestic Department		*International Department*	
Assets	*Liabilities*	*Assets*	*Liabilities*
1. Bank B1 (importer of goods or financial assets)	1. International Department	1. Domestic Department	1. MENA-SI
+500 DZD	+500 DZD	+10 MENA dinars	+10 MENA dinars
2. International Department	2. State (as seller of securities)	2. MENA-SI	2. Domestic Department
+500 DZD	+500 DZD	+10 MENA dinars	+10 MENA dinars

MENA Settlement Institution	
Assets	*Liabilities*
1. Central bank of Algeria (International Department)	1. Central bank of Tunisia (International Department)
+10 MENA dinars	+10 MENA dinars
2. Central bank of Tunisia (International Department)	2. Central bank of Algeria (International Department)
+10 MENA dinars	+10 MENA dinars

Central bank of Tunisia			
Domestic Department		*International Department*	
Assets	*Liabilities*	*Assets*	*Liabilities*
1. International Department	1. Bank B2 (exporter of goods or financial assets)	1. MENA-SI	1. Domestic Department
+10 TND	+10 TND	+10 MENA dinars	+10 MENA dinars
2. Securities	2. International Department	2. Domestic Department	2. MENA-SI
+10 TND	+10 TND	+10 MENA dinars	+10 MENA dinars

exchange rates and make them unstable – the international settlement system will have to make sure that every demand for a currency is simultaneously also a supply of the same currency and for the same amount, for any country involved. To reduce to zero all net demands (and net supplies) on the foreign exchange market, the payments mechanism at the international level must carry out a so-called delivery-versus-payment of securities, every time that a cross-border exchange occurs. In the numerical example considered in this section, the net importing country, Algeria, has to sell an amount of securities (through its state if there is no private resident doing it), in order for this country to finance its net imports of real goods and services. Indeed, only in this case will the country as a whole be led to exert both a demand for and a supply of foreign currency for exactly the same amount and at one and the same point of time. In our numerical example, 500 billion DZD are indeed supplied (in exchange for 10 billion MENA dinars) in payment of Algeria's commercial imports, at the same instant as 500 billion DZD are demanded (against 10 billion MENA dinars) in payment of the securities sold by Algeria to finance its imports of real goods and services. Similarly, 10 billion TND are demanded (in exchange for 10 billion MENA dinars) in payment of Tunisia's trade surplus, at the same time as 10 billion TND are supplied by Tunisia (against 10 billion MENA dinars) in payment of the securities purchased by it from either Algeria or the rest of the world. In Table 11.1, these payments on securities are recorded as shown by the book-keeping entries numbered 2.

Each currency being thus simultaneously supplied and demanded against an identical amount of MENA dinars, exchange rates can never be affected by transactions across borders (be they on product or financial markets). Note that these transactions on securities are induced by the commercial or financial transactions carried out by residents. As such, the former transactions might involve the state of either country (Algeria and/or Tunisia), as there might be no private sector resident willing to sell (or to buy) those securities that are purchased (or sold) by a non-resident (that is to say, a resident in another country). Note also that the securities sold by the net importing country (in our example, Algeria) need not be the securities that are bought by a net exporting country (in our example, Tunisia). This is a point which will be expanded later, after having considered our two other stylised cases, to which we now turn.

Payments between a MENA country and a E(M)U country

Suppose that Tunisia imports from the E(M)U (say, from Germany) goods and/or financial assets worth 10 billion euros or, equivalently, 20 billion Tunisian dinars (assume an exchange rate of 1 euro against 2 TND). In Tunisia, the importer asks the bank (say, Bank B3) to pay 20 billion TND to the German exporter, who holds an account in the German banking system (say, at Bank B4) and is thereby paid in local currency, that is, in euros. In this respect, Bank B3 has to get in touch with its home-country central bank, that is, the central bank of Tunisia, in order for the international transaction to be finally settled. When Bank B3 asks the central bank of Tunisia to pay an amount of 10 billion euros to Bank B4, this payment order gives rise to an entry in both departments at the central bank of Tunisia, as in the previous case: its domestic department enters the transaction in local currency (that is, 20 billion TND), carrying it over to the international department of the same central bank, which enters this payment in MENA dinars (assume that 1 TND = 1 MENA dinar). The result of this purely book-keeping operation is shown in the entries

Table 11.2 The result of an international settlement for E(M)U–MENA trade

Central bank of Tunisia			
Domestic Department		*International Department*	
Assets	*Liabilities*	*Assets*	*Liabilities*
3. Bank B3 (importer of goods or financial assets)	3. International Department	3. Domestic Department	3. MENA-SI
+20 TND	+20 TND	+20 MENA dinars	+20 MENA dinars
4. International Department	4. State (as seller of securities)	4. MENA-SI	4. Domestic Department
+20 TND	+20 TND	+20 MENA dinars	+20 MENA dinars

MENA Settlement Institution	
Assets	*Liabilities*
3. Central bank of Tunisia (International Department)	3. Bundesbank (International Department)
+20 MENA dinars	+20 MENA dinars
4. Bundesbank (International Department)	4. Central bank of Tunisia (International Department)
+20 MENA dinars	+20 MENA dinars

Bundesbank			
Domestic Department		*International Department*	
Assets	*Liabilities*	*Assets*	*Liabilities*
3. International Department	3. Bank B4 (exporter of goods or financial assets)	3. MENA-SI	3. Domestic Department
+10 euros	+10 euros	+20 MENA dinars	+20 MENA dinars
4. Securities	4. International Department	4. Domestic Department	4. MENA-SI
+10 euros	+10 euros	+20 MENA dinars	+20 MENA dinars

numbered 3 in Table 11.2 (where figures are in billions of the relevant monetary unit). As in the previous case, the international settlement of cross-border trade elicits a delivery of securities as shown in Table 11.2 by the entries numbered 4.

As Table 11.2 shows, the corresponding partner of a central bank's international department is not another central bank – as is the case under a correspondent central banking model, which, in fact, can represent only an interim solution to the problem of finally settling cross-border transactions (as noted by the European Central Bank, 1999) – but the international settlement institution that we labelled

MENA-SI. In practice, the international department of the central bank of Tunisia asks the MENA-SI to pay for the country's imports an amount of 20 billion MENA dinars to the account of Germany, which, at the international level, is represented by (the international department of) the Bundesbank. As a result, the international department of the Bundesbank is credited by the MENA-SI with an amount of 20 billion MENA dinars, and carries this flow over to its domestic department, to the benefit of the German exporter, who is paid via Bank B4 in its local currency (10 billion euros) at the prevailing exchange rate. The same reasoning holds, *mutatis mutandis*, for the payment of the German purchase of foreign securities. But we do not need to expand on this payment any further here, as the architecture is the same as that explained above in the case of intra-MENA trade, and the payment will take place through the same mechanics. Let us turn, therefore, to the last stylised case.

Payments between a MENA country and a non-E(M)U country

Suppose that Algeria exports some goods and/or financial assets worth 500 billion DZD to the United States. The relevant book-keeping entries under the proposed new system occur according to the same logic explained above, and are recorded in Table 11.3 with no further need to explain them in any detail (assume that 75 DZD = 1.5 MENA dinars = 1 US dollar (USD)). To repeat only the key analytical point, each autonomous commercial or financial transaction across borders elicits a transaction on securities, implying a transaction by the state of either trading partner in the international settlement system we propose here, if the cross-border financial flows carried out by private residents are not enough to avoid payment deficits, as noted by Machlup (1963: 256).

In this new international payment system, to be headed as well as overseen by an international settlement institution, each national currency is changed into itself – in an absolute exchange – through the purely vehicular emission of an international means of final payment, which has a numerical nature and homogenises all national currencies participating in the system. In this system, all transactions on foreign exchange markets are absolute exchanges, in so far as country *A* recovers its currency as soon as it surrenders this currency in payment of commercial or financial imports from another participating country, *B*. If so, then the regime for international payments becomes a system of stable exchange rates, replacing thereby all forms of exchange rate arrangements existing today – which are unable to guarantee stability on the foreign exchange market, unless they fix exchange rates in an irrevocable way, which elicits, however, a series of macroeconomic issues and drawbacks as noted above.

A last point is in order here. It concerns the quality of those securities that are sold and bought by the general government sector of the countries involved in the new settlement system that we propose. In fact, the main fear that our proposal may elicit is that it could give rise to a series of 'junk bonds.' In particular, the quality of those securities sold by countries having a deficit in their current account might deteriorate over time, so that the new system will not survive the 'market

Table 11.3 The result of an international settlement for US–MENA trade

Central bank of Algeria			
Domestic Department		*International Department*	
Assets	*Liabilities*	*Assets*	*Liabilities*
5. International Department	5. Bank B5 (exporter of goods or financial assets)	5. MENA-SI	5. Domestic Department
+500 DZD	+500 DZD	+10 MENA dinars	+10 MENA dinars
6. Securities	6. International Department	6. Domestic Department	6. MENA-SI
+500 DZD	+500 DZD	+10 MENA dinars	+10 MENA dinars

MENA Settlement Institution	
Assets	*Liabilities*
5. Federal Reserve System (International Department)	5. Central bank of Algeria (International Department)
+10 MENA dinars	+10 MENA dinars
6. Central bank of Algeria (International Department)	6. Federal Reserve System (International Department)
+10 MENA dinars	+10 MENA dinars

Federal Reserve System			
Domestic Department		*International Department*	
Assets	*Liabilities*	*Assets*	*Liabilities*
5. Bank B6 (importer of goods or financial assets)	5. International Department	5. Domestic Department	5. MENA-SI
+6.67 USD	+6.67 USD	+10 MENA dinars	+10 MENA dinars
6. International Department	6. State (as seller of securities)	6. MENA-SI	6. Domestic Department
+6.67 USD	+6.67 USD	+10 MENA dinars	+10 MENA dinars

test,' and is likely to fail in the same way as the EPU did, for creditor countries may not be willing to stockpile these securities as time goes by. To avoid this risk, the multilateral agreement to be signed between countries participating in this new settlement system will have to provide a limit, for instance as a percentage of either total foreign trade or GDP (calculated on a five- or ten-year moving average), beyond which no country is allowed to finance its current account deficit by selling securities – notably, when the country's risk and stock of debt are too high for this country to provide sound collateral – and it must thus cut back on its commercial imports and/or increase its exports of goods and/or services (not least to pay for debt service, that is to say, interest on those securities that the country sold in order to finance its foreign deficits).

In this respect, instead of selling its securities to another country, a country might sell them to the MENA-SI, which would thus act as an international financial intermediary and advance a payment that this very country will benefit from when exporting goods and/or financial assets. If so, there may be two kinds of financial assets behind the entries in Tables 11.1 to 11.3: the paying country's securities sold to the MENA-SI, and the MENA-SI's securities sold to the payee's country. These securities may be denominated in either local currencies or MENA dinars, the crucial point being that settlement of all financial transactions between participating countries occurs using international money as a vehicle, that is, a means of payment, thus transferring the amount of securities from the seller to the buyer.

By selling its own securities (or debt certificates) on the international financial market, the MENA-SI would collect private as well as public capital and would invest it in those MENA countries most in need of economic growth and into which capital would not otherwise flow. Of course, the MENA-SI open-market and lending operations would have to be supervised and to fully respect the principles of sound banking as well as international best practice. Its lending facilities must be limited by some criterion (to be decided at a political level), and an interest rate must be paid by those countries obtaining financial assistance from the MENA-SI. In particular, the interest rate to be paid by countries on their borrowings, from either other countries or the MENA-SI, would depend on the extent of their trade deficits, stock of foreign debts, and capital account imbalances. Clearly, a country recording a financial deficit, in particular a deficit arising from capital account imbalances, is hardly in a position to issue new debt instruments at favourable terms. It must therefore accept the onus of either paying higher rates of interest on new debt or slowing down the national economy by a hike in domestic interest rates in the hope of attracting foreign capital (both short- and long-term).

This framework for regional monetary integration does not solve the problem of how MENA countries participating in the international settlement institution insert the MENA dinar into the current world monetary regime, that is, whether the MENA dinar will be fixed or floated with respect to those currencies that exist outside the MENA region. In fact, this is not an issue, as the MENA dinar is just an international means of payment for MENA central banks, and is out of reach for any other economic agents, be they private sector residents or public sector institutions (see Tables 11.1 to 11.3). All settlements between agents within or across borders will continue to be made in any currency that is permitted by their country's legislation and agreed upon by the contracting parties. For them, it is thus 'business as usual,' apart from the requirement for MENA private banks to get in touch with their local central bank every time a payment occurs across the country's borders, as is shown above through our numerical examples.

Conclusion

This chapter has pointed out that monetary integration does not mean monetary union. Clearly, to integrate countries monetarily does not require abolishing local currencies, to replace them by a single (supranational) currency: a common currency is enough to reach a long-standing goal, that is, exchange rate stability, which is instrumental in order for a country to attract foreign (direct) investment and thereby develop its domestic economy. An important lesson to be drawn from EMU in this regard is to distinguish, as Eichengreen (2005) does, structural preconditions from 'pseudo preconditions' for monetary integration. Among the latter, Eichengreen includes nominal convergence criteria, public deficit ceilings, and sanctions and fines for countries trespassing them. In fact, monetary integration – as an institutional step towards monetary union, which might or might not be accomplished in some near or distant future – requires a structural change, at the international level, as regards final payments of cross-border transactions on either product or financial markets. A new exchange rate arrangement, based on a truly international money, is indeed instrumental in integrating countries monetarily, so as to stabilise exchange rates in the MENA region and, consequently, attract FDI flows, to the benefit of growth and employment in a region that, so far, has been suffering from a lack of foreign private capital. The creation of an international settlement institution in the MENA area is also likely to give more political as well as economic stability to this region, which can be further enhanced by allowing this new institution to issue and sell its own securities or debt certificates. A common currency and the stability of exchange rates implied by our proposal will induce more intra-regional trade, so as to facilitate both convergence and monetary union in line with the literature on the endogeneity of the criteria for optimum currency areas (see De Grauwe and Mongelli, 2005).

Indeed, monetary union between MENA countries along the path that led to EMU is neither possible nor advisable: both political and economic divergences – much more serious within the MENA region than in the EU – point to the necessity to search for alternative strategies for the monetary integration of MENA countries. In fact, financial liberalisation and international capital mobility prove to be incompatible with exchange rate fixity and adoption of a single currency. The solution that this chapter proposes, namely, a multilateral exchange rate arrangement to create a new international monetary institution guaranteeing payment finality for all economic transactions between any participating countries – which requires the emission of a truly international money (that we dubbed 'MENA dinar') as the means of final payment between countries – looks much more promising in order to integrate MENA countries monetarily before long. It also leaves open – in fact, it makes more likely – the possibility of achieving the goal of monetary union, that is the issue of a single currency for a number of (selected) MENA countries, without raising the economic costs that would result from repeating in the MENA region the experience that EU member countries carried out in the recent past, in which they disposed of their local currencies with significantly more pain than gain at the macroeconomic level and in terms of economic performance (see Rossi, 2006). This alternative strategy imposes no straightjacket on economic policies before MENA countries converge (through increasing intra-regional trade), allows individual countries to go at their own speeds as long as they stick to their national currencies, and makes use of the proposed international monetary–financial institution to guarantee exchange rate stability and thereby attract capital inflows, especially at the long-term end of the spectrum (FDI).

Notes

1 The author would like to thank Chrysost Bangaké, Mongi Boughzala, David Cobham, Ghassan Dibeh, Angela Di Maria, Wassim Shahin, Michael Sturm and Abdallah Zouache for their helpful comments, Entela Myftari and Christian Laszewski for valuable research assistance, and Danielle Meuwly for her help with the data set on MENA countries (available from the author on demand). The usual disclaimer applies.

2 The current Barcelona partner countries of the EU are Algeria, Egypt, Israel, Jordan, Lebanon, Morocco, Syria, Tunisia, Turkey, and West Bank and Gaza (both represented by the Palestinian National Authority). EMAs are currently in force in Egypt (since 1 June 2004), Israel (since 1 June 2000), Jordan (since 1 May 2002), Lebanon (since 1 April 2006), Morocco (since 1 March 2000), and Tunisia (since 1 March 1998). The EMA for Algeria is currently in the ratification phase. See http://ec.europa.eu/comm/external_relations/euromed/med_ass_agreemnts.htm.

3 'This is explained mainly by the similar factor endowment of the countries; however, trade barriers, which are to be eliminated as part of the integration process, may also have contributed to this low figure' (Sturm and Siegfried, 2005: 11).

4 According to the World Bank's *Global Development Finance* indicators, between 1998 and 2006 the MENA countries attracted less than five per cent of total net private capital flows to developing countries. In particular, net inward FDI in the MENA region was between 2.1 and 5.6 billion US dollars per year. These figures are the lowest of all the various groups of emerging and developing countries. Indeed, they are even lower than the net inward FDI flows attracted by sub-Saharan Africa over the same period of time.

5 Dollarisation is tantamount to adopting a foreign currency (not necessarily the US dollar) as legal tender in a country, whose currency is thereby removed from circulation and eventually abandoned (currency substitution).

6 As the *Glossary of Terms Used in Payments and Settlement Systems* (Bank for International Settlements, 2003: 45) puts it, a settlement agent is an agent that manages the settlement process (determining settlement positions, monitoring the exchange of payment orders, and so on) for transfer systems or other arrangements that require settlement, whereas a settlement institution is the institution across whose books transfers between participants take place in order to achieve settlement within a settlement system. 'The settlement institution is in the unique position of being able to create a centralised source of settlement funds to the participants of the system. This source is called centralised because the settlement institution is the only counterparty that can influence the total amount of settlement assets that participants hold' (Bank for International Settlements, 2005: 15).

7 The current regime of international payments is a 'non-system', as Williamson (1977: 73) puts it, as reserve-currency countries do not finally pay for their net imports when they surrender an amount of national currencies to the rest of the world. Indeed, '[t]he supply of reserve currencies to other nations depends on *payment* deficits incurred by the reserve countries' (Machlup, 1963: 256, author's emphasis). Payment finality means that 'a seller of a good, or service, or another asset, receives something of equal value from the purchaser, *which leaves the seller with no further claim on the buyer*' (Goodhart, 1989: 26, author's emphasis).

8 Recall that cross-border payments are to be settled according to the RTGS protocol (see above). Securities are financial claims on current or future production of the country issuing them.

9 Clearly, any trade deficit has to be financed, and this can only occur through a sale of securities – provided of course that there is a purchaser for them, otherwise the country must cut back on its net imports of commercial items.

References

Adam, C., and Cobham, D. (2007) 'Exchange Rate Regimes and Trade'. *Manchester School*, 27(s1): 44–63.

Anderton, R., and Skudelny, F. (2001) 'Exchange Rate Volatility and Euro Area Imports'. European Central Bank Working Paper 64.

Angeloni, I., Flad, M., and Mongelli, F. (2005) 'Economic and Monetary Integration of the New Member States: Helping to Chart the Route'. European Central Bank Occasional Paper 36.

Bank for International Settlements (1951) 'From the Intra-European Payments Schemes to the European Payments Union'. *Twenty-First Annual Report*. 214–38. Basle: Bank for International Settlements.

Bank for International Settlements (2003) *A Glossary of Terms Used in Payments and Settlement Systems*. Basle: Bank for International Settlements.

Bank for International Settlements (2005) *New Developments in Large-Value Payment Systems*. Basle: Bank for International Settlements.

Bayoumi, T., Eichengreen, B., and Mauro, P. (2000) 'On Regional Monetary Arrangements for ASEAN'. *Journal of the Japanese and International Economies*, 14: 121–48.

Coffey, P., and Presley, J. (1971) *European Monetary Integration*. London and New York: Macmillan and St. Martin's Press.

Cohen, B. (1998) *The Geography of Money*. Ithaca: Cornell University Press.

Cohen, B. (2002) Monetary Instability: Are National Currencies Becoming Obsolete? in S. McBride, L. Dobuzinskis, M. Cohen and J. Busumtwi-Sam (eds) *Global Instability: Uncertainty and New Visions in Political Economy*. Dordrecht and London: Kluwer Academic Publishers.

Creane, S., Goyal, R., Mobarak, A., and Sab, R. (2004) 'Financial Sector Development in the Middle East and North Africa'. International Monetary Fund Working Paper 04/201.

De Grauwe, P., and Mongelli, P. (2005) 'Endogeneities of Optimum Currency Areas: What Brings Countries Sharing a Single Currency Closer Together?' European Central Bank Working Paper 468.

Dennis, A. (2006) 'The Impact of Regional Trade Agreements and Trade Facilitation in the Middle East North Africa Region'. World Bank Policy Research Working Paper 3837.

Deutsche Bundesbank (2001) 'Monetary Aspects of the Enlargement of the EU'. *Monthly Report*, 53(10): 15–30.

Eichengreen, B. (2005) Real and Pseudo Preconditions for an Asian Monetary Union, in Asian Development Bank (ed.) *Asian Economic Cooperation and Integration: Progress, Prospects, and Challenges*. Manila: Asian Development Bank.

Eichengreen, B., and Bayoumi, T. (1999) Is Asia an Optimum Currency Area? Can it Become One? Regional, Global, and Historical Perspectives on Asian Monetary Relations, in S. Collignon, J. Pisani-Ferry and Y.C. Park (eds) *Exchange Rate Policies in Emerging Asian Countries*. London and New York: Routledge.

European Central Bank (1999) *Correspondent Central Banking Model*. Frankfurt: European Central Bank.

Frankel, J., and Rose, A. (2002) 'An Estimate of the Effect of Common Currencies on Trade and Income'. *Quarterly Journal of Economics*, 117: 437–66.

Goodhart, C. (1989) *Money, Information and Uncertainty* (2nd ed.). Basingstoke: Macmillan.

Gros, D., and Thygesen, N. (1992) *European Monetary Integration: From the European Monetary System to European Monetary Union*. London and New York: Longman and St. Martin's Press.

Kaplan, J., and Schleiminger, G. (1989) *The European Payments Union: Financial Diplomacy in the 1950s*. Oxford: Clarendon Press.

Kenen, P., and Meade, E. (2003) 'EU Accession and the Euro: Close Together or Far Apart?' Institute for International Economics Policy Brief 03/09.

Lahrèche-Révil, A., and Milgram, J. (2006) 'Exchange-rate Policies and Trade in the MENA Countries'. Working Paper 06/07. Grenada: University of Grenada.

McKinnon, R. (2004) 'The World Dollar Standard and Globalisation: New Rules for the Game?' in L. Michelis and M. Lovewell (eds) *Exchange Rates, Economic Integration and the International Economy*. Toronto: Athenian Policy Forum Press.

Machlup, F. (1963) 'Reform of the International Monetary System', in H.G. Grubel (ed.) *World Monetary Reform: Plans and Issues*, Stanford and London: Stanford University Press and Oxford University Press.

Mazzaferro, F., Mehl, A., Sturm, M., Thimann, C., and Winkler, A. (2002) 'Economic Relations with Regions Neighbouring the Euro Area in the "Euro Time Zone"'. European Central Bank Occasional Paper 7.

Rossi, S. (2006) 'The Institution of a Single-Currency Area: Lessons for Asia from the European Monetary Union', in M.G. Plummer and E. Jones (eds) *International Economic Integration and Asia*. Singapore: World Scientific Publishing.

Stiglitz, J. (2004) 'Capital-Market Liberalisation, Globalisation, and the IMF'. *Oxford Review of Economic Policy*, 20(1): 57–71.

Sturm, M., and Gurtner, F. (2007) 'Fiscal Policy in Mediterranean Countries: Developments, Structures and Implications for Monetary Policy'. European Central Bank Occasional Paper 69.

Sturm, M., and Siegfried, N. (2005) 'Regional Monetary Integration in the Member States of the Gulf Cooperation Council'. European Central Bank Occasional Paper 31.

Suardi, M. (2001) 'EMU Asymmetries in the Monetary Policy Transmission'. European Commission Economic Paper 157.

Triffin, R. (1978) 'Gold and the Dollar Crisis: Yesterday and Tomorrow'. *Princeton University Essays in International Finance* 132.

Williamson, J. (1977) *The Failure of World Monetary Reform, 1971–74*. New York: New York University Press.

Index

eBooks

eBooks – at www.eBookstore.tandf.co.uk

A library at your fingertips!

eBooks are electronic versions of printed books. You can store them on your PC/laptop or browse them online.

They have advantages for anyone needing rapid access to a wide variety of published, copyright information.

eBooks can help your research by enabling you to bookmark chapters, annotate text and use instant searches to find specific words or phrases. Several eBook files would fit on even a small laptop or PDA.

NEW: Save money by eSubscribing: cheap, online access to any eBook for as long as you need it.

Annual subscription packages

We now offer special low-cost bulk subscriptions to packages of eBooks in certain subject areas. These are available to libraries or to individuals.

For more information please contact webmaster.ebooks@tandf.co.uk

We're continually developing the eBook concept, so keep up to date by visiting the website.

www.eBookstore.tandf.co.uk